Foundations of Strategy

**Robert M. Grant
and Judith Jordan**

P9-CPY-504

WILEY

John Wiley & Sons, Ltd

This edition first published 2012 by John Wiley & Sons Ltd
© 2012 Robert M. Grant and Judith Jordan

Registered office

John Wiley & Sons Ltd, The Atrium, Southern Gate, Chichester, West Sussex, PO19 8SQ, United Kingdom

For details of our global editorial offices, for customer services and for information about how to apply for permission to reuse the copyright material in this book please see our website at www.wiley.com.

The right of Robert M. Grant and Judith Jordan to be identified as the authors of this work has been asserted in accordance with the Copyright, Designs and Patents Act 1988.

All rights reserved. No part of this publication may be reproduced, stored in a retrieval system, or transmitted, in any form or by any means, electronic, mechanical, photocopying, recording or otherwise, except as permitted by the UK Copyright, Designs and Patents Act 1988, without the prior permission of the publisher.

Wiley publishes in a variety of print and electronic formats and by print-on-demand. Some material included with standard print versions of this book may not be included in e-books or in print-on-demand. If this book refers to media such as a CD or DVD that is not included in the version you purchased, you may download this material at http://booksupport.wiley.com. For more information about Wiley products, visit www.wiley.com.

Designations used by companies to distinguish their products are often claimed as trademarks. All brand names and product names used in this book are trade names, service marks, trademarks or registered trademarks of their respective owners. The publisher is not associated with any product or vendor mentioned in this book. This publication is designed to provide accurate and authoritative information in regard to the subject matter covered. It is sold on the understanding that the publisher is not engaged in rendering professional services. If professional advice or other expert assistance is required, the services of a competent professional should be sought.

Library of Congress Cataloging-in-Publication Data
Grant, Robert M., 1948-
 Foundations of strategy / Robert M. Grant and Judith Jordan.
   p. cm.
 Includes bibliographical references and index.
 ISBN 978-0-470-97127-7 (pbk.)
 1. Strategic planning. 2. Industrial management—Technological innovations. I. Jordan, Judith. II. Title.
 HD30.28.G7214 2012
 658.4'012—dc23

 2011046748

A catalogue record for this book is available from the British Library.

Set in 8.5/12 Myriad Pro by Thomson Digital, India
Printed in Italy by Printer Trento Srl.

Brief contents

Contents

Photo credits

The following images throughout the book have been sourced from Shutterstock images:

Page 1   © Jackiso, sourced from Shutterstock images
Page 12   © Alexander A.Trofimov, sourced from Shutterstock images
Page 22   © Novelo, sourced from Shutterstock images
Page 26   © eddtoro, sourced from Shutterstock images
Page 27   © tony740607, sourced from Shutterstock images
Page 49   © Tom Wang, sourced from Shutterstock images
Page 51   © fantazista, sourced from Shutterstock images
Page 60   © lucadp, sourced from Shutterstock images
Page 62   © David Steele, sourced from Shutterstock images
Page 64   © mangostock, sourced from Shutterstock images
Page 66   © Dmitriy Shironosov, sourced from Shutterstock images
Page 71   © Kirill Kurashov, sourced from Shutterstock images
Page 74   © Racheal Grazias, sourced from Shutterstock images
Page 76   © Dmitry Naumov, sourced from Shutterstock images
Page 80   © Rido, sourced from Shutterstock images
Page 82   © Monkey Business Images, sourced from Shutterstock images
Page 95   © iofoto, sourced from Shutterstock images
Page 105   © dariusl, sourced from Shutterstock images
Page 107   © anyaivanova, sourced from Shutterstock images
Page 119   © Michael D Brown, sourced from Shutterstock images
Page 120   © wavebreakmedia ltd, sourced from Shutterstock images
Page 135   © Raisa Kanareva, sourced from Shutterstock images
Page 142   © nikshor, sourced from Shutterstock images
Page 146   © Emir Simsek, sourced from Shutterstock images
Page 150   © weknow, sourced from Shutterstock images
Page 157   © Kaspars Grinvalds, sourced from Shutterstock images
Page 169   © aragami12345s, sourced from Shutterstock images
Page 177   © WinMaster, sourced from Shutterstock images
Page 180   © Nagy-Bagoly Arpad, sourced from Shutterstock images
Page 183   © hifashion, sourced from Shutterstock images

xii

PHOTO CREDITS

Page 188 © James Thew, sourced from Shutterstock images
Page 209 © EcoPrint, sourced from Shutterstock images
Page 211 © Stephen Rudolph, sourced from Shutterstock images
Page 213 © pressureUA, sourced from Shutterstock images
Page 225 © Gemenacom, sourced from Shutterstock images
Page 229 © Ryabitskaya Elena, sourced from Shutterstock images
Page 253 © JonesHon, sourced from Shutterstock images
Page 256 © Nadiia Ierokhina, sourced from Shutterstock images
Page 258 © Adam Radosavljevic, sourced from Shutterstock images
Page 262 © yuyangc, sourced from Shutterstock images
Page 267 © alexskopje, sourced from Shutterstock images
Page 273 © Christian Delbert, sourced from Shutterstock images
Page 276 © R. Gino Santa Maria, sourced from Shutterstock images
Page 281 © iQoncept, sourced from Shutterstock images
Page 298 © algabafoto, sourced from Shutterstock images
Page 301 © ricardomiguel.pt, sourced from Shutterstock images
Page 307 © cozyta, sourced from Shutterstock images
Page 310 © inxti, sourced from Shutterstock images
Page 316 © Franco Deriu, sourced from Shutterstock images
Page 319 © auremar, sourced from Shutterstock images
Page 322 © Elena Efimova, sourced from Shutterstock images
Page 330 © Denis Vrublevski, sourced from Shutterstock images
Page 336 © alephcomo, sourced from Shutterstock images
Page 361 © qushe, sourced from Shutterstock images
Page 371 © dean bertoncelj, sourced from Shutterstock images
Page 377 © Robert Gooch, sourced from Shutterstock images
Page 387 © Toria, sourced from Shutterstock images
Page 390 © Gabi Moisa, sourced from Shutterstock images
Page 404 © cobalt88, sourced from Shutterstock images
Page 413 © Onur ERSIN, sourced from Shutterstock images
Page 416 © Danny E Hooks, sourced from Shutterstock images
Page 420 © Quayside, sourced from Shutterstock images
Page 422 © wavebreakmedia ltd, sourced from Shutterstock images
Page 434 © Photosani, sourced from Shutterstock images
Page 444 © Dmitriy Shironosov, sourced from Shutterstock images
Page 450 © Afonso Duarte, sourced from Shutterstock images
Page 457 © Patricia Marks, sourced from Shutterstock images
Page 458 © JustASC, sourced from Shutterstock images
Page 467 © Madlen, sourced from Shutterstock images
Page 471 © Rich Carey, sourced from Shutterstock images
Page 477 © Germanskydiver, sourced from Shutterstock images

Preface

Robert Grant's Contemporary Strategy Analysis is one of the market leading text books used on MBA and advanced undergraduate courses around the world. During the continuing development of that text, now in its 7th edition, it has become apparent that there is also considerable demand for a more accessible and concise version of the text. In response to this demand, we have developed Foundations of Strategy as a brand new textbook. While maintaining the accessible writing style, clear approach and sound theoretical depth, this new text is better suited to the needs of both undergraduate students and Masters students requiring a more concise treatment of the subject.

As all those with an interest recognise, the way in which business and management education is delivered continues to evolve and change over time. Strategy modules remain a key part of business and management programmes but are now delivered in a wide variety of different formats, to a diverse range of students using a variety of different technologies. Strategy educators frequently find themselves with the challenge of having to deliver strategy modules in relatively short time frames to students with limited prior knowledge and experience of business and management practice. This text is designed to assist educators and students meet this challenge. Our aim has been to cover the key areas of strategy as concisely as possible without sacrificing intellectual rigour. To that end we have:

- Made clear the learning objectives and provided summary tables against these objectives at the start and end of each chapter.

- Organised the book on the basis of ten chapters

- Provided a range of short cases that students can read and digest quickly and that can be used as an alternative to, or in conjunction, with longer cases available on the web

- Included worked examples relating to the opening case of each chapter demonstrating how theory can be applied to practice in order to gain insight into strategic decision-making.

- Highlighted key concepts in the margin

- Provided a glossary of key terms

The book's organisation

The challenge has been to find a way of balancing brevity and comprehension. We have endeavoured to do this by focusing on selective key topics but explaining them in sufficient depth for students to be stretched intellectually. To assist in achieving this aim we have:

- Included a range of up-to-date examples relating to products and firms with which most students will be familiar in order to capture their interest and enthusiasm

- Included new sections on not-for-profit and public sector strategy to reflect the interests and experience of many students and staff

- Provided suggestions for further reading at the end of each chapter.

Online teaching and learning resources

Visit **www.foundationsofstrategy.com** to access all the teaching and learning materials that accompany this text.

Instructors will find extensive teaching materials such as an **Instructor's Manual**, including **Case Teaching notes**, a **Test Bank** and **PowerPoint slides**. The website also features extra, longer **Case Studies** written by Robert M. Grant as well as **Case Video Clips** with accompanying questions to use in class.

Resources for students include an **interactive eBook of the text** with embedded media including **Self-Test Quizzes**, **Video Clips** and **Glossary Flashcards**.

The authors have chosen to partner with an **Online Simulation** built by Kim Warren. If an instructor adopts this text for class use they can access a special rate per student. For more information follow the link from the Foundations of Strategy website at **www.foundationsofstrategy.com**

The **White Label Restaurant business game** gives students the opportunity to implement strategy within a 'real world' situation, repeatedly and in differing circumstances. Set in an industry familiar to all, students can easily understand how the business works and engage in running it within a short period of time. The game comes with a short case description and teacher material including information on the business's positioning, tying it back to the standard strategy frameworks you may already have covered. The supporting slides set out solid underlying theory, which builds strongly on the resource-based view of the strategy.

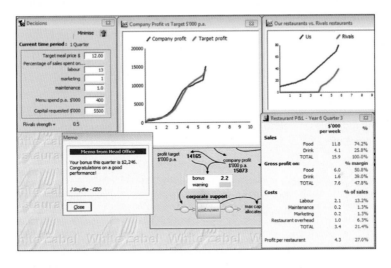

Teams can be offered a range of challenges, such as early start-up, fighting off a new competitor, turning round a business in trouble and managing market maturity. They must also deal with investor expectations in the form of head office targets and rewards that adapt as they move forward. The game can be run as many times as is needed, allowing students to test and save alternative strategies which can form the basis of student assessment.

Case list

Chapter	Opening Case	Closing Case
1. The Concept of Strategy	Strategy and Success: Lady Gaga, James Dyson, Alex Ferguson	The King of Shaves
2. Industry Analysis	The Mobile Phone Industry	Fitness First and the UK Health and Fitness Clubs
3. Resources and Capabilities	Hyundai Motor Company	Harley-Davidson, Inc.
4. The Nature and Sources of Competitive Advantage	Singapore Airlines	The Rise and Fall of Starbucks
5. Business Strategies in Different Industry and Sectoral Contexts	The Evolution of Personal Computers	The World Wild Fund for Nature
6. Technology-based Industries and the Management of Innovation	eBook readers	Nespresso
7. Corporate Strategy	Tesco Bank: From food to finance	Diversification at Disney
8. Global Strategies and the Multinational Corporation	IKEA's International Strategy	Sharp and the Production of Liquid Crystal Displays (LCDs)
9. Realizing Strategy	BP and the Deepwater Horizon Oil Spill	Designing and Redesigning Cisco
10. Contemporary issues in Strategic Management		

1

The concept of strategy

Introduction and objectives

Strategy is about success. This chapter explains what strategy is and why it is important to individuals and organisations in achieving their goals. We will distinguish strategy from planning. Strategy is not a detailed plan or programme of instructions; it is a unifying theme that gives coherence and direction to the actions and decisions of an individual or an organisation.

The principal task of this chapter is to introduce the notion of strategy, to make you aware of some of the key debates in strategy and to present the basic framework for strategy analysis that underlies this book. By the time you have completed this chapter, you will:

- appreciate the contribution that strategy can make to successful performance, both for individuals and for organisations;

- be aware of the origins of strategy and how views on strategy have changed over time;

- be familiar with some of the key questions and terminology in strategy;

- understand the debates that surround corporate values and social responsibility;

- comprehend the basic approach to strategy that underlies this book.

Since the purpose of strategy is to help us to understand success, we start by looking at the role that strategy has played in enabling individuals to achieve their goals. The Opening case provides a brief outline of three individuals' paths to success. While each made his or her name in different fields – Lady Gaga in the music business, James Dyson in design and manufacturing and Alex Ferguson as manager of the football club, Manchester United – their experiences provide us with some important insights into strategy.

Opening case   Strategy and Success: Lady Gaga, James Dyson and Alex Ferguson

Lady Gaga

Stefani Joanne Angelina Germanotta is now better known by her stage name Lady Gaga. Since 2008 she has sold more than 15 million albums, 40 million singles and countless downloads worldwide. In 2010 she became the first living person to achieve 10 million fans on Facebook and her following is still growing. At the same time she has more than 5 million fans on Twitter and is the first, currently performing artist to reach a billion views on YouTube.

Credit: Getty Images

As the eldest daughter of an Italian American family based in New York, she had an interest in music from a relatively early age, taking piano lessons and participating in school musical productions, but accounts of her early life suggest she was a normal student rather than an exceptional talent. Contrary to her current image as a fashion icon, she described her early look as 'a refugee from Jersey Shore, with big black hair, heavy eye makeup and tight revealing clothes'.[1]

She gained early admission to New York University's Tisch School of the Arts but dropped out within a year in order to pursue her music career. It is reported that her father only agreed to pay her rent during this period on the condition that she would re-enrol for Tisch if unsuccessful. She managed, at age 19, to gain a recording contract with the record label Def Jam Recordings but was dropped after just three months. Despite this setback, she continued to write songs and formed a band with her friends, playing in small venues in the Lower East Side of New York. In 2007 she adopted the stage name Lady Gaga (derived from a reference to the song 'Radio Ga Ga' by the band Queen) and with the help of music producer, Rob Fusari and record executive, Vincent Herbert, began to achieve success as a songwriter and vocalist, releasing her debut album, *The Fame*, in 2008.

Whilst Stefani, like many other children, enjoyed performing from an early age, her talents as a songwriter, musician, vocalist and fashion designer cannot be described as exceptional. The visual images she projects are always unusual and her public appearance is always striking but few would consider her a great beauty. The extent of her innovation has also been questioned: she has been criticised by artists such as Grace Jones as being 'imitative' rather than 'original' and, although she has courted controversy to make her name, not everyone considers her a trailblazer. Camille Paglia, writing in the *Sunday Times*,[2] asserts that Gaga 'is more an identity thief than an erotic taboo breaker, a mainstream manufactured product who claims to be singing for the freaks, the rebellious and the dispossessed when she is none of those'. Her journey to worldwide fame has often been compared to that of Madonna. Like Madonna, Lady Gaga recognises herself as a brand. Both trademarked their names early on in their careers and have promoted their brand image relentlessly. Both have maintained control over their image, music and management (Lady Gaga, for example, heads her own creative production team, the Haus of Gaga). Both are exponents of continual reinvention: changing their stage personae and public images frequently as a means of maintaining the interest and involvement of fans and media alike. Lady Gaga is particularly known for the enticing and immersive story worlds she creates for each of her videos and for her extraordinary costumes, including those made from raw meat and plastic bubble wrap. Finally, both have attracted attention – and controversy – through their use of religious, sexual and violent iconography.

Despite the seeming chaos and unpredictability of her rise to fame, Lady Gaga's product development and marketing have been well adapted to the wrenching changes that have transformed, and almost destroyed, the music business over the past decade. Digital technologies and the ease of internet file sharing have drastically reduced the revenues from recorded music, elevating live performances as the dominant revenue source in the music business. Such performances are multimedia events where visual imagery and the overall theatrical experience are at least as important as the music. Most of the money Gaga and her record label earn does not come from video and record sales but from concert tickets. Lady Gaga and her team have also been quick to recognise the opportunities that the internet and social media offer. Her songs are simple to sing in any language and her videos, which also raise revenue through product placements, appeal to any age, gender or nationality. She makes extensive use of social media, such as Facebook and Twitter, to build her fan base and by personally generating the majority of her own online content, she constantly engages with fans and engenders feelings of friendship and loyalty. This loyalty is further reinforced by giving fans the pet name of 'monsters' and releasing video extracts to them prior to more general release. Gaga's second album, *Fame Monster*, was dedicated specifically to her fan base.

Lady Gaga argues that, unlike some other celebrities, she doesn't spend her money on 'mansions' but ploughs it back into her shows. She is reported as favouring what is known as 360 deals, namely contracts in which music labels invest a higher than average amount of money up front, for example in marketing and promotion, but in return keep a percentage of merchandise sales, touring revenue and other earnings that artists traditionally have kept for themselves. It remains to be seen whether Lady Gaga's success will be as enduring as that of individuals like Madonna, Donatella Versace and Grace Jones, who she cites as her muses.

VIDEO

James Dyson

James Dyson, the founder of Dyson Appliances Ltd, is best known as the inventor of the bagless vacuum cleaner, which he invented in the mid-1980s. In March 2011 he ranked as the 420th richest person[3] in the world. His bagless vacuum cleaner is now sold in more than 45 countries worldwide. Together with other innovative products, these produced an annual revenue of £770 million and profits of £190 million.

Dyson's journey in building his multi-million dollar business was by no means a smooth one. He initially trained as a designer, studying furniture, interior and theatre design at the Royal College of Art in London and was set to pursue a career in architecture even though whilst at college he 'accidentally discovered the joys of making things'.[4] His aspirations changed after meeting and working with an inventor and entrepreneur, Jeremy Fry. Dyson says of Fry, 'I was very lucky that the first person I worked for was Jeremy Fry . . . Luckily for me he was an engineer and a manufacturing entrepreneur and definitely a mentor to me. He was key to my success at Dyson. I came from a family of schoolteachers – we knew nothing about business. He taught me what was possible and what wasn't.'[5]

Dyson came up with the idea of creating a bagless vacuum cleaner in 1978 because of being frustrated by the performance of the products that were on the market at that time. He initially came across the 'cyclone' technology, which later formed the basis of his innovative vacuum cleaner design, when he saw sawdust being collected up in a timber yard by giant cyclones. Nonetheless it took him five years from 1979 to 1984 to develop his cleaner and he produced more than 5000 prototypes before his 'dual cyclone' vacuum cleaner met with any success. Dyson patented his product in 1980 even though it took many more years for the bagless vacuum cleaner to finally reach the market. Dyson's next step was to look for a company in the UK or Europe to distribute his product, but he did not find any takers. His innovation was seen as too risky and potentially highly disruptive, particularly given that at this time the bag replacement market was worth over £100 million in the UK alone.

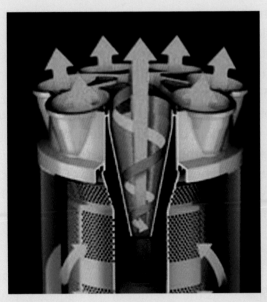

Credit: Reproduced from www.dyson.co.uk with permission from Dyson Limited

Dyson found funding very hard to obtain and in the early years was supported almost entirely by the income of his wife who was an art teacher. Dyson says of those times 'of course there were moments of doubt. I had a young family and I wasn't exactly bringing in a regular income. It wasn't 9 to 5. It was a big risk'.[6] Eventually, in 1985, Dyson entered into a partnership with a Japanese company and his new vacuum cleaner was finally launched in Japan in 1986. It soon became a status symbol in Japanese households, winning design awards. Dyson used the royalties from his sales in Japan to manufacture a new model in his own name in the UK. He borrowed money against his house and worked with four engineers in a shed in his back garden to get his UK business off the ground. He marketed the product on the basis of its features, emphasising the fact that it worked better than competitors' products. He constantly adjusted his product to refine his offering and sales grew.

It soon became evident that to survive the intense competition that existed in the electrical appliance industry Dyson needed to reduce his costs. His factory in the UK was close to his home and he was very much the 'hands-on' type of manager and on first-name terms with most of his employees. He needed to move his production base from the UK to a location with lower labour costs and after a detailed review chose to move manufacturing to Malaysia. Talking about this decision he says 'It really hurt. It was devastating to have to stand up in front of a workforce and tell them that they would be made redundant. It hurt to admit that I couldn't manufacture in Britain . . . But it was the right thing to do if we wanted to stick around'.[7] His steely determination was also evident when Dyson Appliances Ltd entered the US market. In 1999 Hoover, faced with a loss of market share to

Dyson Appliances, launched its Vortex V2500 vacuum cleaner with the tagline 'No bag. No filter replacement. No problems'. Dyson filed a patent infringement lawsuit against Hoover for copying his technology. Hoover filed a countersuit seeking removal of Dyson's patents because his products lacked design and originality. After a long and, at times, bitter battle, the courts found in favour of Dyson and Hoover agreed to pay Dyson damages of around £4 million.[8]

Talking about his vision for the company Dyson says it is 'to become a verb', to transform the language so that people talk about 'Dysoning' rather than 'Hoovering' their homes. Through his leadership the company has continued to innovate bringing out new products such as his Airblade hand dryer and digital slim vacuum, and spends significant sums on R&D. Talking about his approach he says, 'I don't think we have ever thought that we're sustaining something here in the sense that every day we come in is an entrepreneurial day because we're investing more and more in new projects and taking bigger and bigger risks. When we come in it's just as we came in right at the beginning'.[9]

Alex Ferguson

In May 2011, Manchester United Football Club won the English Premier League for the 12th time under their veteran manager, Alex Ferguson. Despite losing to Barcelona in the final of the Champions League, Manchester United retained its position as the second most successful European club of the past decade. Ferguson's relentless pursuit of excellence and painstaking

Credit: Getty Images.

approach to teambuilding is a testament to the power of dedication to systematic, long-term development in business dominated by celebrity, money and the quest for short-term results.

Like many of Britain's leading soccer coaches, Alex Ferguson is a product of the football passion and tradition of Glasgow's Clydeside. After many years as a professional player, his coaching abilities became apparent when, as manager of Aberdeen, he broke the Celtic–Rangers duopoly of Scottish football by winning the Scottish Cup, Scottish League Cup and European Cup Winners Cup.

Appointed manager to Manchester United in 1986, Ferguson systematically rebuilt scouting and youth development and instituted a rigorously disciplined approach to team training. Scouting was extended from its traditional focus in local schools to a global quest for outstanding potential. At the heart of teambuilding was a group of young players – Giggs, Beckham, Scholes, Butt and the Neville brothers – who graduated together from the youth team and provided a nucleus for the first team to which Ferguson added expensive signings from other clubs.

Central themes of Ferguson's approach were:

- Insistence on the highest levels of commitment from team members. Ferguson provided unflinching support for his players while subjecting them to withering criticism if he deemed their efforts were substandard.

- Insisting on the primacy of the team over individual players. 'The best teams stand out because they are teams . . . the individual members have become so fully integrated that the team functions with a single spirit . . . The manager should create a bond among his players that raises their performance to heights that were unimaginable'.[10] This emphasis meant that Ferguson would sell some of his most outstanding players (Beckham, Ronaldo) if he believed that their celebrity created an impediment to team unity.

- Building flexible coordination within the team. Ferguson was a master of team rotation – fielding teams with different configurations of players in order to vary tactics and rest key players.

- Meticulous planning for individual games involving visits to watch opponents play and analysis of videoed games to identify the strengths and weaknesses of opponents.

Case Insight 1.1
Routes to success

Our opening case outlines examples of success in three very different arenas – Lady Gaga in popular entertainment, James Dyson in business and Alex Ferguson in football.

For none of these three examples can success be attributed to overwhelmingly superior resources:

- Lady Gaga possesses vitality, intelligence and imagination, but lacks outstanding talents as a vocalist, songwriter or fashion artist.
- James Dyson had to depend on his wife's salary as an art teacher when he was developing his vacuum cleaner.
- Alex Ferguson built the Manchester United team with comparatively modest expenditures on star players. Manchester United's net expenditures on new players over the past decade are tiny compared to the massive spending of Chelsea, Real Madrid, Inter Milan and Manchester City.

Nor can their success be attributed either exclusively or primarily to luck. All benefited from lucky breaks at critical junctures. More important was the ability to recognise opportunities when they appeared and to have the clarity of direction and the flexibility necessary to exploit these chances.

The key common ingredient in all three success stories was the presence of a soundly formulated and effectively implemented *strategy*. These strategies did not exist as a plan; in most instances the strategy was not even made explicit. Yet, in all three, we can observe a consistency of direction based on a clear understanding of the 'game' being played and a keen awareness of how to manoeuvre into a position of advantage.

- Underpinning Lady Gaga's rise to fame has been a strategy built on commitment, opportunism and a deep understanding of the role that live performances and social media play in developing and sustaining a loyal fan base.
- When James Dyson couldn't find any manufacturers or distributors who would launch his product in the UK he launched it in Japan through catalogue sales and eventually set up his own manufacturing company.
- Alex Ferguson combined old-fashioned virtues of commitment and team spirit with critical insights into the sources of sustained success in top-flight European soccer of the modern era.

The role of strategy in success

What do these examples tell us about the characteristics of a strategy that are conducive to success? In all three stories, four common factors stand out (see Figure 1.1):

1   *Goals that are simple, consistent and long term.* All three examples displayed a single-minded commitment to a clearly recognised goal that was pursued steadfastly over a substantial period of time.

   ● Lady Gaga relinquished the opportunity offered to her by the prestigious Tisch School of Arts to pursue her quest for stardom.

   ● James Dyson persisted for more than five years developing his cleaner, making more than 5000 prototypes.

   ● Alex Ferguson's life appears to be dominated by football and the success of the teams he manages. Although an extremely rich man with a supportive family, other aspects of his life seem to occupy subsidiary roles.

2   *Profound understanding of the competitive environment.* All three cases illustrate strategies around a deep and insightful appreciation of the context in which they were operating.

   ● Fundamental to Lady Gaga's success has been a shrewd understanding of the ingredients of stardom and the basis of popular appeal. This extends from her recognition that she is a 'brand' through to her awareness of the need to manage personally critical elements of media distribution channels. Her focus on live shows, merchandising and social media reflect an acute awareness of the changing nature of the music industry as well as the changing attitudes, styles and social norms of her audiences.

Figure 1.1 Common elements in successful strategies

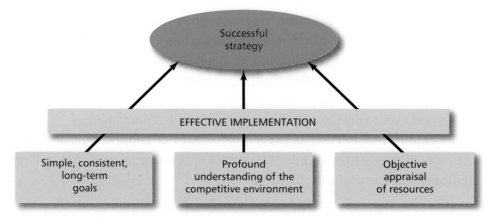

- James Dyson realised the significance of television advertising to sell his product and emphasised the fact that his cleaner, unlike most rival products, did not require the continuing purchase of replacement dust bags. He also moved his manufacturing base from the UK to Malaysia to achieve cost savings.

- Alex Ferguson recognised the new realities of European soccer: the need to look worldwide for talent; the importance of varying teams and tactics in response to complexities of playing in different competitions; the potential for strength through diversity – especially in blending youth with experience; and the merits of psychological warfare both in upsetting opponents and intimidating referees.

3 *Objective appraisal of resources.* All three strategies were effective in exploiting internal strengths, while protecting areas of weakness.

- By positioning herself as a 'performance artist', Lady Gaga exploited her abilities to develop and project her image, to self-promote and to exploit emerging trends, while avoiding being judged simply as a singer or songwriter. Her live performances rely heavily on a large team of highly qualified designers, musicians, vocalists, choreographers and technicians, thus compensating for any weaknesses in her own performing capabilities.

- Dyson realised early on that his product was likely to be imitated by rivals. He battled to achieve patent protection for his inventions and sued Hoover UK for patent infringement, winning significant damages.

- Ferguson is masterful in apprising the talents of both his teams and individual players – including the psychological factors that are so critical to individual performance and team effectiveness.

4 *Effective implementation.* Without effective implementation, the best-laid strategies are of little use. Critical to the success in all three stories is effective leadership in terms of capacity to reach decisions, energy in implementing them and ability to foster loyalty and commitment among subordinates. Each story illustrates the emergence of organisations that allowed effective marshalling of resources and capabilities and quick responses to changes in the competitive environment.

> Without effective implementation, the best-laid strategies are of little use.

These observations about the role of strategy in success can be made in relation to most fields of human endeavour. Whether we look at warfare, chess, politics, sport or business, the success of individuals and organisations is seldom the outcome of a purely random process. Nor is superiority in initial endowments of skills and resources typically the determining factor. Strategies that build on the basic four elements almost always play an influential role.

Look at the 'high achievers' in any competitive area. Whether we review the world's political leaders, the CEOs of the Fortune 500 or our own circles of friends and acquaintances, those who have achieved outstanding success in their careers are seldom those who possessed the greatest innate abilities. Success has gone to those who managed their careers most effectively – typically by combining the four strategic factors mentioned above. They are goal focused; their career goals have taken primacy over the multitude of life's other goals – friendship, love, leisure, knowledge, spiritual fulfilment – which the majority of us spend most of our lives juggling and reconciling. They know the environments within which they play and tend to be fast learners in terms of understanding the keys to advancement. They know themselves in terms of both strengths and weaknesses. And they implement their career strategies with commitment, consistency and determination. As the late Peter Drucker observed: 'we must learn how to be the CEO of our own careers'.[11]

There is a downside, however. Focusing on a single goal may lead to outstanding success, but may be matched by dismal failure in other areas of life.

> Many people who have reached the pinnacles of their careers have led lives scarred by poor relationships with friends and families and stunted personal development. These include Howard Hughes and Jean Paul Getty in business, Richard Nixon and Joseph Stalin in politics, Marilyn Monroe and Elvis Presley in entertainment, Joe Louis and O. J. Simpson in sport and Bobby Fischer in chess. Fulfilment in our personal lives is likely to require broad-based lifetime strategies.[12]

A brief history of strategy

Origins

Enterprises need business strategies for much the same reasons that armies need

military strategies – to give direction and purpose, to deploy resources in the most effective manner and to coordinate the decisions made by different individuals. Many of the concepts and theories of business strategy have their antecedents in military strategy. The term *strategy* derives from the Greek word *strategia*, meaning 'generalship'. However, the concept of

Case Insight 1.2
Strategy versus tactics

James Dyson's decision to move production of his bagless vacuum cleaner to Malaysia is clearly strategic whereas his decision to launch a patent infringement suit against Hoover is less clear cut. The latter decision might be considered tactical in the sense that it was easily *reversible*, indeed Dyson could have dropped the suit at any time. The outcome of the case, however, was very *important* to the company with regard to the sustainability of its competitive advantage and fighting the case required a *significant commitment of resources*. If Dyson had lost his battle with Hoover, this may have opened the floodgates to imitative products that could have challenged the company's market position. We could similarly debate whether Alex Ferguson's decision to sell David Beckham or Lady Gaga's decision to establish Haus of Gaga were tactical or strategic moves. What do you think? In your opinion, does this distinction matter?

strategy did not originate with the Greeks. Sun Tzu's classic *The Art of War*, written in about 500 BC, is regarded as the first treatise on strategy.[13]

Military strategy and business strategy share a number of common concepts and principles, the most basic being the distinction between strategy and tactics. *Strategy* is the overall plan for deploying resources to establish a favourable position; a *tactic* is a scheme for a specific action. Whereas tactics are concerned with the manoeuvres necessary to win battles, strategy is concerned with winning the war. Strategic decisions, whether in military or business spheres, share three common characteristics:

- they are important;
- they involve a significant commitment of resources;
- they are not easily reversible.

The evolution of business strategy

The evolution of business strategy has been driven more by the practical needs of business than by the development of theory. During the 1950s and 1960s, senior executives were experiencing increasing difficulty in coordinating decisions and maintaining

> The evolution of business strategy has been driven more by the practical needs of business than by the development of theory.

control in companies that were growing in size and complexity. Financial budgeting, in the form of annual financial planning and investment appraisal, provided short-term control and project selection but did little to guide the long-term development of the firm. **Corporate planning** (also known as *long-term planning*) was developed during the late 1950s to serve this purpose. Macroeconomic forecasts provided the foundation for the new corporate planning. The typical format was a five-year corporate planning document that set goals and objectives, forecast key economic trends (including market demand, market share, revenue, costs and margins), established priorities for different products and business areas of the firm and allocated capital expenditures. The diffusion of corporate planning was accelerated by a flood of articles and books addressing this new science.[14] The new techniques of corporate planning proved particularly useful for developing and guiding the diversification strategies that many large companies were pursuing during the 1960s. By the mid-1960s, most large US and European companies had set up corporate planning departments.

During the 1970s and early 1980s, confidence in corporate planning and infatuation with scientific approaches to management were severely shaken. Not only did diversification fail to deliver the anticipated synergies, but the oil shocks of 1974 and 1979 ushered in a new era of macroeconomic instability, combined with increased international competition from resurgent Japanese, European and Southeast Asian firms. Faced with a more turbulent business environment, firms could no longer plan their investments, new product introductions and personnel requirements three to five years ahead, simply because they couldn't forecast that far into the future.

The result was a shift in emphasis from planning to strategy making, where the focus was less on the detailed management of companies' growth paths than on positioning the company in markets and in relation to competitors in order to maximise the potential for profit. This transition from corporate planning to what became termed **strategic management** was associated with increasing focus on competition as the central characteristic of the business environment and competitive advantage as the primary goal of strategy.

The emphasis on strategic management also directed attention to business performance. During the late 1970s and into the 1980s, attention focused on sources of profit within the industry environment. Michael Porter of Harvard Business School pioneered the application of industrial organisation economics to analysing industry profitability.[15] Other studies focused on how profits were distributed between the different firms in an industry – in particular the impact of market share and experience upon costs and profits.[16]

During the 1990s, the focus of strategy analysis shifted from the sources of profit in the external environment to the sources of profit within the firm. Increasingly the resources and capabilities of the firm became regarded as the main source of competitive advantage and the primary basis for formulating strategy.[17] This emphasis on what has been called the **resource-based view** of the firm represented a substantial shift in thinking about strategy. Rather than firms pursuing similar strategies, as in seeking attractive markets and favourable competitive positions, emphasis on internal resources and capabilities has encouraged firms to identify how they are different from their competitors and design strategies that exploit these differences. Michael Porter's answer to the question 'What is strategy?', emphasised that: *Competitive strategy is about being different. It means deliberately choosing a different set of activities to deliver a unique mix of value.*[18]

During the first decade of the 21st century, the principles and practice of strategy have been moulded by the uniquely challenging circumstances of a new era. Technology has been a particularly potent force.[19] The beginning of the decade saw the bursting of the TMT (technology, media, telecommunications) bubble and the realisation that the 'new knowledge economy' and internet-based business models did not require a rewriting of the principles of strategy. Nevertheless, technology continues to reshape industries: digital technologies are associated with standards wars,[20] the emergence of 'winner-take-all' markets,[21] and the potential for strategic innovation as firms seek the 'blue oceans' of uncontested market space.[22]

In the face of continuous change and relentless competition, strategy becomes less about building positions of sustained competitive advantage and more about developing the responsiveness and flexibility to create successive temporary advantages. Reconfiguring resources and capabilities to achieve such responsiveness typically requires firms to collaborate within networks of strategic alliances, to reduce hierarchical decision making and to develop high-performance workforces that are capable of exercising discretion in a responsible fashion. In this context, strategy ceases to be the exclusive domain of the top management team but is something that is shaped by, and shapes, the whole membership of the organisation. It is not surprising, therefore, that attention, in recent years, has been drawn to exploring the processes and practices of everyday organisational life that produce strategic outcomes.

> In the face of continuous change and relentless competition, strategy becomes less about building positions of sustained competitive advantage and more about developing the responsiveness and flexibility to create successive temporary advantages.

The continuing challenges of the 21st century, including the recession of 2008–9, are encouraging new thinking about the purpose of business. Disillusion with 'shareholder value capitalism' has been accompanied by renewed interest in corporate social responsibility, ethics, sustainability of the natural environment and the role of social legitimacy in long-term corporate success.

Figure 1.2 summarises the main developments in strategic management over the past 60 years.

Figure 1.2 Evolution of strategic management: dominant themes

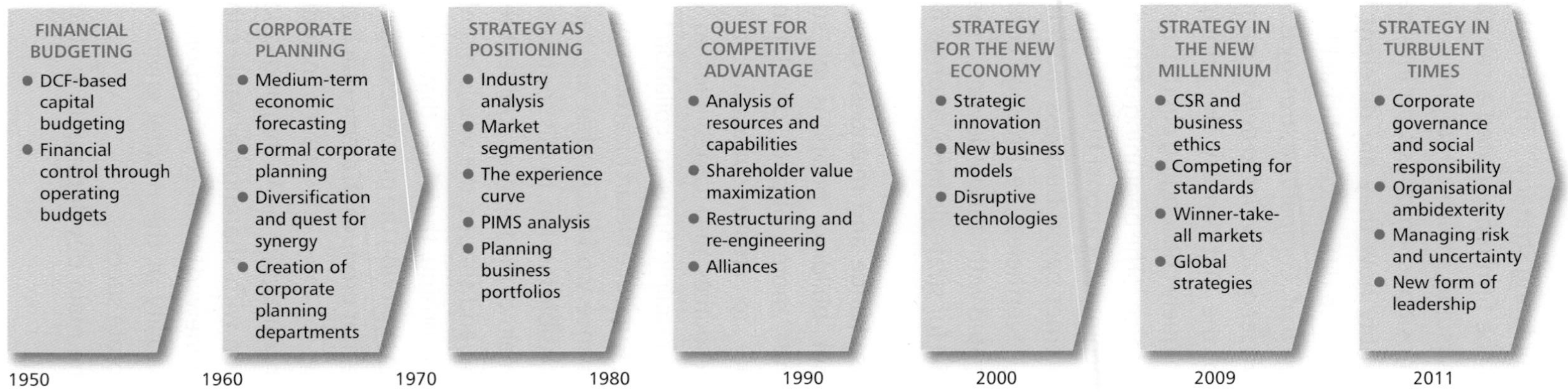

FINANCIAL BUDGETING	CORPORATE PLANNING	STRATEGY AS POSITIONING	QUEST FOR COMPETITIVE ADVANTAGE	STRATEGY FOR THE NEW ECONOMY	STRATEGY IN THE NEW MILLENNIUM	STRATEGY IN TURBULENT TIMES
• DCF-based capital budgeting • Financial control through operating budgets	• Medium-term economic forecasting • Formal corporate planning • Diversification and quest for synergy • Creation of corporate planning departments	• Industry analysis • Market segmentation • The experience curve • PIMS analysis • Planning business portfolios	• Analysis of resources and capabilities • Shareholder value maximization • Restructuring and re-engineering • Alliances	• Strategic innovation • New business models • Disruptive technologies	• CSR and business ethics • Competing for standards • Winner-take-all markets • Global strategies	• Corporate governance and social responsibility • Organisational ambidexterity • Managing risk and uncertainty • New form of leadership
1950	1960	1970	1980	1990	2000	2009	2011

Strategy today

Having looked at the origins of strategy and how views on strategy have changed over time, we are ready to start our exploration of strategy today. We do this by posing a series of basic questions. What is strategy? How might we describe strategy? How do we go about identifying strategies in practice? How is strategy made? What purpose and whose interests does strategy serve? In providing preliminary answers to these questions we introduce a number of key concepts and debates that we return to throughout this book. As you will see when you get further into the subject, strategy is a complex and contested field of study, so answers, which at first sight seem straightforward, can on deeper inspection raise further questions and force us to reflect on some things we might have previously taken for granted. For example, when we address the question of whose interests strategy serves, we find ourselves immediately propelled into considering whose interests strategy *should* serve. Before we get to that debate we need to familiarise ourselves with some basic terminology and concepts and the obvious starting point is with the definition of the term 'strategy' itself.

What is strategy?

In its broadest sense, **strategy** is the means by which individuals or organisations achieve their objectives. Table 1.1 presents a number of definitions of the term strategy. Common to definitions of business strategy is the notion that strategy is focused on achieving certain *goals*; that the critical actions that make up a strategy involve *allocation of resources*; and that strategy implies some *consistency, integration* or *cohesiveness*.

Yet, as we have seen, the conception of firm strategy has changed greatly over the past half century. As the business environment has become more unstable and unpredictable,

Table 1.1 Some definitions of strategy

> ● Strategy: a plan, method, or series of actions designed to achieve a specific goal or effect.
> *– Wordsmyth Dictionary*
>
> ● The determination of the long-run goals and objectives of an enterprise and the adoption of courses of action and the allocation of resources necessary for carrying out these goals.
> *– Alfred Chandler, Strategy and Structure* (Cambridge, MA: MIT Press, 1962)
>
> ● Strategy is the pattern of objectives, purposes, or goals and the major policies and plans for achieving these goals, stated in such a way as to define what business the company is in or is to be in and the kind of company it is or is to be.
> *– Kenneth Andrews, The Concept of Corporate Strategy* (Homewood, IL: Irwin, 1971)

so strategy has become less concerned with detailed plans and more about the quest for success. This is consistent with our starting point to the chapter. If we think back to our three introductory examples – Lady Gaga, James Dyson and Alex Ferguson – none wrote detailed strategic plans, but all possessed clear ideas of what they wanted to achieve and how they would achieve it. This shift in emphasis from *strategy as plan* to *strategy as direction* does not imply any downgrading of the role of strategy. Certainly, in a turbulent environment, strategy must embrace flexibility and responsiveness. But it is precisely in these conditions that strategy becomes more rather than less important. In an environment of uncertainty and change, a clear sense of direction is essential to the pursuit of objectives. When the firm is buffeted by unforeseen threats and where new opportunities are constantly appearing, then strategy becomes a vital tool to navigate the firm through stormy seas.

> In an environment of uncertainty and change, a clear sense of direction is essential to the pursuit of objectives.

When discussing strategy a distinction is commonly made between corporate strategy and business strategy.

- **Corporate strategy** defines the scope of the firm in terms of the industries and markets in which it competes. Corporate strategy decisions include investment in diversification, **vertical integration**, acquisitions and new ventures; the allocation of resources between the different businesses of the firm; and divestments.

- **Business strategy** is concerned with how the firm competes within a particular industry or market. If the firm is to prosper within an industry, it must establish a

Figure 1.3 Corporate versus business strategy

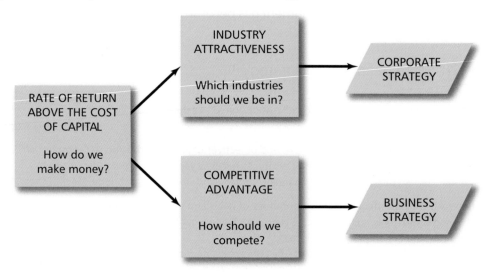

Case Insight 1.3
Corporate versus business strategy

Lady Gaga's extension of her 'brand' from recorded music to the 'Haus of Gaga', Dyson's expansion of its product line from vacuum cleaners to hand driers and Manchester United's sales of merchandise as well as tickets for matches are examples of corporate strategy because they constitute decisions about *where* to compete. In contrast Lady Gaga's frequent changes in her image, James Dyson's close attention to the design, performance and pricing of his vacuum cleaners and Alex Ferguson's team-building activities are examples of business or competitive strategy because they are about *how* to compete.

competitive advantage over its rivals. Hence, this area of strategy is also referred to as *competitive strategy*.

This distinction may be expressed in even simpler terms. The basic question facing the firm is: 'How do we make money?' The answer to this question corresponds to the two basic strategic choices we identified above: 'Where to compete (i.e. in which industries and markets should we be)? and 'How should we compete?' The distinction between corporate strategy and business strategy corresponds to the organisational structure of most large companies. Corporate strategy is typically the responsibility of the top management team and the corporate strategy staff. Business strategy is primarily the responsibility of divisional management.

As an integrated approach to firm strategy, this book deals with both business and corporate strategy. However, our primary emphasis will be on business strategy. This is because the critical requirement for a company's success is its ability to establish competitive advantage. Hence, issues of business strategy precede those of corporate strategy. At the same time, these two dimensions of strategy are intertwined: the scope of a firm's business has implications for the sources of competitive advantage; and the nature of a firm's competitive advantage determines the range of businesses in which it can be successful.

How do we describe a firm's strategy?

These same two questions 'Where is the firm competing?' and 'How is it competing?' also provide the basis upon which we can describe the strategy that a firm is pursuing. The

Case Insight 1.4
Describing Dyson's strategy

Figure 1.4 Describing Dyson's strategy: competing in the present, preparing for the future

<table>
<tr><td>

Static

Where are we competing?

–Product scope: vacuum cleaners, hand dryers, fans and an array of other products

–Geographical scope: product sales in 52 countries

–Vertical scope: a range of products can be purchased direct from Dyson through its web-site.

How are we competing?

–By focussing on invention, design and engineering.

</td><td>

Dynamic

What do we want to become?

–A household name i.e. dysoning rather than hoovering.

What do we want to achieve?

–Sales growth through geographic expansion: 80 countries by 2015.

How will we get there?

–Through high levels of investment in R&D and organic growth.

</td></tr>
</table>

where question has multiple dimensions. It relates to the industry or industries in which the firm is located, the products it supplies, the customer groups it targets, the countries and localities in which it operates and the vertical range of the activities it undertakes.

However, strategy is not simply about competing for today; it is also concerned with competing for tomorrow. This dynamic concept of strategy involves establishing objectives for the future and determining how they will be achieved. Future objectives relate to the overall purpose of the firm (*mission*), what it seeks to become (*vision*) and specific performance targets.

How do we identify a firm's strategy?

Even if we know how to describe a firm's strategy, where do we look to find what strategy a firm is pursuing? Where does information of the type outlined in Case Insight 1.3 come from? Strategy is located in three places: in the heads of the chief executive, senior managers and other members of the organisation; in the top management team's articulations of strategy in speeches and written documents; and in the decisions through which strategy is enacted. Only the last two are observable.

While the most explicit statements of strategy – in board minutes and strategic planning documents – are almost invariably confidential, most companies – public companies in particular – see value in communicating their strategy to employees, customers, investors and business partners – and, inevitably, to the public at large. Collis and Rukstad[23] identify a hierarchy of strategy statements:

- The mission statement is the basic statement of organisational purpose; it addresses 'Why we exist'.

- A statement of principles or values outlines 'What we believe in and how we will behave'.

- The vision statement projects 'What we want to be'.

- The strategy statement articulates 'What our competitive game plan will be'.

Collis and Rukstad argue that the game plan should comprise three definitive components of strategy: *objectives; scope* (where we will compete); and *advantage* (how we will compete).

A version of some or all of these statements is typically found on the corporate pages of companies' websites. The example box on Apple Inc's strategy illustrates this point. More detailed statements of strategy – including qualitative and quantitative medium-term targets – are often found in top management presentations to analysts which are typically included in the 'for investors' pages of company websites. More detailed information on scope (where?) and advantage (how?) can be found in companies' annual reports but this kind of information can be difficult to find for privately owned companies.

The usefulness of public statements of strategy is, however, limited by their role as public relations vehicles – this is particularly evident in vision and mission statements which are frequently grandiose and clichéd. Hence, explicit statements of strategy need to be checked against decisions and actions:

- Where is the company investing its money? Notes to financial statements often provide detailed breakdowns of capital expenditure by region and by business segment.

- What technologies is the company developing? Identifying the patents that a company has filed (using the online databases of the US and EU patent offices) indicates the technological trajectory it is pursuing.

- What new products have been released, major investment projects initiated and/or top management hires made? A company's press releases usually announce these strategic decisions.

Identifying a firm's strategy requires drawing upon multiple sources of information in order to build an overall picture of what the company says it is doing and what it is actually doing.

Featured example 1.1 Apple Computer, Inc: Business strategy

The Company is committed to bringing the best personal computing and music experience to students, educators, creative professionals, businesses, government agencies and consumers through its innovative hardware, software, peripherals, services and internet offerings. The Company's business strategy leverages its unique ability, through the design and development of its own operating system, hardware and many software applications and technologies, to bring to its customers new products and solutions with superior ease-of-use, seamless integration and innovative industrial design. The Company believes continual investment in research and development is critical to facilitate innovation of new and improved products and technologies. Besides updates to its existing line of personal computers and related software, services, peripherals and networking solutions, the Company continues to capitalize on the convergence of digital consumer electronics and the computer by creating innovations like the iPod and iTunes Music Store. The Company's strategy also includes expanding its distribution network to effectively reach more of its targeted customers and provide them a high-quality sales and after-sales support experience.

Source: Apple Computer, Inc., 10-K Report, 2005.

How is strategy made? Design versus emergence

How companies make strategy has been one of the most hotly debated issues in strategic management. Our emphasis on strategy analysis encourages the view that strategy is the result of managers engaging in deliberate, rational analysis. However, strategy may also emerge through adaptation to circumstances. In discussing Lady Gaga's career, we discerned a consistency and pattern to her career decisions that we described as a strategy, yet there is no evidence that she engaged in any systematic strategic planning. Similarly with many successful companies – Wal-Mart's winning strategy built on large store formats, hub-and-spoke distribution, small-town locations and employee motivation was not a product of grand design – it emerged from Sam Walton's hunches and a series of historical accidents.

Henry Mintzberg is a leading critic of rational approaches to strategy design. He distinguishes *intended*, *realised* and *emergent* strategies. **Intended strategy** is strategy as conceived of by the top management team. Even here, intended strategy is less a product of rational deliberation and more an outcome of negotiation, bargaining and compromise among the many individuals and groups involved in the process. However, **realised strategy** – the actual strategy that is implemented – is only partly related to that which was intended (Mintzberg suggests only 10–30% of intended strategy is realised). The primary determinant of realised strategy is what Mintzberg terms **emergent strategy** – the decisions that emerge from the complex processes in which individual managers interpret the intended strategy and adapt to changing external circumstances.[24] According to Mintzberg, not only is rational design an inaccurate account of how strategies are actually formulated, it is a poor way of making strategy.

> *The notion that strategy is something that should happen way up there, far removed from the details of running an organization on a daily basis, is one of the great fallacies of conventional strategic management.*[25]

Featured example 1.2 Honda's entry into the US motorcycle market

Honda's successful entry into the US motorcycle market has provided a central battleground between those who view strategy making as primarily a rational, analytical process of deliberate planning (*the design school*) and those that envisage strategy as emerging from a complex process of organisational decision making (the *emergence or learning school of strategy*).[26] Boston Consulting Group lauded Honda for its single-minded pursuit of a global strategy based on exploiting economies of scale and learning to establish unassailable cost leadership.[27] However, subsequent interviews with the Honda managers in charge of US market entry revealed a different story: a haphazard entry with little analysis and no clear plan.[28] As Mintzberg observes: 'Brilliant as its strategy may have looked after the fact, Honda's managers made almost every conceivable mistake until the market finally hit them over the head with the right formula'.[29]

The emergent approaches to strategy making permit adaptation and learning though continuous interaction between strategy formulation and strategy implementation in which strategy is constantly being adjusted and revised in light of experience.

In practice, strategy making almost always involves a combination of centrally driven rational design and decentralised adaptation. The design aspect of strategy comprises a number of organisational processes through which strategy is deliberated, discussed and decided. In larger companies these include board meetings and a formalised process of strategic planning process supplemented by more broadly participative events such as strategy workshops.

> Strategy is being continually enacted through decisions that are made by every member of the organisation.

At the same time, strategy is being continually enacted through decisions that are made by every member of the organisation – by middle management especially. The decentralised, bottom-up strategy emergence may in fact lead to more formalised strategy formulation. Intel's historic decision to abandon memory chips and concentrate on microprocessors was initiated by incremental decisions taken by business unit and plant managers that were subsequently promulgated by top management into strategy.[30]

In all the companies we are familiar with, strategic planning combines design and emergence – a process that Grant has referred to as **planned emergence**.[31] The balance between the two depends greatly upon the stability and predictability of a company's business environment. The Roman Catholic Church, for example, inhabits a relatively stable environment. For Google, Al Qaeda and Zimbabwe Banking Corporation, however, strategic planning will inevitably be restricted to a few principles and guidelines; the rest must emerge as circumstances unfold. As the business environment becomes more turbulent and less predictable, so strategy making becomes more concerned with guidelines and less with specific decisions. We return to these issues again throughout the book.

What roles does strategy perform?

The transition from corporate planning to strategic management has involved strategy moving from planning departments to the centre of corporate leadership. As such strategy occupies multiple roles within organisations.

STRATEGY AS DECISION SUPPORT We have described strategy as a pattern or theme that gives coherence to the decisions of an individual or organisation. But why can't individuals or organisations make optimal decisions in the absence of such a unifying theme? Consider the 1997 'man-versus-computer' chess epic in which Garry Kasparov was defeated by IBM's 'Deep Blue'.

Deep Blue did not need strategy. Its phenomenal memory and computing power allowed it to identify its optimal moves based on a huge decision tree.[32] Kasparov – although the world's greatest chess player – was subject to *bounded rationality*: his decision analysis was subject to the cognitive limitations that constrain all human beings.[33] For chess players, a strategy offers guidelines and decision criteria that assist positioning and help create opportunities.

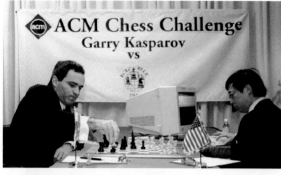

Credit: Getty Images.

Strategy improves decision making in several ways. First, strategy simplifies decision making by *constraining* the range of decision alternatives considered and by acting as a *heuristic* – a rule of thumb – that reduces the search required to find an acceptable solution to a decision problem. Second, a strategy-making process permits the knowledge of different individuals to be pooled and integrated. Third, a strategy-making process facilitates the use of analytic tools – the frameworks and techniques that we will encounter in the ensuing chapters of this book.

STRATEGY AS A COORDINATING DEVICE The greatest challenge of managing an organisation is coordinating the actions of different organisational members. Strategy can promote coordination in several ways. First, it is a communication device. Statements of strategy are a powerful means through which the CEO can communicate the identity, goals and positioning of the company to all organisational members. However, communication alone is not enough. For coordination to be effective, *buy-in* is essential from the different groups that make up the organisation. The strategic planning process can provide a forum in which views are exchanged and consensus developed. Once formulated, the implementation of strategy through goals, commitments and performance targets that are monitored over the strategic planning period also provides a mechanism to ensure that the organisation moves forward in a consistent direction.

STRATEGY AS TARGET Strategy is forward looking. It is concerned not only with how the firm will compete now, but also with what the firm will become in the future. A key purpose of a forward-looking strategy is not only to establish a direction of the firm's development, but also to set aspirations that can *motivate* and *inspire* the members of the organisation. Gary Hamel and

> A key purpose of a forward-looking strategy is not only to establish a direction of the firm's development, but also to set aspirations that can motivate and inspire the members of the organisation.

C. K. Prahalad use the term 'strategic intent' to describe the articulation of a desired leadership position. They argue that: 'strategic intent creates an extreme misfit between resources and ambitions. Top management then challenges the organization to close the gap by building new competitive advantages'.[34] The implication they draw is that strategy should be less about fit and resource allocation and more about *stretch* and **resource leverage**.[35] The evidence from Toyota, Virgin and Southwest Airlines is that resource scarcity may engender ambition, innovation and a 'success-against-the-odds' culture. Jim Collins and Jerry Porras make a similar point: US companies that have been sector leaders for 50 years or more – Merck, Walt Disney, 3M, IBM and Ford – have all generated commitment and drive through setting 'Big, Hairy, Ambitious Goals'.[36] Striving, inspirational goals are typical of most organisations' statements of vision and mission. One of the best known is the goal set by President Kennedy for NASA's space programme: 'before this decade is out, of landing a man on the moon and returning him safely to Earth'. British Airways aspires to be 'The World's Favourite Airline', while Coca-Cola's drive for growth is driven by the quest to 'have a Coca-Cola within arm's reach of everyone in the world'.

STRATEGY AS ANIMATION AND ORIENTATION   Karl Weick[37] popularized the story of a group of soldiers on reconnaissance in the Alps who, after a snow storm, lose their way. They are feeling cold and despondent until one of the party discovers a tattered map in a little used pocket. Finding the map animates the group and gets them walking until they are back on a familiar bearing. On reaching shelter they find that the map was of another mountain range, the Pyrenees. The moral of the story is that the map is like strategy. Often the most important role of strategy is to animate and orientate individuals within organisations so that they are mobilised, encouraged and work in concert with each other to achieve focus and direction even if the plan isn't correct. It helps, of course, to work with a map or a plan that is as accurate as possible.

Strategy: in whose interest? Shareholders versus stakeholders

We have highlighted the multiple roles that strategy plays in organisations and its central role is assisting organisations to achieve their goals, but whilst it is easy to comprehend an individual having personal goals, the notion of organisations having goals is slightly more problematic. Organisations are composed of many different individuals and groups, many of which may have different agendas. As a consequence firms are likely to have multiple goals some of which may, at times, conflict. Nonetheless, at the broadest level, all businesses seek to create value through the activities they undertake. This, of course, invites the questions about what we mean by value and who benefits from the value created. Defining value is not straightforward because it is rarely a matter of objective fact. Perceptions of value arise through the interplay of supply and demand and through processes of negotiation and argument but, in the business world, value is usually assessed in monetary terms through customers' willingness to pay for a good or a service, i.e. value is defined as a measure of the extent to which a good or service is perceived by a customer as meeting his or her needs or wants and is reflected in his or her willingness to pay.

> Organisations are composed of many different individuals and groups, many of which may have different agendas.

The 'value' created by firms is distributed among different parties: employees (wages and salaries), lenders (interest), landlords (rent), government (taxes) and owners (profit). But we need also to remember that firms also create value for their customers to the extent that the satisfaction customers gain exceeds the price they pay (i.e., they derive **consumer surplus**). The purpose of the firm is not only to create this value for customers but also to extract some of it in the form of profit for the firm. Profit is defined as a surplus of revenues over costs and represents that part of the value created by the firm that is available for distribution to its owners. Given that the value added by firms is distributed between these different parties, it is tempting to think of all businesses as operating for the benefit of multiple constituencies. This view of the business organisations as a coalition of interest groups where top management's role to balance these different – often conflicting – interests is referred to as the **stakeholder approach** to the firm.[38]

Balancing the interests of different stakeholders is particularly important for not-for-profit and public sector organisations, because their activities often involve transformations in social situations and citizens' lives. Unfortunately value creation is often much harder to evaluate in these contexts because it is difficult to put a monetary value on the potential benefits that different strategies might confer on stakeholders. Whilst efforts could be made to establish citizens' willingness to pay for things like a reduction in the crime rate or better education using questionnaires or interviews, it is extremely difficult to value services for which no markets exist. Take, for example, a government department's decision to regenerate an inner city area. The authority might try to gauge the value of pursuing this policy by using monetary dimensions like property values or increased rentals for retail premises but the development might also have an aesthetic value (e.g. results in the construction of buildings and spaces that people enjoy looking at and being in) or be valued by the local residents because the regeneration project results in a reduction in crime, improvements to their health and well-being or reductions in road traffic accidents. There are also likely to be winners and losers – those whose outlook is spoiled by new developments, those who benefit from a reduction in traffic past their homes. Deciding how much value has been created and how it has been distributed in the absence of monetarised values to act as common denominator is extremely difficult.

Regardless of whether firms operate in the private or non-private sectors the idea that strategies should be designed in the interests of all stakeholders and that the role of senior managers is to balance competing claims is, at first sight, very appealing but this is a hotly contested issue and not a viewpoint with which everyone would agree.

Strategy: Whose interests should be prioritised?

The notion of the corporation balancing the interests of multiple stakeholders has a long tradition, especially in Asia and continental Europe. By contrast, most English-speaking countries have endorsed shareholder capitalism, where companies' overriding duty is to produce profits for owners. These differences are reflected in international differences in companies' legal obligations. In the US, Canada, the UK and Australia, company boards are required to act in the interests of shareholders. In continental European countries, companies are legally required to take account of the interests of employees, the state and the enterprise as a whole. Whether companies should operate exclusively in the interests of their owners or should also pursue the goals of other stakeholders is an ongoing debate.

During the 1990s, 'Anglo-Saxon' shareholder capitalism was in the ascendancy – many continental European and Japanese companies changed their strategies and corporate governance to increase their responsiveness to shareholder interests. However, during the 21st century, shareholder value maximisation became associated with short-termism, financial manipulation (Enron, WorldCom), excessive CEO compensation and the failures of risk management that precipitated the 2008–9 financial crisis – issues we return to in more detail in the final chapter of this book. The responsibilities of business to employees, customers, society and the natural environment are central ethical and social issues.

VIDEO

Featured example 1.3 The Kraft takeover of Cadbury: shareholders versus stakeholders

Cadbury plc was a globally recognised confectionery company, second only to the Mars-Wrigley group in size worldwide. Its brands included Crunchie, Flake, Creme Eggs, Roses and Milk Tray to name but a few. In its long history Cadbury's had acquired many other companies but in February 2010 the company itself became an acquisition target, was taken over by the US food giant, Kraft, and ceased to exist as an independent corporate entity.

The business was originally founded by John Cadbury in 1824 selling tea, coffee and drinking chocolate. The retail business flourished and John, recognising an opportunity, extended his activities into the production of cocoas and drinking chocolates and formed the partnership, Cadbury Brothers of Birmingham, with his brother Benjamin. The business gained particular momentum in the1850s when a reduction in the high rate of import tax on cocoa and chocolate, meant the Cadbury Brothers' products, which had hitherto been the preserve of the wealthy due to their high cost, became more affordable to the general public. Around this time master confectioner, Frederic Kinchelman, joined the business, bringing with him his recipes and production secrets and this allowed Cadbury's to move into the chocolate-covered, confectionery products that eventually became the basis of its growth and development.

When the founder's health deteriorated the business was taken over by his sons who by the 1870s decided that they needed to move to larger premises. They acquired land just outside Birmingham, which was close to a canal and a recently constructed railway line, and their new Bournville factory opened in 1879. John's sons, like their father and uncle, were Quakers, that is to say members of a protestant religious group that rejected ritual and formal creed and had a commitment to social reform. Acting in the Quaker philanthropic tradition, George Cadbury (one of John's sons) bought land adjacent to

Credit: Getty Images.

◀ the new factory and built a model village for workers at his own expense in order to 'alleviate the evils of more cramped living conditions'. His aim was to operate a profitable company that cared for and nurtured its employees. The company retained its commitment to social philanthropy over time and was known for its caring attitude to its workers and for its charitable works, for example, its sustainable cocoa-growing projects in Africa and other parts of the world. The company ethos proved so enduring that in 2010, when faced with the hostile bid from Kraft, the then chief executive of Cadbury, Todd Stitzer, argued that his firm was the embodiment of a distinctive style of 'principled capitalism' that was 'woven into its fabric' by its founders. He saw the Cadbury culture as something distinctive that contributed to the company's competitive success and argued that this advantage would be lost if the company were acquired by Kraft.

Kraft eventually acquired control of Cadbury in February 2010 for £11.5 billion but the takeover was particularly controversial. Cadbury workers protested on the streets, the Royal Bank of Scotland was fiercely criticised for lending Kraft the money to close the deal and a few politicians tried to have the takeover blocked on competition grounds. At the heart of the debate over Cadbury's future was disagreement about whose interests were being served. Those who wished to block the bid argued that past history suggested that Kraft would prioritise shareholders' interests above those of other stakeholders and in the pursuit of profit would negate everything that Cadbury had previously stood for. Others saw no such conflict, arguing that doing good is good for business and, anyway, firms that do not pay attention to shareholders' interests do not survive.

In practice the extent to which firms take a narrow (shareholder) or broad (stakeholder) view of their purpose is probably more a matter of pragmatics than arbitrary choice. For example in competitive labour markets firms that failed to take their employees into account would soon find themselves incurring costs of high labour turnover, Similarly firms that failed to take the interests of customers or suppliers into account would soon find themselves disadvantaged relative to competitors with different policies. In practice what is important is the priority given to different groups and senior managements' judgement calls on the trade-offs required to satisfy important interest groups.

Profit and purpose

As the Cadbury example illustrates there is more to business than making money. Profit maximisation (enterprise value maximisation, to be more precise) provides a convenient foundation for building our tools of strategy analysis, yet it is not the goal that inspired Henry Ford to build a business that precipitated a social revolution.

> I will build a motor car for the great multitude . . . It will be so low in price that no man making good wages will be unable to own one and to enjoy with his family the blessing of hours of pleasure in God's great open spaces . . . When I'm through, everyone will be able to afford one and everyone will have one.[39]

We saw in our opening case that Lady Gaga, James Dyson and Alex Ferguson were not so much driven by the desire for riches as for the desire to create. The world's most consistently successful companies in terms of profits and shareholder value tend to be those that are motivated by factors other than profit. A succession of studies point to the role of strategic intent, vision and ambitious goals in driving sustained corporate success.[40] Indeed, the converse may also be true – the companies that are most focused on profitability and the creation of shareholder value are often remarkably unsuccessful at achieving those goals.

> The world's most consistently successful companies in terms of profits and shareholder value tend to be those that are motivated by factors other than profit.

Why does the pursuit of profit so often fail to realise its goal? First, profit will only be an effective guide to management action if managers know what determines profit. Obsession with profitability can blinker managers' perception of the real drivers of superior performance. Conversely, a strategic goal 'to build a motor car for the great multitude that everyone will be able to afford' (Ford), or to 'build great planes' (Boeing), or to 'become the company most known for changing the worldwide poor quality image associated with Japanese products' (Sony, 1950s) may lead a company to direct its efforts towards the sources of competitive advantage within its industry – ultimately leading to superior long-term profitability.

Some companies have kept alive a keen sense of purpose – it is embedded in organisational culture and implicit in strategy and in the behaviour of corporate leaders. However, sustaining a sense of purpose typically requires articulation in explicit statements of mission, vision and purpose. For example:

- Google's mission is: 'to organize the world's information and make it universally accessible and useful'.

- 'The IKEA vision is to create a better everyday life for the many people. We make this possible by offering a wide range of well-designed, functional home furnishing products at prices so low that as many people as possible will be able to afford them'.

- SAP strives to define and establish undisputed leadership in the emerging market for business process platform offerings and accelerate business innovation powered by IT for companies and industries worldwide.

- Gaia House (a Buddhist retreat centre in England) 'exists for the liberation of all beings from greed, hatred and delusion'.

The second factor concerns motivation. Success is the result of coordinated effort. The goal of maximising the return to stockholders is unlikely to inspire employees and other company stakeholders and it's unlikely to be especially effective in inducing cooperation and unity between them. Dennis Bakke, founder of the international power company AES, offers the following analogy:

Profits are to business as breathing is to life. Breathing is essential to life, but is not the purpose for living. Similarly, profits are essential for the existence of the corporation, but they are not the reason for its existence.[41]

A sense of purpose is common to most new, entrepreneurial enterprises and is also very evident in numerous non-private sector organisations, for example charities like Oxfam or campaigning organisations like Greenpeace. But what about established companies? What happens to the sense of purpose that was presumably present at their founding?

Is organisational purpose instilled at birth, or can companies choose or adapt their *raison d'être* during the course of their lives? Certainly many of the companies that are most closely identified with clarity of purpose – HP, Johnson & Johnson, Walt Disney – have a sense of mission that is little changed from that articulated by their founders. Yet, Cynthia Montgomery argues that 'forging a compelling organisational purpose' is the ongoing job of the CEO – indeed, it is the 'crowning responsibility of the CEO'.[42] The challenge is to link change with continuity. Some of the most successful corporate turnarounds have been engineered by corporate leaders – Gerstner at IBM, Eisner at Walt Disney – who have renewed and redirected organisational purpose while appealing to a continuity of tradition and values. We re-engage with this debate in Chapter 9 when we explore how strategy is realised in practice.

The debate over corporate social responsibility

This issue of 'whose interests should strategy serve' has re-emerged in recent years as part of the debate over **corporate social responsibility** (CSR). What are a company's obligations to society as a whole?

In a sharp rebuttal to calls for business to address the broader problems of society, free-market economist, Milton Friedman declared CSR to be both unethical and undesirable. Unethical because it involved management spending owners' money on projects that owners had not approved of; undesirable because it involved corporate executives determining the interests of society. Once business enterprises accept responsibility for society, does this justify support for political groups, for religious movements, for elitist universities? According to Friedman:

> There is one and only one social responsibility of business – to use its resources and engage in activities designed to increase its profits so long as it stays within the rules of the game, which is to say, engages in open and free competition without deception or fraud.[43]

Despite these arguments, companies are increasingly accepting responsibilities that extend well beyond the immediate interests of their owners. The case for CSR is based both on ethics and efficacy. Ethical arguments about management responsibility depend, ultimately, upon what we conceive the firm to be. William Allen contrasts two different notions of the public corporation: *'the property conception'*, which views the firm as a set of assets owned by stockholders and the *'social entity conception'*, which views the firm as the community of individuals that is sustained and supported by its relationships with its social, political, economic and natural environment.[44] The **'firm as property'** view implies that management's responsibility is to operate in the interests of shareholders. The **'firm as social entity'** implies a responsibility to maintaining the firm within its overall network of relationships and dependencies. Charles Handy dismisses the 'firm as property' view as a hangover from the 19th century – in the 21st century shareholders invest in companies but are not 'owners' in any meaningful sense. To regard profit as the purpose for which companies exist, he argues, is a tragic confusion.[45]

The approach taken in this book

Narrowing the focus

In order to make progress in developing analytical tools for designing successful strategies, in the first instance, we narrow our focus by limiting our discussions to private sector firms operating in market economies and assuming that such firms operate in the interests of their owners by seeking to maximise profits in the long run. Why do we make these assumptions and how do we justify them? Our initial focus is on private sector firms because the foundations of mainstream strategy lie in analysis of competition and firms' quests to outperform their rivals. Strategy takes on a very different meaning and requires a very different approach in non-competitive, public policy contexts. Whilst strategy is always bound up with issues of power and politics, these issues often loom particularly large within the public and not-for-profit sectors. In a short 'foundational'

> The foundations of mainstream strategy lie in analysis of competition and firms' quests to outperform their rivals.

text of this nature we cannot hope to do justice to the extensive debates around the 'politics of strategy' so we narrow our terms of reference to make the task manageable. We do, however, provide some discussion of the challenges of strategy formulation and implementation in public and not-for-profit sectors in Chapter 5 but confine ourselves to exploring the key characteristics of public and not-for-profit organisations and the extent to which concepts and frameworks developed in the private sector have been adapted to fit this context.

We justify our second simplifying assumption, namely that companies operate in the interests of their owners by seeking to maximise profits over the long term by pointing to four key considerations:

1   *Competition.* Competition erodes profitability. As competition increases, the interests of different stakeholders converge around the goal of survival. Survival requires that, over the long term, the firm earns a rate of profit that covers its cost of capital: otherwise it will not be able to replace its assets. Over half of the USA's publicly listed companies do not cover their cost of capital.[46] Across many sectors of industry, the heat of international competition is such that few companies have the luxury of pursuing goals that diverge from profit maximisation.

2   *The market for corporate control.* Management teams that fail to maximise the profits of their companies will be replaced by teams that do. In the 'market for corporate control', companies that underperform financially suffer a declining share price that acquirers – other public companies or private equity funds – will use as a basis for personnel replacement. In addition, activist investors, both individuals (Carl Icahn,

Kirk Kerkorian) and funds (such as California Public Employees' Retirement System, The Children's Investment Fund) put pressure on boards of directors to improve shareholder returns. One result has been increased turnover of chief executives.[47]

3 *Convergence of stakeholder interests.* Even beyond a common interest in the survival of the firm, there is likely to be more community of interests than conflict of interests among different stakeholders. Profitability over the long term requires loyalty from employees, trusting relationships with suppliers and customers, and support from governments and communities. The argument that firms require legitimacy in order to survive and prosper is reinforced by evidence that firms that pursue ethical principles and corporate social responsibility achieve superior financial performance.[48]

4 *Simplicity.* A key problem of the stakeholder approach is that considering multiple goals and specifying trade-offs between them vastly increases the complexity of decision making.[49] Virtually all the major tools of business decision making, from pricing rules to discounted cash flow analysis, are rooted in the assumption of profit maximisation. Adopting stakeholder goals risks opening the door to political wrangling and management paralysis.

Assuming that firm strategy is directed primarily toward making profit doesn't mean that we have to accept that profit is the sole motivation driving business enterprises. As we noted earlier in the chapter, the goals driving the architects of the world's great enterprises – Henry Ford at Ford Motor Company, Bill Gates at Microsoft and Nicolas Hayek of Swatch – are seldom financial. The dominant drivers tend to be the fulfilment of a vision and the desire to make a difference in the world. Nevertheless, even when business goals transcend mere money making, their achievement requires enterprises that are commercially successful – this requires the adoption of strategies that generate profit.

The basic framework for strategy analysis

Figure 1.5 shows the basic framework for strategy analysis that we shall use throughout the book. The four elements of a successful strategy that we outlined at the start of this chapter and illustrated in Figure 1.1 are recast into two groups – the firm and the industry environment – with strategy forming a link between the two. The firm embodies three sets of these elements: goals and values ('simple, consistent, long-term goals'); resources and capabilities ('objective appraisal of resources'); and structure and systems ('effective implementation').

The industry environment ('profound understanding of the competitive environment') represents the core of the firm's external environment and is defined by the firm's

Figure 1.5 The basic framework: strategy as a link between the firm and its environment

relationships with customers, competitors and suppliers. Hence, we view strategy as forming a link between the firm and its external environment.

Fundamental to this view of strategy as a link between the firm and its external environment is the notion of **strategic fit**. For a strategy to be successful, it must be consistent with the firm's external environment and with its internal environment – its goals and values, resources and capabilities and structure and systems. As we shall see, the failure of many companies is caused by lack of consistency with either the internal or external environment. General Motors' long-term decline is a consequence of a strategy that has failed to break away from its long-established ideas about multi-brand market segmentation and adapt to the changing market for cars. In other cases, many companies have failed to align their strategies to their internal resources and capabilities. A critical issue for Nintendo in the coming years will be whether it possesses the financial and technological resources to continue to compete head-to-head with Sony and Microsoft in the market for video game consoles.

> For a strategy to be successful, it must be consistent with the firm's external environment and with its internal environment – its goals and values, resources and capabilities and structure and systems.

We address the notion of 'fit' in the next three chapters, looking first at the external environment, then at the firm's internal environment and finally bringing them together in a discussion of business strategy.

Summary

This chapter has covered a great deal of ground. If you are feeling a little overwhelmed, not to worry: we shall be returning to most of the themes and issues raised in the subsequent chapters of the book. Through the examples provided in our opening case and our subsequent discussion we have sought to show you the links between strategy and success and to outline the different ways of thinking about strategy. By posing a series of fundamental questions we have uncovered a number of central debates. Is strategy about planning or about recognising patterns? Is strategy formulation the prerogative of the top management team or something that emerges? Whose interests does strategy serve and, equally importantly, whose interests should it serve?

The strategic issues that individuals face in their careers and firms face in their business operations are too complex to lend themselves to simple solutions and as we progress through this book and introduce an array of analytical tools and techniques, you will soon come to appreciate that the purpose of studying strategy is not to provide quick-fix answers (there aren't any!) but to understand better the issues. Most of the analytical concepts and techniques we introduce in this and subsequent chapters are designed to help us identify, classify and understand the principal factors relevant to strategic decisions. Often one of the most useful contributions strategic analysis makes is to enable us to make a start at problems. It helps us to find those initial threads that are the key to untangling complex knots.

We have seen that strategy is about providing common purpose, committing resources and creating value, so inevitably strategy is bound up with ethical questions. What values and principles should a business organisation adopt? What are a business organisation's broader obligations to society as a whole? As we progress through the illustrative cases and chapters of this book, we will see that strategic decisions always have an ethical dimension and the pursuit of shareholder as opposed to broader stakeholder interests remains a hotly contested debate. We will also see that the pursuit of wider social and environmental goals does not necessarily have to conflict with shareholder interests. Strategy's main concern is about creating value for the future and this requires identifying and exploiting the fundamental drivers of value in a principled way. This is the challenge we address in the next two chapters starting with the analysis of the business environment.

Summary table

Learning objectives	Summary
Appreciate the contribution that strategy can make to successful performance, both for individuals and for organisations	Using the life stories of Lady Gaga, James Dyson and Alex Ferguson to illustrate, we argue that success is associated with strategy. In particular success is linked to: adoption of goals that are simple, consistent and long term; having a profound understanding of the competitive environment; objective appraisal of resources; and effective implementation

Learning objectives	Summary
Be aware of the origins of strategy and how views on strategy have changed over time	Strategy derives from the Greek word *strategia* but its roots are believed to lie with the art of war. Strategy has been driven by the practical needs of business and has moved from a focus on corporate planning to an emphasis on strategic management
Be familiar with some of the key questions and terminology in strategy	We have outlined six key questions: What is strategy? How can strategy be described? How can strategy be identified? How is strategy made? What roles does strategy play? Whose interests does strategy serve? And in our discussion of these topics we have introduced a range of key terms
Understand the debates that surround corporate values and social responsibility	Our discussion of whose interests strategy serves led to a further discussion on whose interests strategy should serve – shareholders or stakeholders? We reviewed the arguments on both sides
Comprehend the basic approach to strategy that underlies this book	Our approach focuses primarily on private sector for-profit firms

Further reading

In his 1996 article Michael Porter provides an excellent discussion on the difference between strategy and operational effectiveness and in a later article he provides some good insights into current debates about shareholder versus stakeholder values and corporate social responsibility. Campbell and Yeung's (1991) article on mission and vision is something of a classic, making clear the distinction between a firm's mission and attempts to create a 'sense of mission'. Henry Mintzberg's work is the obvious starting point for deeper insight into the ways in which strategy is made.

Campbell, A. and Yeung, S. (1991). Creating a sense of mission. *Long Range Planning*, 24(4), 10–20.

Mintzberg, H. (1985). Of strategies: deliberate and emergent. *Strategic Management Journal*, 6, 257–72.

Porter, M. E. (1996). What is strategy? *Harvard Business Review*, 74(6), 61–78.

Porter, M. E. (2006). Strategy and society: the link between competitive advantage and corporate social responsibility. *Harvard Business Review*, 84(2), 78–92.

QUIZ

Visit your enhanced ebook at **www.foundationsofstrategy.com** for self test quiz questions

Self-study questions

1   Choose a company that has recently been celebrated in the media for its success and examine its performance in relation to the four characteristics of successful strategies (clear, consistent, long-term objectives; profound understanding of the environment; objective appraisal of resources; and effective implementation),

2   The discussion of the evolution of business strategy established that the characteristics of a firm's strategic plans and its strategic planning process are strongly influenced by the volatility and unpredictability of its external environment. On this basis, what differences would you expect in the strategic plans and strategic planning processes of the Coca-Cola Company and Google Inc?

3   Select a firm and use internet resources to identify and describe its strategy. Use the template provided in Case Insight 1.4 to structure your answer.

4   What is your career strategy for the next five years? To what extent does your strategy fit with your long-term goals, the characteristics of the external environment and your own strengths and weaknesses?

5   'Firms abandon shareholder value maximisation in favour of some woolly notion of stakeholder satisfaction at their peril'. Discuss, explaining the benefits and drawback of firms acting primarily in the interests of shareholders.

GLOSSARY

Visit your enhanced ebook at **www.foundationsofstrategy.com** for key term flashcards

Closing case The King of Shaves

VIDEO

Will King, the founder of the King of Shaves brand first got the idea for his business in 1998. From its humble beginnings in the bedroom of his

© The King of Shaves Company Ltd. Reproduced with permission.

girlfriend's flat, King has managed to build the company into a multi-million dollar brand taking on the corporate giants, Wilkinson Sword and Gillette.

Will King

Will King refers to himself during his early school years as 'a bit of a loner'.[50] His parents, who were teachers, were highly supportive of their children and Will described himself as having a 'thrifty, yet comfortable, upbringing'. He didn't like school and recounts that, 'I felt that I didn't fit in as I couldn't tell jokes, was rubbish at football, cricket and rugby, always being last to be picked. I wasn't that bright either. Sure, I was probably in the upper 25% in terms of effort, but attainment was always a challenge'. In his teenage years he did, however, discover a passion for sailing and got his first taste of success when he became one of the UK's youngest ever qualified sailing instructors and won a number of prizes in dinghy races. He went on to study at degree level but is quick to point out that his results were 'very average'. After graduating he got a job selling advertising space in *Marketing* magazine, a niche that suited him well. On starting his first job he reports setting himself the goal of doubling his salary, getting a company car and owning a flat within a year. He managed to do all three.

The shaving market in 1993

In 1993 the UK was just coming out of recession and the men's toiletries market was pretty flat, having shown little or no growth in the previous three years. The shaving market comprised two distinct product areas – shaving products such as soaps, gels and foam; and shaving instruments such as razors and razor blades. At that time shaving technology was still pretty traditional. Men mainly used hard soap and a soft brush to create lather and shaved with a standard razor. The 1960s had seen the introduction of aerosol technology that created a foam that could be directly applied to the face and shaving gels first made their appearance in the

1990s but, overall, shaving 'technology' had remained unchanged for many years. The market was dominated by two large players, Gillette and Wilkinson Sword. Gillette sold $1 billion of foams and gels worldwide but only made $50 million profit[51] from these activities, concentrating most of its efforts instead on shaving 'hardware' rather than 'software'. Similarly Wilkinson Sword focused most of its attention on shaving systems rather than shaving creams. There was little or no product differentiation and what there was wasn't well communicated.

The launch of King of Shaves

By the early 1990s King had moved on from *Marketing* magazine but the company to which he had moved hit bad times and he was made redundant. His experience of redundancy made him feel angry but also determined to avoid repeating this experience by becoming his own boss. He started looking around for self-employment opportunities and made some initial connections with specialist clothing manufacturers with a view to becoming a distributor.

King had always had a problem shaving. He had sensitive skin and, after shaving, he often got razor burn that caused his skin to become itchy and sore. With time on his hands after losing his job he was spending a lot of time at his girlfriend's flat and noticed she used essential oils for her dry skin. She suggested trying these oils for his shaving rash and it worked.

Realising that he had found a solution to his problem, he was keen to turn his discovery into a market opportunity so he created and registered the King of Shaves brand name and developed a distinctive plastic bottle. One of the great advantages of shaving oil was that only a small amount was needed for a good shave. This meant that only 10 millilitres or so of oil was required to deliver 50 to 100 shaves, but filling and packing containers was something of a challenge. Fate and luck conspired to enable Will to find both a supplier of the oils he needed and also a manufacturer who was willing to produce prototypes bottles. He hand-filled close to 10,000 bottles in his kitchen, using a 'gunk pump' that dispensed accurate amounts of oil per

© *The King of Shaves Company Ltd. Reproduced with permission.*

stroke, supplied to him by a friend in the yacht business. Two other challenges remained, however, finding the money to launch his product and finding a well-known retailer who would distribute his product.

The money problem was solved by persuading his family and friends to invest relatively small sums in the business. Of particular note is the partnership he entered into with Hiten Dayal, a management consultant who had worked with the US consultancy Booz Allen Hamilton and whom King had met when Dayal was brought in as a consultant to King's former (failing) employer. King approached Dayal, more commonly known by the nickname Herbie, to be one of the initial investors in his new business proposition. Speaking about that time Dayal said, 'when Will came to me with a small bottle of shaving oil and told me it helped his razor burn and it would maybe help others, I naturally regarded it as a possible business idea. This despite the fact that it was a completely different technology from shaving foam, looked completely different, went under a brand name no-one had heard of and we had absolutely no money to market it. On top of that we were going to compete with one of the biggest and best known companies in the world and we would need shelf space from the UK's biggest retailers – in which we had no contacts whatsoever. Analytically it didn't stack up. What did stack up was the enthusiasm and optimism Will brought with that first bottle. Having watched him at work on other businesses in the past it was clear that he was a doer and that if the business failed it wouldn't be for the lack of trying'.[52] Herbie went on to become the chairman of the company.

The problem of finding a retail outlet that would stock the product was solved, when after much time and effort, King persuaded Harrods, a prestigious London department store, to stock his shaving oil. Will used the deal with Harrods to persuade other retailers to follow suit and eventually managed to get his product into large retail chains in the UK. By 1995 sales had risen to £58,000.

Growing the company

In the early days the business lacked the financial resources to launch marketing campaigns so King focused on word of mouth and 'viral' marketing using social network sites on the web. King acquired the domain name shave.com for $35 in 1995 and made extensive use of 'free' platforms such as Facebook and Twitter. Recognising the power of social media the company has continued to focus much of its marketing efforts through these channels with King writing a regular blog to keep in direct contact with his customers. By 2010 according to the Industrial Research Institute the King of Shaves brand was the third-largest selling shaving preparation by value in the UK behind Gillette and Nivea. Talking about his approach King has said: 'You have to have a clear objective. For instance, because King of Shaves is a brand that is in the UK and is globalising and social media is a global phenomenon, we can use it to promote our brand in the markets we want to be in'. By 2010 the King of Shaves brand was stocked in 30,000 stores worldwide including the United States, Japan, Australia, New Zealand, Brazil and South Africa and the company entered into a partnership with Remington to make greater inroads into the shaving 'hardware' (razors and razor blades) market in the US.

Over time the company has not only expanded geographically, it has also extended its product range, launching a non-aerosol gel in a plastic tube in 1996 and a range of men's skincare products for Boots, a health and beauty product retailer, in 1997. They began to realise they were creating a 'premium mass segment of the shaving and skin care market', i.e. they were producing products that were widely available but more expensive than some of the alternatives. The range was further extended into products for women (under the brand name Queen of Shaves) and razors (under the brand name Azor). In the razor market, dominated by large multinationals, the approach was to challenge the pricing tactics of the established companies who tended to sell razor handles at very low prices and made the majority of profit on replacement cartridges. The price of the cartridges for King's Azor razor was reportedly less than half that of rival brands.

The approach to strategy

Describing the company strategy Will King has stated, 'we don't really follow a strategy other than the desire to turn King of Shaves into a global "billion" dollar brand, delivering the world's best shave to the billions of men and women in the world who shave. In terms of how we work, Herbie and I are quite different, come from different backgrounds and have very different skills sets'. He adds that: 'we (Herbie and I) act as knowledge vacuum cleaners, i.e. constantly seeing what the hell is going on around us. We are quite paranoid, in terms of being overtaken and constantly strive to be the best. We sit next to each other, talk the whole time, he does some stuff, I do other stuff. We don't really "work" but think about a year and a half in advance'. In other presentations he has emphasised the importance of enjoying the business you are in, as he puts it, 'Life is for living, loving and laughing not just working 12 hours a day wondering if you are ever going to get anywhere'.[53]

◀ *Case questions*

● How would you account for Will King's success in building the King of Shaves' business?

● What role do you think 'luck' has played in his success?

● Distinguish between the following concepts using examples drawn from the case:

  – corporate and competitive strategy;

  – strategy and tactics.

● How would you describe King of Shaves' strategy and the process by which it is formulated?

● In what ways might pressures for firms to become more socially responsible affect the King of Shaves' business?

Notes

1 www.deepbottle.com/best-lady-gaga-fashion-styles. Accessed 22 September 2011.

2 Camille Paglia, 'Lady Gaga and the death of sex', *Sunday Times Magazine* (12 September, 2010). www.thesundaytimes.co.uk/sto/public/magazine/article389697. ece. Accessed 22 September 2011.

3 www.forbes.com/wealth/billionaires. Accessed 22 June 2011.

4 The Richard Dimbleby Lectures – Engineering the Difference by James Dyson (9 December, 2004). www.bbc.co.uk/pressoffice/pressreleases/stories/2004/12_december/09/dyson.shtml. Accessed 22 September 2011.

5 Bill Magee, 'Two heads, one mind'. *Director Magazine* (November, 2006). www.director.co.uk/MAGAZINE/2006/11%20Nov/mentoring_60_4.html.

6 Views expressed in an interview reported in the article 'Ask the expert: Dyson', *Financial Times* (14 November 2005).

7 www.guardian.co.uk/business/2005/feb/28/science.g2. Accessed 22 June 2011.

8 www.independent.co.uk/news/business/news/dyson-sweeps-up-pound6m-hoover-payout-613146.html. Accessed 22 June 2011.

9 www.businessdynamics.org.uk/gen/ymtnoe45jmxuakywlwoliq5509112004103113.pdf. Accessed 22 September 2011.

10 A. Ferguson, *Managing My Life: An Autobiography* (London: Hodder & Stoughton, 1999).

11 P. F. Drucker, 'Managing oneself', *Harvard Business Review* (March–April, 1999): 65–74.

12 Stephen Covey (*The Seven Habits of Highly Effective People*, Simon & Schuster, 1989) advises us to start at the end – to visualise our own funerals and imagine what we would like the funeral speakers to say about us and our lives. On this basis, he recommends that we develop lifetime mission statements based on the multiple roles that we occupy in life.

13 Sun Tzu, *The Art of Strategy: A New Translation of Sun Tzu's Classic 'The Art of War'*, trans. R. L. Wing (New York: Doubleday, 1988).

14 During the late 1950s, *Harvard Business Review* featured a number of articles on corporate planning, e.g. D. W. Ewing, 'Looking around: long-range business planning', *Harvard Business Review* (July–August 1956): 135–46; B. Payne, 'Steps in long-range planning', *Harvard Business Review* (March–April 1957): 95–101.

15 M. E. Porter, *Competitive Strategy* (New York: Free Press, 1980).

16 Boston Consulting Group, *Perspectives on Experience* (Boston: Boston Consulting Group, 1978).

17 R. M. Grant, 'The resource-based theory of competitive advantage: implications for strategy formulation', *California Management Review* 33 (Spring 1991): 114–35; D. J. Collis and C. Montgomery, 'Competing on resources: strategy in the 1990s', *Harvard Business Review* (July–August 1995): 119–28.

18 M. E. Porter, 'What is strategy?' *Harvard Business Review* (November–December 1996): 64.

19 C. Christensen, *The Innovator's Dilemma* (Boston: Harvard Business School Press, 1997).

20 C. Shapiro and H. R. Varian, *Information Rules* (Boston: Harvard Business School Press, 1998).

21 R. H. Frank and P. J. Cook, *The Winner-Take-All Society* (New York: Penguin, 1997).

22 W. C. Kim and R. Mauborgne, 'Creating new market space', *Harvard Business Review* (January–February 1999): 83–93.

23 D. J. Collis and M. G. Rukstad, 'Can you say what your strategy is?' *Harvard Business Review* (April 2008): 63–73.

24 See H. Mintzberg, 'Patterns of strategy formulation', *Management Science* 24 (1978): 934–48; 'Of strategies: deliberate and emergent', *Strategic Management Journal* 6 (1985): 257–72; and *Mintzberg on Management: Inside Our Strange World of Organizations* (New York: Free Press, 1988).

25 H. Mintzberg, 'The fall and rise of strategic planning', *Harvard Business Review* (January–February 1994): 107–14.

26 The two views of Honda are captured in two Harvard cases: *Honda [A]* (Boston: Harvard Business School, Case No. 384049, 1989) and *Honda [B]* (Boston: Harvard Business School, Case No. 384050, 1989).

27 Boston Consulting Group, *Strategy Alternatives for the British Motorcycle Industry* (London: Her Majesty's Stationery Office, 1975).

28 R. T. Pascale, 'Perspective on strategy: the real story behind Honda's success', *California Management Review* 26, no. 3 (Spring 1984): 47–72.

29 H. Mintzberg, 'Crafting strategy', *Harvard Business Review* 65 (July–August 1987): 70.

30 R. A. Burgelman and A. Grove, 'Strategic dissonance', *California Management Review* 38 (Winter 1996): 8–28.

31 R. M. Grant, 'Strategic planning in a turbulent environment: evidence from the oil and gas majors', *Strategic Management Journal* 14 (June 2003): 491–517.

32 'Strategic intensity: a conversation with Garry Kasparov', *Harvard Business Review* (April 2005): 105–13.

33 The concept of bounded rationality was developed by Herbert Simon ('A behavioral model of rational choice', *Quarterly Journal of Economics* 69 (1955): 99–118).

34 G. Hamel and C. K. Prahalad, 'Strategic intent', *Harvard Business Review* (May–June 1989): 63–77.

35 G. Hamel and C. K. Prahalad, 'Strategy as stretch and leverage', *Harvard Business Review* (March–April 1993): 75–84.

36 J. C. Collins and J. I. Porras, *Built to Last: Successful Habits of Visionary Companies* (New York: HarperCollins, 1995).

37 K. E. Weick, *Sensemaking in Organizations* (Thousand Oaks, CA: Sage, 1995: 54).

38 T. Donaldson and L. E. Preston, The stakeholder theory of the corporation, *Academy of Management Review* 20 (1995): 65–91.

39 See www.abelard.org/ford.

40 J. Collins and J. Porras, 'Building your company's vision', *Harvard Business Review* (September–October, 1996): 65–77.

41 Author's interview.

42 C. A. Montgomery, 'Putting leadership back into strategy, *Harvard Business Review* (January, 2008): 54–60.

43 M. Friedman, *Capitalism and Freedom* (Chicago: University of Chicago Press, 1963). See also: M. Friedman, 'The social responsibility of business is to increase its profits', *New York Times Magazine* (13 September 1970).

44 W. T. Allen, 'Our schizophrenic conception of the business corporation', *Cardozo Law Review* 14 (1992): 261–81.

45 C. Handy, 'What's a business for?' *Harvard Business Review* (December, 2002): 133–43.

46 Stern Stewart & Co, *Russell 3000 Annual Ranking Data*, 2003 (2004).

47 Weber Shandwick, Global CEO turnover rises 10% in past 12 months according to new study', (March 3, 2008), www.webershandwick.com; M. Wiersema, 'Holes at the top: why CEO firings backfire', *Harvard Business Review* (December 2002): 66–78; S. N. Kaplan and B. Minton, "How CEO turnover changed," NBER Working Paper No. 12465 (August, 2006).

48 S. L. Hart and M. B. Milstein, 'Global sustainability and the creative destruction of industries', *Sloan Management Review* 41 (Fall, 1999): 23–33; M. Orlitzky, F. L. Schmidt and S. L. Rynes, 'Corporate social and financial performance: a meta-analysis', *Organization Studies* 24 (Summer, 2003): 403–41.

49 J. Figuero, S. Greco and M. Ehrgott, *Multiple Criteria Decision Analysis: State of the Art Surveys* (Berlin: Springer, 2005).

50 W. King, *The King of Shaves* (London: Headline, 2009).

51 R. Ouellet, *Knowledge and Merchandising Inc. Ltd – Case Study* (Reims Management School, 2006).

52 King, W. (2009) *The King of Shaves Story* (London: Headline, 2009: 18–19).

53 http://annualconvention.iod.com/tips.

Industry analysis

Introduction and objectives

In this chapter we explore the external environment of the firm. In Chapter 1 we observed that profound understanding of the competitive environment is a critical ingredient of a successful strategy. We further noted that business strategy is essentially a quest for profit. The primary task for this chapter is to identify the sources of profit in the external environment. The firm's proximate environment is its industry environment; hence the primary focus of this chapter is on industry analysis.

By the time you have completed this chapter you will:

● Be familiar with a number of frameworks used to analyse an organisation's external environment and understand how the structural features of an industry influence competition and profitability;

● Be able to use evidence on structural trends within industries to forecast changes in competition and profitability and to develop appropriate strategies for the future;

● Understand the value and challenge of undertaking industry analysis and be able to provide a critique of Porter's five forces framework;

● Be able to analyse competition and customer requirements in order to identify opportunities for competitive advantage within an industry (*key success factors*).

Opening case The Mobile Phone Industry

VIDEO

Mobile phones have been one of the most significant growth industries in the world over the past two decades. During the 1990s the growth in handset sales in North America, Europe and Japan averaged close to 50% each year and generated massive profits and shareholder value for the early leaders such as Motorola, Ericsson, Nokia and Siemens. During the late 1980s and into the 1990s these firms dominated the design, production and marketing of mobile phones and had a strong presence in the mobile communications infrastructure business. These manufacturers invested huge sums in research and development to improve performance and to reduce the size of mobile phones and their success moved the mobile phone from being a niche product limited to business and professional users to one with mass market appeal.

As this industry developed profound changes took place in its competitive structure and profitability. Over time technology and the requirements of end-users grew in sophistication and the handset became an increasingly complex device. It proved virtually impossible for any single handset  manufacturer to retain leading expertise in the rapidly evolving array of hardware and software technologies associated with this product. As a consequence the industry witnessed an influx of new, more specialised firms, producing software and components that were assembled by branded and own equipment manufacturing (OEM) firms. Overall the industry fragmented with the early leaders predominantly transforming themselves into systems integrators and assemblers supporting a hinterland of more specialist firms producing components, sub-assemblies and software.

There has also been cross entry into this market by established telecom equipment manufacturers (Lucent, Alcatel) and consumer electronics companies (Sony, Sharp, LG, Samsung, Hitachi, Toshiba, Matsushita) as well as the emergence of some new international players. This latter group includes a number of manufacturers from Taiwan (HTC, BenQ) and mainland China (Huawei, ZTE, Lenovo) – many of these recent entrants were former contract manufacturers now supplying under their own brands. During 2007–8, the world handset market was further shaken up by the introduction of the smartphone, particularly Apple's introduction of the iPhone and Google's development of the Android mobile operating system.

In addition, the handset manufacturers face strong vertical bargaining power from both suppliers and customers. On the demand side wireless service providers have become major distributors of mobile handsets, offering end-users discounted phones when they sign up for call packages. Service providers, like Vodafone, Orange and Verizon, are engaged in a continuous struggle with the handset manufacturers for pre-eminence in consumer brand loyalty and seek to strengthen their bargaining power by ordering specially designed handsets manufactured under their own brands. At the other end of the supply chain the manufacturers are dealing with powerful suppliers including the suppliers of digital signalling chips and operating systems (Microsoft, Symbian, Palm).

Overall these trends have been depressing industry profitability, despite continued demand growth especially in emerging markets. During 2000–5 the industry leaders – Nokia, Motorola, Sony Ericsson and Samsung – earned an average pre-tax margin of 20.2% on their sales of mobile devices; by 2006–8 this had fallen to 8.9% with Motorola incurring substantial losses. There have also been departures from the industry including Phillips, Siemens, Mitsubishi and Sanyo. The structural trends that have eroded profitability over the past decade seem likely to continue in the near future. It is likely that market saturation will spread from established to more recently developed markets, like China and India. Despite the prospect of excess manufacturing capability, there is a risk that new entry will continue to boost the already excessive number of mobile phone suppliers. Widespread outsourcing by the leading suppliers to contract manufacturers in Asia and elsewhere means that there are many firms with the manufacturing capability and know-how ready to enter the market with their own brands.

There are two major uncertainties facing producers: firstly, the future of product differentiation; and, secondly, the balance of bargaining power between handset manufacturers and service providers. With regard to product differentiation, there are two conflicting forces: the growing demand for low-cost, technologically unsophisticated handsets in emerging markets suggests that there will be increasing commoditisation; but the technological opportunities provided by 3G and 4G technologies and the mobile internet offer the possibility of greater differentiation. Although advancing technologies and multi-functionality (e.g. mobile phone as a device for internet access, GPS, TV and music) may allow some firms to gain an advantage, most forms of differentiation in this market appear short-lived as other firms quickly imitate. Already the distinction between smartphones such as RIM's Blackberry and Apple's iPhone and mainstream mobile phones is disappearing. It seems that, as a result of market power and control over distribution, the service producers, at present, still hold the balance of vertical power in this market, but as the industry continues to evolve firms designing and producing handsets may strengthen their position. Much will depend on which side has greater control over technology.

From environmental analysis to industry analysis

The **business environment** of a firm consists of all the external influences that affect its decisions and performance. Given the vast number and range of external influences, how can managers hope to monitor, let alone analyse, environmental conditions? The starting point is some kind of system or framework for organising information. For example, environmental influences can be classified by *source* – e.g. political, economic, social and technological factors ('PEST analysis') – or by *proximity* – the 'micro-environment' or 'task environment' can be distinguished from the wider influences that form the 'macro-environment'.[1]

PEST analysis, in particular, has become popular as an environmental scanning framework because it provides a simple yet systematic approach to identifying those factors that are likely to shape the competitive conditions within an industry. Recognising these 'basic forces' is important in understanding and predicting how an industry might change and evolve over time and is a key initial step in thinking about future scenarios and the opportunities and threats that the industry might face. Case Insight 2.1 provides an example of PEST analysis based on the opening case.

Case Insight 2.1
Example of a PEST analysis

Some illustrative examples of the PEST factors affecting firms in the mobile handset industry

Political

- *Licences* – the way governments select companies to provide access to the wireless spectrum for 3G and 4G services affects not only the service operators but also the nature and level of demand for different types of handsets.
- *Standardisation* – a number of mobile phone manufacturers have agreed to a standard connector for charging phone batteries. This makes life easier for end-users but may also contribute to the commoditisation of mobile phones, i.e. the process by which mobile phones become indistinguishable from one another and consumers buy solely on the basis of price.
- *Restrictions on usage* – governments place restrictions on the use of mobile phones, for example on aeroplanes or whilst driving a car. Given that the products of all the handset manufacturers are subject to the same restrictions, these constraints are unlikely to affect the competitive position of a particular handset firm but may provide incentives for new technologies to be developed or might limit the extent to which handsets are substituted for products such as car satellite navigation systems.

Economic

- *The level of economic activity* – during the recent recession overall sales of mobile phones slowed significantly but smartphone sales remained buoyant.[2] This suggests that mobile handset providers may be differentially affected by economic fluctuations according to the mix of handsets they offer.
- *The rapid take-up of mobile technologies in developing economies* – mobile connections offer a more economical and efficient solution than land lines to communications infrastructure problems in many countries including Africa and India. The geographic focus of different handset manufacturers may have significant implications for their growth rates.

Social

- *Health scares* – concerns have been raised about the amount of radio waves that people can safely absorb into their bodies when talking on a mobile phone. The mobile handset producers obviously need to be aware of the latest research and adopt appropriate risk management policies.
- *Changes in fashion* – mobile phones are increasingly being viewed as a fashion accessory by younger age groups which creates both opportunities and challenges for handset designers.

Technological

- The mobile handset industry is characterised by rapid changes in technology which invariably creates winners and losers. Technological improvements that are on the horizon include extensions to battery life, the development of 4G systems and more secure encryption.

Though systematic, continuous scanning of the whole range of external influences might seem desirable, extensive environmental analysis incurs high costs and creates information overload. Merely listing large numbers of external factors that in some way influence firms' operations and performance is rarely helpful. Rather, the key to effective environmental analysis is to distinguish the vital from the merely important. For example, although all the PEST factors listed in Case Insight 2.1 have an impact on firms in the mobile handset industry, some are clearly more important than others. Restrictions on the use of mobile phones on aircraft clearly have fewer consequences than global recessions or technological breakthroughs. For PEST analysis to be worthwhile those undertaking the analysis need to exercise judgement and keep in mind the purpose of the exercise, which is to identify those factors that are likely to be the *most important* in shaping industry conditions. It is to industry conditions we turn next but before we start it is worthwhile reminding ourselves of some basic principles.

First, for a firm to make a profit it must create value for customers. Hence, it must understand its customers. Second, in creating value, the firm acquires goods and services from suppliers. Hence, it must understand its suppliers and manage relationships with them. Third, the ability to generate profitability depends on the intensity of competition among firms that compete for the same value-creating opportunities. Hence, the firm must

> The core of the firm's business environment is formed by its relationships with three sets of players: customers, suppliers and competitors. This is its industry environment.

Figure 2.1 From PEST analysis to industry analysis

understand competition. Thus, the core of the firm's business environment is formed by its relationships with three sets of players: customers, suppliers and competitors. This is its industry environment.

This is not to say that macro-level PEST factors such as general economic trends, changes in demographic structure or social and political trends are unimportant to strategy analysis. These factors are critical determinants of the threats and opportunities a company will face in the future, but the key issue is how these more general environmental factors affect the firm's industry environment (Figure 2.1).

Consider the threat of global warming. For most companies this is not an important strategic issue (at least, not for the next 100 years). However, for the producers of cars, global warming is a vital issue. But, to analyse the strategic implications of global warming, the car manufacturers need to trace its implications for their industry environment. For example, what will be the impact on consumers and their preferences? Will there be a switch from private to public transportation? With regard to competition, will there be new entry by manufacturers of electric vehicles into the car industry? Will increased R&D costs cause the industry to consolidate?

The determinants of industry profit: demand and competition

The starting point for industry analysis is a simple question: what determines the level of profit in an industry?

The prerequisite for profit is the creation of value for the customer. Value is created when the price the customer is willing to pay for a product exceeds the costs incurred by the firm. But value creation does not translate directly into profit. The surplus of value over cost is distributed between customers and producers by the forces of competition. The stronger the competition among producers, the more of the surplus is received by customers in **consumer surplus** and the less is the surplus received as **producer surplus**. A single supplier of bottled water at an all-night rave can charge a price that fully exploits the dancers' thirst. If there are many suppliers of bottled water, then, in the absence of competitor complicity, competition causes the price of bottled water to fall toward the cost of supplying it.

Even when producers earn a surplus, this is not necessarily captured in profits. Where an industry has powerful suppliers – monopolistic suppliers of components or employees united by a strong labour union – a substantial part of the surplus may be appropriated by these suppliers (the profits of suppliers or premium wages of union members).

The profits earned by the firms in an industry are thus determined by three factors:

- the value of the product to customers;
- the intensity of competition;
- the bargaining power of the producers relative to their suppliers.

Industry analysis brings all three factors into a single analytic framework.

Analysing industry attractiveness

Table 2.1 shows the profitability of different US industries. Some industries (such as tobacco and pharmaceuticals) consistently earn high rates of profit; others (motor vehicles and parts, entertainment) earn much lower rates of profit or fail to cover their cost of capital (airlines). The basic premise that underlies industry analysis is that the level of industry profitability is neither random nor the result of entirely industry-specific influences – it is determined by the systematic influences of the industry's structure. The pharmaceutical industry and the personal computer industry not only supply very different products, they also have very different structures, which make one highly profitable and the other a nightmare of price competition and weak margins. The pharmaceutical industry produces highly differentiated products bought by price-insensitive consumers and new products receive monopoly privileges in the form of patents. The personal computer industry comprises many firms, produces commoditised products and is squeezed by powerful suppliers (e.g. Intel and Microsoft).

Small markets can often support much higher profitability than large markets – for the simple reason that small markets can more easily be dominated by a single firm. Featured Example 2.1 offers examples of niche markets that are havens from the rigours of fierce competition.

Table 2.1 The profitability of US industries, 2000–10

Industry	Median ROE 2000–10 (%)	Leading companies
Tobacco	33.5	Philip Morris Intl., Altria, Reynolds American
Household and personal products	27.8	Procter & Gamble, Kimberly-Clark, Colgate-Palmolive
Pharmaceuticals	20.5	Pfizer, Johnson & Johnson, Merck
Food consumer products	20.0	PepsiCo, Kraft Foods, General Mills
Food services	19.9	McDonald's, Yum Brands, Starbucks
Medical products and equipment	18.5	Medtronic, Baxter International, Boston Scientific
Petroleum refining	17.6	ExxonMobil, Chevron, ConocoPhillips
Mining, crude oil production	16.3	Occidental Petroleum, Devon Energy
Securities	15.9	KKR, BlackRock, Charles Schwab
Chemicals	15.7	Dow Chemical, Du Pont, PPG
Aerospace and defence	15.7	Boeing, United Technologies, Lockheed Martin
Construction and farm equipment	14.5	Caterpillar, Deere, Illinois Tool Works
IT services	14.1	IBM, Computer Sciences, SAIC
Specialty retailers (non-apparel)	13.9	Home Depot, Costco, Lowe's
Communications equipment	13.1	Cisco Systems, Motorola, Qualcomm
Healthcare insurance and managed care	13.1	United Health Group, Wellpoint, Aetna
Commercial banks	12.4	Bank of America, JP Morgan Chase, Citigroup
Engineering, construction	12.3	Fluor, Jacobs Engineering, KBR
Computers, office equipment	12.1	Hewlett-Packard, Apple, Dell Computer
Diversified financials	12.	General Electric, Fannie Mae
General merchandisers	11.6	Wal-Mart, Target, Sears Holdings
Energy	11.4	AES, AEP, Constellation Energy,

Industry	Median ROE 2000–10 (%)	Leading companies
Pipelines	11.1	Plains All-American, Enterprise Products, Oneok
Utilities: gas and electric	10.6	Execon, Southern, NextEra
Packaging and containers	10.2	Ball, Crown Holdings, Owens-Illinois
Automotive retailing and services	9.8	AutoNation, Penske, Hertz
Food and drug stores	9.6	CVS, Kroger, Walgreen
Insurance: property and casualty	9.5	Berkshire Hathaway, AIG, Allstate
Insurance: life and health	8.7	MetLife, Prudential, Aflac
Hotels, casinos, resorts	8.5	Marriott International, Caesars, Las Vegas Sands
Metals	8.2	Alcoa, US Steel, Nucor
Semiconductors and electronic components	7.7	Intel, Texas Instruments, Jamil Circuit
Forest and paper products	7.3	International Paper, Weyerhaeuser, Domtar
Food Production	5.2	Archer Daniels Midland, Tyson Foods, Smithfield
Telecommunications	5.8	Verizon, AT&T, Sprint-Nextel
Motor vehicles and parts	4.4	GM, Ford, Johnson Controls
Entertainment	3.9	Time Warner, Walt Disney, News Corporation
Airlines	−11.3	AMR, UAL, Delta Airlines

Notes:

1 Median ROE for each industry averaged across the 11 years 2000–10.

2 Industries with fewer than five or firms were excluded (with the exception of tobacco). Also omitted were industries that were substantially redefined during the period.

Source: Data from Fortune 1000 by industry.

Featured example 2.1 Chewing tobacco, sausage skins and slot machines: the joys of niche markets

UST Inc was the most profitable company in the S&P500 over the period 2003–8 (in 2008 it was acquired by Altria, the owner of Philip Morris) with an average annual ROIC (operating profit as percentage of total assets less current liabilities) of 63%. What's the secret of UST's profitability? It controls 78% of the US market for 'smokeless tobacco' (chewing tobacco and snuff), with brands such as Skoal, Copenhagen and Red Seal. Despite its association with a bygone era of cowboys and farm workers, chewing tobacco has been a growth market in the US. UST's long-established brands, its distribution through tens of thousands of small retail outlets and restrictions on advertising tobacco products have created formidable barriers to entry into this market.

Devro plc, based in the Scottish village of Moodiesburn, is the world's leading supplier of collagen sausage skins ('casings'). 'From the British "banger" to the Chinese lap cheong, from the French merguez to the South American chorizo, Devro has a casing to suit all product types'. Its overall world market share is around 60%, with about 80% of the UK and Australian markets. In recent years its ROIC has averaged 18% and its return on equity 20%.

International Game Technology (IGT) based in Reno, Nevada, is the world's dominant manufacturer of slot machines for casinos. ITG maintains its 70% US market share through close relations with casino operators and a continuous flow of new products. With heavy investment in R&D, new product saturation, tight control over distribution and servicing and a policy of leasing rather than selling machines, IGT offers little opportunity to rivals. During 2004–7, IGT earned an average ROE of 31%.

Sources: **www.ustinc.com**, **www.devro.com**, **www.igt.com**.

Figure 2.2 Porter's five forces of competition framework

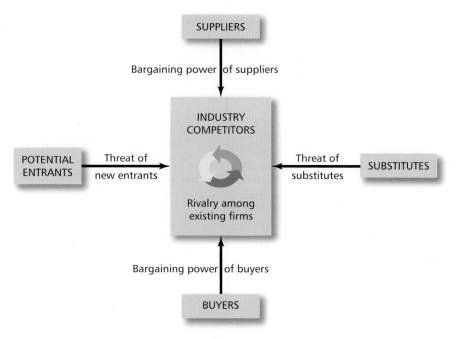

Porter's five forces of competition framework

A helpful, widely used framework for classifying and analysing the factors that determine the intensity of competition and levels of competition in different industries was developed by Michael Porter of Harvard Business School.[3] Porter's five forces of competition framework views the profitability of an industry (as indicated by its rate of return on capital relative to its cost of capital) as determined by five sources of competitive pressure. These five forces of competition include three sources of 'horizontal' competition: competition from substitutes, competition from entrants and competition from established rivals; and two sources of 'vertical' competition: the power of suppliers and power of buyers (see Figure 2.2).

The strength of each of these competitive forces is determined by a number of key structural variables, as shown in Figure 2.3.

Competition from substitutes

The price customers are willing to pay for a product depends, in part, on the availability of substitute products. The absence of close substitutes for a product, as in the case of petrol or cigarettes, means that consumers are comparatively insensitive to price (i.e. demand is inelastic with respect to price). The existence of close substitutes means that customers will switch to substitutes in response to price increases for the product (i.e. demand is elastic with respect to price). The internet has provided a new source of substitute

Figure 2.3 The structural determinants of the five forces of competition

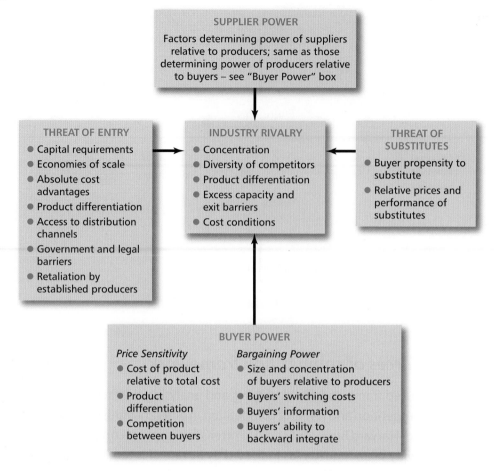

competition that has proved devastating for a number of established industries. Travel agencies, newspapers and telecommunication providers have all suffered devastating competition from internet-based substitutes.

The extent to which substitutes depress prices and profits depends on the propensity of buyers to substitute between alternatives. Most power users are indifferent as to how their electricity is generated. Hence, wind farms face strong substitute competition from electricity generated by natural gas, coal and nuclear power. In the US, the steep decline in natural gas prices between July 2008 and July 2011 as a result of the boom in shale gas has sharply reduced the profitability of the wind farms.

The threat of entry

If an industry earns a return on capital in excess of its cost of capital, it will act as a magnet to firms outside the industry. If the entry of new firms is unrestricted, the rate of profit will fall toward its competitive level. The US bagel industry faced a flood of new entrants in the late 1990s that caused a sharp decline in profitability.[4] We also see the impact of entry restrictions in many professions. Why, on average, do orthodontists earn higher salaries than general dentists? The explanation lies, in part, with the need for qualified dentists to obtain a further licence to practise orthodontics. Restrictions on the number of licences create barriers to entry.

Threat of entry rather than actual entry may be sufficient to ensure that established firms constrain their prices to the competitive level. Eurostar is currently the only company offering a high speed passenger rail service through the Channel Tunnel which links Britain and France. Yet, Eurostar may be unwilling to exploit its monopoly power to the full given that European liberalisation legislation means that other rail operators will soon be able to extend their operations to this route. An industry where no barriers to entry or exit exist is *contestable*: prices and

> Threat of entry rather than actual entry may be sufficient to ensure that established firms constrain their prices to the competitive level.

profits tend towards the competitive level, regardless of the number of firms within the industry.[5] Contestability depends on the absence of **sunk costs** – investments whose value cannot be recovered on exit. An absence of sunk costs makes an industry vulnerable to 'hit-and-run' entry whenever established firms raise their prices above the competitive level.

In most industries, however, new entrants cannot enter on equal terms with those of established firms. A **barrier to entry** is any advantage that established firms have over entrants. The height of a barrier to entry is usually measured as the unit cost disadvantage faced by would-be entrants. The principal sources of barriers to entry are discussed below.

CAPITAL REQUIREMENTS   The capital costs of getting established in an industry can be so large as to discourage all but the largest companies. The duopoly of Boeing and Airbus in large passenger jets is protected by the huge capital costs of establishing R&D, production and service facilities for supplying these planes. Similarly with the business of launching commercial satellites: the costs of developing rockets and launch facilities make new entry highly unlikely. In other industries, entry costs can be modest. For example running a fitness boot camp in a local park requires very little capital, which is one reason why many such programmes have sprung up in recent years. Similarly the costs of internet ventures such as price comparison websites are typically small. Across the service sector more generally, start-up costs tend to be low. For example, start-up costs for a franchised pizza outlet begin at $120,000 for a Domino's and $638,000 for a Pizza Hut.[6]

ECONOMIES OF SCALE In industries that are capital or research or advertising intensive, efficiency requires large-scale operation. The problem for new entrants is that they are faced with the choice of either entering on a small scale and accepting high unit costs, or entering on a large scale and bearing the costs of underutilised capacity. In the car industry, cost efficiency means producing at least three million vehicles a year. As a result, the only recent entrants into volume car production have been state-supported companies (e.g., Proton of Malaysia and Maruti of India). The main source of **scale economies** is new product development costs. Thus, developing and launching a new model of car typically costs over $1.5 billion. Airbus's A380 superjumbo cost about $18 billion to develop and must sell about 400 planes to break even. Once Airbus had committed to the project, then Boeing was effectively excluded from the superjumbo segment of the market.

ABSOLUTE COST ADVANTAGES Established firms may have a unit cost advantage over entrants irrespective of scale. **Absolute cost advantages** often result from the acquisition of low-cost sources of raw materials. Saudi Aramco's access to the world's biggest and most accessible oil reserves give it an unassailable cost advantage over Shell, Exxon Mobil and BP, whose costs per barrel are at least four times those of Saudi Aramco. Absolute cost advantages may also result from economies of learning. Sharp's cost advantage in LCD flat screen TVs results from its early entry into LCDs and its speed in moving down the learning curve.

PRODUCT DIFFERENTIATION In an industry where products are differentiated, established firms possess the advantages of brand recognition and customer loyalty. The percentage of US consumers loyal to a single brand varies from under 30% in batteries, canned vegetables and garbage bags, up to 61% in toothpaste, 65% in mayonnaise and 71% in cigarettes.[7] New entrants to such markets must spend disproportionately heavily on advertising and promotion to gain levels of brand awareness and brand goodwill similar to that of established companies. One study found that, compared to early entrants, late entrants into consumer goods markets incurred additional advertising and promotional costs amounting to 2.12% of sales revenue.[8]

ACCESS TO CHANNELS OF DISTRIBUTION For many new suppliers of consumer goods, the principal barrier to entry is likely to be gaining distribution. Limited capacity within distribution channels (e.g., shelf space), risk aversion by retailers and the fixed costs associated with carrying an additional product result in retailers being reluctant to carry a new manufacturer's product. The battle for supermarket shelf space between the major food processors (typically involving 'slotting fees' to reserve shelf space) further disadvantages new entrants. One of the most important competitive impacts of the internet has been allowing new businesses to circumvent barriers to distribution.

GOVERNMENTAL AND LEGAL BARRIERS   Economists from the Chicago School claim that the only effective barriers to entry are those created by government. In taxicabs, banking, telecommunications and broadcasting, entry usually requires a licence from a public authority. From medieval times to the present day, companies and favoured individuals have benefited from governments granting them an exclusive right to ply a particular trade or offer a particular service. In knowledge-intensive industries, patents, copyrights and other legally protected forms of intellectual property are major barriers to entry. Xerox Corporation's monopolisation of the plain-paper copier industry until the late 1970s was protected by a wall of over 2000 patents relating to its xerography process. Regulatory requirements and environmental and safety standards often put new entrants at a disadvantage to established firms because compliance costs tend to weigh more heavily on newcomers.

RETALIATION   Barriers to entry also depend on the entrants' expectations as to possible retaliation by established firms. Retaliation against a new entrant may take the form of aggressive price-cutting, increased advertising, sales promotion or litigation. The major airlines have a long history of retaliation against low-cost entrants. Southwest and other budget airlines have alleged that selective price cuts by American and other major airlines amounted to predatory pricing designed to prevent its entry into new routes.[9] To avoid retaliation by incumbents, new entrants may seek initial small-scale entry into less visible market segments. When Toyota, Nissan and Honda first entered the US car market, they targeted the small car segments, partly because this was a segment that had been written off by the Detroit Big Three as inherently unprofitable.[10]

THE EFFECTIVENESS OF BARRIERS TO ENTRY   Industries protected by high entry barriers tend to earn above average rates of profit.[11] Capital requirements and advertising appear to be particularly effective impediments to entry.[12]

The effectiveness of barriers to entry depends on the resources and capabilities that potential entrants possess. Barriers that are effective against new companies may be ineffective against established firms that are diversifying from other industries.[13] Google has used its massive web presence as a platform for entering a number of other markets – including Microsoft's seemingly impregnable position in browsers and Apple's in the smartphone market.

Rivalry between established competitors

For most industries, the major determinant of the overall state of competition and the general level of profitability is competition among the firms within the industry. In some industries, firms compete aggressively – sometimes to the extent that prices are pushed below the level of costs and industry-wide losses are incurred. In other industries, price competition is muted and rivalry focuses on advertising, innovation and other non-price dimensions. The intensity of competition between established firms is the result of interactions between six factors. Let us look at each of them.

CONCENTRATION   Seller concentration refers to the number and size distribution of firms competing within a market. It is most commonly measured by the **concentration ratio**: the combined market share of the leading producers. For example, the four-firm concentration ratio (*CR4*) is the market share of the four largest producers. In markets dominated by a single firm (e.g., Microsoft in PC operating systems, or UST in the US smokeless tobacco market), the dominant firm can exercise considerable discretion over the prices it charges.

Where a market is dominated by a small group of leading companies (an oligopoly), price competition may also be restrained, either by outright collusion or more commonly through 'parallelism' of pricing decisions.[14] Thus, in markets dominated by two companies, such as alkaline batteries (Duracell and Energizer), colour film (Kodak and Fuji) and soft drinks (Coca-Cola and Pepsi), prices tend to be similar and competition focuses on advertising, promotion and product development. As the number of firms supplying a market increases, coordination of prices becomes more difficult and the likelihood that one firm will initiate price-cutting increases. However, despite the frequent observation that the exit of a competitor reduces price competition, while the entry of a new competitor stimulates it, there is little systematic evidence that seller concentration increases profitability. Richard Schmalensee concluded that: 'The relation, if any, between seller concentration and profitability is weak statistically and the estimated effect is usually small'.[15]

DIVERSITY OF COMPETITORS   The extent to which a group of firms can avoid price competition in favour of collusive pricing practices depends on how similar they are in their origins, objectives, costs and strategies. The cosy atmosphere of the US car industry prior to the advent of import competition was greatly assisted by the similarities of the companies in terms of cost structures, strategies and top management mindsets. The intense competition that affects the car markets of Europe and North America today is partly due to the different national origins, costs, strategies and management styles of the competing firms. Similarly, the key challenge faced by OPEC is agreeing and enforcing output quotas among member countries that are sharply different in terms of objectives, production costs, politics and religion.

PRODUCT DIFFERENTIATION   The more similar the offerings among rival firms, the more willing are customers to switch between them and the greater the inducement for firms to cut prices to boost sales. Where the products of rival firms are virtually indistinguishable, the product is a *commodity* and price is the sole basis for competition. Commodity industries such as agriculture, mining and petrochemicals tend to be plagued by price wars and low profits. By contrast, in industries where products are highly differentiated (perfumes, pharmaceuticals, restaurants, management consulting services), price competition tends to be weak, even though there may be many firms competing.

EXCESS CAPACITY AND EXIT BARRIERS   Why does industry profitability tend to fall so drastically during periods of recession? The key is the balance between demand and capacity. Unused capacity encourages firms to offer price cuts to attract new business. Excess capacity may be cyclical (e.g. the boom–bust cycle in the semiconductor industry); it may also be part of a structural problem resulting from overinvestment and declining demand. In these latter situations, the key issue is whether excess capacity will leave the industry. **Barriers to exit** are costs associated with capacity leaving an industry. Where resources are durable and specialised and where employees are entitled to job protection, barriers to exit may be substantial.[16] In the European and North American car industry excess capacity together with high exit barriers have devastated industry profitability. Conversely, rapid demand growth creates capacity shortages that boost margins.

COST CONDITIONS: SCALE ECONOMIES AND THE RATIO OF FIXED TO VARIABLE COSTS   When excess capacity causes price competition, how low will prices go? The key factor is cost structure. Where **fixed costs** are high relative to **variable costs**, firms will take on marginal business at any price that covers variable costs. The consequences for profitability can be disastrous. In the airline industry, the emergence of excess capacity almost invariably leads to price wars and industry-wide losses. The willingness of airlines

The market for DRAM (dynamic random access memory) chips, used in electronic goods such as laptop computers and home games consoles, illustrates the link between demand, costs, and industry profitability well. Demand for DRAM chips is closely correlated with global levels of economic activity whereas the supply of DRAM chips is constrained by the size of fabrication plants and the rate at which production capacity can be ramped up. When demand is buoyant, it is difficult to add extra manufacturing capacity quickly. Similarly when demand falls away, because of the massive set-up costs and distinctive production processes of this industry, manufacturers cannot withdraw or cut back production easily or quickly. Between January and September 2010 DRAM prices fluctuated between a low of US$1.19 for a standard chip to and a high of US$4.5 with consequent effects on the profitability of DRAM chip producers such as Fujitsu (Japan), Samsung (Korea), Vanguard (Taiwan) and Virtium (US).

to offer heavily discounted tickets on flights with low bookings reflects the very low variable costs of filling empty seats. During the recession in 2009, the industries that suffered the most drastic falls in profitability (cars, mining, hotels) tended to be those where fixed costs are high and firms are willing to accept additional business at any price that covers variable costs.

Scale economies may also encourage companies to compete aggressively on price in order to gain the cost benefits of greater volume. If scale efficiency in the car industry means producing four million cars a year, a level that is currently achieved by only five companies, the outcome is a battle for market share as each firm tries to achieve critical mass.

Bargaining power of buyers

The firms in an industry compete in two types of markets: in the markets for inputs and in the markets for outputs. In input markets firms purchase raw materials, components and financial and labour services. In the markets for outputs firms sell their goods and services to customers (who may be distributors, consumers or other manufacturers). In both markets the transactions create value for both buyers and sellers. How this value is shared between them in terms of profitability depends on their relative economic power. Let us deal first with output markets. The strength of buying power that firms face from their customers depends on two sets of factors: buyers' price sensitivity and relative bargaining power.

> The firms in an industry compete in two types of markets: in the markets for inputs and in the markets for outputs.

BUYERS' PRICE SENSITIVITY   The extent to which buyers are sensitive to the prices charged by the firms in an industry depends on four main factors:

- The greater the importance of an item as a proportion of total cost, the more sensitive buyers will be about the price they pay. Beverage manufacturers are highly sensitive to the costs of aluminium cans because this is one of their largest single cost items. Conversely, most companies are not sensitive to the fees charged by their auditors, since auditing costs are a tiny fraction of total company expenses.

- The less differentiated the products of the supplying industry, the more willing the buyer is to switch suppliers on the basis of price. The manufacturers of T-shirts and light bulbs have much more to fear from Tesco's buying power than have the suppliers of perfumes.

- The more intense the competition among buyers, the greater their eagerness for price reductions from their sellers. As competition in the world car industry has intensified, so component suppliers face greater pressures for lower prices.

- The more critical an industry's product to the quality of the buyer's product or service, the less sensitive are buyers to the prices they are charged. The buying power of personal computer manufacturers relative to the manufacturers of microprocessors (Intel and AMD) is limited by the vital importance of these components to the functionality of PCs.

RELATIVE BARGAINING POWER   Bargaining power rests, ultimately, on refusal to deal with the other party. The balance of power between the two parties to a transaction depends on the credibility and effectiveness with which each makes this threat. The key issue is the relative cost that each party sustains as a result of the transaction not being consummated. A second issue is each party's expertise in managing its position. Several factors influence the bargaining power of buyers relative to that of sellers:

- *Size and concentration of buyers relative to suppliers*. The smaller the number of buyers and the bigger their purchases, the greater the cost of losing one. Because of their size, health maintenance organisations (HMOs) can purchase healthcare from hospitals and doctors at much lower cost than can individual patients. Empirical studies show that buyer concentration lowers prices and profits in the supplying industry.[17]

- *Buyers' information*. The better informed buyers are about suppliers and their prices and costs, the better they are able to bargain. Doctors and lawyers do not normally display the prices they charge, nor do traders in the bazaars of Tangier and Istanbul. Keeping customers ignorant of relative prices is an effective constraint on their buying power. But knowing prices is of little value if the quality of the product is unknown. In the markets for haircuts, interior design and management consulting, the ability of buyers to bargain over price is limited by uncertainty over the precise attributes of the product they are buying.

- *Ability to integrate vertically*. In refusing to deal with the other party, the alternative to finding another supplier or buyer is to do it yourself. Large food-processing companies such as Heinz and Campbell Soup have reduced their dependence on the manufacturers of metal cans by manufacturing their own. The leading retail chains have increasingly displaced their suppliers' brands with their own-brand products. Backward integration need not necessarily occur – a credible threat may suffice.

Bargaining power of suppliers

Analysis of the determinants of relative power between the producers in an industry and their suppliers is comparable to analysis of the relationship between producers and their buyers. The only difference is that it is now the firms in the industry that are the buyers and the producers of inputs that are the suppliers. The key issues are the ease with which the firms in the industry can switch between different input suppliers and the relative bargaining power of each party.

Because raw materials, semi-finished products and components are often commodities supplied by small companies to large manufacturing companies, their suppliers usually lack bargaining power. Hence, commodity suppliers often seek to boost their bargaining power through cartelisation (e.g., OPEC, the International Coffee Organisation and farmers' marketing cooperatives). A similar logic explains labour unions. Conversely, the suppliers of complex, technically sophisticated components may be able to exert considerable bargaining power. The dismal profitability of the personal computer industry may be attributed to the power exercised by the suppliers of key components (processors, disk drives, LCD screens) and the dominant supplier of operating systems (Microsoft).

Case Insight 2.2
Porter's five forces framework applied to the mobile handset industry

Competition from substitutes

Although it might be argued that fixed-line telephones are a substitute for mobiles, the relationship between these two forms of telephone communication

---

is ambiguous. On the one hand mobiles may be used instead of landlines, particularly in countries like Africa where demand for fixed lines remains unsatisfied. On the other hand in many countries the increased use of fixed-line telephones is positively associated with the use of mobile phones suggesting a complementary relationship. Many service providers promote landline and mobile telephone services as a bundled package.

The functionality of mobile handsets has been extended significantly and most phones now include features such as built-in cameras, music players and global positioning software. This brings handsets into competition with a range of other, more specialist products, for example digital cameras, MP3 players and GPS systems. By the same token other electronic devices offer some of the functionality of mobile phones, for example the development of voice over internet protocols, used in services such as Skype, means that personal computers can be used for voice and visual communication. It remains to be seen which sets of product features customers will want integrated in a single device although there is a tendency for manufacturers to overshoot with respect to performance requirements and offer customers features which they don't use and are reluctant to pay for.

Overall strength of the force: moderate to low.

The threat of entry

The initial growth and profitability of the handset industry has attracted a wide variety of potential entrants and entry has been facilitated by structural changes that have lowered barriers. As the industry has 'unbundled', i.e. changed from one dominated by large vertically integrated firms to one characterised by a diverse array of more specialist firms, so the industry's cost structure has changed. Assemblers of modular products are able to compete on similar terms so small companies enjoy similar costs to larger firms. In addition new entrants from counties like China and Taiwan have advantages in terms of lower factor costs and considerable experience in manufacturing low-cost modular products.

Overall strength of the force: high.

Rivalry between established competitors

Seller concentration varies between countries, for example in the UK three smartphone vendors – RIM, Apple and HTC – took close to a 40% share of the market in 2011.[18] In India, by contrast, Nokia had 36% of the handset market in the second quarter 2010 but this was down from its previous high of over 50% because of the inroads made by Chinese and Indian vendors at the low end of the market. According to recent estimates there were 68 new vendors in the Indian market, who together accounted for approximately 41% of phone shipments in the latter part of 2010.[19] Many of these new vendors positioned themselves to meet the needs of India's rural population, providing low-priced phones with features such as MP3 players and FM radio.

In the market as a whole it has proved increasingly difficult for firms to compete on product characteristics and functionality because different vendors can quickly gain access to the same components and sub-assemblies.

Overall strength of the force: high.

Buyer and supplier power

Handset producers are dependent on component suppliers at one end of their supply chain and mobile phone retailers at the other, with the added complication that network operators, like Vodafone and T-Mobile, distribute large numbers of handsets as part of their call packages. Whilst many of the components needed to assemble handsets are widely available, some critical components, such as the chipsets that are at the heart of mobile phones are controlled by a few large semiconductor firms who have potential bargaining strength, particularly when the market is buoyant.

On the retail side mobile phone handsets are sold through specialist high-street stores, supermarkets and online. In addition, in many countries, handsets are offered to end-users at discounted rates when they sign up for call packages with particular mobile phone network providers. Significant volumes of handsets are sold in this way through network providers' retail outlets, giving service providers a certain degree of bargaining strength vis à vis the handset manufacturers. There are, however, significant numbers of mobile network operators worldwide and the degree of competition between them varies from country to country so the relative bargaining strength of handset producers and distributors is likely to differ according to national and local arrangements.

Overall strength of the force: moderate to high.

Applying industry analysis

Once we understand how industry structure drives competition, which in turn determines industry profitability, we can apply this analysis in one of three ways. First, to forecast industry profitability in the future; second, to position the firm in relation to the competitive forces it faces; and, third, to find ways of changing industry structure for the better.

Forecasting industry profitability

We can use industry analysis to understand why profitability has been low in some industries and high in others but, ultimately, our interest in industry analysis is not to explain the past, but to predict the future. Investment decisions made today will commit resources to an industry for a decade or more – hence, it is critical that we are able to predict what industry profitability is likely to be in the future. Current profitability tends to be a poor indicator of future profitability. However, if an industry's profitability is determined by the structure of that industry, then we can use observations of the structural trends in an industry to forecast the likely changes in competition and profitability. Given that changes in industry structure tend to be long term and are the result of fundamental shifts in customer buying behaviour, technology and firm strategies, we can use our current observations to identify emerging structural trends.

> Ultimately, our interest in industry analysis is not to explain the past, but to predict the future.

To predict the future profitability of an industry, our analysis proceeds in three stages:

1   Examine how the industry's current and recent levels of competition and profitability are a consequence of its present structure.

2   Identify the trends that are changing the industry's structure. Is the industry consolidating? Are new players seeking to enter? Are the industry's products becoming more differentiated or more commoditised? Will additions to industry capacity outstrip growth of demand?

3   Identify how these structural changes will affect the five forces of competition and resulting profitability of the industry. Will the changes in industry structure cause competition to intensify or to weaken? Rarely do all the structural changes move competition in a consistent direction – typically, some factors will cause competition to increase; others will cause competition to moderate. Hence, determining the overall impact on profitability is likely to be a matter of judgement.

VIDEO

Featured example 2.2 The future of horse racing

On 10 April 2010 around 60,000 people crammed in to Oaklawn, a 106-year-old horse racing track in central Arkansas, USA to watch the Arkansas Derby, an event which has become a preview for the more famous Kentucky Derby that takes place three weeks later. Attendance was up by 38% on the previous year but the town of Oaklawn, which has a population of just under 40,000, wasn't built for such crowds so enterprising locals turned their lawns and shop fronts into car parking slots at $20–25 a go.[20]

Whilst events like the Arkansas and Kentucky Derbies in the US, the Grand National in the UK and the Melbourne Cup in Australia are as popular as ever, horse racing in general is going through more turbulent times. Whilst sometimes celebrated as the 'sport of kings', horse racing is a business like any other business and is subject to fluctuations in its fortunes as the external environment changes.

One of the biggest factors triggering change in recent years has been the introduction of the internet. The first online gambling site started in 1995 but such sites have grown rapidly in number and there are now estimated to be in excess of 2000 in existence. The advent of online gambling has not only increased the number of places a 'punter' can place a bet, it has also changed the way in which horse racing takes place.

Horse racing as a sport is heavily dependent on money from betting. Practically every national racing association in the world takes a cut from bets placed on races. In Britain, for example, 10% of bookmakers' profits go to a statutory body that distributes these funds to British horse racing interests, for example the money goes to increase prize money, to support race tracks and horse breeders, to fund work in veterinary science and so on. However, revenues from these kinds of levies are falling. Not only does the internet provide an extended range of opportunities for those who wish to gamble to bet on sports other than horse racing but, more importantly, it means that betting on horse racing does not necessarily take place through bookmakers or at race tracks.

Britain and Australia have permitted the development of betting exchanges which allow people to bet with each other rather than going through licensed bookmakers. The companies that run betting exchanges charge the users a small commission in much the same way that eBay does. In Britain one of the largest of these exchange providers is Betfair. Around 90% of bets placed through exchanges and more than half the bets made online in Britain are now through Betfair. Many traditional bookmakers are beginning to shut up shop, preferring to offer odds through Betfair to avoid taxes and levies. As a consequence the flow of funds into the horse racing industry is diminishing and, overall, the sport is in decline. Whilst headline events still draw the crowds, everyday racing is much harder to sustain.

Some argue that this would have happened anyway. Bookmakers have always looked for ways of avoiding taxes and levies. For example, the bookmakers, Ladbrokes and William Hill, have already moved their betting operations from Britain to Gibraltar, where they are exempt from paying levies and the tax on betting is 2% rather than 15%. The answer they argue is in finding a new revenue model and paying closer attention to what the 'punters' want. Whilst the transformation that is taking place in the industry has taken some stakeholders by surprise, the impact of these environmental changes on competition has long been predicted.

Positioning the company

Recognising and understanding the competitive forces that a firm faces within its industry allows managers to position the firm where competitive forces are weakest. The record industry with its reliance on sales of CDs has been devastated by the substitute competition in the form of digital downloads, piracy and file sharing. Yet not all segments of the recorded music business have been equally affected. The old are less inclined to turn to digital downloading than younger listeners with the result that classical music, country and golden oldies have become comparatively more attractive than pop and hip-hop genres.

Porter describes the success of US truck-maker, PACCAR, in sheltering itself against the bargaining power of fleet buyers. By focusing on the preferences of independent owner-operators – for example by providing superior sleeping cabins, higher specification

> Recognising and understanding the competitive forces that a firm faces within its industry allows managers to position the firm where competitive forces are weakest.

seats, a roadside assistance programme – PACCAR has consistently been able to earn the higher rate of return in the industry.[21]

Effective positioning requires the firm to anticipate changes in the competitive forces likely to impact the industry. Between 2006 and 2008, the pornographic video industry suffered a massive revenue decline as customers turned to free websites that featured user-generated content. A leading survivor in the industry is Vivid Entertainment which has invested in its brand and in high-quality production in an effort to differentiate its DVDs from that available on free websites. Vivid has also initiated legal moves – suing AEBN, owner of PornTube – for copyright infringement.[22]

Strategies to alter industry structure

Understanding how the structural characteristics of an industry determine the intensity of competition and the level of profitability provides a basis for identifying opportunities for changing industry structure to alleviate competitive pressures. The first issue is to identify the key structural features of an industry that are responsible for depressing profitability. The second is to consider which of these structural features are amenable to change through appropriate strategic initiatives. For example:

- The remarkable profit revival in the world steel industry between 2002 and 2008 was mainly the result of rising demand, however, it was also supported by the rapid consolidation of the industry, led by Mittal Steel.[23]

- Excess capacity was a major problem in the European petrochemicals industry. Through a series of bilateral plant exchanges, each company built a leading position within a particular product area.[24]

- In the US airline industry, the major airlines have struggled to change an unfavourable industry structure. In the absence of significant product differentiation, the airlines have used frequent-flier schemes to build customer loyalty. Through hub-and-spoke route systems, the companies have achieved dominance of particular airports: American at Dallas-Fort Worth, US Airways at Charlotte NC and Northwest at Detroit and Memphis. Mergers and alliances have reduced the numbers of competitors on many routes.[25]

- Building entry barriers is a vital strategy for preserving high profitability in the long run. A primary goal of the American Medical Association has been to maintain the incomes of its members by controlling the numbers of doctors trained in the United States and imposing barriers to the entry of doctors from overseas.

Case Insight 2.3
Using industry analysis

Describing industry structure

The mobile phone industry comprises a series of complex linked activities, ranging from the purchase of generic hardware and software components, through the design of the device, the integration of components with the mobile platform and operation system, the physical assembly and production of the handset to marketing and after-sales service. Some companies are integrated across more stages of activities than others making the boundaries of the industry quite difficult to draw. The five forces analysis helps us to sort out the different players and their relationships, and to understand the structural changes that have eroded industry profitability in recent years.

Forecasting industry profitability

Our prior analysis suggests, all other things being equal, that the mobile phone business is likely to become increasingly unattractive over time as profitability moves away from the handset manufacturers to the suppliers of those critical components that perform the key functions that end-users value.

Positioning the company

Competitive forces have resulted in the mobile phone industry becoming increasingly commoditised with intense price competition emerging between suppliers. A number of firms, most notably Apple, have endeavoured to position themselves in parts of the market which offer greater potential for more attractive rates of return, namely the high price, smartphone segment where competition, temporarily, has been less intense.

Strategies to alter industry structure

When Apple initially launched the iPhone in June 2007 in the US, the company announced an exclusive agreement with cellular service provider AT&T. Exclusive deals between manufacturers and network operators were not the norm in this industry at that time. More typical was the arrangement by which manufacturers

▶

sold phones to network operators who in turn heavily discounted the price of handsets to end-users who took up contacts with them. This traditional arrangement had the effect of reinforcing the bargaining power of the network operators relative to the handset manufacturers. Apple attempted to change the rules of the game by offering AT&T exclusive rights in return for a revenue sharing agreement. Whilst the details of the arrangement were secret, commentators suggest that Apple received around 10% of AT&T's iPhone revenue. In the event, the arrangement didn't persist over time because the advantages to Apple of reaching a wider market by collaborating with a larger number of network operators were greater than the revenue derived from the exclusivity arrangement.

Key issues and challenges

The five forces model offers a systematic approach to analysing competition and provides managers with a great of deal of practical insight into the industry environments in which they operate, but Porter's framework is not without its critics. The criticisms tend to take two forms. Some commentators argue that the model offers too simplified a view of product/market competition; it omits important variables and cannot be applied to the dynamic and complex realities of many industries without significant modification or supplementary analysis. Others suggest that the premise on which the model is based is flawed and not supported by strong empirical evidence. We explore these sets of arguments in the next section.

Defining the industry

The first stage of industry analysis is to identify the key elements of the industry's structure and, in principle, this is a simple task. It requires identifying who are the main players – the producers, the customers, the suppliers and the producers of substitute goods – then examining some of the key structural characteristics of each of these groups that will determine competition and bargaining power.

In some sectors, particularly those that are service based, it can be difficult to get a clear picture of the industry and technological change is also causing boundaries to blur.

In many industries the identity of the different groups of players is straightforward but, in others, this is more problematic. In some sectors, particularly those that are service based, it can be difficult to get a clear picture of the industry and technological change is also causing boundaries to blur.

It used to be relatively easy to distinguish the main players in the music industry (the group of firms that sold recordings and performances of music) and to see a clear difference between companies like EMI, who produced music and retailers like HMV who sold CDs and other physical media such as tapes and videos. The digital revolution has blurred these boundaries and these distinctions are no longer clear-cut. Artists can now, if they choose, bypass recording companies and promote their music using websites like YouTube and music recording is no longer tied to the production of physical products, therefore consumer electronics companies like Apple have become music retailers. In the music industry, like many others, technological change is reshaping the ways in which value-adding activities are divided between firms and new configurations are evolving. During transitions such as these, defining industry boundaries becomes more complex and difficult.

To get to grips with delineating industry boundaries, we first need to clarify what we mean by the term 'industry'. Economists define an industry as a group of firms that supplies a market. Hence, a close correspondence exists between markets and industries. From the economist's perspective the key to defining market boundaries is **substitutability**. Substitutability can be defined on either the demand or the supply side. Let us start with the demand side and consider the market within which Jaguar Cars, a subsidiary of Tata Motors, competes. Most of us would take it as given that Jaguar is in the car industry, but its cars are high end and relatively expensive so would not normally be one of the cars considered, for instance, by a family looking to purchase a small car. It is more likely to be seen as a substitute for a BMW 7 series or an Audio A8 than a Ford Focus. If customers are only willing to substitute between Jaguars and other makes of luxury cars, then Jaguar's relevant market is luxury cars rather than the car market as a whole. But we need also to consider substitution from the supply side. If manufacturers find it easy to switch their production from family sedans to luxury cars, such supply-side substitutability would suggest that Jaguar is competing within the broader car market. The ability of Toyota, Nissan and Honda to penetrate the luxury car market suggests that supply-side substitutability between mass-market cars and specialty cars is moderately high.

The same considerations apply to the geographical boundaries of markets. Should Jaguar view itself as competing in a single global market or in a series of separate national or regional markets? The criterion here again is substitutability. If customers are willing and able to substitute cars available on different national markets, or if manufacturers are willing and able to divert their output among different countries to take account of differences in margins, then a market is global. The key test of the geographical boundaries of a market is price: if price differences for the same product between different locations tend to be eroded by demand-side and supply-side substitution, then these locations lie within a single market.

In practice, drawing the boundaries of markets and industries is a matter of judgement that depends on the purposes and context of the analysis. If Tata is considering the pricing and market positioning of its Jaguar cars, it must take a micro-level approach that defines markets around each model, in each country and in relation to different categories of customer (e.g., distinguishing between sales to car rental companies and sales to individual consumers). In considering decisions over investments in technology, component plants and new products, Tata will view Jaguar as one part of its Tata Motors business and will define its market as global and extending across its full range of models. The longer term the decisions are that it is considering, the more broadly it will wish to consider its markets, since substitutability is higher in the long run than in the short term. Fortunately, the precise delineation of the boundaries of a market or industry is seldom critical to the outcome of our analysis so long as we remain alert to external influences.

Case Insight 2.4
Defining the industry

On the demand side the mobile phone industry appears to be clearly defined. Mobile phone handsets are distinctive products that can easily be distinguished from most other ICT products, but even in this market boundaries are beginning

to blur slightly. In the recent past phone handsets had more or less the same features and consumers chose between leading suppliers, such as Nokia, Motorola or Samsung. However, the introduction of smart-phones has added more complexity to the industry. Most phone users probably do not consider a basic mobile phone to be a good substitute for a smartphone such as the iPhone or a Samsung Galaxy. If we were therefore undertaking industry analysis in order to explore Apple's position in the mobile phone industry we might choose to delineate the boundaries of the industry in terms of smartphones, rather than the broader category of mobile phones. But, we might need to keep a watchful eye on developments in tablet computing in case end-users start to see these different devices as substitutes for each other.

On the supply side the boundaries of the mobile phone industry are even less clear-cut. Manufacturers of electronic goods can easily switch between different products, for example the Taiwanese company HTC has become a leading manufacturer of smartphones but started out making notebook computers. Most producers of traditional handsets have now upgraded to the assembly of smartphones as well.

Choosing an appropriate level of analysis

The difficulty of drawing industry boundaries and the need to define industries broadly or narrowly depending on the kinds of questions we are seeking to answer means that sometimes it is helpful to undertake more detailed, disaggregated analysis. One of the main approaches to 'within-' or 'intra-' industry analysis is market segmentation.

Segmentation is the processes of partitioning a market on the basis of characteristics that are likely to influence consumers' purchasing behaviour and segmentation analysis is concerned with evaluating competitive conditions within segmented submarkets. Segmentation is particularly important if competition varies across these different submarkets such that some are more attractive than others. A company can avoid some of the problems of an unattractive industry by judicious segment selection. In the intensely competitive personal computer industry, Dell has used its highly flexible direct distribution system to target products, geographical areas and customers that offer the best margins: 'We cut the market and then cut it again, looking for the most profitable customers to serve,' says CEO Kevin Rollins.[26]

The purpose of segmentation analysis is to identify attractive segments, to select strategies for different segments and to determine how many segments to serve. The analysis proceeds in five stages:

- *Identify possible segmentation variables*. Essentially segmentation decisions are choices about which customers to serve and what to offer them, hence segmentation variables relate to the characteristics of customers and the product. The most appropriate segmentation variables are those that partition the market most distinctly in terms of limits to substitution by customers (demand-side substitutability) and producers (supply-side substitutability). Price differentials are

> Essentially segmentation decisions are choices about which customers to serve and what to offer them.

a good guide to market segments. Thus, in the car industry, colour is probably not a good segmentation variable (white and red Honda Civics sell at much the same price); size is a better segmentation variable (full-size cars sell at a price premium over sub-compact cars).

- *Construct a segmentation matrix.* Typically segmentation analysis generates far too many segmentation variables so it is necessary to reduce the number of variables to make the analysis more manageable. This is usually done by selecting only those variables that are most important or that are closely correlated with each other. Reducing the number of variables allows individual segments to be identified in a two- or three-dimensional matrix.

- *Analyse segmentation attractiveness.* Profitability within a segment is determined by the same structural forces that determine profitability within the industry as a whole so the five forces analysis can be applied to individual market segments.

- *Identify key success factors in each segment.* By analysing buyers' purchase criteria and the basis of competition within individual segments we can identify what a firm needs to do well in order to be successful in a particular segment.

- *Analyse the attraction of broad versus narrow scope.* A firm needs to decide whether it wishes to be a segment specialist or compete across multiple segments. The advantage of a broad over a narrow focus depends on the similarity of key success factors and the presence of shared costs.

Case Insight 2.5
Choosing an appropriate level of analysis

In the opening case we chose to examine the mobile phone market as a whole but we could have looked in more detail at the competitive conditions influencing a particular subset of the handsets market if that better suited the purpose of our analysis. This market can be segmented in many different ways and for example segmentation can be undertaken on the basis of:

- use motivations – communication, information, entertainment, e.g. handset used primarily for phone and text, feature phones, designer phones;
- product attributes – price, functionality;

- user characteristics – age, lifestyle;
- geography – e.g. UK, US, India.

A number of these variables are correlated, for example user motivation, lifestyle and price may cluster together. Consumers who use their mobile phones intensively and access a wide variety of functions are likely to be in a particular age group and to select more expensive handsets. Clustering attributes allows the number of segmentation variables to be reduced so that two or three attributes of key importance can be represented in a segmentation matrix. For example in mobile phones we might consider product attributes and geography to be two key characteristics and we can construct a two-dimensional segmentation matrix on this basis. Having established such a matrix, the aim is to understand why some segments may be more profitable than others. Using Porter's five forces framework to analyse each of the individual segments we might find, for example, that there are a large number of established firms and many new entrants piling in to the 'basic phone' market in India depressing profitability in this segment, whereas the smartphone market in the UK is dominated by a few large multinational players who through their branding and collaborative arrangements with network operators may have succeeded in earning above-average profits. These particular examples are for illustrative purposes only and are obviously oversimplified. In practice, segmentation analysis and construction of segmentation matrices (see Figure 2.4 for an example) requires systematic market research and a detailed and comprehensive review of relevant product and consumer characteristics.

Figure 2.4 Illustrative segmentation matrix for the mobile phone market

		Geographic market				
		Africa	China	Europe	India	U.S.
Product attributes	Smartphones					
	Designer phones					
	Feature phones*					
	Basic, low-priced phones					

*Feature phones refers to handsets that have more functions or attributes than a basic phone, e.g. they allow users to play games, take photos, play music, but do not have the full capability of a smartphone.

Adding additional forces?

The Porter framework identifies the suppliers of substitute goods and services as one of the forces of competition that reduces the profit available to the firms within an industry.

> While the presence of substitutes reduces the value of a product, complements increase value.

However, economic theory identifies two types of relationship between different products: substitutes and complements. Complements have the opposite effect to substitutes. While the presence of substitutes reduces the value of a product, complements increase value. For example, the availability of ink cartridges for my printer transforms its value to me.

Given the importance of complements to most products – the value of my car depends on the availability of petrol, insurance and repair services – our analysis of the competitive environment needs to take them into account. The simplest way is to add a sixth force to Porter's framework (see Figure 2.5).[27]

Where products are close complements, they have little value to customers individually – customers value the whole system. But how is the value shared between the producers of the different complementary products? Bargaining power and its deployment are the key.

During the early 1990s, Nintendo earned huge profits from its video game consoles. Although most of the revenue and consumer value was in the software – mostly supplied by independent developers – Nintendo was able to appropriate most of the profit potential of the entire system through establishing dominance over the games developers. Nintendo used its leadership in the console market and ownership of the console operating system to enforce restrictive developer licences to software producers of games and maintain tight control over the manufacture and distribution of games cartridges (from which Nintendo earned a large royalty).[28]

Where two products are complements to one another, profit will accrue to the supplier that builds the stronger market position and reduces the value contributed by the other. How is this done? The key is to achieve monopolisation, differentiation and shortage of supply in one's own product, while encouraging competition, commoditisation and excess capacity in the production of the complementary product. IBM is attempting to shift the balance of power between hardware and software producers through its promotion of Linux and other open-source software programs. By pressing to differentiate its hardware products while commoditising software, it can reduce the power of Microsoft and gain a bigger share of the profit returns from systems of hardware and software.[29]

It has also been suggested that the government should be added to the model as an additional force, indeed Michael Porter considered this possibility when he presented

Figure 2.5 Five forces, or six?

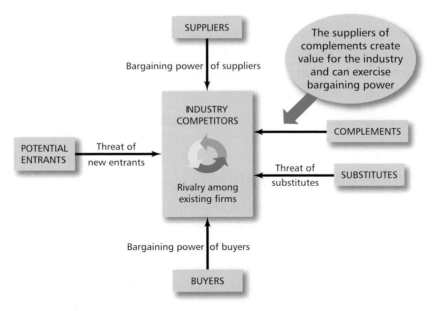

his framework in his book *Competitive Advantage* published in 1980.[30] Governments can have a strong impact on industry profitability. For example, the announcement in 2010 by the Australian government of proposals to raise taxes on the profits of mining companies like Rio Tinto and BHP Billiton resulted in an immediate fall in the valuation of these companies. Whilst the government can directly affect industry attractiveness, as the mining example illustrates, it also has a powerful influence on each of the other five forces. The majority of analysts view the government as having such a pervasive influence on all aspects of industry competition that its influence is best captured through the existing five forces rather than added as a sixth.

Case Insight 2.6
Dealing with missing factors

It is self-evident that mobile phones are only of value to users when used in conjunction with wireless network services. The futures of mobile phone manufacturers and mobile phone network operators are so firmly intertwined that to analyse one industry requires knowledge of the other. The issue by national

▶

governments of 3G licences also illustrates the impact of complements and the government on industry attractiveness. Smartphones require wireless licences to be in place for the phones to work. Government decisions on what licences to issue, to whom and at what price clearly influence the nature of competition, the market and overall industry profitability.

Dealing with dynamic competition

Using five forces analysis to predict industry profitability presupposes that industry structure is relatively stable and determines competitive behaviour in a predictable way, but this ignores the dynamic forces of innovation and entrepreneurship which transform industry structure. Joseph Schumpeter, one of the great economists of the early twentieth century, viewed competition as a 'perennial gale of creative destruction' through which favourable industry structures – monopoly in particular – contain the seeds of their own destruction by attracting incursions from new and established firms deploying innovatory strategies and innovatory products to unseat incumbents.[31] The key consideration is the speed of structural change in the industry – if structural transformation is rapid, the five forces model has limited predictive value.

In practice, Schumpeter's process of 'creative destruction' tends to be more of a breeze than a gale. In established industries, entry occurs so slowly that profits are undermined only gradually,[32] while changes in industrial concentration tend to be slow.[33] One survey observed: 'the picture of the competitive process . . . is, to say the least, sluggish in the extreme.'[34] As a result, both at the firm and the industry level, profits tend to be highly persistent in the long run.[35]

What about recent decades? Has accelerating technological change and intensifying international competition reinforced the processes of 'creative destruction'? Rich D'Aveni argues that a general feature of industries today is **hypercompetition**: 'intense and rapid competitive moves, in which competitors must move quickly to build [new] advantages and erode the advantages of their rivals.'[36] If industries are hypercompetitive, their structures are likely to be less stable than in the past, superior profitability will tend to be transitory and the only route to sustained superior performance is through continually recreating and renewing competitive advantage.

Despite the plausibility of this thesis and everyday observations that markets are becoming more volatile and market leadership more tenuous, systematic evidence of this trend is elusive. One large-scale statistical study concluded: 'The heterogeneity and volatility of competitive advantage in US manufacturing industries has steadily and astonishingly increased since 1950. Industry structures are destabilizing. These results suggest that a shift towards hypercompetition has indeed occurred'.[37] This volatility is observed not just in technology-intensive and manufacturing industries.[38] However, another study found a 'lack of widespread evidence . . . that markets are more unstable now than in the recent past'.[39]

Does industry matter?

The central theme of industry analysis is that, because of underlying structural conditions, some industries are intrinsically more profitable than others. By extension, one might be tempted to argue that firms located in profitable industries are likely to be more profitable than those that are not. But is there evidence to support this view? There are many examples of businesses that succeed in lacklustre industries, for example, in the opening case we noted the forces depressing profitability in the mobile phone market but saw that Apple, with its iPhone, bucked this trend, at least in the short term. Statistical evidence suggests that industry environment is a relatively minor determinant of a firm's profitability. Studies of the sources of inter-firm differences in profitability have produced very different results (see Table 2.2) – but all acknowledge that industry factors account for a minor part (less than 20%) of variation in return on assets among firms. Put simply, the correct choice of firm strategy may be more important than the correct choice of industry.

> Put simply, the correct choice of firm strategy may be more important than the correct choice of industry.

From industry attractiveness to competitive advantage: identifying key success factors

The five forces framework allows us to determine an industry's potential for profit. But how is industry profit shared between the different firms competing in that industry? Let us look explicitly at the sources of competitive advantage within an industry. In subsequent chapters we develop a more comprehensive analysis of competitive advantage. Our goal here is to identify those factors within the firm's market environment that determine the firm's ability to survive and prosper – its **key success factors**.[40]

Our approach to identifying key success factors is straightforward and commonsense. To survive and prosper in an

> To survive and prosper in an industry, a firm must meet two criteria: first, it must supply what customers want to buy; second, it must survive competition.

industry, a firm must meet two criteria: first, it must supply what customers want to buy; second, it must survive competition. Hence, we may start by asking two questions:

● What do our customers want?

● What does the firm need to do to survive competition?

To answer the first question we need to look more closely at customers of the industry and to view them, not as a threat to profitability because of their buying power, but as the purpose of the industry and its underlying source of profit. This requires that we enquire: Who are our customers? What are their needs? How do they choose between competing

Table 2.2 What determines inter-firm differences in profitability? The role of industry

	Percentage of variance in firms' return on assets explained by:		
	Industry effects	Firm effects	Unexplained variance
Schmalensee (1985)	19.6%	0.6%	79.9%
Rumelt (1991)	4.0%	44.2%	44.8%
McGahan & Porter (1997)	18.7%	31.7%	48.4%
Hawawini *et al.* (2003)	8.1%	35.8%	52.0%
Roquebert *et al.* (1996)	10.2%	55.0%	32.0%
Misangyi *et al.* (2006)	7.6%	43.8%	n.a.

Notes:

'Firm effects' combine business unit and corporate effects.
The rows do not sum to 100% because other sources of variance are not reported.

Source: R. Schmalensee, 'Do markets differ much?' *American Economic Review* 75 (1985): 341–51; R. P. Rumelt, 'Does industry matter much?' *Strategic Management Journal* 12 (1991): 167–85; A. M. McGahan and M. E. Porter, 'How much does industry matter, really?' *Strategic Management Journal* 18 (1997): 15–30; G. Hawawini, V. Subramanian and P. Verdin, 'Is firms' profitability driven by industry or firm-specific factors? A new look at the evidence', *Strategic Management Journal* 24 (2003): 1–16; J. A. Roquebert, R. L. Phillips and P. A. Westfall, 'Markets vs. management: what drives profitability?' *Strategic Management Journal* 17 (1996): 633–64; V. F. Misangyi, H. Elms, T. Greckhamer and J. A. Lepine, 'A new perspective on a fundamental debate: a multilevel approach to industry, corporate and business unit effects', *Strategic Management Journal* 27 (2006): 571–90.

Figure 2.6 Identifying key success factors

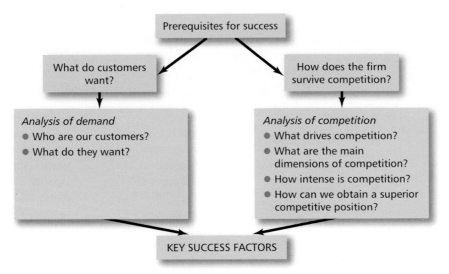

offerings? Once we recognise the basis of customers' preferences, we can then identify the factors that confer success upon the individual firm. For example, if consumers choose supermarkets on the basis of price, then cost efficiency is the primary basis for competitive advantage and the key success factors are the determinants of inter-firm cost differentials.

The second question requires that we examine the nature of competition in the industry. How intense is competition and what are its key dimensions? Thus, in airlines, it is not enough to offer low fares, convenience and safety. Survival requires sufficient financial strength to survive the intense price competition that accompanies cyclical downturns.

A basic framework for identifying key success factors is presented in Figure 2.6. Application of the framework to identify key success factors in three industries is outlined in Table 2.3.

The value of success factors in formulating strategy has been scorned by some strategy scholars. Pankaj Ghemawat observes that the 'whole idea of identifying a success factor and then chasing it seems to have something in common with the ill-considered medieval hunt for the philosopher's stone, a substance that would transmute everything it touched into gold'.[41] Our goal is not to identify 'generic strategies' that can guarantee success, simply to recognise commonalities in customer motivation and the nature of competition. In the fashion clothing business we identified key success factors (see Table 2.3). However, unique resources and capabilities applied to common success factors results in the adoption of very different strategies.

Table 2.3 Identifying key success factors: steel, fashion clothing and supermarkets

	What do customers want? (analysis of demand)	How do firms survive competition? (analysis of competition)	Key success factors
Steel	• low price • product consistency • reliability of supply • specific technical specifications for special steels	• commodity products, excess capacity, high fixed costs, excess capacity, exit barriers and substitute competition mean intense price competition and cyclical profitability • cost efficiency and financial strength essential	• Cost efficiency requires: large-scale plants, low-cost location, rapid capacity adjustment • alternatively, high technology, small-scale plants can achieve low costs through flexibility and high productivity • differentiation through technical specifications and service quality
Fashion clothing	• diversity of customer preferences in terms of garment type, style, quality, colour • customers willing to pay premium for brand, style, exclusivity and quality • mass market, highly price sensitive	• low barriers to entry and exit, low seller concentration and buying power of retail chains imply intense competition • differentiation can yield substantial price premium, but imitation is rapid	• combining differentiation with low costs • differentiation requires speed of response to changing fashions, style, reputation and quality
Supermarkets	• low prices • convenient location	• intensity of price competition depends on number and proximity of competitors	• cost efficiency requires manufacture in low-wage countries

- wide range of products adapted to local preferences
- fresh/quality produce, good service, ease of parking, pleasant ambience

- bargaining power a critical determinant of cost of bought-in goods

- low costs require operational efficiency, scale-efficient stores, large aggregate purchases, low wage costs
- differentiation requires large stores (to allow wide product range), convenient location, familiarity with local customer preferences

Table 2.4 Key success factors

	Standard phones	**Smartphones**
What the customer wants?	Low price Reliability	High speed data download Wide range of 'apps' Fashionable design
How the firm survives competition?	Commodity market – excess production capacity, intense price competition Cost efficiency paramount	Low barriers to entry and exit, buying power of wireless service providers strong, provision of complementary products important, Differentiation can yield substantial price premium but imitation is rapid
Key success factors	Systems integration capability Industrial design capability Low cost manufacturing skills	Fashion design Partnerships with content providers Strong R&D

Summary

In Chapter 1 we established that a profound understanding of the competitive environment is a critical ingredient of a successful strategy. In this chapter we have developed a systematic approach to analysing a firm's industry environment in order to evaluate the industry's profit potential and to identify sources of competitive advantage. The centrepiece of this chapter has been Porter's five forces of competition framework which links the structure of an industry to the competitive intensity within it and to the profitability that it realises. We have also introduced the notion of key success factors as a way of starting to get to grips with the question of how industry profits are shared between different firms competing in that industry.

By applying Porter's framework to some specific examples we have revealed some of the challenges and limitations of the approach, recognising, in particular, the need to exercise judgement when deciding how to define the scope of industry analysis and how finely grained such analysis needs to be. We have noted the potential for complementary products to add value and that we need to expand our strategy tool kit when it comes to looking at highly dynamic business environments. These are issues we return to in Chapters 5 and 6.

Summary table

Learning objectives	Summary
You will be familiar with various approaches to analysing an organisation's external environment and understand how the structural features of an industry influence competition and profitability	You have been introduced to a systematic approach to analysing a firm's industry environment using PEST and Porter's five forces framework. PEST analysis aims to identify those factors that are most likely to shape the competitive conditions within an industry. The five forces framework classifies those features of an industry that drive competition and profitability. Although every industry is unique, industry attractiveness is the result of the systematic influences of the structure of that industry
You will be able to use evidence on structural trends within industries to forecast changes in competition and profitability and to develop appropriate strategies for the future	The five forces framework can be used to explore future as well as current competitive conditions. It is useful for predicting industry profitability, positioning the firm in relation to these forces and identifying how the firm can improve industry attractiveness. Firm strategies can shape, as well as be shaped by, industry structure
You will understand the value and challenge of undertaking industry analysis and be able to provide a critique of Porter's five forces framework	Through practical applications of Porter's five forces framework, we became aware of some of the practical challenges of using the model, in particular the problems associated with defining markets and selecting an appropriate level of analysis. We noted the possible need to augment the model by including a sixth force in certain contexts, for example in markets where complementary

	products play a significant role. We also recognised the limitations of the framework in dealing with highly dynamic market conditions and in providing a complete explanation of variations in profitability between firms
You will be able to analyse competition and customer requirements in order to identify opportunities for competitive advantage within an industry (*key success factors*)	By combining the analysis of industry competition with a close examination of customer wants we were able to see how to identify key success factors, namely what firms need to do well to succeed in a particular industry

Further reading

In this particular area of study it is well worth returning to classic books and articles to gain a deeper understanding of the subject and to appreciate how debates have developed over time. That said, Ofek and Wathieu's short article in the *Harvard Business Review* gives some up-to-date examples of recent trends and the perils of ignoring them and Michael Porter's 2008 article in the same journal provides an easy alternative to reading his original work which was published in his 1980 book entitled *Competitive Strategy*. In his more recent article he reaffirms and extends his five forces framework and comments on the practicalities of using this approach. It is often assumed that dominant firms or firms acting together can change their industry structure. Michael Jacobides introduces the notion of architectural advantage and suggests that all firms can potentially influence industry structure.

The problems of defining markets and undertaking segmentation analysis are of key importance to marketeers so most standard marketing texts cover this area reasonably comprehensively. However, Gadiesh and Gilbert point out that markets are usually disaggregated horizontally by product, geography and customer group, but they can also be segmented vertically by identifying different value chain activities.

Gadiesh, O and Gilbert, J. L. (1998). Profit pools: a fresh look at strategy. *Harvard Business Review*, May–June, 139–47.

Ofek, E and Wathieu, L. (2010). Are you ignoring trends that could shake up your business? *Harvard Business Review*, 88 (7/8), 124–31.

Jacobides, M. G. (2008). Building architectural advantage: don't just compete *in* your sector. Shape your sector and win! AIM White Paper, London Business School.

Porter, M. E. (2008). The five competitive forces that shape strategy. *Harvard Business Review*, 57, 57–71.

Visit your enhanced ebook at **www.foundationsofstrategy.com** for self test quiz questions

QUIZ

Self-study questions

1   In September 2010 Blockbuster, a provider of a DVD rental service, filed for bankruptcy, blaming heightened competition for its demise. Use Porter's five forces of competition framework to evaluate Blockbuster's claim that competition has intensified in the DVD rental market over time and to explain the forces that drive competition in this industry.

2   'The practical application of Porter's framework reveals its many limitations'. Discuss and suggest ways in which some of the limitations you identify might be overcome.

3   Aldi is a discount supermarket chain that has over 8000 retail stores worldwide including the UK, mainland Europe, Scandinavia, the US and Australia. Although Aldi operates internationally, most shoppers choose between retailers located within a few miles of each other. For the purposes of analysing profitability and competitive strategy should Aldi consider the discount retailing industry to be global, national or local?

4   How would you segment the restaurant market in your home town? How would you advise someone thinking of starting a new restaurant what segments might be most attractive in terms of profit potential?

5   What do you think are the key success factors in the:

●   pizza delivery industry?

●   Formula One racing industry?

Visit your enhanced ebook at **www.foundationsofstrategy.com** for key term flashcards

GLOSSARY

Closing case Fitness First and the UK Health and Fitness Club Industry

On a Monday morning in September 2011, Duncan Tatton-Brown, the chief financial officer of Fitness First Ltd, was preparing for a meeting with his CEO, Colin Waggett. The purpose of the meeting was to determine the capital expenditure budget for Fitness First's UK health club business over the next four years. John Gamble, managing director of Fitness First, had proposed a programme of expansion and upgrading aimed at maintaining and strengthening Fitness First's leadership position in the UK health club sector.

Tatton-Brown was concerned that circumstances in the UK health club industry – notably slowing growth and rising competition – would make it difficult to earn a satisfactory return on new investment.

Fitness First Ltd

Fitness First began in 1993 as a single health and fitness club founded by Mike Balfour. In 1996, the company was floated on London's AIM market and with the funds raised began rapid expansion throughout the UK and into Germany and Belgium. During 2000–3, global expansion accelerated with the acquisition of health club chains in Australia and Hong Kong and entry into Spain, Malaysia, France, Holland and Italy. However, rapid expansion strained the finances of Fitness First and, following a steep fall in its share price, it was acquired by Cinven, a private equity firm in 2003. After a two-year period of financial restructuring and strategic refocusing, Fitness First was sold to another private equity group, BC Partners, in November 2005 for £835 million.

In 2011, Fitness First Ltd claimed to be the world's largest private health and fitness club operator with 474 clubs and around 1.3 million members. The UK accounted for 150 of these at the end of 2010, down from 161 the previous year. The UK generated £156.4 million in revenue during 2009, 20% of the world total for Fitness First.

◄ *The UK health club industry*

Development

As in other countries, gymnasiums with facilities for weight lifting and general exercise and for sports such as gymnastics, boxing, wrestling and judo had long been a feature of the social infrastructure of urban Britain. Gymnasiums were operated both by local government authorities and non-for-profit clubs.

The emergence of health club chains owned and operated as a business enterprise dates back to the early 1980s and is associated with the rise of the 'yuppie' (young urban professional) social and cultural group.

The contrast between the new health clubs and the old gyms was stark. Gyms were typically scruffy, male-only facilities with limited equipment and very basic changing and showering facilities. The private health clubs featured sophisticated, technologically advanced exercise equipment; saunas and steam rooms; individual and group instruction in a range of activities from yoga to weight training; individual consultation through personal trainers; and luxurious relaxation facilities including cafes and juice bars.

Early entrants into the industry were typically start-up companies which began with a single establishment then used venture capital funds to expand. These were often founded by individual enthusiasts and former sports personalities.

Holmes Place in 1980, David Lloyd Leisure in 1982, Fitness First in 1993 and Esporta in 1994 were early leaders of the industry. The typical pattern for these start-up companies was to grow initially with venture capital finance, then list on the London Stock Exchange or AIM market. Subsequently, many were bought out by private equity firms. The general perception was that health clubs were a growth industry and as a result there appeared to be no shortage of equity capital to fund both new and established ventures. In addition a number of established companies entered the industry. Richard Branson's Virgin Group entered the business in 1992 when it acquired South Africa's Health and Racquet Club. JJB Sports, a retail sportswear chain, opened JJB Sports Clubs (later to become DW Sports Fitness) and several hotel chains (including Marriott and Hilton) introduced health clubs within their hotels.

While the leading chains owned and operated their individual health clubs, a number of franchise chains had been established, several of them international. For example, Kieser Training, a Swiss-based company with 120 franchised outlets worldwide, was seeking franchisees in the UK. For a 400–600 square metre facility, the investment cost was estimated at around £400,000.[42]

Most health clubs comprised an exercise room equipped with a range of exercise equipment, activity rooms, a pool, sauna and steam rooms, changing rooms and a lounge with refreshment facilities. Services offered included training and specialised classes, physiotherapy and consultation services.

Facilities, costs and pricing

Clubs differed in the sophistication and luxury and in the range of equipment and services they offered. Some clubs emphasised particular sports. For example the David Lloyd club emphasised racquet sports (tennis, badminton and squash). Some clubs were women only.

While a small fitness club comprising an exercise room and changing facilities could be opened in leased premises for a start-up cost of around £300,000, a full-service health club of the type offered by the major chains involved an investment of in excess of a million pounds. The principal costs were (i) converting the premises to install facilities such as a pool, Jacuzzi, showers and so forth and (ii) equipment. Exercise machines have advanced substantially in sophistication and cost – individual items of equipment can cost over £20,000. Leading suppliers include Life Fitness (USA) and Technogym (Italy).

The typical pricing policy for health clubs is through annual membership contracts. These typically involve a one-time registration fee and a monthly fee of between £30 and £60. Because the costs of operating a health club are much the same irrespective of usage, health club operators were under considerable pressure to generate revenue through signing up new members. Competition takes multiple forms. While health clubs are reluctant to compete on published membership fees, substantial discounts from list prices are offered. Initial sign-up fees were often waived, generous incentives were given to existing members for introducing new members, low-cost family deals and off-peak memberships were common and heavily discounted multiyear membership deals were offered.

An important source of profit for the industry was from consumers who signed up for membership but subsequently used their clubs little if at all. However, this source of revenue was under attack. In a May 2011 court ruling, membership contracts of more than one year were declared unenforceable. The court found that the membership contracts of Ashbourne Management Services Ltd (which drew up membership agreements and then collects members' payments for over 700 gym clubs) were 'designed and calculated to take advantage of the naivety and inexperience of the average consumer using gym clubs at the lower end of the market' and 'a trap into which the average consumer is likely to fall'.[43]

The pressure to cut membership fees was increased by growing competition from local authority-owned gyms and sports centres. Many local authorities had invested heavily in sports and fitness centres, including the upgrading of existing swimming pools with the addition of new gym facilities. Typically these public sports and fitness facilities were much cheaper than private health clubs, even if they did offer less luxury and fewer services. However, public fitness centres were often larger and offered superior facilities (e.g. full-size swimming pools). Table 2.5 shows some comparisons.

The leading companies

Table 2.6 shows the UK's leading health club operators in terms of numbers of clubs. Table 2.7 gives financial information on five companies.

Recent developments

After two decades of rapid growth, after 2000 the industry appeared to be maturing. The growth in new club memberships slowed considerably. Between 2009 and 2011 the number of private health club subscriptions was virtually static at about 4.4 million. However, the total number of clubs had continued to grow, which meant that most clubs operated with substantial excess capacity.

Clearly, the industry's development had been hit by the financial crisis of 2007–9: during a period of depressed consumer expenditure and rising unemployment, private gym subscriptions were viewed by many as a dispensable luxury. Looking ahead, the prospects of a return to the growth rates of earlier decades seemed remote. There was the growing body of evidence that suggested that UK economic growth and consumer spending would remain sluggish for some time into the future, with fears of a 'double-dip' recession exacerbated by the depressed state of the UK housing market. Many clubs were reporting that the existing members who did not renew their annual subscriptions far outweighed new sign ups.

Table 2.5 Private and public health and fitness clubs in the UK, 2011

	Private	Public
Number of clubs	3,146	2,706
Number of members	4.43m.	2.91m.
Average monthly fee	£30.39	£43.38

Sources: 'Private gyms fall behind as low-cost and public options pick up speed', The Times (30 May 2011).

Table 2.6 Top 10 UK private health and fitness club club operators, January 2011

Company	No. of clubs	Owner
Fitness First	150	BC Partners
LA Fitness	79	Mid Ocean Partners
David Lloyd Leisure	76	London & Regional / Caird Capital
Virgin Active	69	Virgin Group
DW Sports Fitness	60	DW Fitness
Bannatyne's	59	Bannatyne Fitness
Esporta	53	Société Générale
Nuffield Health Fitness & Wellbeing	51	BC Partners
Living Well	47	Hilton Partners
Marriott Leisure Club	44	Marriott International

Source: 'Private gyms fall behind as low-cost and public options pick up speed', *The Times* (30 May 2011): 33.

Since 2000, there has been substantial consolidation on the industry. Virgin Active acquired the Holmes Place chain, David Lloyd Leisure merged with Next Generation Clubs and in 2011 Virgin Active acquired Esporta. David Stalker, chief executive of the Fitness Industry Association, predicted 'more competition and further consolidation of the market.'[44]

There was an additional factor that was a particular concern to Tatton-Brown and other members of Fitness First's senior management team. Recent years had seen the entry of a new breed of low-cost health club chains. In September 2010 there were 10 low-cost gym chains operating in Britain. However, the category seemed poised to expand following the announcement that the Easy Group, owner of easyJet budget airline would establish a chain of easyGym budget health clubs.[45] The biggest UK budget gym operator, The Gym Group, offered monthly membership for £14.99 and one-day membership for £5. Like The Gym Club, Pure Gym was expanding rapidly: during 2011 and 2012 it planned to grow from 15 to 45 clubs. Another budget chain, Fit4less with a £16.99 monthly fee, was seeking franchisees in locations across the UK.

▶

Table 2.7 Selected financial data for leading UK private health and fitness club operators

	Fitness First Ltd.		David Lloyd Leisure Ltd.			Virgin Active Ltd.		Bannatyne Fitness Ltd.		LA Fitness Ltd.	
	2009	2008	2009	2008		2010	2009	2010	2009	2010	2009
Revenue £m	34.42	27.55	204.88	207.83		72.96	73.05	89.06	88.57	n.a.	n.a.
Operating profit £m	(85.04)*	18.70	(16.81)	30.59		13.85	12.26	17.62	19.82	2.75	1.60
Net profit £m	(83.07)*	33.44	23.06	301.18+		4.25	11.18	7.87	6.39	2.75	1.60
Capital employed £m	416.85	497.82	483.50	470.85		91.54	87.07	210.71	212.30	61.94	59.15
Shareholders' equity £m	360.73	444.79	472.97	449.91		91.33	87.07	51.29	43.42	11.05	8.30
ROCE^	4.4%	3.8%	(3.5%)	6.5%		15.1%	14.1%	8.3%	9.3%	4.4%	2.7%
ROE^	5.5%	7.5%	4.9%	3.1%		4.7%	12.9%	15.3%	14.7%	24.9%	19.3%

Notes: * After £103.18 exceptional administrative expense
+ Includes £287.29 million profit on disposal of fixed assets
^ Excluding exceptional items;
ROCE = operating profit/capital employed;
ROE = net profit/shareholders' equity

Source: Annual reports from Companies' House (www.companieshouse.gov.uk)

As Duncan Tatton-Brown walked towards his chief executive's office, he reflected on the many forces that were impacting the UK health club industry. After three decades of growth and development, the industry was entering a period of uncertainty and change. At the same time, as the leading company in the industry, Fitness First was not powerless in face of these changes. Tatton-Brown wondered how Fitness First might influence the course of the industry's evolution and how it might position itself to take advantage of the changes occurring within the sector.

Case questions

- How attractive is the UK health and fitness club industry in terms of its profit potential? Apply Porter's five forces of competition framework to the industry to justify your answer.

- How might this industry be segmented? Advise Fitness First on those segments that appear the most attractive.

- In what ways might Fitness First influence the course of the industry's evolution to its own advantage?

- What do you think are the key success factors in this industry?

Notes

1 B. Eilert, 'Ignite your strategic planning process with a PEST analysis', *Strategy Knowledge* (http://strategyknowhow.bnet.com/ PEST_analysis_primer.html), September 2004.

2 N. Clark, 'Smartphone sales continue to buck recession', *The Independent* (24 February 2010).

3 M. E. Porter, 'The five competitive forces that shape strategy', *Harvard Business Review* 57 (January 2008): 57–71.

4 'For bagel chains, investment may be money in the hole', *Wall Street Journal* (30 December 1997): B8.

5 W. J. Baumol, J. C. Panzar and R. D. Willig, *Contestable Markets and the Theory of Industry Structure* (New York: Harcourt Brace Jovanovich, 1982). See also Michael Spence, 'Contestable markets and the theory of industry structure: a review article', *Journal of Economic Literature* 21 (September 1983): 981–90.

6 'Annual Franchise 500', *Entrepreneur* (January 2009).

7 'Brand loyalty is rarely blind loyalty', *Wall Street Journal* (19 October 1989): B1.

8 R. D. Buzzell and P. W. Farris, 'Marketing costs in consumer goods industries', in H. Thorelli (ed.), *Strategy – Structure – Performance* (Bloomington, IN: Indiana University Press, 1977): 128–9.

9 In October 1999, the Department of Justice alleged that American Airlines was using unfair means in attempting to monopolize air traffic out of Dallas-Fort Worth (http://www.aeroworldnet.com/1tw05179.htm).

10 M. Lieberman ('Excess capacity as a barrier to entry', *Journal of Industrial Economics* 35, June 1987: 607–27) argues that, to be credible, the threat of retaliation needs to be supported by incumbents holding excess capacity giving them the potential to flood the market.

11 See for example: J. S. Bain, *Barriers to New Competition* (Cambridge, MA: Harvard University Press, 1956) and H. M. Mann, 'Seller concentration, entry barriers and rates of return in thirty industries', *Review of Economics and Statistics* 48 (1966): 296–307.

12 W. S. Comanor and T. A. Wilson, *Advertising and Market Power* (Cambridge: Harvard University Press, 1974); J. L. Siegfried and L. B. Evans, 'Empirical studies of entry and exit: a survey of the evidence', *Review of Industrial Organization* 9 (1994): 121–55.

13 G. S. Yip, 'Gateways to entry', *Harvard Business Review* 60 (September–October 1982): 85–93.

14 F. M. Scherer and D. R. Ross, *Industrial Market Structure and Economic Performance*, 3rd edn (Boston: Houghton Mifflin, 1990); R. M. Grant, 'Pricing behaviour in the uk wholesale market for petrol. A 'structure-conduct analysis', *Journal of Industrial Economics* 30 (March 1982).

15 R. Schmalensee, 'Inter-industry studies of structure and performance', in R. Schmalensee and R. D. Willig, *Handbook of Industrial Organisation*, 2nd edn (Amsterdam: North Holland, 1988): 976; M. A. Salinger, 'The concentration-margins relationship reconsidered', *Brookings Papers: Microeconomics* (1990): 287–335.

16 The problems caused by excess capacity and exit barriers are discussed in C. Baden-Fuller (ed.), *Strategic Management of Excess Capacity* (Oxford: Basil Blackwell, 1990).

17 S. H. Lustgarten, 'The impact of buyer concentration in manufacturing industries', *Review of Economics and Statistics* 57 (1975): 125–32; T. Kelly and M. L. Gosman, 'Increased buyer concentration and its effects on profitability in the manufacturing sector', *Review of Industrial Organisation* 17 (2000): 41–59.

18 T. Kang, 'UK handset vendor market share by operator: Q1 2011', Strategy Analytics. www.strategyanalytics.com/default.aspx?mod=reportabstractviewer&a0=6406. Accessed 2 July 2011.

19 www.cio.com/article/649863/Nokia_8217_S_market_Share_Drops_Further_in_ India. Accessed 2 July 2011.

20 'Lengthening odds. New betting options imperil horseracing's future', *The Economist* (8 July 2010).

21 M. E. Porter, 'The five competitive forces that shape strategy', op cit.

22 'Rude awakening', *FT Weekend, Financial Times* (4/5 October 2008): 16–23.

23 'Globalization or concentration?' *Business Week* (8 November 2004): 54; 'Mittal: blood, steel and empire building', *Business Week* (13 February 2006).

24 J. Bower, *When Markets Quake* (Boston: Harvard Business School Press, 1986).

25 M. Carnall, S. Berry and P. Spiller, 'Airline hubbing, costs and demand', in D. Lee (ed.), *Advances in Airline Economics* vol. 1 (Elsevier, 2006).

26 O. Gadiesh and J. L. Gilbert, 'Profit pools: a fresh look at strategy', *Harvard Business Review* (May–June1998): 146.

27 A. Brandenburger and B. Nalebuff, *Co-opetition* (New York: Doubleday, 1996) propose an alternative framework, the *value net*, for analysing the impact of complements.

28 See A. Brandenburger and B. Nalebuff, 'The right game: use game theory to shape strategy', *Harvard Business Review* (July–August, 1995): 63-4 and A. Brandenburger, J. Kou and M. Burnett, *Power Play (A): Nintendo in 8-bit Video Games* (Harvard Business School Case No. 9-795-103, 1995).

29 C. Baldwin, S. O'Mahony and J. Quinn, *IBM and Linux (A)* (Harvard Business School Case No. 903-083, 2003).

30 M. E. Porter, *Competitive Advantage* (New York: Free Press, 1980).

31 J. A. Schumpeter, *The Theory of Economic Development* (Cambridge, MA: Harvard University Press, 1934).

32 R. T. Masson and J. Shaanan, 'Stochastic dynamic limit pricing: an empirical test', *Review of Economics and Statistics* 64 (1982): 413–22; R. T. Masson and J. Shaanan,

'Optimal pricing and threat of entry: Canadian evidence', *International Journal of Industrial Organization* 5 (1987): 520–35.

33 R. Caves and M. E. Porter, 'The dynamics of changing seller concentration', *Journal of Industrial Economics* 19 (1980): 1–15; P. Hart and R. Clarke, *Concentration in British Industry* (Cambridge: Cambridge University Press, 1980).

34 P. A. Geroski and R. T. Masson, 'Dynamic market models in industrial organization', *International Journal of Industrial Organization* 5 (1987): 1–13.

35 D. C. Mueller, *Profits in the Long Run* (Cambridge: Cambridge University Press, 1986).

36 R. D'Aveni, *Hypercompetition: Managing the Dynamics of Strategic Maneuvering* (New York: Free Press, 1994): 217–18.

37 L. G. Thomas and R. D'Aveni, 'The rise of hypercompetition in the U.S. manufacturing sector, 1950–2002'. Tuck School of Business, Dartmouth College, Working Paper #2004-11 (2004).

38 R. R. Wiggins and T. W. Ruefli, 'Schumpeter's ghost: is hypercompetition making the best of times shorter?' *Strategic Management Journal* 26 (2005): 887–911.

39 G. McNamara, P. M. Vaaler and C. Devers, 'Same as it ever was: the search for evidence of increasing hypercompetition', *Strategic Management Journal* 24 (2003): 261–78.

40 The term was coined by Chuck Hofer and Dan Schendel, *Strategy Formulation: Analytical Concepts* (St Paul: West Publishing, 1977): 77. They defined key success factors as 'those variables that management can influence through its decisions and that can affect significantly the overall competitive positions of the firms in an industry'.

41 P. Ghemawat, *Commitment: The Dynamic of Strategy* (New York: Free Press, 1991): 11.

42 www.franchisesales.com/franchisees/kieser-training-franchise. Accessed 2 July 2011.

43 http://oft.gov.uk/news-and-updates/press/2011/60-11. Accessed 13 October 2011.

44 'Private gyms fall behind as low-cost and public options pick up speed', *The Times*, 30 May 2011: 32–3.

45 Easy brand arrives. *Healthclub Management* (September 2010): 3.

Resources and capabilities

Introduction and objectives

In this chapter, we shift our focus from the external environment to the internal environment. We look within the firm and concentrate our attention on the resources and capabilities that firms possess. In doing so, we build the foundations for our analysis of competitive advantage which began in Chapter 2 with the discussion of key success factors.

By the time you have completed this chapter you will be able to:

- appreciate the role of a firm's resources and capabilities as a basis for formulating strategy;

- identify and appraise the resources and capabilities of a firm;

- evaluate the potential for a firm's resources and capabilities to confer sustainable competitive advantage;

- use the results of resource and capability analysis to formulate strategies that exploit internal strengths while defending against internal weaknesses;

- identify the means through which a firm can develop its resources and capabilities;

- recognise the difficulties that managers face in developing the resources and capabilities of the organisation.

VIDEO **Opening case** Hyundai Motor Company

A man goes into a parts' garage:

Man: 'Can I have a windshield wiper for a Hyundai, please?'
Parts man: 'Yeah, that seems like a fair swap'

Question: Why do Hyundai's have heated rear windows?
Answer: To keep your hands warm whilst you're pushing it[1]

In 2009 the Hyundai Automotive Group, which comprises Hyundai Motors and its affiliate company Kia Motors, overtook Ford to become the world's fourth largest car manufacturer by sales.[2] Despite being in the midst of a global recession, this South Korean car manufacturer managed to double its net profit and to increase its sales by 11% on the previous year. This was quite an achievement for a company that some years previously had been the butt of many jokes of the kind illustrated at the start of this case. Hyundai's emergence as a world-class car producer is a remarkable example of capability development over a short period of time.

Hyundai first started producing cars in 1967. The firm began by assembling a Ford compact car on a knockdown basis,[3] but it rapidly assimilated foreign technology and within 30 years it had acquired sufficient capability to develop its own car designs, launching the Accent in 1994 and the Avante in 1995. Hyundai's path to becoming a credible car producer in the highly competitive and crowded world car market closely mimicked that of its Japanese rival, Toyota, namely it entered with a limited product range at the low end of the market and gradually broadened both its product range and its market scope.

The company, as a latecomer to the market, recognised its need to acquire key capabilities and set about obtaining these through a series of phased developments. Each phase of the development process was characterised by clear objectives in terms of product outcomes, tight time deadlines, precise responsibilities assigned to development teams, explicit recognition of the

◀ **Figure 3.1** Key phases in Hyundai's development process

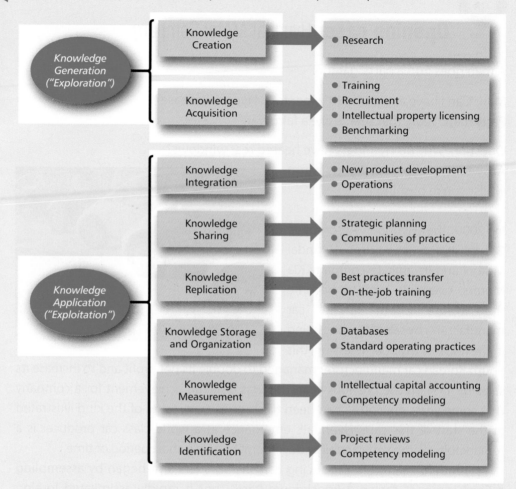

capabilities that needed to be developed in each phase and an atmosphere of impending crisis should the project not succeed.[4] Figure 3.1 provides a summary of key phases in Hyundai's development process.

Having established itself as an independent car manufacturer, Hyundai sought to become truly world class when Chung Mong Koo took over as chairman of the company in 1999. Chung instituted a strategy of rapid international expansion because, despite the considerable progress that had been made, the company sales remained heavily reliant on the domestic (South Korean) market. By global standards this market was small and did not afford the company the advantages of scale and scope needed to compete aggressively with established car producers like General Motors, Volkswagen and others. The company had invested early on in a few overseas production facilities but even by the year 2000 output from these plants constituted a very small part of the company's overall sales. Chung faced two main challenges, first building Hyundai's production and research capabilities abroad and second enhancing the company's market knowledge and marketing skills. The latter constituted a particular problem for Hyundai. On a visit to the USA Chung had been shocked to find that his company was perceived as producing shoddy products. Although the quality of Hyundai cars, in line with its mastery of key car manufacturing capabilities, had steadily improved over time and the company was well regarded in Korea, public perceptions of quality were slow to change outside the domestic market. In rapidly growing markets like China, this poor brand image was particularly damaging because consumers lacked experience of car purchase and had little access to the kinds of objective data provided by consumer advisory groups on the performance and reliability of different makes of cars. As a consequence Hyundai cars were commonly viewed as low status and second best.[5]

Hyundai had limited experience of overseas operations but recognised its need to develop its capabilities in this arena. In particular the firm lacked local expertise in market research and customer service. It sought to fill this gap by recruiting talented individuals with relevant experience gained in other parts of the car industry and, in the case of China, by entering a joint venture with a domestic firm. Hyundai established production plants in India (Chennai), the USA (Alabama), Europe (Slovakia) and China (Beijing) and carefully customised its product offerings to different countries. For example in China Hyundai initially entered the market by producing a mid-sized model in order to foster an upmarket image. The outward appearance of this model was then changed to ensure that it would enhance the perceived status of its owner and plush interiors for the rear seats were added because, in China, it was common for owners of mid-sized cars to have chauffeurs. The company also adjusted the structure and height of the cars to local road conditions.[6] In India it developed a variant of its Ato model that took into consideration India's climate (high temperatures and high humidity in many areas) and poor road conditions.

Chung sought to overcome the perceptions of poor quality by introducing a 10-year/100,000 mile warranties for Hyundai vehicles, a tight, quality control programme worldwide and a five-star ranking system for suppliers. Consumer perceptions were slow to change but the company's policies met with significant success. Hyundai began to win quality awards for its models and as Figure 3.2 illustrates is now ranked above average in the well-recognised, annual quality study carried by J.D. Power and Associates.

◀ **Figure 3.2** J.D. Power and Associates 2010 U.S. Initial Quality Study (IQS)

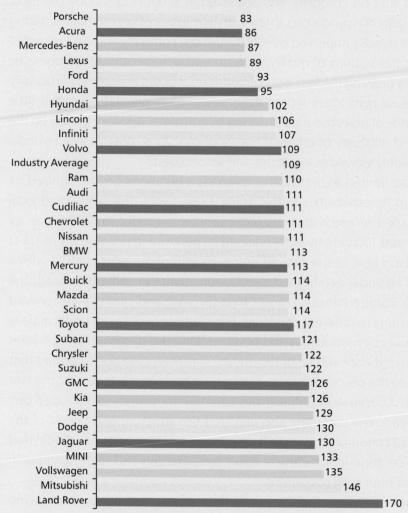

**J.D. Power and Associates
2010 U.S. Initial Quality Study℠ (IQS)**

2010 Nameplate IQS Ranking
Problems per 100 Vehicles

Nameplate	Problems per 100 Vehicles
Porsche	83
Acura	86
Mercedes-Benz	87
Lexus	89
Ford	93
Honda	95
Hyundai	102
Lincoin	106
Infiniti	107
Volvo	109
Industry Average	109
Ram	110
Audi	111
Cudiliac	111
Chevrolet	111
Nissan	111
BMW	113
Mercury	113
Buick	114
Mazda	114
Scion	114
Toyota	117
Subaru	121
Chrysler	122
Suzuki	122
GMC	126
Kia	126
Jeep	129
Dodge	130
Jaguar	130
MINI	133
Vollswagen	135
Mitsubishi	146
Land Rover	170

Source : J.D. Power and Associates 2010 U.S. Initial Quality Study℠

Charts and graphs extracted from this press release must be accompanied by a statement identifying J.D. Power and Associates as the publisher and the J.D. Power and Associates 2010 U.S. Initial Quality Study℠ as the source. Rankings are based on numerical scores, and not necessarily on statistical significance. No advertising or other promotional use can be made of the information in this release of J.D. Power and Associates survery results without the express prior written consent of J.D. Power and Associates.

The role of resources and capabilities in strategy formulation

We saw in Chapter 1 that strategy is concerned with matching a firm's resources and capabilities to the opportunities that arise in the external environment. In Chapter 2 our emphasis was on the identification of profit opportunities in the external environment of the firm. In this chapter, our emphasis shifts from the interface between strategy and the external environment towards the interface between strategy and the **internal environment** of the firm – more specifically, the relationship between strategy and the **resources** and **capabilities** of the firm (see Figure 3.3). Moving from the external to the internal is a logical way of proceeding with our exploration of strategy but also resonates with a theme we noted in Chapter 1: the trend over time from seeing sources of profit as lying mainly in the external environment to seeing sources of profit being located within firms. There are two main reasons why this shift in emphasis has occurred. First, as firms' industry environments have become more unstable, so internal resources and capabilities rather than external market focus have been viewed as a more secure base for formulating strategy. Second, it has become increasingly apparent that **competitive advantage** rather than industry attractiveness is the primary source of superior profitability.

> Competitive advantage rather than industry attractiveness is the primary source of superior profitability.

Basing strategy on resources and capabilities

During the 1990s, ideas concerning the role of resources and capabilities as the principal basis for firm strategy and the primary source of profitability merged into what has become known as the **resource-based view** of the firm.[7]

Figure 3.3 Analysing resources and capabilities: the interface between strategy and the firm

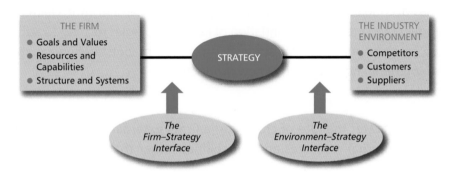

To understand why the resource-based view has had a major impact on strategy thinking, let us go back to the starting point for strategy formulation: typically some statement of the firm's identity and purpose (often expressed in a mission statement). Conventionally, firms have answered the question 'what is our business?' in terms of the market they serve: 'who are our customers?' and 'which of their needs are we seeking to serve?' However, in a world where customer preferences are volatile and the identity of customers and the technologies for serving them are changing, a market-focused strategy may not provide the stability and constancy of direction needed to guide strategy over the long term.[8] When the external environment is in a state of flux, the firm itself, in terms of its bundle of resources and capabilities, may be a much more stable basis on which to define its identity.

In their 1990 landmark paper, 'The Core Competence of the Corporation,' C. K. Prahalad and Gary Hamel pointed to the potential for capabilities to be the 'roots of competitiveness', source of new products and foundation for strategy.[9] Examples of this are shown below.

> Honda Motor Company is the world's biggest motorcycle producer and a lead supplier of cars, but it has never defined itself either as a motorcycle company or a motor vehicle company. Since its founding in 1948, its strategy has been built around its expertise in the development and manufacture of engines; this capability has successfully carried it from motorcycles to a wide range of gasoline-engine products.
>
> Canon Inc had its first success producing 35 mm cameras. Since then it has gone on to develop fax machines, calculators, copy machines, printers, video cameras, camcorders, semiconductor manufacturing equipment and many other products. Almost all Canon's products involve the application of three areas of technological capability: precision mechanics, microelectronics and fine optics.
>
> 3M Corporation expanded from sandpaper, into adhesive tapes, audio and videotapes, road signs, medical products and floppy disks. Its product list now comprises over 30,000 products. Is it a conglomerate? Certainly not, claims 3M. Its vast product range rests on a foundation of key technologies relating to adhesives, thin-film coatings and materials sciences supported by outstanding capability in the development and launching of new products.

In general, the greater the rate of change in a firm's external environment, the more likely it is that internal resources and capabilities rather than external market focus will provide a secure foundation for long-term strategy. In fast-moving, technology-based industries, new companies are built around specific technological capabilities. The markets where these capabilities are applied are a secondary consideration. Motorola, the Texas-based supplier of wireless telecommunications equipment, semiconductors and direct satellite communications, has undergone many transformations, from being a leading provider of TVs and car radios to its current focus on telecom equipment. Yet, underlying these transformations has been a consistent focus on wireless electronics.

> The greater the rate of change in a firm's external environment, the more likely it is that internal resources and capabilities rather than external market focus will provide a secure foundation for long-term strategy.

When a company faces the imminent obsolescence of its core product, should its strategy focus on continuing to serve fundamental customer needs or on deploying its resources and capabilities in other markets?

Olivetti, the Italian typewriter manufacturer, was a pioneer in electronic computers during the 1960s, yet was unable to establish long-term viability in either mainframes or personal computers.[10] Rather than maintain its focus on serving the word-processing needs of business, should Olivetti sought to have exploited its electro-mechanical and precision engineering capabilities in other product markets?

Eastman Kodak's dominance of the world market for photographic products based on chemical imaging has been threatened by digital imaging. Over the past 25 years, Kodak has invested billions of dollars developing digital technologies and digital imaging products. Yet profits and market leadership in digital imaging remain elusive for Kodak. Might Kodak have been better off sticking with its chemical know-how and developing its interests in specialty chemicals, pharmaceuticals and healthcare?[11]

The difficulties experienced by established firms in adjusting to technological change within their own markets are well documented – in typesetting and in disk-drive manufacturing, successive technological waves have caused market leaders to falter and allowed new entrants to prosper.[12]

The remainder of this chapter outlines a resource-based approach to strategy formulation. Fundamental to this approach is a thorough and insightful understanding of the resources and capabilities of a firm. It is important to distinguish between resources

Figure 3.4 The links among resources, capabilities and competitive advantage

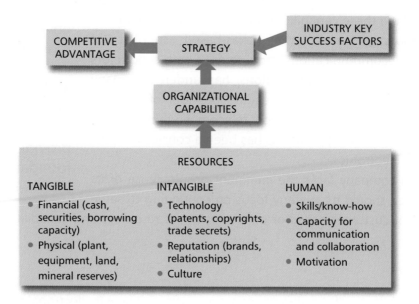

Resources are the productive assets owned by the firm; capabilities are what the firm can do.

and capabilities: resources are the productive assets owned by the firm; capabilities are what the firm can do. Individual resources do not confer competitive advantage alone, they must work together to create organisational capability. It is capability that is the essence of superior performance. Figure 3.4 shows the relationship among resources, capabilities and competitive advantage. Such understanding provides a basis for selecting a strategy that exploits key resource and capability strengths of an organisation – or an individual (see Example 3.1).

Identifying the organisation's resources

In order to evaluate a firm's resources and capabilities we need first to identify and classify them, but drawing up an inventory of a firm's resources can be surprisingly difficult. No such document exists within the accounting or management information systems of most corporations. The corporate balance sheet provides a limited view of a firm's resources – it comprises mainly financial and physical resources. To take a wider view of a firm's resources it is helpful to identify three principal types of resource: tangible, intangible and human resources.

Featured example 3.1 Focusing strategy around core capabilities: Lyor Cohen on Mariah Carey

2001 was a disastrous year for Mariah Carey. Her first movie, *Glitter*, was a flop, the soundtrack was Carey's most poorly received album in a decade, her $80 million recording contract was dropped by EMI and she suffered a nervous breakdown.

Lyor Cohen, the aggressive, workaholic chief executive of Island Def Jam records was quick to spot an opportunity: 'I cold-called her on the day of her release from EMI and I said, I think you are an unbelievable artist and you should hold your head up high', says Cohen. 'What I said stuck on her and she ended up signing with us'.

His strategic analysis of Carey's situation was concise: 'I said to her, what's your competitive advantage? A great voice, of course. And what else?

Credit: Getty Images.

You write every one of your songs – you're a great writer. So why did you stray from your competitive advantage? If you have this magnificent voice and you write such compelling songs, why are you dressing like that, why are you using all these collaborations [with other artists and other songwriters]? Why? It's like driving a Ferrari in first – you won't see what that Ferrari will do until you get into sixth gear'.

Cohen signed Carey in May 2002. Under Universal Music's Island Def Jam Records, Carey returned to her core strengths: her versatile voice, song-writing talents and ballad style. Her next album, *The Emancipation of Mimi*, was the biggest-selling album of 2005 and in 2006 she won a Grammy award.

Source: 'Rap's unlikely mogul', *Financial Times* (5 August 2002). Reproduced with permission.

Tangible resources

Tangible resources are the easiest to identify and evaluate: financial resources and physical assets are identified and valued in the firm's financial statements. Yet, balance sheets are renowned for their propensity to obscure strategically relevant information and to under- or overvalue assets. Historic cost valuation can provide little indication of an asset's market value. For example Disney's movie library had a balance sheet value of $5.4 billion in 2008, based on production costs. Its land assets (including its 28,000 acres in Florida) were valued at a paltry $1.2 billion.

However, the primary goal of resource analysis is not to value a company's assets, but to understand their potential for creating competitive advantage. Information that British Airways possessed fixed assets valued at £8 billion in 2010 is of little use in assessing their strategic value. To assess British Airways' ability to compete effectively in the world airline industry we need to know about the composition of these assets: the location of land and buildings, the types of plane, the landing slots and gate facilities at airports and so on.

Once we have fuller information on a company's tangible resources we explore how we can create additional value from them. This requires that we address two key questions:

1 *What opportunities exist for economising on their use?* It may be possible to use fewer resources to support the same level of business, or to use the existing resources to support a larger volume of business. In the case of British Airways, there may be opportunities for consolidating administrative offices and engineering and service facilities. Improved inventory control may allow economies in inventories of parts and fuel. Better control of cash and receivables permits a business to operate with lower levels of cash and liquid financial resources.

2 *What are the possibilities for employing existing assets more profitably?* Could British Airways generate better returns on some of its planes by redeploying them into cargo carrying? Should British Airways seek to redeploy its assets from Europe and the North Atlantic to Asia-Pacific? Might it reduce costs in its European network by reassigning routes to small franchised airlines?

Intangible resources

For most companies, intangible resources are more valuable than tangible resources. Yet, in company financial statements, intangible resources remain largely invisible. The exclusion or undervaluation of intangible resources is a major reason for the large

Table 3.1 Major companies with the highest market-to-book ratios, December 2006

Company	Valuation ratio	Country	Company	Valuation ratio	Country
Yahoo! Japan	72.0	Japan	Coca-Cola	7.8	US
Colgate-Palmolive	20.8	US	Diageo	7.4	UK
GlaxoSmithKline	13.4	UK	3M	7.3	US
Anheuser-Busch	12.6	US	Nokia	6.7	Finland
eBay	11.2	US	Sanofi-Aventis	6.3	France
SAP	10.8	Germany	AstraZeneca	5.9	UK
Yahoo!	10.7	US	Johnson & Johnson	5.7	US
Dell Computer	10.0	US	Boeing	5.7	US
Sumitomo Mitsui Financial	8.8	Japan	Eli Lily	5.6	US
Procter & Gamble	8.4	US	Cisco Systems	5.5	US
Qualcomm	8.3	US	Roche Holding	5.5	Switz.
Schlumberger	8.2	US	L'Oreal	5.3	France
Unilever	8.1	Neth./UK	Altria	5.2	US
PepsiCo	8.0	US	Novartis	5.1	Switz.

Note: the table includes companies with the highest market capitalisation as a proportion of balance sheet net asset value among the top 200 companies of the world with the largest market capitalisation at the end of 2006.

and growing divergence between companies' balance sheet valuations ('book values') and their stock market valuations (see Table 3.1). Among the most important of these undervalued or unvalued intangible resources are brand names. Table 3.2 shows companies owning brands valued at $15 billion or more.

Table 3.2 The world's most valuable brands, 2010

Rank	Brand	Brand value in 2010 ($ billion)	Change from 2009	Country of origin
1	Coca-Cola	70.4	2%	US
2	IBM	64.7	7%	US
3	Microsoft	60.9	7%	US
4	Google	43.6	36%	US
5	GE	42.8	-10%	US
6	McDonald's	33.6	+4%	US
7	Intel	32.0	+4%	US
8	Nokia	29.5	-15%	Finland
9	Disney	28.7	+1%	US
10	Hewlett-Packard	26.9	+12%	US
11	Toyota	26.2	-16%	Japan
12	Mercedes-Benz	25.2	+6%	Germany
13	Gillette	23.3	+2%	US
14	Cisco	23.2	+5%	US
15	BMW	22.3	+3%	Germany
16	Louis Vuitton	21.9	+4%.	France
17	Apple	21.1	+37%	US
18	Marlboro	20.0	+5%	US
19	Samsung	19.5	+11%	South Korea
20	Honda	18.5	+4%	Japan

Note: Brand values are calculated as the net present value of future earnings generated by the brand.
Source: Interbrand.

Brand names and other trademarks are a form of reputational asset: their value is in the confidence they instil in customers. Different approaches can be used to estimate brand value (or 'brand equity'). One method takes the price premium attributable to a brand, multiplies it by the brand's annual sales volume, then calculates the present value of this revenue stream. The brand valuations in Table 3.2 are based upon the operating profits for each company (after taxation and a capital charge), estimating the proportion attributable to the brand and then capitalising these returns.

Brand names and other trademarks are a form of reputational asset: their value is in the confidence they instil in customers.

The value of a company's brands can be increased by extending the range of products over which a company markets its brands. Johnson & Johnson, Samsung and General Electric derive considerable economies from applying a single brand to a wide range of products. As a result, companies that succeed in building strong consumer brands have a powerful incentive to diversify – e.g. Nike's diversification from athletic shoes into apparel and sports equipment.[13]

Like reputation, technology is an intangible asset whose value is not evident from most companies' balance sheets. Intellectual property – patents, copyrights, trade secrets and trademarks – comprise technological and artistic resources where ownership is defined in law. Over the past 20 years, companies have become more attentive to the value of their intellectual property. For IBM (with the world's biggest patent portfolio) and Qualcomm (with its patents relating to CDMA digital wireless telephony), intellectual property is the most valuable resource that they own.

Human resources

Human resources of the firm comprise the expertise and effort offered by employees. Like intangible resources, human resources do not appear on the firm's balance sheet – for the simple reason that the firm does not own its employees; it purchases their services under employment contacts. The reason for including human resources as part of the resources of the firm is their stability – although employees are free to move from one firm to another (most employment contracts require any more than a month's notice on the part of the employee) – in practice most employment contracts are long term. In the US the average length of time an employee stays with an employer is 4 years, in Europe it is longer – ranging from 8 years in Britain to 13 in Greece.[14]

Most firms devote considerable effort to appraising their human resources. This appraisal occurs at the hiring stage when potential employees are evaluated in relation to the requirements of their job and as part of an

ongoing appraisal process of which annual employee reviews form the centrepiece. The purposes of appraisal are to assess past performance for the purposes of compensation and promotion, set future performance goals and establish employee development plans. Trends in appraisal include greater emphasis on assessing results in relation to performance targets (e.g. management-by-objectives) and broadening the basis of evaluation (e.g. 360-degree appraisal).

Over the past decade, human resource evaluation has become far more systematic and sophisticated. Many organisations have established assessment centres specifically for the purpose of providing comprehensive, quantitative assessments of the skills and attributes of individual employees and increasingly appraisal criteria are based upon empirical research into the components and correlates of superior job performance. **Competency modelling** involves identifying the set of skills, content knowledge, attitudes and values associated with superior performers within a particular job category, then assessing each employee against that profile.[15] An important finding of research into HR competences is the critical role of psychological and social aptitudes in determining superior performance: typically these factors outweigh technical skills and educational and professional qualifications. Recent interest in emotional intelligence reflects growing recognition of the importance of interpersonal skills and emotional awareness.[16] Overall, these finding explain the growing trend among companies to 'hire for attitude; train for skills'.

The ability of employees to harmonise their efforts and integrate their separate skills depends not only on their interpersonal skills but also the organisational context. This organisational context as it affects internal collaboration is determined by a key intangible resource: the culture of the organisation. The term **organisational culture** is notoriously ill defined. It relates to an organisation's values, traditions and social norms. Building on the observations of Peters and Waterman that 'firms with sustained superior financial performance typically are characterised by a strong set of core managerial values that define the ways they conduct business',[17] Jay Barney identifies organisational culture as a firm resource of great strategic importance that is potentially very valuable.[18]

Identifying the organisation's capabilities

Resources are not productive on their own. A brain surgeon is close to useless without a radiologist, anaesthetist, nurses, surgical instruments, imaging equipment and a host of other resources. To perform a task, a team of resources must work together.

Case Insight 3.1

Illustrative examples of resources classified by type for the Hyundai Motor Company

Resource category	Illustrative example	Strategic relevance
Tangible resources	Hyundai currently owns and operates three car production bases in Korea and has invested in seven overseas manufacturing plants in China, Europe, India and the US. Plans are well underway to establish additional production plants in Russia and Brazil	The company has established offshore manufacturing bases in both established and emerging markets. This makes the company less vulnerable to trade conflicts and helps it to accumulate local market knowledge
Intangible resources	Brand: Hyundai has sought to build its brand over time. Whereas in the 80s and 90s its brand was generally regarded as weak (as we have seen from the jokes that circulated about Hyundai cars), by 2010 the value of Hyundai brand had increased significantly. It is now considered one of the top 100 most valuable brands worldwide[19]	Brand image is critically important to car manufacturers, particular in fast-growing economies like India and China where many consumers are purchasing cars for the first time and associate brand recognition with quality and status
Human resources	The company employs over 75,000 people worldwide. In order to gain the expertise needed to build its own models, it recruited experienced senior staff who had worked in the European and the US car industry. On the production side the company usually	The ability to recruit and retain the services of talented designers and engineers is critical to the company's ongoing success but keeping total labour costs as low as possible is also very important.

▶

chooses to locate its overseas manufacturing plants in the less developed areas of its target regions in order to keep labour costs down. For example in the US Hyundai located its plant in Alabama rather than in the traditional car production area around Detroit because labour costs were lower and the workforce was less unionised. In Europe Hyundai has located its manufacturing plant in the Czech Republic

The car industry is intensively competitive and in order to succeed producers need to offer consumers value for money. Car manufacturers whose costs exceed the industry average are unlikely to thrive in such an aggressively competitive global market place

An **organisational capability** is a 'firm's capacity to deploy resources for a desired end result'.[20] Just as an individual may be capable of playing the violin, ice skating and speaking Mandarin, so an organisation may possess the capabilities needed to manufacture widgets, distribute them globally and hedge the resulting foreign exchange exposure. We use the terms capability and competence interchangeably.[21]

Our primary interest is in those capabilities that can provide a basis for competitive advantage. Selznick used **distinctive competence** to describe those things that an organisation does particularly well relative to its competitors.[22] Prahalad and Hamel coined the term core competences to distinguish those capabilities fundamental to a firm's strategy and performance.[23] **Core competences**, according to Hamel and Prahalad, are those that:

- make a disproportionate contribution to ultimate customer value, or to the efficiency with which that value is delivered; and

- provide a basis for entering new markets.[24]

Prahalad and Hamel criticise US companies for emphasising product management over competence management. They compare the strategic development of Sony and RCA in consumer electronics. Both companies were failures in the home video market. RCA introduced its videodisk system, Sony its Betamax videotape system. For RCA, the failure of its first product marked the end of its venture into home video systems and heralded a progressive retreat from the consumer electronics industry. RCA was acquired by GE and later sold to Thomson of France. Sony, on the other hand, acknowledged the failure of Betamax, but continued to develop its capabilities in video technology and produced a string of successful video products including camcorders, digital cameras and the PlayStation game console.

Classifying capabilities

Before focusing upon capabilities that are distinctive or core, it is helpful to take a comprehensive look at an organisation's capabilities. To identify a firm's capabilities, we need to have some basis for classifying and disaggregating its activities. Two approaches are commonly used:

1   A **functional analysis** identifies organisational capabilities in relation to each of the principal functional areas of the firm. Table 3.3 classifies the principal functions of the firm and identifies organisational capabilities located within each function, giving examples of firms that are widely recognised for their capabilities in particular functions.

Table 3.3 A functional classification of organisational capabilities

Functional area	Capability	Exemplars
Corporate functions	Financial control	Exxon Mobil, PepsiCo
	Management development	General Electric, Shell
	Strategic innovation	Google, Haier
	Multidivisional coordination	Unilever, Shell
	Acquisition management	Cisco, Systems, Luxottica
	International management	Shell, Banco Santander
Management information	Comprehensive, integrated MIS network linked to managerial decision making	Wal-Mart, Capital One, Dell Computer

Research & development	Research	IBM, Merck
	Innovative new product development	3M, Apple
	Fast-cycle new product development	Canon, Inditex (Zara)
Operations	Efficiency in volume manufacturing	Briggs & Stratton, YKK
	Continuous improvements in operations	Toyota, Harley-Davidson
	Flexibility and speed of response	Four Seasons Hotels
Product design	Design capability	Nokia, Apple
Marketing	Brand management	Procter & Gamble, Altria
	Building reputation for quality	Johnson & Johnson
	Responsiveness to market trends	MTV, L'Oreal
Sales and distribution	Effective sales promotion and execution	PepsiCo, Pfizer
	Efficiency and speed of order processing	L. L. Bean, Dell Computer
	Speed of distribution	Amazon.com
	Customer service	Singapore Airlines, Caterpillar

In Case Insight 3.2 we illustrate how this 'functional' approach might be used to audit Hyundai's capabilities. In some areas Hyundai's capabilities are equivalent to those of other car firms; in others Hyundai has developed capabilities that are distinctive. We refer to capabilities that are common to all car manufacturers as threshold capabilities because they comprise the essential set of capabilities that any firm needs to compete and survive in its chosen industry.

Case Insight 3.2
Some illustrative examples of Hyundai's capabilities by function

Function	Illustrative capability
Corporate functions	*International management:* the rapid design, build and start-up of offshore manufacturing plants *Financial management:* the willingness and ability to commit significant financial resources in order to acquire market share and achieve long-term success
Management information	*A threshold capability:* Hyundai's capabilities in this function appear to be in line with that of other car manufacturers rather than distinctive
Research & development	*Product & process improvements:* 5% of Hyundai's revenue is devoted to expenditure on R&D in comparison to a 4% average for European car manufacturers. Hyundai's main capabilities seem to lie in upgrading products and implementing process improvements rather than technological leadership per se
Operations	*Planning & scheduling:* the company is noted for its ability to coordinate and schedule production activities across its supply chain. It also has a capability in low-cost production
Product design	*Global product development:* Hyundai has developed its ability to quickly adapt its product offerings to local requirements
Marketing	*Threshold competence:* Hyundai has had to work hard to catch up with its rivals in terms of marketing. It has found it necessary to allocate more resources to marketing than many of its competitors in order to counter its former 'cheap car' image. The company bases its marketing campaigns on extensive market research and examination of market trends and has been successful in raising its market share. Hyundai has successfully linked marketing and operations by being the first company to introduce 10-year warranties on its cars. Although this initiative was initially prompted by the need to overcome consumers' concerns about the quality of Hyundai cars skilful marketing created a virtue out of a necessity

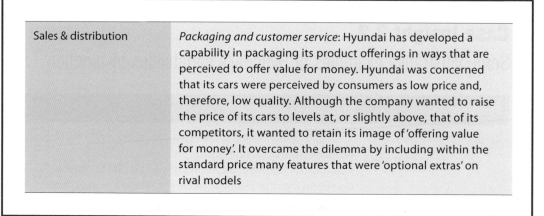

Sales & distribution	*Packaging and customer service*: Hyundai has developed a capability in packaging its product offerings in ways that are perceived to offer value for money. Hyundai was concerned that its cars were perceived by consumers as low price and, therefore, low quality. Although the company wanted to raise the price of its cars to levels at, or slightly above, that of its competitors, it wanted to retain its image of 'offering value for money'. It overcame the dilemma by including within the standard price many features that were 'optional extras' on rival models

2   **Value chain analysis** separates the activities of the firm into a sequential chain. Michael Porter's representation of the value chain distinguishes between primary activities (those involved with the transformation of inputs and interface with the customer) and support activities (see Figure 3.5). Porter's generic value chain identifies a few broadly defined activities that can be separated to provide a more detailed identification of the firm's activities (and the capabilities that correspond to each activity). Case Insight 3.3 shows how this might look for firms like Hyundai operating in the car industry. Thus, marketing might include market research, test marketing, advertising, promotion, pricing and dealer relations.[25] By exploring different activities and, most crucially, the linkages between them it is possible to gain a sense of an organisation's main capabilities.

Figure 3.5 Porter's value chain

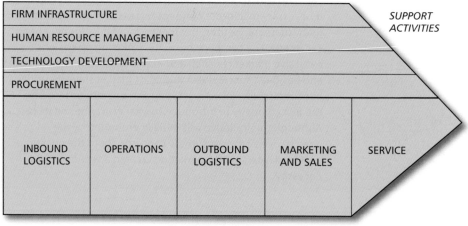

Case Insight 3.3
Using Porter's value chain to explore the capabilities of firms in the car industry

Type of activity	Generic value chain label	Illustrative examples of activities and associated capabilities required in the car industry
Primary activities	Inbound logistics	Purchasing
		Supply chain management
		Component manufacture
	Operations	Design and product development
		Assembly
		Flexible manufacturing
		Quality control
	Outbound logistics	Distribution coordination and support
		Dealer relationships and management
	Marketing & sales	Market research
		Test marketing
		Advertising
		Promotion
		Pricing
	Service	Warranty and car servicing arrangements
		Parts
		Recycling

Support activities	Infrastructure	Integration of the value chain
		Global communications
		Customer focused approach
		Risk management
	Human resource management	Training and skills development
		Staff recruitment and retention
		Staff appraisal and performance management
	Technology development	Technology managed design and manufacturing
		Integrated management information systems
		Technology linked manufacture and sales
	Procurement	Database management and IT controlled purchasing of parts and sub-assemblies
		Inventory management
		Supply chain integration and coordination

The nature of capability

We noted earlier that drawing up an inventory of a firm's resources can be challenging. Identifying organisational capabilities poses an even greater problem because capabilities are much more elusive. Apple's distinctive capability in the design of consumer electronic products that combine pleasing aesthetics with a superior user interface is evident from its iMac, iPod and iPhone products – but where within Apple is this capability located? To better understand organisational capabilities, let us take a look at their structure.

CAPABILITY AS PROCESS AND ROUTINE

Organisational capability requires the efforts of various individuals to be integrated with one another and with capital equipment, technology and other resources. But how does this integration occur? Productive activity within an organisation involves coordinated actions undertaken by teams of people engaged in a series of productive tasks. We refer to the sequence of actions through which a specific task is performed as an **organisational process**. The sequences that comprise organisational processes can be mapped using a flowchart.[26] For example, the process of fixing bugs in the operating system developed by a large computer company involved a sequence of 30 distinct activities that began with problem recognition and ended with changes in software documentation.[27]

A key feature of almost all the processes performed by an organisation is their routinised nature. **Routinisation** is an essential step in translating directions and operating practices into capabilities – only by becoming routine do processes become efficient and reliable. In every McDonald's restaurant, operating manuals provide precise directions for a comprehensive range of tasks, from the placing of the pickle on the burger to the maintenance of the milkshake machine. In practice, the operating manuals are seldom referred to – through continuous repetition, tasks become routinised.

These organisational routines – 'regular and predictable behavioral patterns [comprising] repetitive patterns of activity'[28] – are viewed by evolutionary economists as the fundamental building blocks of what firms are and what they do. It is through the adaptation and replication of routines that firms develop. Like individual skills, organisational routines develop through learning-by-doing. Just as individual skills become rusty when not exercised, so it is difficult for organisations to retain coordinated responses to contingencies that arise only rarely. Hence, there may be a trade-off between efficiency and flexibility. A limited repertoire of routines can be performed highly efficiently with near-perfect coordination. The same organisation may find it extremely difficult to respond to novel situations.[29]

THE HIERARCHY OF CAPABILITIES

Whether we start from a functional or value chain approach, the capabilities that we identify are likely to be broadly defined: operational capability, marketing capability, supply chain management capability. However, having recognised that capabilities are the outcome of processes and routines, it is evident that these broadly defined capabilities can be broken down into more specialist capabilities. For example, marketing capabilities can be separated into market research capability, product launch capability, advertising capability, pricing capability, dealer relations capability – and others too. We can also recognise that even broadly defined functional capabilities integrate to form wider cross-functional capabilities: new product development, business development, the provision of customer solutions. What we observe is a hierarchy of capabilities where more general, broadly defined capabilities are formed from the integration of more specialised capabilities. For example:

- A hospital's capability in treating heart disease depends on its integration of capabilities relating to patient diagnosis, physical medicine, cardiovascular surgery, pre- and post-operative care, as well as capabilities relating to training, information technology and various administrative and support functions.

- Toyota's manufacturing capability – its system of 'lean production' – integrates capabilities relating to the manufacture of components and sub-assemblies, supply chain management, production scheduling, assembly, quality control procedures, systems for managing innovation and continuous improvement and inventory control.

Appraising resources and capabilities

So far, we have established what resources and capabilities are, how they can provide a long-term focus for a company's strategy and how we can go about identifying them. However, given our emphasis on strategy as a quest for profit, the next stage of our analysis is to appraise the potential for resources and capabilities to earn profits for the company.

The profits that a firm obtains from its resources and capabilities depend on three factors: their abilities to establish a competitive advantage; to sustain that competitive advantage; and to appropriate the returns to that competitive advantage. Each of these depends on a number of resource characteristics. Figure 3.6 shows the key relationships.

Establishing competitive advantage

For a resource or capability to establish a competitive advantage, two conditions must be present:

1 *Scarcity.* If a resource or capability is widely available within the industry, then it may be essential to compete, but it will not be a sufficient basis for competitive advantage. In oil and gas exploration, new technologies such as directional drilling and 3D seismic analysis are critical to reducing the costs of finding new reserves. However, these technologies are widely available from oilfield service and IT companies. As a result, such technologies are 'needed to play', but they are not *sufficient to win*.

2 *Relevance.* A resource or capability must be relevant to the key success factors in the market. British coal mines produced some wonderful brass bands. Unfortunately, musical capabilities did little to assist the mines in meeting competition from cheap

Figure 3.6 Appraising the strategic importance of resources and capabilities

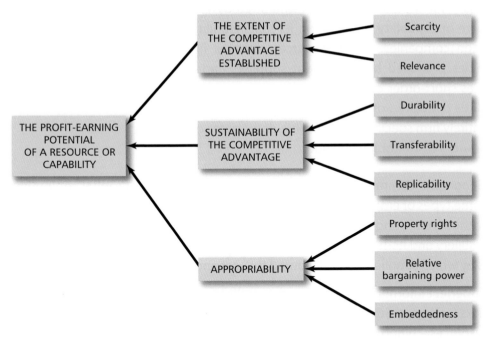

imported coal and North Sea gas. As retail banking shifts toward automated teller machines and online transactions, so the retail branch networks of the banks have become less relevant for customer service.

Sustaining competitive advantage

The profits earned from resources and capabilities depend not just on their ability to establish competitive advantage, but also on how long that advantage can be sustained. This depends on whether resources and capabilities are durable and whether rivals can imitate the competitive advantage they offer. Resources and capabilities are imitable if they are transferable or replicable.

Durability. Some resources are more durable than others and therefore are a more secure basis for competitive advantage. The increasing pace of technological change is shortening the useful life span of most resources including capital equipment and proprietary technologies. Brands, on the other hand, can show remarkable resilience to time. Heinz sauces, Kellogg's' cereals, Guinness stout, Burberry raincoats and Coca-Cola have all been market leaders for over a century.

> The profits earned from resources and capabilities depend not just on their ability to establish competitive advantage, but also on how long that advantage can be sustained.

Transferability. The simplest means of acquiring the resources and capabilities necessary for imitating another firm's strategy is to buy them. The ability to buy a resource or capability depends on its transferability – the extent to which it is mobile between companies. Some resources, such as finance, raw materials, components, machines produced by equipment suppliers and employees with standardised skills (such as short-order cooks and auditors), are transferable and can be bought and sold with little difficulty. Some resources are not easily transferred (or 'immobile') – either they are entirely firm specific, or their value depreciates on transfer.[30]

Sources of immobility include:

- Geographical immobility of natural resources, large items of capital equipment and some types of employees may make it difficult for firms to acquire these resources without relocating themselves. The competitive advantage of the Laphroaig distillery and its 10-year-old, single-malt whiskey is its water spring on the Isle of Islay which supplies water flavoured by peat and sea spray.

- Imperfect information regarding the quality and productivity of resources creates risks for buyers. Such imperfections are especially important in relation to human resources – hiring decisions are typically based on very little knowledge of how the new employee will perform. Sellers of resources have better information about the characteristics of the resources on offer than potential buyers – this creates a 'lemons problem' for firms seeking to acquire resources in that there is information asymmetry between the seller and the buyer.[31] Jay Barney has shown that different valuations of resources by firms can result in their being either underpriced or overpriced, giving rise to differences in profitability between firms.[32]

- Complementarity between resources means that the detachment of a resource from its 'home team' causes it to lose productivity and value. Thus, if brand reputation is associated with the company that created it, a change in ownership of the brand erodes its value. The sale of Jaguar Cars, first to Ford and then to Tata Motors of India has almost certainly eroded its brand value.[33]

- Organisational capabilities, because they are based on teams of resources, are less mobile than individual resources. Even if the whole team can be transferred (in investment banking it has been commonplace for whole teams of analysts or mergers and acquisitions specialists to defect from one bank to another), the dependence of the team on a wider network of relationships and corporate culture may pose difficulties for recreating the capability in the new company.

Replicability. If a firm cannot buy a resource or capability, it must build it. In financial services, most innovations in new derivative products can be imitated easily by competitors. In retailing too, competitive advantages that derive from store layout, point-of-sale technology, charge cards and extended opening hours can also be copied easily by competitors.

Less easily replicable are capabilities based on complex organisational routines. Federal Express's national, next-day delivery service and Nucor's system for steel manufacturing that combines efficiency with flexibility are complex capabilities based on unique corporate cultures.

Some capabilities appear simple but prove difficult to replicate. Throughout the 1980s and 1990s, General Motors struggled to understand and replicate the Toyota lean production system. The Terumi joint venture between the two companies gave GM a bird's-eye view of Toyota's system in operation. Yet, after two decades of benchmarking, capital investment and employee training, GM was still lagging in efficiency quality and flexibility.[34]

Even where replication is possible, incumbent firms benefit from the fact that resources and capabilities that have been accumulated over a long period can only be replicated at disproportionate cost by would-be imitators. Dierickx and Cool identify two major sources of **incumbency advantage**:

- Asset mass efficiencies occur where a strong initial position in technology, distribution channels or reputation facilitates the subsequent accumulation of these resources.

- Time compression diseconomies are the additional costs incurred by imitators when attempting to accumulate rapidly a resource or capability. Thus, 'crash programmes' of R&D and 'blitz' advertising campaigns tend to be less productive than similar expenditures made over a longer period.[35]

Case Insight 3.4
Building competitive advantage at Hyundai

As a latecomer to the car market Hyundai faced a considerable hurdle in trying to establish itself as a global car manufacturer. Acquiring appropriate resources such as finance, plant and equipment, component parts and skilled workers were not too much of a problem because these resources were transferable and easily purchased, but acquiring appropriate capabilities was a more difficult matter. Developing capabilities in areas such as product design and quality assurance is not straightforward because it requires a newcomer to replicate complex organisational routines that established firms have developed over many years. Hyundai overcame this challenge by recruiting experts from other car companies and by making a clear long-term commitment to develop the required capabilities in a focused and systematic way. The company studied and replicated the most effective practices of rivals having first using benchmarking and competitor intelligence to establish which firms were 'best in class'.

Although Hyundai was able to gain a foothold in the car market, the advantages possessed by the incumbent firms limited the company's competitiveness during its early years of operation. For example, Hyundai lacked the advantages that existing firms reaped from scale economies, established brand identities and pre-existing distribution channels. Entry into the car industry was costly for Hyundai and required the firm to make a considerable long-term financial and management commitment to the business. This long-term commitment was possible because Hyundai was part of South Korea's 'chaebol' system. Chaebols are large, conglomerate, family-controlled firms with strong ties to government. Chaebols received considerable economic and political support from the South Korean government in the 1980s and early 1990s and this support enabled Hyundai to invest heavily in the capital-intensive car industry without being under pressure to make short-term returns. Although, over time, Hyundai has succeeded in enhancing its competitive position, it is worth noting that the quality problems that arose in the early years as Hyundai attempted to increase its production and develop its competence as a car manufacturer had an enduring effect on the company's brand image and required the firm to commit significant additional funds to marketing and customer service initiatives.

Appropriating the returns to competitive advantage

Who gains the returns generated by superior capabilities? We should normally expect that such returns accrue to the owner of that capability. However, ownership is not always clear-cut: capabilities depend heavily on the skills and efforts of employees – who are not owned by the firm. For companies dependent on human ingenuity and know-how, the mobility of key employees represents a constant threat to their competitive advantage (see Example 3.2). In investment banks and other human capital-intensive firms, the struggle between employees and shareholders to capture a greater share of profits has come into sharp relief in debates about individual bonuses following the financial meltdown of 2008. The

> Capabilities depend heavily on the skills and efforts of employees – who are not owned by the firm.

Featured example 3.2 When your competitive advantage walks out the door: Gucci

On 10 September 2001, French retailer Pinault Printemps Redoute (PPR) agreed to acquire Gucci Group – the Italian-based fashion house and luxury goods maker. On 4 November 2003 the managers and shareholders of the two companies were stunned to learn that chairman Domenico De Sole and vice chairman Tom Ford would be leaving Gucci in April 2004.

The duo had masterminded Gucci's transformation from a near-bankrupt family firm with an over-extended brand into one of the world's hottest fashion houses. As creative director, Tom Ford had established Gucci as a style leader and hired young designers such as Stella McCartney and Alexander McQueen. De Sole's astute leadership had instituted careful planning and financial discipline and built Gucci's global presence – especially in Asia.

How great a blow was De Sole and Ford's departure to the parent PPR? In principle, a new CEO and new head of design could be hired. In practice, talent of the class of De Sole and Ford was rare – especially a combination of designer and CEO who could collaborate around a shared vision.

The stock market's reaction was ominous. On 3 November 2003 Gucci's share price was $86.10; on 6 November it had fallen to $84.60. However, in the absence of PPR's guarantee to acquire Gucci's shares at $85.52, analysts estimated that Gucci would be trading at around $74. The implication was that Gucci was worth $1.2 billion less without De Sole and Ford than with them.

Source: Adapted from articles in the *Financial Times* during 5–8 November 2003.

prevalence of partnerships (rather than joint-stock companies) in professional service industries (lawyers, accountants and management consultants) reflects the desire to avoid conflict between owners and its human resources.

The less clearly defined are property rights in resources and capabilities, the greater the importance of relative bargaining power in determining the division of returns between the firm and its individual members. In the case of team-based organisational capabilities, this balance of power between the firm and an individual employee depends crucially on the relationship between individuals' skills and organisational routines. The more deeply embedded are individual skills and knowledge within organisational routines and the more they depend on corporate systems and reputation, the weaker the employee is relative to the firm.

Conversely, the more closely an organisational capability is identified with the expertise of individual employees and the more effective those employees are at deploying their bargaining power, the better able employees are to appropriate surpluses. If the individual employee's contribution to productivity is clearly identifiable, if the employee is mobile and if the employee's skills offer similar productivity to other firms, the employee is in a strong position to appropriate most of his or her contribution to the firm's value added.

Did the $32.5 million over five years paid to the footballer, David Beckham, fully exploit his value to LA Galaxy? In most professional sports, it appears that strategies based exclusively on signing superstar players result in the players appropriating most of the rents, with little surplus available for the clubs – this was certainly the fate of Real Madrid, Chelsea and Manchester City football clubs in recent years. The emphasis by investment banks and consulting companies upon the capabilities of their teams, rather than upon the role of star employees is a strategy for improving the bargaining power of the firm relative to that of its key employees.

Putting resource and capability analysis to work: a practical guide

We have covered the principal concepts and frameworks for analysing resources and capabilities. How do we put this analysis into practice? We now offer a simple, step-by-step approach to how a company can appraise its resources and capabilities and then use the appraisal to guide strategy formulation.

Step 1: Identify the key resources and capabilities

To draw up a list of the firm's resources and capabilities, we can begin from outside or inside the firm. From an external focus, we begin with key success factors (see Chapter 2).

What factors determine why some firms in an industry are more successful than others and on what resources and capabilities are these success factors based?

Suppose we use this approach to analyse the resources and capabilities of Hyundai. We can start with key success factors in the world car industry: low-cost production; attractively designed new models embodying the latest technologies; and the financial strength to weather the cyclicality and heavy investment requirements of the industry. What capabilities and resources do these key success factors imply? They would include manufacturing capabilities, new product development capability, effective supply chain management, global distribution, brand strength, scale-efficient plants with up-to-date capital equipment, a strong balance sheet and so on. To organise and categorise these various resources and capabilities, it is helpful to switch to the inside of Hyundai using either a functional approach (as we did in Case Insight 3.2) or the value chain approach (illustrated in Case Insight 3.3). Case Insight 3.5 shows how we might work through this step for Hyundai. The first column of the table in Case Insight 3.5 lists Hyundai's principal resources and capabilities, which are derived from prior analyses of the types illustrated in Case Insights 3.1–3.3.

Step 2: Appraising resources and capabilities

Resources and capabilities need to be appraised against two key criteria. First is their importance: which resources and capabilities are most important in conferring sustainable competitive advantage? Second, where are our strengths and weaknesses as compared to competitors?

Case Insight 3.5
Appraising Hyundai's resources and capabilities

	Importance[1]	Hyundai's relative strength[2]	Comments
RESOURCES			
R1. Finance	6	6	Net profits are up despite general downturn in the car industry. It has a triple B credit rating with Standard & Poor which is around the industry

▶

			average. The company has benefited recently from the weakness in its domestic currency, the won, but currency fluctuations can also work against the firm
R2. Technology	7	4	Despite some technical strengths, Hyundai is not a leader in automotive technology
R3. Plant and equipment	8	9	The company has invested heavily in establishing new plants and, as a late comer to the market, has been able to invest in locations that provide a low-cost manufacturing base
R4. Location	4	5	Plants in key low-cost growth markets (China, India, Brazil) but labour costs in the Korean manufacturing base have risen over time and the company has faced industrial disputes with a unionised workforce in its home country
R5. Distribution (dealership network)	8	7	Geographically extensive distribution with special strength in emerging markets. Hyundai has experimented with new dealership arrangements which, though at an early stage of introduction, seem to be successful
R6. Brands	6	4	Despite making significant progress, the company still suffers from its past image of being a producer of low-price, low-quality cars which is hampering its move into the luxury end of the car market

			and affecting sales in regions where status is as important as price and reliability
CAPABILITIES			
C1. Product development	8	9	Has a growing reputation for producing products that are customised to local requirements and in tune with market trends
C2. Purchasing and supply chain management	7	8	Has restructured its supplier network and introduced extensive quality control procedures in conjunction with suppliers
C3. Engineering	7	5	Whilst the company has significantly improved the reliability of its cars and added a significant number of new products to its range, it is perceived as a follower rather than a leader in engineering terms
C4. Manufacturing	8	8	A low-cost producer that has significantly improved the reliability of its cars. Its production figures are now comparable with leading companies in the industry
C5. Financial management	6	5	In keeping with its chaebol heritage the firm has placed more emphasis on market share and long-term sustainability than short-term profitability and returns to shareholders
C6. R&D	5	4	Spends 5% of its revenue on R&D but is not regarded as a leader in automotive innovation

C7. Marketing and sales	9	7	As a consequence of the challenges it has faced with regard to its brand image Hyundai is very sensitive to the market and to emerging market trends. It is improving its brand management and manages its advertising and promotion with increasing dexterity. Nonetheless the company still finds itself in the position of playing 'catch up'
C8. Government relations	4	8	These relationships are particularly important in emerging markets. The company is sensitive to cultural issues (for example it requires its operatives working in China to learn Chinese) and places emphasis on establishing local supply networks. These kinds of policies have fostered good relationships with host governments
C9. Strategic management	7	9	The company's management team has a track record of identifying key success factors and adopting a systematic and focused approach to |acquiring new capabilities

Both scales range from 1 to 10 (1 = very low, 10 = very high).
Hyundai's resources and capabilities are compared against those of GM, Ford, Toyota, DaimlerChrysler, Nissan, Honda, Fiat and PSA, where 5 represents parity. The ratings are based on the author's subjective judgement.

ASSESSING IMPORTANCE

The temptation in assessing which resources and capabilities are most important is to concentrate on customer choice criteria. What we must bear in mind, however, is that our ultimate objective is not to attract customers, but to make superior profit through establishing a sustainable competitive advantage. For this purpose we need to look beyond customer choice to the underlying strategic characteristics of resources and capabilities. To do this we need to look at the set of appraisal criteria outlined in the previous section on 'Appraising Resources and Capabilities'.

> Our ultimate objective is not to attract customers, but to make superior profit through establishing a sustainable competitive advantage.

In the case of Hyundai, many resources and capabilities are essential to compete in the business, but several of them are not scarce (for example, total quality management capability and technologically advanced assembly plants have become widely diffused within the industry), while others (such as IT capability and design capability) are outsourced to external providers – either way, they are 'needed to play' but not 'needed to win'. On the other hand, resources such as brand strength and a global distribution network and capabilities such as fast-cycle new product development and global logistics capability, cannot be easily acquired or internally developed – they are critical to establishing and sustaining advantage. In column 2 of Case Insight 3.5 we provide our subjective ranking of the importance of different resources and capabilities.

ASSESSING RELATIVE STRENGTHS

Objectively appraising the comparative strengths and weaknesses of a company's resources and capabilities relative to competitors is difficult. In assessing their own competences, organisations frequently fall victim to past glories, hopes for the future and their own wishful thinking. The tendency towards arrogance among companies – and their senior managers – means that business success often sows the seeds of its own destruction.[36] Among the failed industrial companies in the US and Europe are many whose former success blinded them to their stagnating capabilities and declining competitiveness: examples include the cutlery producers of Sheffield, England and the integrated steel giants of the US.

To identify and appraise a company's capabilities, managers must look both inside and outside. Internal discussion can be valuable in sharing insights and evidence and building consensus regarding the organisation's resource and capability profile. The evidence of history can be particularly revealing in reviewing instances where the company has performed well and those where it has performed poorly: do any patterns appear? In column 3 of Case Insight 3.5 we provide our subjective rankings of the relative strength of Hyundai with respect to different resources and capabilities.

Finally, to move the analysis from the subjective to the objective level, **benchmarking** is a powerful tool for quantitative assessment of performance relative to that of competitors. Benchmarking is 'the process of identifying, understanding and adapting outstanding practices from organisations anywhere in the world to help your organisation improve its performance.'[37] Benchmarking offers a systematic framework and methodology for identifying particular functions and processes and then for comparing their performance with other companies.

Ultimately, appraising resources and capabilities is not about data, it's about insight and understanding. Every organisation has some activity where it excels or has the potential to excel. For FedEx, it is a system that guarantees next-day delivery anywhere within the United States. For BMW, it is the ability to integrate world-class engineering with design excellence and highly effective marketing. For McDonald's, it is the ability to supply millions of hamburgers from thousands of outlets throughout the world, with remarkable uniformity of quality, customer service and hygiene. For General Electric, it is a system of corporate

management that reconciles coordination, innovation, flexibility and financial discipline in one of the world's largest and most diversified corporations. All these companies are examples of highly successful enterprises. One reason why they are successful is that they have recognised what they can do well and have based their strategies on their strengths. For poor-performing companies, the problem is not necessarily an absence of distinctive capabilities, but a failure to recognise what they are and to deploy them effectively.

> Ultimately, appraising resources and capabilities is not about data, it's about insight and understanding.

BRINGING TOGETHER IMPORTANCE AND RELATIVE STRENGTH

Putting together the two criteria – importance and relative strength – allows us to highlight a company's key strengths and key weaknesses. Having provided a partial (and hypothetical) identification and appraisal of Hyundai's resources and capabilities during the period 2000–10 in relation to the two criteria of importance and relative strength outlined above, Case Insight 3.6 then brings these two criteria together into a single display. Dividing this display into four quadrants allows us to identify those resources

Case Insight 3.6
Appraising Hyundai's resources and capabilities (hypothetical)

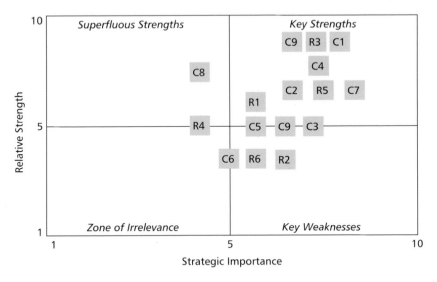

Note: The figure is based on the ratings of resources and capabilities in Case Insight 3.5.

and capabilities that we may regard as key strengths and those that we may identify as key weaknesses. For example, our assessment suggests that the modern, well-located plants, product development and clear strategic intent are key strengths of Hyundai, while brand image (rapidly improving but historically poor) and technology (historically a follower rather than a leader) are key weaknesses.

Step 3: Developing strategy implications

Our key focus is on the two right-hand quadrants of Case Insight 3.6. How do we exploit our key strengths most effectively? What do we do about our key weaknesses in terms of both upgrading them and reducing our vulnerability to them? Finally, what about our 'inconsequential' strengths? Are these really superfluous, or are there ways in which we can deploy them to greater effect?

EXPLOITING KEY STRENGTHS
Having identified resources and capabilities that are important and where our company is strong relative to competitors, the key task is to formulate our strategy to ensure that

these resources are deployed to the greatest effect. If product development is a key strength of Hyundai, then it makes sense for the company to differentiate itself from competitors by customising its products to meet local demands. If the company has modern, efficient and flexible plants at the same time as offering locally customised products it may be able to offer customers 'value for money' in terms of its pricing strategy.

To the extent that different companies within an industry have different capability profiles, this implies differentiation of strategies within the industry. Thus, Toyota's outstanding manufacturing capabilities and fast-cycle new product development, VW's engineering excellence and Peugeot's design flair suggest that each company should be pursuing a distinctively different strategy.

MANAGING KEY WEAKNESSES

What does a company do about its key weaknesses? It is tempting to think of how companies can upgrade existing resources and capabilities to correct such weaknesses. However, converting weakness into strength is likely to be a long-term task for most companies as we have seen in the Hyundai case. In the short to medium term, a company is likely to be stuck with the resources and capabilities that it inherits from the previous period.

The most decisive – and often most successful – solution to weaknesses in key functions is to outsource. Thus, in the car industry, companies have become increasingly selective in the activities they perform internally.

We shall consider the vertical scope of the firm at greater depth in Chapter 7. Through clever strategy formulation a firm may be able to negate the impact of its key weaknesses. In the Hyundai case, the company decided to offer a 10-year warranty on its cars and more recently to offer its US customers an option that they can return their car without

During the 1930s, Ford was almost completely vertically integrated. At its massive River Rouge plant, which once employed over 100,000 people, coal and iron ore entered at one end, completed cars exited at the other. In 2004, Ford opened its Dearborn Truck Plant on the old River Rouge site. The new plant employed 3200 Ford workers and an equal number of suppliers' employees. Almost all component production was outsourced along with a major part of design, engineering, assembly, IT and security. In athletic shoes and clothing, Nike undertakes product design, marketing and overall 'systems integration', but manufacturing, logistics and many other functions are contracted out.

money owing if they are made redundant or declared bankrupt within one year of their purchase. This has gone a long way to overcoming potential customers' initial reluctance to purchase a Hyundai car, particularly during a period of recession and economic turbulence.

WHAT ABOUT SUPERFLUOUS STRENGTHS?

What about those resources and capabilities where a company has particular strengths, but these don't appear to be important sources of sustainable competitive advantage? One response may be to lower the level of investment from these resources and capabilities. If a retail bank has a strong, but increasingly underutilised, branch network, this may be an opportunity to prune its real estate assets and invest in IT approaches to customer services.

In the same way that companies can turn apparent weaknesses into competitive strengths, so it is possible to develop innovative strategies that turn apparently inconsequential strengths into valuable resources and capabilities.

Capcom, a Japanese developer and publisher of popular video games such as Street Fighter and Resident Evil, started out manufacturing and distributing arcade game machines. Whilst their initial focus was on producing coin-operated electronic machines based on simple 'scroll and shoot' games, the company soon recognised that it was their subsidiary skill in developing the games rather than the machines that offered the greatest potential.

Developing resources and capabilities

As we have seen in Chapter 2, the circumstances in which firms find themselves change over time. Technology and consumer tastes change, the economic climate alters, key personnel retire or leave the organisation and, as a consequence, firms need to develop new resources and capabilities. Whilst there are undoubtedly many challenges faced in acquiring new resources we nonetheless know a lot about how to approach acquiring resources; be they tangible (e.g. acquiring raw materials or plant and equipment), intangible (e.g. building a brand or managing intellectual capital) or human (e.g. recruiting and retaining the services of talented individuals). However, organisational capabilities are a different matter altogether. Possibly the most difficult problem in developing capabilities is that we know little about the linkage between resources and capabilities. One observation that is confirmed repeatedly across very different fields of competitive endeavour is that capabilities are not simply an outcome of the resources upon which they are based.

In sport it is common to see resource-rich teams failing to match the achievements of teams that create strong capabilities from modest resources. In European football, teams built with modest finances and without the acquisition of top-class players (Arsenal, Bayern Munich, PSV Eindhoven and Valencia) frequently outplay star-studded teams built from massive finance outlays (Chelsea, Real Madrid, Manchester City and Inter Milan).

International competition tells a similar story; it is small, resource-poor countries that regularly outperform the pre-eminent national teams. At the Beijing Olympics, the US sprint relay teams – despite having some of the world's fastest runners – failed to win a single medal.

It is the same in business: the firms that demonstrate the most outstanding capabilities are not necessarily those with the greatest resource endowments.

- In cars, GM has four times the output of Honda and four times the R&D expenditure, yet, over the past three decades, it is Honda, not GM, that has been the world leader in power train technology.

- In animated movies, the most successful productions in recent years were by newcomers Pixar (*Toy Story*, *The Incredibles*) and Aardman Animations (*Wallace and Gromit*) rather than by industry giant, Walt Disney.

- In telecom equipment it was the upstart Cisco, rather than established incumbents Alcatel-Lucent, Ericsson and Siemens, that established leadership in the new era of package switching.

That said, there is one resource that does seem to be critical to the development of capabilities: managers with the requisite knowledge for capability building. While there is a great deal that we do not know about why some companies have developed certain capabilities to higher levels than other firms, one thing is clear – managers play a critical role in nurturing and shaping those capabilities. Among the founders of new companies, a substantial number have prior managerial experience within the same sector.[38] In new industries, the best-performing firms are often those whose founders had prior experience in closely related sectors.[39] It is reasonable to suppose that the key knowledge that these entrepreneurs carry with them is an understanding of what it takes to build key organisational capabilities.

Path dependency and the role of early experiences

If organisational capability is not simply the result of the application of resources, what determines the capabilities in which a firm achieves distinctiveness? If we examine the types of capability that make different firms distinctive in their particular industries (the companies listed in Table 3.2 for example), one obvious feature is that these capabilities have developed over significant periods of time. In many cases we can trace the origins of a distinctive capability (or 'core competence') to the circumstances which prevailed during the founding and early development of the company. In other words, organisational capability is path dependent – a company's capabilities today are the result of its history.[40]

> Organisational capability is path dependent –
> a company's capabilities today are the result of its history.

Consider Wal-Mart Inc, the world's biggest retailer. How did it develop its outstanding capability in supply chain logistics? This super-efficient system of warehousing, distribution and vendor relationships was not the result of careful planning and design; it evolved from the circumstances that Wal-Mart faced during its early years of existence. Its small-town locations in Arkansas and Oklahoma, resulted in unreliable delivery from its suppliers, consequently Wal-Mart established its own distribution system. Similarly with its remarkable commitment to cost efficiency. Its management systems are undoubtedly important, but ultimately it is Wal-Mart's origins in the rural South and the values and personality of its founder, Sam Walton, that sustains its obsession with cutting cost and eliminating waste.

Consider too the world's largest oil and gas majors (see Table 3.4). Despite long histories of competing together in the same markets, with near-identical products and similar strategies, the majors display very different capability profiles. Industry leaders Exxon and Royal Dutch Shell exemplify these differences. Exxon (now Exxon Mobil) is known for its outstanding financial management capabilities exercised through rigorous investment controls and unrelenting cost efficiency. Shell is known for its decentralised, international management capability which allows it to adapt to different national environments and to become an 'insider' wherever it does business. These differences can be traced back to the companies' 19th-century origins. Exxon (then Standard Oil New Jersey) acted as holding company for Rockefeller's Standard Oil Trust exercising responsibility for overall financial management. Shell was established to sell Russian oil in China and the Far East, while Royal Dutch was established to exploit Indonesian oil reserves. With head offices thousands of miles away in Europe, both parts of the group developed a decentralised, adaptable management style.

Table 3.4 Distinctive capabilities as a consequence of childhood experiences: the oil majors

Company	Distinctive capability	Early history
Exxon	Financial management	Exxon's predecessor, Standard Oil (NJ), was the holding company for Rockefeller's Standard Oil Trust
Royal Dutch Shell	Coordinating a decentralised global network of 200 operating companies	Shell Transport & Trading headquartered in London and founded to sell Russian oil in China and the Far East Royal Dutch Petroleum headquartered in The Hague; founded to exploit Indonesian reserves
BP	'Elephant hunting'	Discovered huge Persian reserves, went on to find Forties field (North Sea) and Prudhoe Bay (Alaska)
ENI	Deal making in politicised environments	The Enrico Mattei legacy; the challenge of managing government relations in post-war Italy
Mobil	Lubricants	Vacuum Oil Co. founded in 1866 to supply patented petroleum lubricants

The linkage between resources and capabilities

These observations are troubling for ambitious top managers anxious to adapt and regenerate their companies: if a firm's capabilities are determined during the early stages of its life, is it really possible to develop the new capabilities needed to meet the challenges of tomorrow?

To explore this question let us look more closely at the structure of organisational capability. Capabilities, we observed, involve coordination between organisational members such that they integrate their skills with one another and with a variety of other resources. We can distinguish formal and informal dimensions of this coordination. The literature on organisational routines emphasises the informal dimension. Routinisation involves 'repetitive patterns of activity', that are 'ordinarily accomplished without conscious awareness'.[41]

Two factors contribute to the efficiency and effectiveness with which teams of individuals perform these repetitive patterns of activity. The first is organisational learning. Coordination is perfected through repetition. The more complex the task, the greater the gains from learning-by-doing. The second is culture, one of the intangible resources of the firm that plays a pivotal role. The capacity for organisational members to comprehend one another and collaborate together without continual managerial direction depends upon shared perceptions, common values and behavioural norms – all elements of the complex phenomenon that we refer to as organisational culture.

Are organisational capabilities rigid or dynamic?

If capabilities develop over long time periods, are embodied within organisational structure and embedded within organisational culture, they act as barriers to a firm's ability to change. The more highly developed a firm's organisational capabilities are, the narrower its repertoire and the more difficult it is for the firm to adapt them to new circumstances. Because Dell Computers' direct sales model was so highly developed, Dell found it difficult to adapt to selling though retail outlets as well. Thus, Dorothy Leonard argues that core capabilities are simultaneously core rigidities – they inhibit firms' ability to access and develop new capabilities.[42]

> Core capabilities are simultaneously core rigidities – they inhibit firms' ability to access and develop new capabilities.

The idea that capabilities impose rigidities on firms has been challenged from two directions:

- *Flexibility in organisational routines.* The notion that routines are fixed patterns of interaction that function through automatic stimulus–response mechanisms has been undermined by studies that demonstrate that even basic operations display variation and the capacity to adapt.[43]

- *Dynamic capability.* Many companies are able to adapt to changing circumstances. The capacity to change may itself be regarded as an organisational capability. David Teece and his colleagues introduced the term **dynamic capabilities** to refer to a 'firm's ability to integrate, build and reconfigure internal and external competences to address rapidly changing environments'.[44] Defining precisely what is a dynamic capability has proven contentious. Eisenhardt and Martin consider dynamic capabilities to be any capabilities that allow an organisation to reconfigure its resources in order to adapt and change.[45] Winter and Zollo are more precise: a dynamic capability is a 'higher level' process through which the firm modifies its operating routines.[46]

What is agreed is that dynamic capabilities are far from common. For most companies highly developed capabilities in existing products and technologies create barriers to developing capabilities in new products and new technologies. When adapting to radical change within an industry, or in exploiting entirely new business opportunities, are new firms at an advantage or disadvantage to established firms? It depends on whether the change or the innovation is competence enhancing or competence destroying.

In TV manufacturing, the most successful new entrants were existing producers of radios – the new technology was compatible with their capabilities. However, in most new industries, the most successful firms tend to be start-ups rather than established firms. In personal computers, it was newcomers such as Dell, Acer, Compaq and Gateway that emerged as most successful during the 1990s. Among established firms, relatively few (IBM, Hewlett-Packard and Toshiba) went on to significant success. Many others (e.g., Xerox, GE, Texas Instruments, AT&T and Olivetti) exited. In wireless telephony, too, it was start-ups – Vodafone, McCaw Cellular, Orange – that were more successful than established telephone companies.[47]

Approaches to capability development

So, how do companies go about developing new capabilities? Our focus here is on the internal development of capabilities. However, we need to acknowledge that firms can also import capabilities from outside – either by acquisition or alliance. Let us begin with a brief review of the issues involved in acquiring and accessing other firms' capabilities, before considering alternative approaches to the internal development of organisational capability.

Acquiring capabilities: mergers, acquisitions and alliances

Acquiring a company that has already developed the desired capability can short-circuit the tortuous process of capability development. Among the many motives for corporate acquisition, obtaining another company's capabilities is common – especially in technologically fast-moving environments where established firms target specific technical capabilities. Microsoft's adaptation to the internet and its entry into video games was facilitated by multiple acquisitions. Each year, Microsoft hosts its VC Summit, where venture capitalists from all over the world are invited to market their companies. In building digital imaging capabilities, Eastman Kodak has made a host of acquisitions over the past 10 years. Acquisitions are also used for obtaining other types of capability: the attraction of Gillette to P&G was to a great extent because of Gillette's new product development capability.

However, using acquisitions as a means of extending a company's capability base involves major risks. To begin with acquisitions are expensive. In addition to the acquisition premium that must be paid, the targeted capability comes with a mass of additional resources and capabilities that are most likely surplus to requirements for the acquiring firm. Most important, once the acquisition has been made, the acquiring company must find a way to integrate the acquiree's capabilities with its own. All too often, culture clashes, personality clashes between senior managers or incompatibility of management systems can result in the degradation or destruction of the very capabilities that the acquiring company was seeking. Selecting and integrating company acquisitions is itself an organisational capability. Cisco Systems' 136 acquisitions between 1996 and 2004 were critical to its expanding its base of technological and product development capabilities.[48]

These costs and risks add to the attractions of strategic alliances as a targeted and cost-effective means to access another company's capabilities. A strategic alliance is a cooperative relationship between firms involving the sharing of resources in pursuit of common goals. Long-running technical collaboration between HP and Canon has allowed both firms to enhance their printer technology. Prior to acquisition in 2005, Pixar's alliance with Disney allowed it to access Disney's marketing and distribution capabilities.

A key issue that arises in the formation and management of strategic alliances is whether their purpose is to gain access to the capabilities of the partner firm or to acquire those capabilities through one partner learning from the other.[49] The strategic alliance between Intel and DreamWorks Animation allows each company to access the other's capabilities in order to jointly develop next-generation stereoscopic 3D films.[50] Conversely, General Motors' NUMMI joint venture with Toyota to make cars at the former GM Fremont, California plant was primarily motivated by GM's desire to learn about the Toyota Production System.[51] Where both alliance partners are trying to acquire one another's capabilities, the result may well be a 'competition for competence' that ultimately destabilises the relationship.[52]

It is tempting to view strategic alliances as a quick and low-cost means of extending the capabilities available to a firm. However, managing alliance relationships is itself a critically important organisational capability. **Relational capability** comprises building trust, developing inter-firm knowledge-sharing routines and establishing mechanisms for coordination.[53] The more a company outsources its value chain activities to a network of alliance partners, the more it needs to develop the 'systems integration capability' to coordinate and integrate the dispersed activities.[54]

Internal development: focus and sequencing

We have observed that, to build organisational capability, obtaining the necessary resources is the easy part. The challenge is in integrating these resources in order to do something. Indeed, achieving excellence in resources may militate against achieving high levels of integration. At London's Arsenal Football Club, manager Arsene Wenger sold his star players, Patrick Viera and Thierry Henry, on the basis that their presence inhibited a coordinated effort from his young team.

Integrating resources into capabilities, we have seen, requires organisation and management systems and is facilitated by culture and strategic intent. The implication is that capability development needs to be systematic. It needs to bring together the requisite human and non-human resources, locate these resources within a suitable organisational unit, establish the processes that perform the capability, allow these processes to develop through routinisation, design management systems that support the capability and lead the entire effort through appropriate strategic intent.[55]

Achieving this complex task is likely to mean that an organisation must limit the number and scope of the capabilities that it is attempting to create at any point of time. Hamel and Prahalad argue that the key to developing superior capabilities is 'resource leveraging'. Two key components of this leveraging are, first, 'concentrating resources' by focusing the efforts of each group, department and business unit on specific priorities, then 'accumulating resources' through 'mining experience' in order to accelerate learning.[56]

Focusing implies developing capabilities sequentially. Thus, complex capabilities can be developed incrementally through several stages and, in order to develop multiple capabilities, it is advisable to target no more than a few capabilities in each time period.

Given our limited knowledge about how capabilities are created and are developed, companies often find it helpful to focus their capability development efforts, not on the organisational capabilities themselves, but on developing and supplying the products that utilise those capabilities. A trajectory through time of related, increasingly sophisticated products allows a firm to develop the 'integrative knowledge' that is at the heart of organisational capability.[57] Matsushita utilises this approach in developing operational capabilities in countries where it is establishing plants for the first time:

In every country batteries are a necessity, so they sell well. As long as we bring a few advanced automated pieces of equipment for the processes vital to final product quality, even unskilled labor can produce good products. As they work on this rather simple product, the workers get trained and this increased skill level then permits us to gradually expand production to items with increasingly higher technology levels, first radios, then televisions.[58]

Where a company is developing an entirely new area of business, such an approach can allow the sequential upgrading of products to be linked to targeting specific capabilities. The opening case, Hyundai Motors, provides a clear illustration of a targeted approach which is explored in a little more detail in Case Insight 3.7.

Case Insight 3.7
Capabilities development at Hyundai

The Hyundai Motor Company has displayed a remarkable ability to develop new capabilities over time, first in its bid to become a world-class car manufacturer and second in its pursuit of international expansion. Between 1967 and 1997 it set out to systematically develop its capabilities in a series of compressed phases, focusing first on assembly and manufacturing capabilities and latterly on global logistics and lifecycle engineering. To achieve its goal Hyundai also recruited designers and engineers who had worked for car companies in the UK and Europe and benchmarked itself against its rivals. Since 2000 the company has sought to develop its quality control, market research, brand and international management capabilities and has set about this in a similarly targeted fashion. In China it has developed its operations as a joint venture with Beijing Automotive and like most companies it outsources much of its marketing and advertising to professional agencies, but the company has also set up brand management groups internally and recruited talented marketing personnel who have car industry experience in the US and Europe. It is interesting to note that the family connections that characterise the company appear to extend into the company's choice of agency, Innocean, the majority shareholder of which is reported to be Seong-i Chung, the chief executive's daughter.[59]

Summary

We have shifted the focus of our attention from the external to the internal environment of the firm. This internal environment comprises many features of the firm, but for the purposes of strategy analysis, the key issue is what the firm *can do*. This means looking at the resources of the firm and the way resources combine to create organisational capabilities. Our interest is the potential for resources and capabilities to establish sustainable competitive advantage. Systematic appraisal of a company's resources and capabilities provides the basis for formulating (or reformulating) strategy. How can the firm deploy its strengths to maximum advantage? How can it minimise its vulnerability to its weaknesses? Figure 3.7 provides a simplified view of the approach to resource analysis developed in this chapter.

Although much of the discussion has been heavy on concepts and theory, the issues are practical. The management systems of most firms devote meticulous attention to the physical and financial assets that are valued on their balance sheets; much less attention has been paid to the critical intangible and human resources of the firm and even less to the identification, appraisal and development of organisational capability. In this chapter our emphasis has been on identifying, assessing and deploying a firm's existing resources and capabilities but we have also considered how resources and capabilities can be developed for the future. Most senior managers are now aware of the importance of their resources and capabilities, but the techniques of identifying, assessing and developing them are still woefully underdeveloped.

Figure 3.7 Summary: a framework for analysing resources and capabilities

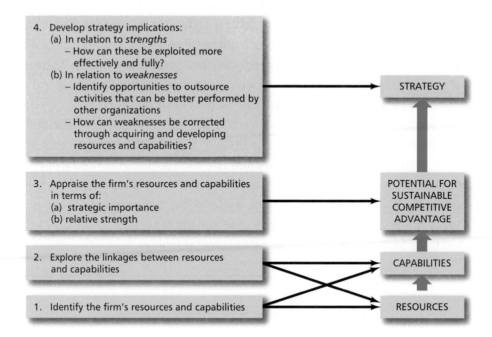

Summary table

Learning objectives	Summary
Appreciate the role of a firm's resources and capabilities as a basis for formulating strategy	Whilst the emphasis in Chapter 2 was on the external environment, this chapter highlights the importance of internal resources and capabilities. The interface between strategy and the internal environment of the firm has come increasingly to be seen as important because the external environment is perceived to have become more unstable and because research has indicated that competitive advantage rather than industry attractiveness is the primary source of superior profitability
Identify and appraise the resources and capabilities of a firm	Resources are what the firm 'has' or 'owns', capabilities are what the firm can 'do'. Different ways of identifying and appraising resources and capabilities include functional and hierarchical classification schema and value chain analysis
Evaluate the potential for a firm's resources and capabilities to confer sustainable competitive advantage	The profit-earning potential of a resource or capability depends on the extent to which it can be used to establish a competitive advantage. The key factors determining this potential are summarised in Figure 3.6

Use the results of resource and capability analysis to formulate strategies that exploit internal strengths while defending against internal weaknesses	A step-by-step approach to appraising resources and capabilities is outlined in the chapter together with an illustrative example based on the Hyundai Motor Company
Identify the means through which a firm can develop its resources and capabilities	Whilst we know much about the ways in which firms develop or acquire new resources, our knowledge of the ways in which new capabilities are acquired and developed is much more limited. Firms may acquire capabilities through mergers, takeovers or alliances or they may choose to develop capabilities internally

Further reading

Classic articles which outline the central tenets of the resource-based view include:

Barney, J. B. (1991). Firms' resources and sustained competitive advantage. *Journal of Management*, 17, 99–120.

Grant, R. (1991). The resource-based theory of competitive advantage. *California Management Review*, 33, 114–35.

Peteraf, M. A. (1993). The cornerstones of competitive advantage: a resource-based view. *Strategic Management Journal*, 14, 179–92.

An excellent critique and defence of the resource-based view is provided in the exchange between Richard Priem and John Butler on the one hand and Jay Barney on the other in the 2001 Issue 1 of the *Academy of Management Review*:

Priem, R. and Butler, J. (2001). Is the resource-based 'view' a useful perspective for strategic management research? *Academy of Management Review*, 26(1), 22–40.

Barney, J. (2001). Is the resource-based 'view' a useful perspective for strategic management research: yes? *Academy of Management Review*, 26(1), 41–56.

More recently attention has focused on the notion of dynamic capabilities and, in particular, on the way in which such capabilities are developed and sustained. A seminal article here is:

Teece, D. J., Pisano, G. and Shuen, A. (1997). Dynamic capabilities and strategic management. *Strategic Management Journal*, 18, 509–33.

Barreto also provides a recent review and critique of research in this area.

Barreto, I. (2010). Dynamic capabilities: a review of past research and an agenda for the future. *Journal of Management*, 36(1), 256–80.

QUIZ

Visit your enhanced ebook at **www.foundationsofstrategy.com** for self test quiz questions

Self-study questions

1   In recent years Google has expanded from an internet search engine to a company that operates across a broad range of internet services, including email, photo management, satellite maps, digital book libraries, blogger services and telephony. To what extent has Google's strategy focused on its resources and capabilities rather than specific customer needs? What are Google's principal resources and capabilities?

2   Through our opening case 'The Hyundai Motor Company' and the associated Case Insights (see particularly Case Insight 3.4) we have explored the ways in which Hyundai has improved its competitive position over time. In your opinion, does Hyundai have a sustainable competitive advantage? Justify your answer with reference to the resource-based view of the firm.

3   Given the profile of Hyundai's resources and capabilities outlined in Case Insight 3.5 and taking in to consideration your answer to the previous self-study question, what strategy recommendations would you offer Hyundai ?

4   Apply the approach outlined in the section 'Putting Resource and Capability Analysis to Work' to your own place of study. Begin by identifying the resources and capabilities relevant to success in the market for business education, appraise the resources and capabilities of your institution (e.g. your business school or university department), then make strategy recommendations regarding such matters as the programmes to be offered and the overall positioning and differentiation of the school or department and its offerings.

5   Identify two sports teams: one that is rich in resources (e.g. talented players) but whose capabilities (as indicated by performance) have been poor; one that is resource-poor but has displayed strong team capabilities. What clues can you offer as to the determinants of capabilities among sports teams?

GLOSSARY

Visit your enhanced ebook at **www.foundationsofstrategy.com** for key term flashcards

VIDEO

Closing case Harley-Davidson, Inc

On 1 May 2009, Keith Wandell took over as CEO of Harley-Davidson, Inc. He faced a dramatically different situation from that which had greeted his predecessors. The financial year 2008 had seen Harley's first decline in revenue since 1984 and a sharp drop in motorcycle shipments. After decades of customer waiting lists and insufficient production capacity, Wandell now had to lay off employees and amalgamate plants in order to cut capacity.

In its annual general report for 2009 the company announced a 23.1% drop in revenue from the previous year and a full year net loss of $55.1 million. Not only was the firm facing a drop in demand but a large proportion of Harley's sales were financed by loans from its own financial services subsidiary. Unable to securitise its customer loans, Harley was forced to retain more of these loans on its own balance sheet. With rising default rates on consumer credit, Harley was perceived as much more risky than it previously had been.

Wandell viewed these problems as cyclical. Already the credit markets and macroeconomic forecasts were pointing to the US economy bottoming out and then recovering. Moreover, even with sharply reduced profits, Harley was still the world's most profitable motorcycle company in 2008 with a return on average equity of 29%. What concerned Wandell more were the longer term threats to Harley's business.

Harley's long-term profit growth depended on its ability to keep expanding the sales of its high-priced, heavyweight motorcycles. With the US accounting for 69% of Harley's motorcycle revenues and with the US government and US households facing a painful rebuilding of their balance sheets over the next decade, it seemed likely that the demand for luxury leisure products costing between $8000 and $26,000 would continue to be subdued.

The opportunity for Harley to grow its market share at the expense of rivals was limited by

▶

the fact that Harley already accounted for more than 50% of the US heavyweight motorcycle market. Indeed, Harley's own market might be vulnerable to competition. While no other company could replicate the emotional attachment of riders to the 'Harley Experience', there was always the risk that motorcycle riders might seek a different type of experience and become more attracted to the highly engineered sports models produced by European and Japanese manufacturers. Such concerns were fuelled by demographic trends. Harley's core market was the baby-boomer generation – and this cohort was moving more towards retirement homes than outdoor sports.

A brief history of Harley-Davidson: fall and rise

1903–81: From birth to maturity

Harley-Davidson, Inc. was founded in 1903 by William Harley and brothers William, Arthur and Walter Davidson. Harley's 1903 model was made in the Davidson family shed and had a three-horsepower engine. In 1909 Harley introduced its first two-cylinder, V-twin engine, featuring the deep, rumbling sound for which Harley motorcycles are renowned. In 1953, the closure of Indian Motorcycle Manufacturing Company meant that Harley-Davidson was the sole survivor of the 150 US motorcycle producers that had existed in 1910.

The post-war era saw new challenges for Harley-Davidson. Growing affluence and the rise of youth culture created a growing demand for motorcycles. However, this was satisfied primarily by imports: first the British (by 1959, BSA, Triumph and Norton took 49% of the US market); then the Japanese. Initially Harley benefited from the rebirth of motorcycling as a leisure activity. Soon Harley was facing direct competition: in 1969 Honda introduced its four-cylinder CB750, a huge technical advance on anything produced by Harley or the British. In the same year, Harley-Davidson was acquired by AMF. An expansion of production capacity to 75,000 units a year led to horrendous product quality problems followed by losses and a loss of leadership of the US heavyweight motorcycle market.

1981–2008: Rebirth

In 1981, Harley's senior managers, led by Vaughn Beals, organised a leveraged buyout of AMF's Harley-Davidson subsidiary. Harley emerged as an independent, privately owned company, heavily laden with debt. The buyout coincided with a severe recession and soaring interest rates. Harley's sales fell and during 1981 and 1982, it lost a total of $60 million. Only by drastically cutting costs and gaining temporary protection from Japanese imports did Harley survive.

At the same time, the management team devoted itself to rebuilding production methods and working practices. Managers visited several Japanese car plants and carefully studied Toyota's just-in-time (JIT) system. Less than four months after the buyout, Harley management began a pilot JIT inventory and production-scheduling programme called 'MAN' (Materials-As-Needed) in its Milwaukee engine plant. The objective was to reduce inventories and costs and improve quality control. Within a year, all Harley's manufacturing operations were being converted to JIT: components and sub-assemblies were 'pulled' through the production system in response to final demand.

With revamped production methods and a new spirit of cooperation between workers and management, Harley increased sales and returned to profitability allowing it to go public in 1986. With increased investment in new models, plants and its dealership network, Harley's share of the super-heavyweight market (over 850 cc) grew from about 30% in 1986, to over 60% in 1990. The 1990s saw uninterrupted growth in the heavyweight motorcycle market and a continued increase in Harley's market share. The company's biggest challenge continued to be balancing production capacity with surging demand for its products. To overcome this constraint, in 1996, the company announced dramatically increased production capacity by opening new plants, launched new models and began to explore international markets.

Harley in 2009
The brand

Harley's top management team considered that the Harley-Davidson image and the loyalty it engendered among its customers were its greatest assets. Harley-Davidson was an archetype of American style. The famed spread eagle signified not just the brand of one of the world's oldest motorcycle companies, but an entire lifestyle with which it was associated. Together with a few other companies – including Walt Disney and Levi Strauss – Harley had a unique relationship with American culture. The values that Harley represented – individuality, freedom and adventure – could be traced back to the cowboy and frontiersman of yesteryear and before that to the quest that brought people to America in the first place. As the sole surviving American motorcycle company from the pioneering days of the industry, Harley-Davidson represented a tradition of US engineering and manufacturing.

This appeal of the Harley brand was central not just to the company's marketing, but also to its strategy as a whole. The central thrust of the strategy

◀ was reinforcing and extending the relationship between the company and its consumers. Harley-Davidson had long recognised that it was not selling motorcycles, it was selling the Harley Experience. However, since the 1980s, the demographic and socioeconomic profile of Harley customers had shifted substantially: once blue-collar youngsters, Harley owners were now middle aged and middle class.

The products

Harley's commitment to traditional design features may be seen as making a virtue out of necessity. Its smaller corporate size and inability to share R&D across cars and bikes (unlike Honda and BMW) limited its ability to invest in technology and new products. As a result, Harley lagged far behind its competitors in the application of automotive technologies: its motorcycles not only looked old-style, much of the technology was old-style. Harley's engines were most representative of its technological backwardness. Long after Honda had moved to multiple valves per cylinder, overhead camshafts, liquid cooling and electronic ignition, Harley continued to rely on air-cooled push-rod engines. In suspension systems, braking systems and transmissions too, Harley lagged far behind Honda, Yamaha and BMW. Nevertheless, Harley was engaged in constant upgrading – principally incremental refinements to its engines, frames and gearboxes aimed at improving power delivery and reliability, increasing braking power and reducing vibration. Harley also accessed automotive technology through alliances with other companies, including Porsche AG, Ford and Gemini Racing Technologies.

Despite being a technological laggard, Harley was very active in new product development and the launching of new models. Most of Harley's product development efforts were limited to style changes, new paint designs and engineering improvements, but between 2000 and 2008 Harley had accelerated technological progress and introduced more radical new product developments. Some of the initiatives, for example, the extension of the product line to lighter-weight bikes appealing to younger riders (the Buell products) and the acquisition of an Italian bike company (MV Agusta), were short-lived. The dramatic downturn in sales caused Wandell and his team to rethink their strategy and to announce their exit from the Buell range and the selloff of MV Agusta.

Central to Harley's product strategy was the idea that every Harley rider would own a unique, personalised motorcycle through offering a wide range of customisation opportunities. Reconciling product differentiation with scale economies was a continuing challenge for Harley. The solution was to offer a wide range of customisation options while standardising on key components. For example, among the different Harley-Davidson models there were three engine types, four basic frames, four styles of gas tank and so on.

The Harley product line also covered a wide price range. The Sportster model was positioned as an entry-level bike beginning at $6,999, less than one-third of the price of the Ultra Classic Electra Glide, with 'custom colouring' at $22,159. Top of the price range was the three-wheeler Tri-Glide at $31,994 (including non-black paint and a reverse gear).

Distribution

Upgrading Harley's distribution network was central to its transformation strategy of the 1980s and 1990s. At the time of the buyout, many of Harley's 620 US dealerships were operated by enthusiasts, with erratic opening hours, a poor stock of bikes and spares, and indifferent customer service. If Harley was in the business of selling a lifestyle and an experience, then dealers played a pivotal role in delivering that experience. Moreover, if Harley's target market had shifted towards mature, upper income individuals – Harley needed to provide a retail experience commensurate with the expectations of this group.

Harley's dealer development programme increased support for dealers while imposing higher standards of pre- and after-sales service and requiring better dealer facilities. The dealers were obliged to carry a full line of Harley replacement parts and accessories and to perform services on Harley bikes. Training programmes helped dealers to meet the higher service requirements and encouraged them to recognise and meet the needs of the professional, middle-class clientele that Harley was now courting. Harley pioneered the introduction of new services to customers. These included test ride facilities, rider instruction classes, motorcycle rental, assistance for owners in customising their bikes through dealer-based design centres and chrome consultants and insurance services. Close to 85% of Harley dealerships in the US were exclusive – far more than for any other motorcycle manufacturer. Harley believed that the quality and effectiveness of its dealer network was a key determinant of the strong demand for its products.

Other products

Sales of parts, accessories and 'general merchandise' (clothing and collectibles) represented 20% of total revenue in 2008 – much higher than for any other

◀ motorcycle company. Clothing sales included not just traditional riding apparel, but also a wide range of men's, women's and children's leisure apparel.

Only a small proportion of the clothing, collectibles and other products bearing the Harley-Davidson trademark were sold through the Harley dealership network. Most of the 'general merchandising' business represented licensing of the Harley-Davidson name and trademarks to third-party manufacturers of clothing, giftware, jewellery, toys and other products. L'Oréal offered a line of Harley-Davidson cologne. To expand sales of licensed products, Harley opened a number of 'secondary retail locations' which sold clothing, accessories and giftware, but not motorcycles. Harley-Davidson Financial Services was established to supply credit, insurance and extended warranties to Harley dealers and customers. Between 2000 and 2007 it was Harley's most rapidly growing source of profit, contributing almost 12% of operating profit in 2007. However, the credit crunch hit the business hard.

Operations

As already noted, Harley-Davidson development during the 1980s and 1990s focused heavily on upgrading its manufacturing operations. Investment in plant and equipment included the introduction of advanced process technologies and capacity expansion. Particular emphasis was placed on developing manufacturing capabilities through total quality management, just-in-time scheduling, CAD/CAM and the devolution of responsibility and decision making to the shopfloor. Harley's capacity for efficiency was limited, however, by its dispersed manufacturing operations and its low production volumes. The company lacked the buying power of Honda and BMW, and bought-in, customised components accounted for a large proportion of manufacturing costs. To offset its lack of purchasing power Harley fostered close relations with its key suppliers and placed purchasing managers at senior levels within its management structure. In 2009, in response to its deteriorating financial position, Harley announced a programme of plant consolidation and further restructuring that would eliminate about 2,400 jobs and reduce costs by about $250 million annually.

People and management

Central to Harley-Davidson's renaissance was the creation of a new relationship between management and employees. Following the management buyout in 1981, Harley's new management team systematically rethought management–employee relationships, employee responsibilities and organisational structure.

The result was a transformation in employee commitment and job satisfaction. Harley's employee relations focused on involvement, self-management, open communication and the provision of generous health and leave benefits.[60]

Meeting the challenges of tomorrow

Despite Wandell's optimism that Harley would bounce back from the recession, the company was facing a number of longer term problems: its core customers were growing older and buying new bikes less often; its decision to ramp up production to meet unmet demand had had the unintended effect of diminishing the exclusivity of the brand; its 'American frontier' image did not necessarily translate well in overseas markets; and its attempts at broadening its product-market scope were adding to its current problems. The company now faced some significant choices – should it stay focused on what it does best or make smaller more affordable bikes that were more appealing to younger riders and overseas markets?

Case questions

● How would you account for Harley's transformation from a failing to a highly successful company in the 1980s? What resources and capabilities did the company need to develop in order to effect this change?

● Using some of the tools and techniques introduced in this chapter, assess Harley's principal resources and capabilities at the case date.

● What strategy recommendations would you offer Harley-Davidson's management team on the basis of your answer to question 2.

Notes

1 http://5feitir.blogcentral.is/sida/2009452. Accessed 27 December 2010.

2 'Hyundai defies downturn to post record profits', *Financial Times* (28 January 2010).

3 Assembling cars on a knockdown basis refers to a practice which is common in the automotive industry whereby a kit containing all or most of the parts required to produce a car are sold to a foreign affiliate or licensees. The affiliates assemble the parts to produce the final product.

4 L. Kim, 'Crisis construction and organizational learning: capability building in catching-up at Hyundai Motors', *Organizational Science* (1998): 506–21.

5 S. Holchandani, 'Mass marketing to class marketing: Hyundai's underlying dilemma', Amity Research Center Case Study (2009).

6 Hyunai Motor Company in China, Stanford Graduate Business School Case IB-91 (2008).

7 The 'resource-based view' is described in J. B. Barney, 'Firm resources and sustained competitive advantage', *Journal of Management* 17 (1991): 99–120; J. Mahoney and J. R. Pandian, 'The resource-based view within the conversation of strategic management', *Strategic Management Journal* 13 (1992): 363–80; M. A. Peterlaf, 'The cornerstones of competitive advantage: a resource-based view', *Strategic Management Journal* 14 (1993): 179–92; R. M. Grant, 'The resource-based theory of competitive advantage', *California Management Review* 33 (1991): 114–35.

8 Ted Levitt ('Marketing myopia', *Harvard Business Review*, July–August 1960: 24–47) proposed that firms should define their strategies on the basis of customer needs rather than products, e.g. railroad companies should view themselves as in the transportation business. However, this fails to address the resource implication of serving these broad customer needs.

9 C. K. Prahalad and G. Hamel, 'The core competence of the corporation', *Harvard Business Review* (May–June 1990): 79–91.

10 E. Danneels, B. Provera and G. Verona, 'Legitimizing exploration: Olivetti's transition from mechanical to electronic technology', Management Department, Bocconi University, 2008; also 'Olivetti reinvents itself once more', *Wall Street Journal* (22 February 1999): A.1.

11 'Eastman Kodak: meeting the digital challenge', in R. M. Grant, *Cases to Accompany Contemporary Strategy Analysis*, 6th edn (Oxford: Blackwell, 2008).

12 M. Tripsas, 'Unraveling the process of creative destruction: complementary assets and incumbent survival in the typesetter industry', *Strategic Management Journal* 18, Summer Special Issue (1997): 119–42; J. Bower and C. M. Christensen, 'Disruptive technologies: catching the wave', *Harvard Business Review* (January–February 1995): 43–53.

13 Economies of scope in brands can also be exploited by licensing. Harley-Davidson licenses its brands to the manufacturers of apparel, toys, cars and toiletries.

14 *Economic Survey of the European Union, 2007* (Paris: OECD, 2007).

15 E. Lawler, 'From job-based to competency-based organizations', *Journal of Organizational Behavior* 15 (1994): 3–15; L. Spencer, D. McClelland and S. Spencer, *Competency Assessment Methods: History and State of the Art* (Hay/McBer Research Group, 1994); L. Spencer and S. Spencer, *Competence At Work: Models for Superior Performance* (New York: Wiley, 1993).

16 D. Goleman, *Emotional Intelligence* (New York: Bantam, 1995).

17 T. J. Peters and R. H. Waterman, *In Search of Excellence: Lessons from America's Best-Run Companies* (New York: Harper & Row, 1982).

18 J. Barney, 'Organisational culture: can it be a source of sustained competitive advantage?' *Academy of Management Review* 11 (1986): 656–65.

19 Ranked as 65th in 2010 by Interbrand. www.interbrand.com/en/best-global-brands. Accessed 27 December 2010.

20 C. E. Helfat and M. Lieberman, 'The birth of capabilities: market entry and the importance of prehistory', *Industrial and Corporate Change* 12 (2002): 725–60.

21 G. Hamel and C. K. Prahalad argue (*Harvard Business Review*, May–June 1992: 164–5) that 'the distinction between competences and capabilities is purely semantic'.

22 P. Selznick, *Leadership in Administration: A Sociological Interpretation* (New York: Harper & Row, 1957).

23 C. K. Prahalad and G. Hamel, 'The core competence of the corporation', op. cit.

24 G. Hamel and C. K. Prahalad, letter, *Harvard Business Review* (May–June 1992): 164–5.

25 Porter's value chain is the main framework of his *Competitive Advantage* (New York: Free Press, 1984). McKinsey & Company refers to the firm's value chain as its 'business system'. See: C. F. Bates, P. Chatterjee, F. W. Gluck, D. Gogel and A. Puri, 'The Business System: a new tool for strategy formulation and cost analysis', in *McKinsey on Strategy* (Boston: McKinsey & Company, 2000).

26 T. W. Malone, K. Crowston, J. Lee and B. Pentland, 'Tools for inventing organisations: toward a handbook of organisational processes', *Management Science* 45 (1999): 425–43.

27 K. Crowston, 'A coordination theory approach to organisation design', *Organization Science* 8 (1997): 157–75.

28 R. R. Nelson and S. G. Winter, *An Evolutionary Theory of Economic Change* (Cambridge, MA: Belknap, 1982).

29 As a result, specialists perform well in stable environments while generalists do well in variable conditions. J. Freeman and M. Hannan, 'Niche width and the dynamics of organizational populations', *American Journal of Sociology* 88 (1984): 1116–45.

30 See Richard Caves' discussion of 'specific assets' in 'International corporations: the industrial economics of foreign investment', *Economica* 38 (1971): 1–27.

31 G. Akerlof, 'The market for lemons: qualitative uncertainty and the market mechanism', *Quarterly Journal of Economics* 84 (1970): 488–500.

32 J. B. Barney, 'Strategic factor markets: expectations, luck and business strategy', *Management Science* 32 (October 1986): 1231–41.

33 'Is India Bad for Jaguar', *Time* (14 December 2007).

34 K. Ichijo and I. Nonaka, *Knowledge Creation and Management* (New York: Oxford University Press, 2006): 127–8; 'The open secret of success', *The New Yorker* (12 May 2008).

35 I. Dierickx and K. Cool, 'Asset stock accumulation and sustainability of competitive advantage', *Management Science* 35 (1989): 1504–13.

36 Benchnet: The Benchmarking Exchange (www.benchnet.com).

37 www.capom.com. Accessed 18 July 2011.

38 C. B. Schoonhoven and E. Romanelli, 'The local origins of new firms' in C. B. Schoonhoven and E. Romanelli (Eds), *The Entrepreneurship Dynamic* (Stanford: Stanford University Press, 2001): 40–67.

39 S. Klepper, 'the capabilities of new firms and the evolution of the U.S. car industry', *Industrial and Corporate Change* 11 (2001): 645–6.

40 B. Wernerfelt, 'Why do firms tend to become different?' in Constance Helfat (Ed.) *Handbook of Organizational Capabilities* (Oxford: Blackwell, 2006): 121–33.

41 R. R. Nelson and S. G. Winter, *An Evolutionary Theory of Economic Change* (Cambridge, MA: Belknap, 1982): 15, 97.

42 D. Leonard-Barton, 'Core capabilities and core rigidities', *Strategic Management Journal*, Summer Special Issue (1992): 111–26.

43 M. S. Feldman and B. T. Pentland, 'Reconceptualizing organizational routines as a source of flexibility and change', *Administrative Science Quarterly* 48 (2003): 94–118.

44 D. J. Teece, G. Pisano, and A. Shuen, 'Dynamic capabilities and strategic management', *Strategic Management Journal* 18 (1997): 509–33.

45 K. M. Eisenhardt and J. A. Martin, 'Dynamic capabilities: what are they?' *Strategic Management Journal* 21 (2000): 1105–21 and H. Volberda, *Building the Flexible Firm* (Oxford: Oxford University Press, 1998).

46 M. Zollo and S. G. Winter, 'Deliberate learning and the evolution of dynamic capabilities', *Organization Science* 13 (2002): 339–51; S. G. Winter, 'Understanding dynamic capabilities', *Strategic Management Journal* 24 (2003): 991–5.

47 Established firms typically fail to survive radical innovation. See, for example, R. M. Henderson and K. B. Clark, 'Architectural innovation: the reconfiguration of existing product technologies and failure of established firms', *Administrative Science Quarterly* 35 (1990): 9–30; C. Christensen, 'The rigid disk drive industry: a history of commercial and technological turbulence', *Business History Review* 67 (1993): 531–88; M. Tripsas, 'Unravelling the process of creative destruction: complementary assets and incumbent survival in the typesetter industry', *Strategic Management Journal* 18 (Summer Special Issue, 1997): 119–42; A. Henderson, 'Firm strategy and age dependence: a contingent view of the liabilities of newness, adolescence and obsolescence', *Administrative Science Quarterly* 44 (1999): 281–314.

48 C. E. Helfat, S. Finkelstein, W. Mitchell, M. A. Peteraf, H. Singh, D. J. Teece, S. G. Winter, *Dynamic Capabilities: Understanding Strategic Change in Organizations* (Malden, MA: Blackwell Publishing, 2007): Chapter 6.

49 See, for example, A. Mody, 'Learning through alliances', *Journal of Economic Behavior and Organization* 20 (1993): 151–70; D. C. Mowery, J. E. Oxley and B. S. Silverman, 'Strategic alliances and interfirm knowledge transfer', *Strategic Management Journal* 17, Winter Special Issue (1996): 77–93; A. C. Inkpen and M. M. Crossan, 'Believing is seeing: joint ventures and organizational learning', *Journal of Management Studies* 32 (1995): 595–618.

50 Intel News Release, *Intel, Dreamworks Animation Form Strategic Alliance to Revolutionize 3-D Filmmaking Technology* (8 July 2008), www.intel.com/pressroom/archive/releases/20080708corp.htm. Accessed 3 July 2009.

51 J. A. Badaracco, *The Knowledge Link: How Firms Compete Through Strategic Alliances* (Boston: Harvard Business School Press, 1991).

52 G. Hamel, 'Competition for competence and interpartner learning within international strategic alliances', *Strategic Management Journal* 12, Summer Special Issue (1991): 83–103.

53 P. Kale, J. H. Dyer and H. Singh, 'Alliance capability, stock market response and long term alliance success', *Strategic Management Journal* 23 (2002): 747–67; C. E. Helfat et al. *Dynamic Capabilities* op. cit.: Chapter 5.

54 A. Prencipe, 'Corporate strategy and systems integration capabilities' in A. Prencipe, A. Davies and M. Hobday, *The Business of Systems Integration* (Oxford University Press, 2003): 114–32.

55 A. Bakhru and R. M. Grant, 'A managerial process model of organizational capability development: evidence from new e-commerce businesses', CROMA Discussion Paper, Bocconi University, Milan, 2008.

56 G. Hamel and C. K. Prahalad, *Competing for the Future* (Boston: Harvard Business School Press, 1994).

57 C. E. Helfat and Ruth S. Raubitschek, 'Product sequencing: co-evolution of knowledge, capabilities and products', *Strategic Management Journal* 21 (2000): 961–79. The parallel development of capabilities and products has also been referred to as 'dynamic resource fit'. See: H. Itami, *Mobilizing Invisible Assets* (Boston: Harvard University Press, 1987): 125.

58 A. Takahashi, *What I Learned from Konosuke Matsushita* (Tokyo: Jitsugyo no Nihonsha, 1980); in Japanese, quoted by Itami, op. cit.: 25.

59 J. Tylee, 'Hyundai plans London agency', *Campaign* (3 March 2006).

60 Stephen Roth, 'Harley's goal: unify union and management', *Kansas City Business Journal* (16 May 1997).

4

The nature and sources of competitive advantage

Introduction and objectives

In this chapter, we integrate and develop the elements of competitive advantage that we have analysed in prior chapters. We noted in earlier chapters that a firm can earn superior profits either by locating in an attractive industry or by establishing a competitive advantage over its rivals. Of these two, competitive advantage is the more important. As competition has intensified across almost all industries, very few industry environments can guarantee secure returns; hence, the primary goal of a strategy is to establish a position of competitive advantage for the firm.

Chapters 2 and 3 have provided the two primary building blocks for our analysis of competitive advantage. In Chapter 2 we analysed the *external* sources of competitive advantage: the key success factors within a market. In Chapter 3 we analysed the *internal* sources of competitive advantage: the potential for the firm to establish and sustain a competitive advantage on the basis of its resources and capabilities.

This chapter looks more deeply at competitive advantage. We focus on the dynamic relationship between competitive advantage and the competitive process. Competition provides the incentive for establishing advantage and is the means by which advantage is worn away. By understanding the characteristics of competition in a market we can identify the opportunities for, and the challenges to, competitive advantage.

By the time you have completed this chapter you will be able to:

- understand the meaning of the term 'competitive advantage' and identify the circumstances in which a firm can create a competitive advantage over a rival;

- predict the potential for competition to wear away competitive advantage through imitation;

- recognise how resource conditions create imperfections in the competitive process that offer opportunities for competitive advantage;

- distinguish the two primary types of competitive advantage: cost advantage and differentiation advantage;

- use the value chain framework to analyse potential sources of cost and differentiation advantage and to recommend strategies for enhancing competitiveness;

- appreciate the pitfalls of being 'stuck in the middle' and the challenge of achieving effective differentiation and low cost.

Opening case Singapore Airlines

Over the past four decades Singapore Airlines (SIA) has developed an enviable reputation for providing its passengers with a high-quality air travel experience. The company prides itself on being the 'most awarded airline', a title it has gained through winning many prizes for its customer service standards. SIA has, for example, been acknowledged as the 'World's Best Airline' by *Condé Nast Traveler* 21 times out of the total of 22 times the title has been awarded and was ranked 27th in *Fortune* magazine's 'World's Most Admired Companies' in 2010. What is perhaps less well known is that SIA is also one of the most cost-effective operators in the airline business. The data listed in Table 4.1 illustrates this fact.

The company can trace its roots back to 1947 but really took off as an independent entity in the early 1970s when it severed its ties to Malaysian Airlines. During the 1970s the company grew rapidly, extending its scheduled routes from its Singapore hub to many destinations in India and Asia. In the 1980s it added routes to the US, Canada and Europe and continues to expand its network. Since its incorporation in 1972 SIA has been partly owned by the Singapore government that has a 'golden share' but operationally it is free from government intervention.

SIA has based its strategy on two main pillars – its planes and its people. In terms of its aircraft, the company tries to keep its fleet 'young'. In 2009, for example, the average age of the SIA fleet was 74 months as opposed to the industry average of around 160 months.[1] SIA was the first airline to launch the Airbus A380 high-capacity jet and although there was an initial delay in receiving the aircraft from Airbus, due to development problems, these additions to the fleet have proved

Table 4.1 Costs of available seat kilometres (ASK) between 2001 and 2009 in US cents

Airline	Costs per ASK (US cents)
Singapore Airlines	4.58
Full service European airlines	8–16
US airlines	7–8
Asian airlines	5–7

Source: Heracleous, L. and Wirtz, J. (2010). Singapore Airlines' balancing act. *Harvard Business Review*, July–August, 145–9. Reproduced by permission of Harvard Business Publishing.

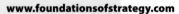

Reproduced by permission of Singapore Airlines

successful. The policy of operating a young fleet also means that SIA's aircraft are more fuel efficient and require less repair and maintenance than those of its rivals. Heracleous and Wirtz[2] report that 'in 2008 repairs accounted for 4% of SIA's total costs compared with 5.9% for United Airlines and 4.8% for American Airlines'. SIA's aircraft also spend less time in hangars and more time in the air – 13 hours, on average per day versus the industry average of 11.3%.

In terms of its people, the Singapore International Airlines group as a whole (including cargo, repair and maintenance service, etc.) employed just under 22,000 people in 2010/11, of which 13,600 were employed by the passenger airline business. While the company pays only average Singapore wages, it manages to attract first-class university graduates because it has a reputation for offering excellent training and experience. The company spends around $70 million a year putting each of its employees through 110 hours of retraining annually. Much of this training is focused on embedding the culture of customer service into everything employees do. Staff are, for example, trained to appreciate subtle cultural differences and to look for clever ways of personalising passengers' flying experience – for example noticing that a laptop is out of power or a mother needs assistance with her child. As a consequence crew members who leave the company usually find it easy to find employment with other operators.

Whilst emphasis is given to customer service, any opportunity to cut costs, however small, is taken. The headquarters of the airline is housed in modest premises near the airport and the central 'head count' is kept to a minimum. Training takes place within the airline's offices and is delivered by senior members of the airline's own crew rather than by outside trainers. Staff are encouraged to find ways of reducing waste and bonus schemes are in place that incentivise cost-cutting behaviour. For example, even though two brands of high-quality champagne are available to business class travellers, cabin crew are encouraged to pour drinks from whichever bottle is open unless the passenger requests a specific brand. Similarly, pots of jam, which cabin crew noticed were frequently wasted, are now provided only on request. To make sure that cabin crew can give passengers personal attention SIA flights usually carry more flight attendants than other airlines, but this is reported to add only about 5% to labour costs and as an expense that contributes strongly to the airline's reputation for excellent customer service allows SIA to compete on factors other than price.

SIA tries to achieve both differentiation and cost saving through its approach to innovation. The company is willing to experiment and is fast to adopt any incremental innovations that improve customer service. It was, for example, one of the first airlines to introduce fully reclining seats (slumberettes), in-flight mobile telephone and fax services and biometric technology to simplify and speed up check-in times following a series of global health scares. However, unlike some of its rivals, it has not developed highly customised and sophisticated yield management and other back-office software, preferring instead to buy 'off the shelf' tried-and-tested applications. It has also outsourced responsibility for maintaining non-strategic hardware and software to low-cost service providers in India.

Whilst the company seems to have very successfully reconciled the seemingly contradictory strategies of cost minimisation and differentiation, it does face problems. The company dominates the business class market segment on many of its routes and it is this segment that is particularly sensitive to the level of economic activity. For the first time in 2009 SIA posted a full-year loss and its load factors were below the industry average.[3] The company has responded by cutting staff, reducing working hours and reviewing its routes and schedules. It remains to be seen whether the distinctive culture of the company that supports its dual strategy remains intact when the company attempts to simultaneously operate budget and full service airlines.

The emergence of competitive advantage

To understand how **competitive advantage** emerges, we must first understand what competitive advantage is. Most of us can recognise competitive advantage when we see it: Wal-Mart has a competitive advantage in discount retailing within the US; Toyota has a competitive advantage in making mass-produced cars; SAP has a competitive advantage in enterprise resource planning (ERP) software. Defining competitive advantage is troublesome. At a basic level we can define it as follows:

When two or more firms compete within the same market, one firm possesses a competitive advantage over its rivals when it earns (or has the potential to earn) a persistently higher rate of profit.

The problem here is that if we identify competitive advantage with superior profitability, why do we need the concept of competitive advantage at all? The key difference is that competitive advantage may not be revealed in higher profitability – a firm may forgo current profit in favour of investment in market share, technology, customer loyalty or executive perks.[4] In the long run, competition eliminates differences in profitability between competing firms but external and internal changes can create short-term opportunities for creating an advantage (see Figure 4.1).

External sources of change

For an external change to create competitive advantage, the change must have differential effects on companies because of their different resources and capabilities or strategic positioning.

Figure 4.1 The emergence of competitive advantage

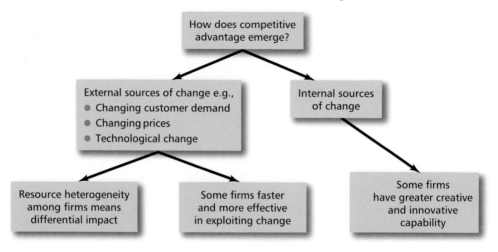

The global financial downturn of 2008–9 affected all car manufacturers but the US 'big three' – General Motors, Ford and Chrysler – were hit harder than many of their European and Asian rivals because their market position had already been weakened by a decline in demand for their vehicles. The sales of US car producers were skewed towards sales of sports utility vehicles (SUVs) and pickup trucks that had, until the 2000s, been very popular with American consumers and offered high profit margins. In the period 2003–8 the price of oil tripled and consumers turned away from these 'gas guzzlers'[5] to smaller more fuel-efficient cars. With fewer small cars in their product portfolios, US car manufacturers lost out to European and Asian rivals. The world financial crisis of 2008 hit the 'big three' when they were already struggling with falling sales and mounting debts and pushed these firms to the edge of bankruptcy.

The extent to which external change creates competitive advantage and disadvantage depends on the magnitude of the change and the extent of firms' strategic differences. The more turbulent an industry's environment, the greater the number of sources of change, and the greater the differences in firms' resources and capabilities, the greater the dispersion of profitability within the industry. In the world tobacco industry, the external environment is fairly stable and the leading firms pursue similar strategies with similar resources and capabilities. Hence, competitive advantages, as reflected in inter-firm profit differentials, tend to be small. The toy industry, on the other hand, comprises a diverse group of firms that experience unpredictable shifts in consumer preferences and technology. As a result, profitability differences are wide and variable.

Competitive advantage from responsiveness to change

The competitive advantage that arises from external change also depends on firms' ability to respond to change. Any external change creates opportunities for profit, including opportunities for new business initiatives (what is known as **entrepreneurship**).

Responsiveness involves one of two key capabilities. The first is the ability to anticipate changes in the external environment. The second is speed. An unexpected rain shower creates an upsurge in the demand for umbrellas. Those street vendors who are quickest to position themselves outside a busy train station will benefit most.

> The competitive advantage that arises from external change also depends on firms' ability to respond to change.

As markets become more turbulent and unpredictable, so speed of response through greater flexibility has become increasingly important as a source of competitive advantage. The first requirement for quick response capability is information. As conventional economic and market forecasting has become less effective, so companies rely increasingly on 'early warning systems' through direct relationships with customers, suppliers and even competitors. The second requirement is short cycle times that allow information on emerging market developments to be acted upon speedily.

In fashion retailing, fast response to emerging fashion trends is critical to success. Zara, the chain of retail clothing stores owned by the Spanish company Inditex, has pioneered leading-edge fashion clothes for budget-minded young adults through a tightly integrated vertical structure that cuts the time between a garment's design and retail delivery to under three weeks (against an industry norm of three to six months).[6]

The notion of speed as a source of competitive advantage was pioneered by the Boston Consulting Group with its concept of **time-based competition**.[7] However, it was the advent of the internet, real-time electronic data exchange and wireless communication that facilitated radical improvements in response capability across the business sector as a whole.

Case Insight 4.1

Singapore Airlines: gaining or losing competitive advantage as a consequence of external change

Singapore Airlines' policy of investing in new aircraft sets it apart from many of its rivals but also means that external change affects it in different ways. By being the first company to introduce the Airbus 380 aircraft on long-haul flights, it altered its cost structure and load factors. The A380 is able to seat significantly more passengers than rival aircraft, but being a larger aircraft it consumes more fuel. The key to a profitable operation rests with the number of seats that are occupied. If the plane is full then, on a per seat kilometre basis, the aircraft is very fuel efficient; if the plane has few passengers then fuel costs per seat kilometre are high. SIA has deployed its A380s on routes where load factors are substantially higher than its network average, for example, Singapore to London, and as long as passenger traffic holds up this is a cost-effective strategy. The introduction of these new aircraft therefore gives SIA an advantage over rivals with older fleets when fuel prices increase, but only if SIA can keep load factors high, meaning it is more vulnerable to falling passenger numbers on key routes.

Competitive advantage from innovation: 'new game' strategies

The changes that create competitive advantage may also be generated internally through innovation. Innovation not only creates competitive advantage, it also provides a basis for overturning the competitive advantage of other firms. Although innovation is typically thought of as new products or processes that embody new technology, a key source of competitive advantage is strategic innovation – new approaches to doing business including new business models.

Strategic innovation typically involves creating value for customers from novel products, experiences or modes of product delivery. Thus in the retail sector competition is driven by a constant quest for new retail concepts and formats. This may take the form of: big-box stores with greater variety (Toys-R-Us, Staples, PetSmart); augmented customer service (John Lewis, Nordstrom); and novel approaches to display and store layout (Sephora in cosmetics).

Strategic innovation may also be based on redesigned processes and novel organisational designs as shown in the examples below.

> A key source of competitive advantage is strategic innovation – new approaches to doing business including new business models.

In the US steel industry, Nucor achieved unrivalled productivity and flexibility by combining new process technologies, flat and flexible organisational structures and innovative management systems. Since 1997, it has been the biggest steel producer in the US.

Southwest Airlines' point-to-point, no-frills airline service using a single type of plane and flexible, non-union employees has made it the only consistently profitable airline in North America and the model for budget airlines throughout the world.

Nike built its large and successful businesses on a business system that totally reconfigured the shoe industry's traditional value chain – notable by outsourcing manufacturing and concentrating upon design and marketing, and orchestrating a vast global network of producers, logistics providers and retailers.

Apple's resurgence during 2003–6 was the result of its reinvention of the recorded music business by combining an iconic MP3 player with its iTunes music download service.

How do we go about shaping innovative strategies? Strategic innovations tend to involve pioneering along one or more dimensions of strategy:

- *New industries.* Some companies launch products which create a whole new market. Xerox created the plain-paper copier industry; Freddie Laker pioneered budget air travel; Craig McCaw and McCaw Communications launched the mass market for wireless telephony. For Kim and Mauborgne, creating new markets is the purest form of *blue ocean strategy* – the creation of 'uncontested market space'.[8]

- *New customer segments.* Creating new customer segments for existing product concepts can also open up vast new market spaces. Apple did not invent the personal computer, but it launched the market for computers in the home. The video cassette recorder was developed by Ampex for use in television studios; Sony and Matsushita's innovation was in introducing VCRs for the home. The success of the Nintendo Wii video games console has been based upon extending video gaming into new customer segments.

- *New sources of competitive advantage.* As Kim and Mauborgne acknowledge, most successful blue ocean strategies do not launch whole new industries, but introduce novel approaches to creating customer value. Thus, Dell's strategic innovation was an integrated system for ordering, assembling and distributing PCs that permitted unprecedented customer choice and speed of order fulfilment. Cirque du Soleil has reinvented the circus business as a multimedia entertainment spectacle that meshes technology with highly developed acrobatic and choreographic capabilities.[9]

McKinsey & Company show that a key element of strategic innovation – what they call new game strategy – involves reconfiguring the industry value chain in order to change the 'rules of the game' within a market.[10] For example, Canon's successful penetration of the plain-paper copier market during 1973–6, was based upon a strategy that was radically different from that of the incumbent, Xerox. While Xerox's dominance was based upon large machines which used dry toner and were leased to customers, Canon introduced small machines that used liquid toner and were sold outright to customers.[11] In their study of rejuvenation among mature firms, Charles Baden-Fuller and John Stopford observe that strategic innovation often involves combining performance dimensions that were previously viewed as conflicting. For example, Richardson, a UK kitchen knife producer, used an innovative design, process innovation and a lean, entrepreneurial management to supply kitchen knives that combined price competitiveness, durability, sharpness and responsive customer service.[12] However, according to Gary Hamel, even innovative strategies are subject to imitation. He argues that the most durable forms of competitive advantage are those that derive from management innovation such as Procter & Gamble's invention of modern brand management and Toyota's lean production system.[13]

Sustaining competitive advantage

Once established, competitive advantage is subject to erosion by competition. The speed with which competitive advantage is undermined depends on the ability of competitors to challenge either by imitation or innovation. Imitation is the most direct form of competition; thus, for competitive advantage to be sustained over time, barriers to imitation must exist. Rumelt uses the term **isolating mechanisms** to describe the barriers that protect a firm's profits from being driven down by the competitive process.[14] The more effective these isolating mechanisms are, the longer competitive advantage can be sustained against the onslaught of rivals. In most industries the erosion of the competitive advantage of industry leaders is a slow process: inter-firm profit differentials often persist for period of a decade or more.[15] However, some commentators argue that, over time, competition in many industries has intensified and this has accelerated the erosion of profit.[16]

> Imitation is the most direct form of competition; thus, for competitive advantage to be sustained over time, barriers to imitation must exist.

To identify the sources of isolating mechanisms, we need to examine the process of competitive imitation. For one firm successfully to imitate the strategy of another, it must meet four conditions:

- *Identification.* The firm must be able to identify that a rival possesses a competitive advantage.

- *Incentive.* Having identified that a rival possesses a competitive advantage (as shown by above-average profitability), the firm must believe that by investing in imitation, it too can earn superior returns.

- *Diagnosis.* The firm must be able to diagnose the features of its rival's strategy that give rise to the competitive advantage.

- *Resource acquisition.* The firm must be able to acquire through transfer or replication the resources and capabilities necessary for imitating the strategy of the advantaged firm.

Figure 4.2 illustrates these stages and the types of isolating mechanism that exist at each stage.

Identification: obscuring superior performance

A simple barrier to imitation is to obscure the firm's superior profitability. According to George Stalk of the Boston Consulting Group, 'one way to throw competitors off balance

Figure 4.2 Sustaining competitive advantage: types of isolating mechanism

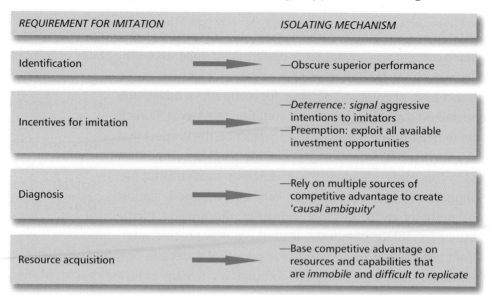

REQUIREMENT FOR IMITATION	ISOLATING MECHANISM
Identification	—Obscure superior performance
Incentives for imitation	—*Deterrence: signal* aggressive intentions to imitators —Preemption: exploit all available investment opportunities
Diagnosis	—Rely on multiple sources of competitive advantage to create 'causal ambiguity'
Resource acquisition	—Base competitive advantage on resources and capabilities that are *immobile* and *difficult to replicate*

is to mask high performance so rivals fail to see your success until it's too late'.[17] For example, in the 1948 movie classic *The Treasure of the Sierra Madre*, Humphrey Bogart and his partners went to great lengths to obscure their find from other gold prospectors.[18]

For firms that dominate a niche market, one of the attractions of remaining a private company is to avoid disclosing financial performance. Few food processors realised just how profitable cat and dog food could be until the UK Monopolies Commission revealed that the leading firm, Pedigree Petfoods (a subsidiary of Mars Inc.) earned a return on capital employed of 47%.[19]

Avoiding competition through avoiding disclosure of a firm's profits is much easier for a private than a public company. For Mars Ltd, the nondisclosure of financial results may help the firm in protecting its highly profitable pet food and confectionery businesses.

Deterrence and pre-emption

A firm may avoid competition by undermining the incentives for imitation. If a firm can persuade rivals that imitation will be unprofitable, it may be able to avoid competitive challenges.

Reputation is critically important in making threats credible. Brandenburger and Nalebuff argue that in the aspartame market, NutraSweet's aggressive price war against the Holland Sweetener Company deterred other would-be entrants.[20]

A firm can also deter imitation by pre-emption – occupying existing and potential strategic niches to reduce the range of investment opportunities open to the challenger. Pre-emption can take many forms:

- Proliferation of product varieties by a market leader can leave new entrants and smaller rivals with few opportunities for establishing a market niche. Between 1950 and 1972, for example, the six leading suppliers of breakfast cereals introduced 80 new brands into the US market.[21]

- Large investments in production capacity ahead of the growth of market demand also pre-empt market opportunities for rivals. Monsanto's heavy investment in plants for producing NutraSweet ahead of its patent expiration was a clear threat to would-be producers of generic aspartame.

- Patent proliferation can protect technology-based advantage by limiting competitors' technical opportunities. In 1974, Xerox's dominant market position was protected by a wall of over 2000 patents, most of which were not used. When IBM introduced its first copier in 1970, Xerox sued it for infringing 22 of these patents.[22]

The ability to sustain competitive advantage through pre-emption depends on the presence of two flaws in the competitive process. First, the market must be small relative to the minimum efficient scale of production, such that only a very small number of competitors is viable. Second, there must be first-mover advantage that gives an incumbent preferential access to information and other resources, putting rivals at a disadvantage.

Diagnosing competitive advantage: 'causal ambiguity' and 'uncertain imitability'

If a firm is to imitate the competitive advantage of another, it must understand the basis of its rival's success. In most industries, there is a serious identification problem in linking superior performance to the strategic decisions that generate that performance. Consider the remarkable success of Wal-Mart in discount retailing. For Wal-Mart's struggling competitor, Sears Holdings (owner of the Kmart

> If a firm is to imitate the competitive advantage of another, it must understand the basis of its rival's success.

chain of discount stores), it is easy to point to the differences between Wal-Mart and itself. As one Wal-Mart executive commented: 'Retailing is an open book. There are no secrets. Our competitors can walk into our stores and see what we sell, how we sell it, and for how much'. The difficult task is to identify which differences are the critical determinants of superior profitability. Is it Wal-Mart's store locations (typically in small towns with little direct competition)? Its tightly integrated supply chain? Its unique management system? The information system that supports Wal-Mart's logistics and decision-making practices? Or is it a culture built on traditional rural American values of thrift and hard work?

The problem for Kmart/Sears is what Lippman and Rumelt refer to as **causal ambiguity**.[23] The more multidimensional a firm's competitive advantage and the more it is based on complex bundles of organisational capabilities, the more difficult it is for a competitor to diagnose the determinants of success. The outcome of causal ambiguity is **uncertain imitability**: where there is ambiguity associated with the causes of a competitor's success, any attempt to imitate that strategy is subject to uncertain success.

Recent research suggests that the problems of strategy imitation may run even deeper. Capabilities are the outcome of complex combinations of resources and different capabilities that interact together to confer competitive advantage. Work on complementarities among firms' activities suggests that these interactions extend across the whole range of management activities.[24] Michael Porter and Nicolaj Siggelkow quote Urban Outfitters as an example of a unique 'activity system' (see Example 4.1).[25] If company success is the outcome of a complex configuration of strategy, structure, management systems, personal leadership and a host of business processes, the implication is that imitation may well be impossible.

One of the challenges for the would-be imitator is deciding which management practices are generic best practices and which are 'contextual' – i.e. complementary with other management practices. For example, if we consider Sears Holdings' deliberation of which of Wal-Mart's management practices to imitate in its Kmart stores, some practices (e.g. employees required to smile at customers, point-of-sale data transferred direct into the corporate database) are likely to be generically beneficial. Others, such as Wal-Mart's 'everyday low prices' pricing policy, low advertising sales ratio and hub-and-spoke distribution, are likely to be beneficial only when combined with other practices.[26]

Acquiring resources and capabilities

Having diagnosed the sources of an incumbent's competitive advantage, the imitator can mount a competitive challenge only by assembling the resources and capabilities necessary for imitation. As we saw in Chapter 3, a firm can acquire resources and capabilities in two ways: it can buy them or it can build them. The period over which a competitive advantage can be sustained depends critically on the time it takes to acquire and mobilise the resources and capabilities needed to mount a competitive challenge.

Featured example 4.1 Urban outfitters

During the three years to January 2009, Urban Outfitters Inc, which comprises 130 Urban Outfitters stores (together with the Anthropologie and Free People chains) has grown at an average of 20% annually and earned a return on equity of 21%. The company describes itself as: 'targeting well-educated, urban-minded, young adults aged 18 to 30 through its unique merchandise mix and compelling store environment . . . We create a unified environment in our stores that establishes an emotional bond with the customer. Every element of the environment is tailored to the aesthetic preferences of our target customers. Through creative design, much of the existing retail space is modified to incorporate a mosaic of fixtures, finishes and revealed architectural details. In

our stores, merchandise is integrated into a variety of creative vignettes and displays designed to offer our customers an entire look at a distinct lifestyle'.

According to Michael Porter and Nicolaj Siggelkow, Urban Outfitters offers a set of management practices that are both distinctive and highly interdependent. The urban-bohemian-styled product mix which includes clothing, furnishings and gift items are displayed within bazaar-like stores each of which have a unique design. To encourage frequent customer visits, the layout of each store is changed every two weeks, creating a new shopping experience whenever customers return. Emphasising community with its customers, it forgoes traditional forms of advertising in favour of blogs and word-of-mouth transmission. Each practice makes little sense on its own, but together they represent a distinctive, integrated strategy. Attempts to imitate Urban Outfitters' competitive advantage would most likely fail because of the difficulty of replicating every aspect of the strategy then integrating them in the right manner.

Sources: Urban Outfitters Inc. 10-K Report to January 31, 2009 (Washington: SEC, 2008); M. E. Porter and N. Siggelkow, 'Contextuality within activity systems and sustainable competitive advantage', *Academy of Management Perspectives* 22 (May 2008): 34–56.

Case Insight 4.2
Is Singapore Airlines' competitive advantage sustainable?

In the opening case to this chapter we have argued that SIA has outperformed its rivals by referring to the number of awards it has achieved and the fact that it has consistently achieved returns that are well in excess of the industry average. Its success has been based on its systematic design and development of a cost-effective approach to service excellence, supported by investments in its fleet, customer-focused innovation and staff training and development. But how sustainable is SIA's advantage? Can its approach be identified and replicated easily by competitors?

It would appear relatively straightforward for other airlines to unpick SIA's strategy – indeed we have attempted to do that in our analysis – and they too can invest in new aircraft, staff training, new ticketing and check-in technologies and so on. What is much more difficult to identify and copy is the culture of cost-effective service excellence ingrained in the company and its people and the complex sets of linkages between SIA's different activities that create a virtuous circle of improvement. SIA's unique activity system is embedded in a way in that its 'profit conscious' approach is made explicit in its vision statement (to be the most profitable rather than the largest airline), is evident in the way staff are rewarded, is highlighted in staff training and is reinforced by its emphasis on feedback and benchmarking. Cabin crew members work together for significant periods of time and form closely-knit teams, experienced staff deliver in-house staff training and the giving and receiving of feedback is encouraged – all of which creates a climate where there is peer pressure to perform. When these linked activities are combined with investment in a modern fleet and the infrastructure of its hub airport, Changi, in Singapore and put together with a successful track record of implementing customer-focused innovation, the whole becomes greater than the sum of the parts and much more difficult for competitors to imitate.

Businesses that require the integration of a number of complex, team-based routines may take years to reach the standards set by industry leaders. General Motors' attempt to transfer team-based, lean production from its NUMMI joint venture with Toyota at Fremont, California, to the GM Van Nuys plant 400 miles to the south involved complex management problems that remained unsolved two years later.[27]

Conversely, where a competitive advantage does not require the application of complex, firm-specific resources, imitation is often fast. In financial services, most new products are copied quickly by competitors. Collateralised debt obligations (CDOs), the derivative securities that played a central role in the 2008 financial crisis, were developed first by Drexel Burnham Lambert. During the late 1990s, several leading investment banks began issuing CDOs and by 2005 the annual volume of new CDOs exceeded $500 billion.[28]

A key issue for would-be imitators is the extent to which **first-mover advantage** exists within the market. The idea of first-mover advantage is that the initial occupant of a strategic position or niche gains access to resources and capabilities that a follower cannot match. This is either because the first-mover is able to pre-empt the best resources, or can use early entry to build superior resources and capabilities.[29] We shall return to the issue of first-mover advantage when we consider competitive advantage in technology-based industries (in Chapter 6).

Types of competitive advantage: cost and differentiation

A firm can achieve a higher rate of profit (or potential profit) over a rival in one of two ways: either it can supply an identical product or service at a lower cost, or it can supply a product or service that is differentiated in such a way that the customer is willing to pay a price premium that exceeds the additional cost of the differentiation. In the former case, the firm possesses a **cost advantage**; in the latter, a **differentiation advantage**. In pursuing cost advantage, the goal of the firm is to become the cost leader in its industry or industry segment. Cost leadership requires that the firm 'must find and exploit all sources of cost advantage . . . [and] . . . sell a standard, no-frills product'.[30] Differentiation by a firm from its competitors is achieved 'when it provides something unique that is valuable to buyers beyond simply offering a low price'.[31]

Figure 4.3 illustrates these two types of advantage.

Figure 4.3 Sources of competitive advantage

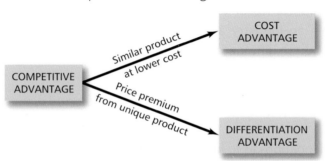

Table 4.2 Features of cost leadership and differentiation strategies

Generic strategy	Key strategy elements	Resource and organisational requirements
Cost leadership	Scale-efficient plants Design for manufacture Control of overheads and R&D Process innovation Outsourcing (especially overseas) Avoidance of marginal customer accounts	Access to capital Process engineering skills Frequent reports Tight cost control Specialisation of jobs and functions Incentives linked to quantitative targets
Differentiation	Emphasis on branding advertising, design, service, quality and new product development	Marketing abilities Product engineering skills Cross-functional coordination Creativity Research capability Incentives linked to qualitative performance targets

The two sources of competitive advantage define two fundamentally different approaches to business strategy. A firm that is competing on low cost is distinguishable from a firm that competes through differentiation in terms of market positioning, resources and capabilities, and organisational characteristics. Table 4.2 outlines some of the principal features of cost and differentiation strategies.

Strategy and cost advantage

There are seven principal determinants of a firm's unit costs (cost per unit of output) relative to its competitors; we refer to these as **cost drivers** (see Figure 4.4).

The relative importance of these different cost drivers varies across industries, across firms within an industry and across the different activities within a firm. By examining each of these different cost drivers, in relation to a particular firm we can do the following:

● Analyse a firm's cost position relative to its competitors and diagnose the sources of inefficiency.

● Make recommendations as to how a firm can improve its cost efficiency.

Figure 4.4 The drivers of cost advantage

187

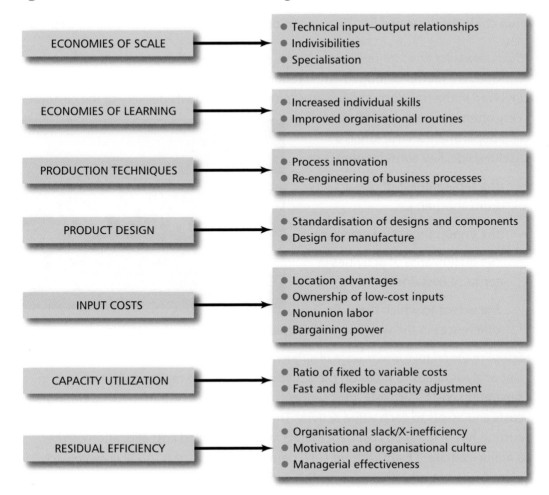

The value chain is a useful framework with which to undertake this analysis. As we saw in Chapter 3 every business may be viewed as a chain of activities. Analysing costs requires breaking down the firm's value chain to identify:

- The relative importance of each activity with respect to total cost.

- The cost drivers for each activity and the comparative efficiency with which the firm performs each activity.

- How costs in one activity influence costs in another.

- Which activities should be undertaken within the firm and which activities should be outsourced.

The principal stages of value chain analysis for cost advantage

A **value chain analysis** of a firm's cost position comprises the following six stages:

1 *Break down the firm into separate activities.* Determining the appropriate value chain activities is a matter of judgement. It requires understanding the chain of processes involved in the transformation of inputs into output and its delivery to the customer. Very often, the firm's own divisional and departmental structure is a useful guide. Key considerations are:

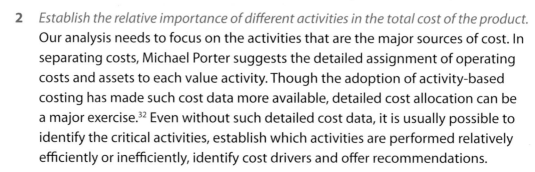

   – the separateness of one activity from another;

   – the importance of an activity;

   – the dissimilarity of activities in terms of cost drivers;

   – the extent to which there are differences in the way competitors perform the particular activity.

2 *Establish the relative importance of different activities in the total cost of the product.* Our analysis needs to focus on the activities that are the major sources of cost. In separating costs, Michael Porter suggests the detailed assignment of operating costs and assets to each value activity. Though the adoption of activity-based costing has made such cost data more available, detailed cost allocation can be a major exercise.[32] Even without such detailed cost data, it is usually possible to identify the critical activities, establish which activities are performed relatively efficiently or inefficiently, identify cost drivers and offer recommendations.

3 *Compare costs by activity.* To establish which activities the firm performs relatively efficiently and which it does not, benchmark unit costs for each activity against those of competitors.

4 *Identify cost drivers.* For each activity, what factors determine the level of cost relative to other firms? For some activities, cost drivers are evident simply from the nature of the activity and the composition of costs. For capital-intensive activities such as the operation of a body press in an car plant, the principal factors are likely to be capital equipment costs, weekly production volume and downtime between changes of dyes. For labour-intensive assembly activities, critical issues are wage rates, speed of work and defect rates.

5 *Identify linkages.* The costs of one activity may be determined, in part, by the way in which other activities are performed. Xerox discovered that its high service costs

relative to competitors reflected the complexity of design of its copiers, which required 30 different interrelated adjustments.

6   *Identify opportunities for reducing costs.* By identifying areas of comparative inefficiency and the cost drivers for each, opportunities for cost reduction become evident. For example:

–   If scale economies are a key cost driver, can volume be increased? One feature of Caterpillar's cost-reduction strategy was to broaden its model range and begin selling diesel engines to other vehicle manufacturers in order to expand its sales base.

–   Where wage costs are the issue, can wages be reduced either directly or by relocating production?

–   If a certain activity cannot be performed efficiently within the firm, can it be outsourced?

Case Insight 4.3
Using the value chain to explore Singapore Airlines' cost-saving initiatives and opportunities

Porter's category	Illustrative examples of airline activity fitting Porter's categories	Illustrative cost-saving opportunities and initiatives
Inbound logistics	Aircraft Fuel Food and drink	Young fleet – in 2009 the average age of SIA's aircraft was 74 months compared to an industry average of 160 months New aircraft significantly more fuel efficient Staff trained to spot ways of eliminating waste in food and drink
Operations	Airport and gate operations Ticketing Flight scheduling Baggage handling Repair and maintenance	In 2008 repairs accounted for 4% of SIA's total costs, close to 1% point lower than its main rivals

Outbound logistics	Flight connections Partnerships and alliances with other operators	Routes are constantly being added and subtracted from the company's route map
Marketing & sales	Promotion advertising	The company's success in achieving awards promotes the company in promoting its brand
Service	Pre and post flight service	Online booking of meals and seats allows for better forward planning. Social media are used as a low-cost way of reinforcing the relationship with customers
Firm infrastructure	Management systems – yield management, IT services, budgeting, etc.	Small headquarters located in low-cost site
HRM	Recruitment and reward Training	Training undertaken by senior cabin crew members rather than third parties and takes place on SIA's own premises. Training emphasises 'waste control' – no cost saving considered too small. The staff reward scheme with bonuses based on company profitability encourages staff to engage in cost savings Labour costs are lower than many of its rivals because it pays average Singaporean wages but attracts a high calibre of applicant
Technology development	IT systems	Non-strategic IT services e.g. end-user support for desktops etc. outsourced to low-cost service providers Buys tried-and-tested software systems 'off the shelf' rather than customised or leading-edge applications
Procurement	Acquisition of aircraft	A culture of hard bargaining for anything from aircraft to the negotiation of hotel rates for crew member stays when overseas

Strategy and differentiation advantage

A firm differentiates itself from its competitors when it provides something unique that is valuable to buyers beyond simply offering a low price. **Differentiation advantage** occurs when a firm is able to obtain from its differentiation a price premium in the market that exceeds the cost of providing the differentiation.

Every firm has opportunities for differentiating its offering to customers, although the range of differentiation opportunities depends on the characteristics of the product. A car or a restaurant offers greater potential for differentiation than cement, wheat or memory chips. These latter products are called 'commodities' precisely because they lack physical differentiation. Yet, even commodity products can be differentiated in ways that create customer value: 'Anything can be turned into a value-added product or service for a well-defined or newly created market', claims Tom Peters.[33] Consider the following:

- Cement is the ultimate commodity product, yet Cemex, the Mexican-based supplier of cement and ready-mix concrete, has established itself as the world's biggest supplier using a strategy that emphasises 'building solutions'. One component of this strategy is ensuring that 98% of its deliveries are on time (compared to 34% for the industry as a whole).[34]

- Online bookselling is inherently a commodity business – any online bookseller has access to the same titles and the same modes of distribution. Yet, Amazon has exploited the information generated by the business to offer a range of value-adding services: best-seller lists, reviews and customised recommendations.

The lesson is this: differentiation is not simply about offering different product features, it is about identifying and understanding every possible interaction between the firm and its customers, and asking how these interactions can be enhanced or changed in order to deliver additional value to the customer.

Analysing differentiation requires looking at both the firm (the supply side) and its customers (the demand side). While supply-side analysis identifies the firm's potential to create uniqueness, the critical issue is whether such differentiation creates value for customers, and whether the value created exceeds the cost of the differentiation.

> The lesson is this: differentiation is not simply about offering different product features, it is about identifying and understanding every possible interaction between the firm and its customers, and asking how these interactions can be enhanced or changed in order to deliver additional value to the customer.

Principal stages of value chain analysis for differentiation advantage

In much the same way as we used the value chain to analyse the potential for a firm to gain a cost advantage relative to its rivals so we can use this framework to analyse opportunities for differentiation advantage. This involves four principal stages:

1   *Construct a value chain for the firm and the customer.* It may be useful to consider not just the immediate customer, but also firms further downstream in the value chain. If the firm supplies different types of customers – for example, a steel company may supply steel strip to car manufacturers and white goods producers – draw separate value chains for each of the main categories of customer.

2   *Identify the drivers of uniqueness in each activity.* Assess the firm's potential for differentiating its product by examining each activity in the firm's value chain and identifying the variables and actions through which the firm can achieve uniqueness in relation to competitors' offerings. Figure 4.5 identifies sources of differentiation within Porter's generic value chain.

3   *Select the most promising differentiation variables for the firm.* Among the numerous drivers of uniqueness that we can identify within the firm, which one should be

Figure 4.5 Using the value chain to identify differentiation potential on the supply side

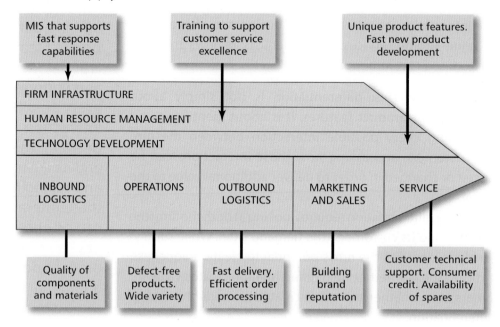

selected as the primary basis for the firm's differentiation strategy? On the supply side, there are three important considerations.

- First, we must establish where the firm has greater potential for differentiating from, or can differentiate at lower cost than, rivals. This requires some analysis of the firm's internal strengths in terms of resources and capabilities.

- Second, to identify the most promising aspects of differentiation, we also need to identify linkages among activities, since some differentiation variables may involve interaction among several activities. Thus, product reliability is likely to be the outcome of several linked activities: monitoring purchases of inputs from suppliers, the skill and motivation of production workers, and quality control and product testing.

- Third, the ease with which different types of uniqueness can be sustained must be considered. The more differentiation is based on resources specific to the firm or skills that involve the complex coordination of a large number of individuals, the more difficult it will be for a competitor to imitate the particular source of differentiation. Thus, offering business class passengers wider seats and more legroom is an easily imitated source of differentiation. Achieving high levels of punctuality represents a more sustainable source of differentiation.

4   *Locate linkages between the value chain of the firm and that of the buyer.* The objective of differentiation is to yield a price premium for the firm. This requires that the firm's differentiation creates value for the customer. Creating value for customers requires either that the firm lowers customers' costs, or that customers' own product differentiation is facilitated. Thus, by reorganising its product distribution around quick response technologies, Procter & Gamble has radically reduced distribution time and increased delivery reliability. This permits retailers to reduce costs of inventory while simultaneously increasing their reliability to shoppers through lowering the risk of stockouts. To identify the means by which a firm can create value for its customers it must locate the linkages between differentiation of its own activities and cost reduction and differentiation within the customer's activities. Analysis of these linkages can also evaluate the potential profitability of differentiation. The value differentiation created for the customer represents the maximum price premium the customer will pay. If the provision of just-in-time delivery by a component supplier costs an additional €1000 a month but saves an car company €6000 a month in reduced inventory, warehousing and handling costs, then it should be possible for the component manufacturer to obtain a price premium that easily exceeds the costs of the differentiation.

Case Insight 4.4

Using the value chain to explore Singapore Airlines' differentiation opportunities and initiatives

Porter's generic categories	Illustrative examples of airline activity fitting Porter's categories	Illustrative examples of differentiation opportunities and initiatives
Inbound logistics	Aircraft Fuel Food and drink	Young fleet means a greater % of arrivals and departures are on time Food and drink customised to individuals' preferences through use of online booking system
Operations	Airport and gate operations Ticketing Flight scheduling Baggage handling	Employs more cabin crew than other airlines so that more personal attention can be given to customers in-flight
Outbound logistics	Flight connections Partnerships and alliances with other operators	Introduction of a non-stop business class only service between Singapore and New York in 2007
Marketing & sales	Promotion Advertising	Use of customer relationship management (CRM) system in conjunction with training of cabin crew to personalise passengers' in-flight experience
Service	Pre and post flight service	Loyalty marketing
Firm infrastructure	Management systems – yield management, IT services, budgeting, etc.	The constant reinforcement of a culture of customer service Use of the CRM system to personalise the customer experience
HRM	Recruitment and reward Training	The company attracts first-class university students who like the idea of working for a leading local company. The company invests heavily in training and enhancement of staff skills
Technology development	IT systems	SIA has invested in those technologies that improve the customer experience. For example, after the scares over the

		SARS epidemic, SIA invested in biometric technology to speed up check-in
Procurement	Acquisition of aircraft	Has pioneered the introduction of brand new aircraft, like the Airbus A380, to its fleet and has used this to generate publicity and to enhance its reputation as a leading airline. For example the launch of the A380 service was accompanied by a charity auction of the first seats

The aim of the analysis is not merely to identify and classify different elements of SIA's overall differentiation strategy but to spot where opportunities exist for further differentiation and to reinforce linkages between different parts of the value chain. For example allowing passengers to state their preferences through online booking of meals when combined with judicious use of the CRM system and careful training of staff allows the airline to both 'personalise' and 'standardise' customer service.

By combining the two types of competitive advantage with the firm's choice of scope – broad market versus narrow segment – Michael Porter has defined three generic strategies: cost leadership, differentiation and focus (see Figure 4.6). Porter views cost leadership and differentiation as mutually exclusive strategies. A firm that attempts to pursue both is 'stuck in the middle':

The firm stuck in the middle is almost guaranteed low profitability. It either loses the high-volume customers who demand low prices or must bid away its profits to get this business from the low-cost firms. Yet it also loses high-margin business – the cream – to the firms who are focused on high-margin targets or have achieved differentiation overall. The firm that is stuck in the middle also probably suffers from a blurred corporate culture and a conflicting set of organisational arrangements and motivation system.[35]

In practice, few firms are faced with such stark alternatives. Differentiation is not simply an issue of 'to differentiate or not to differentiate'. All firms must make decisions as to which customer requirements to focus on, and where to position their product or service in the market. A cost leadership strategy typically implies a narrow-line, limited-feature, standardised offering. However, such a positioning does not necessarily imply that the product or service is an undifferentiated commodity. In the case of IKEA furniture and Southwest Airlines, a low-price, no-frills offering is also associated with clear market positioning and a unique brand image. The VW Beetle shows that a low-cost, utilitarian,

Figure 4.6 Porter's generic strategies

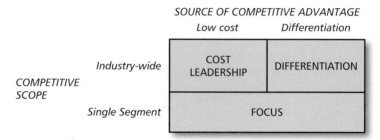

mass-market product can achieve cult status. At the same time, firms that pursue differentiation strategies cannot be oblivious to cost.

In most industries, market leadership is held by firms that maximise customer appeal by reconciling effective differentiation with low cost – Toyota in cars, McDonald's in fast food, Nike in athletic shoes. Cost leaders are frequently not market leaders but smaller competitors with minimal overheads, non-union labour and cheaply acquired assets. In oil refining, the cost leaders tend to be independent refining companies rather than integrated giants such as Exxon Mobil or Shell. In car rental, the cost leader is more likely to be Rent-A-Wreck (a division of Bundy American Corporation) rather than Hertz or Avis. Simultaneously pursuing differentiation, cost efficiency and innovation was a key element in the global success of Japanese companies in cars, motorcycles, consumer electronics and musical instruments. Reconciling different performance dimensions has been facilitated by new management techniques. For example, total quality management has refuted the perceived trade-off between quality and cost.

> In most industries, market leadership is held by firms that maximise customer appeal by reconciling effective differentiation with low cost.

Case Insight 4.5
Singapore Airlines: reconciling differentiation with low costs

Porter argues that it is impossible for a firm to sustain cost leadership and differentiation over a sustained period of time without becoming 'stuck in the middle'.

He bases this claim on the fact that such strategies usually entail contradictory investments, different organisational processes and different organisational mindsets. The SIA case illustrates that many companies do not face such stark alternatives and that by developing appropriate cultures, thinking creatively and strategically about investment decisions and paying attention to the details the best performing companies often manage to reconcile what at first sight appear to be contradictory strategies. For example by allowing customers to state their food preferences in advance the airline offers them a personalised service whilst at the same time eliminating waste. By speeding up the check-in process, the airline enhances the travel experience of its passengers but also improves punctuality and reduces the costs incurred by delays.

Summary

Making money in business requires establishing and sustaining competitive advantage. Both these conditions for profitability demand profound insight into the nature and process of competition within a market. Competitive advantage depends critically on the presence of some faults in the competitive process – under perfect competition, profits are transitory. Our analysis of the imperfections of the competitive process has drawn us back to the resources and capabilities that are required to compete in different markets and to pursue different strategies. Sustaining competitive advantage depends on the existence of isolating mechanisms: barriers to rivals' imitation of successful strategies. The greater the difficulty that rivals face in accessing the resources and capabilities needed to imitate or substitute the competitive advantage of the incumbent firm, the greater the sustainability of that firm's competitive advantage. Hence, one outcome of our analysis is to reinforce the argument made in Chapter 3: the characteristics of a firm's resources and capability are fundamental to its strategy and its performance in decision making and long-term success.

Summary table

Learning Objectives	Summary
Understand the term 'competitive advantage' and identify the circumstances in which a firm can create a competitive advantage over a rival	When two or more firms compete within the same market one firm possesses a competitive advantage over its rivals when it earns (or has the potential to earn) a persistently higher rate of profit. Firms can create a competitive advantage when some kind of imperfection exists in the competitive process

Predict the potential for competition to wear away competitive advantage through imitation	In the long run competition wears away differences in profitability between firms but external and internal change can both create opportunities for advantage and destroy them
Recognise how resource conditions create imperfections in the competitive process which offer opportunities for competitive advantage	Firms owning resources or having capabilities that are in some way unique and offer the firm some protection against imitation by rivals
Distinguish the two primary types of competitive advantage: cost advantage and differentiation advantage	A firm can achieve competitive advantage either by supplying an identical product or service at a lower cost or by supplying a product or service that is differentiated in such a way that the customer is willing to pay a premium price. Differentiation has some attraction over low cost as a basis for competitive advantage because it is less vulnerable to being overturned by changes in the external environment and is often more difficult to replicate
Use the value chain framework to analyse potential sources of cost and differentiation advantage and to recommend strategies for enhancing competitiveness	The value chain views the firm as a series of linked activities and is an insightful tool for understanding sources of competitive advantage in an industry and for assessing the competitive position of a particular firm
Appreciate the pitfalls of being 'stuck in the middle' and the challenge of achieving effective differentiation and low cost	According to Porter cost leadership and differentiation are mutually exclusive strategies and firms that are 'stuck in the middle' are almost guaranteed low profitability. Most firms do not face such stark alternatives. The most successful firms are often those who have managed to differentiate themselves in a highly cost-effective manner

Further reading

Jay Barney has developed a popular framework (VRIO) for analysing internal capabilities, the sustainability of competitive advantage, which is outlined in his article:

Barney, J. B. (1991). Firm resources and sustained competitive advantage. *Journal of Management*, 17(1), 99–120.

Michael Porter's original work is well worth reading as he provides a clear exposition of his basic arguments, particularly in Chapter 2 where he outlines his notion of generic strategies and the concept of being 'stuck in the middle'.

Porter, M. (1980). *Competitive Strategy: Techniques for Analysing Industries and Competitors*. New York: Free Press

The article by Cronshaw *et al.*, whilst now rather dated in terms of its examples, nonetheless provides a nice critique of the concept of 'being stuck in the middle' and the problems of interpreting some of Porter's terminology.

Cronshaw, M., Evans, D. and Kay, J. (1994). On being stuck in the middle: or good food costs less at Sainsbury's. *British Journal of Management*, 5(1), 19–32.

Loizos Heracleous and Jochen Wirtz have produced two articles that provide excellent detailed accounts of Singapore Airlines' strategy and organisation. They are:

Heracleous, L. and Wirtz, J. (2009). Strategy and organization at Singapore Airlines: achieving sustainable advantage through dual strategy. *Journal of Air Transport Management*, 15, 274–9.

Heracleous, L. and Wirtz, J. (2010). Singapore Airlines' balancing act. *Harvard Business Review*, July–August, 145–9.

QUIZ

Visit your enhanced ebook at **www.foundationsofstrategy.com** for self test quiz questions

Self-study questions

1   The chief executive of Singapore Airlines, Goh Choon Phong, recently announced the company's plan to launch a new budget airline[36] to compete with new low-cost operators like AirAsia and Jetstar, who have rapidly increased their market share in the region. What challenges do you think Singapore Airlines will face in operating both a budget and a full-service airline?

2   Consider the implications for a business school of adopting a cost leadership strategy. How would a business school implementing a cost-leadership strategy differ from a business school pursuing a differentiation strategy in terms of its market position, resources and capabilities and organisational characteristics?

3 Apple has been highly successful in dominating the market for touch screen tablet computers with its iPad product. Can Apple sustain its leadership in this market? If so, how?

4 Illy, the Italian-based supplier of quality coffee and coffee-making equipment, is launching an international chain of gourmet coffee shops. What advice would you offer Illy for how it can best build competitive advantage in the face of Starbucks' market leadership?

5 Target (the US discount retailer), H&M (the Swedish fashion clothing chain) and Primark (the UK discount clothing chain) have pioneered 'cheap chic' – combining discount store prices with fashion appeal. What are the principal challenges of designing and implementing a 'cheap chic' strategy? Design a 'cheap chic' strategy for a company entering another market, e.g. restaurants, sports shoes, cosmetics or office furniture.

GLOSSARY

Visit your enhanced ebook at **www.foundationsofstrategy.com** for key term flashcards

VIDEO

Closing case The Rise and Fall of Starbucks

When Howard Schultz stepped down as chief executive officer in 2000, Starbucks' revenue and income were soaring. During his decade and a half in the role he had transformed the business, changing it from an enterprise based on the local Seattle market to a multi-million dollar organisation with more than 17,000 stores in 150 countries. Unfortunately his successor, Jim Donald, did not meet with such success. By the time Donald left the company in 2008 and Schultz returned to his former position, Starbucks' share price had dropped by almost 50% and there was a comparable decline in its operating income.

The rise of Starbucks: wake up and smell the coffee

The first Starbucks store was opened in Seattle in 1971 selling coffee beans and coffee-making equipment. Howard Schultz joined the company in 1982 and after a holiday in Italy became enthusiastic about using Starbucks to develop the Italian coffee-drinking culture in America. The owners of Starbucks were not convinced with the wisdom of Schultz's idea so he left to set up his own coffee shop. Later, when the opportunity arose, Schultz acquired his former employers' business and set about building the Starbucks brand.

In line with his earlier vision, Schultz sought to introduce Americans to a more sophisticated coffee-drinking experience. Starbucks chose only to offer coffee made from high-quality beans (Arabica rather the Robusta beans that were more commonly used in the US at that time); it developed a distinct taste by developing a house style of roasting coffee beans, introduced a new language for ordering coffee and experimented with innovative coffee-based drinks. One of the company's early TV advertising campaigns invited viewers to wake up and smell the coffee, encouraging them to see themselves as part of this new urbane, coffee-drinking culture. The coffee shops were designed in a manner that was both comfortable and stylish with an emphasis on customer service. The aim was to create an ambiance that was chic, welcoming but slightly exclusive, justifying the premium prices charged.

To develop the right culture time and money was spent on recruiting, training and retaining suitable staff. Employees working in the retail outlets were known as 'baristas' and were trained in coffee-making techniques and encouraged to be knowledgeable about the coffee in general and Starbucks' products in particular. US staff received generous healthcare benefits and employees who worked for more than 20 hours a week were able to participate in equity holdings.

The company also placed great emphasis on social responsibility – it sourced its beans according to 'fair trade' principles, supported environmental projects at home and abroad and encouraged its staff to get involved in community activities.

Credit: Getty Images

Between 1993 and 2009 the company grew rapidly, increasing its revenues from $160 million in 1993 to $10 billion by 2009. First the company expanded over North America but then it moved into more distant countries in Europe and Asia. The expansion was so rapid that jokes circulated about Starbucks opening additional Starbucks in the toilets of its coffee shops. As the expansion progressed so practices within the company started to change and the chain began to move away from some of its original ways of doing things. For example, in a number of outlets the company switched from hand-pulled espresso machines to the automatic variety which helped to speed up service but diminished the spectacle of coffee making.

The fall of Starbucks: four bucks is dumb

A number of factors came together in the mid- to late 2000s to slow Starbucks' growth. Starbucks' success alerted others to the attractiveness of the markets and there had been a rapid growth in competition. Between 2000 and 2005, the number of coffee shops in the United States increased by 70%, reaching a total of 21,400, approximately one shop for every 14,000 Americans.[37] Similar trends were also apparent in other countries. Not only did Starbucks meet competition from new entrants, but it also came under pressure from companies like McDonald's and Dunkin Donuts that had traditionally operated at the lower end of the market. The phrase 'four bucks is dumb' comes from a billboard campaign by McDonald's suggesting that Starbucks coffee was over-priced and customers could achieve better value for money at McDonald's. A billboard containing this message was placed in easy sight of Starbucks' headquarters in Seattle. As well as pressure from rivals moving upmarket, competition was also getting tougher at the top end. As Howard Schultz acknowledged in an interview[38] with *Harvard Business Review*, 'At the higher end were independents who went to school on Starbucks and there was this feeling of "Let's support the local companies". So Starbucks was being squeezed to the middle and that is an undesirable place to be'. At the same time that competitive pressures were growing, problems emerged further down the supply chain. The average wholesale price for coffee increased significantly between 2000 and 2010, in part due to adverse conditions, like weather, in coffee-growing countries.[39]

Starbucks not only sold coffee through its cafes but it also sold coffee beans and coffee-making equipment for use in the home. The company foresaw a trend towards home consumption and extended its presence in this market. Through a deal with Kraft Foods it moved into distributing and retailing its coffee and coffee products through specialist grocery stores and it also extended its product range by introducing a bottled Frappuccino drink, a home espresso machine and an instant coffee called Via. These moves, however, did not protect the company from a considerable drop in its sales when the global economy went into recession, following the 2008 banking crisis. To add to its problems, Starbucks also found itself targeted by environmental campaigners who questioned the company's environmental record and circulated rumours about the company's alleged malpractice through social media. For example Schultz found himself receiving phone calls from journalists about a claim that Starbucks was wasting millions of gallons of precious water through the processes it used to sanitise its equipment.

Overall, perhaps one of Starbucks' biggest failings was complacency. As Howard Schultz puts it 'success is not sustainable if it is defined by how big you become or by growth for growth's sake. Success is very shallow if it doesn't have emotional meaning. I think it was herd mentality – a reason for being that somehow became linked to PE, the stock price and a group of people who think they are invincible. Starbuck's isn't the first company that has happened to, thankfully we caught it in time'.

Regaining momentum
Schultz stepped back into the CEO role in 2008 in an attempt to get Starbucks back on track. He and his team made immediate decisions to close certain stores and lay off some of the staff but much of the emphasis was directed at trying to

◀ revitalise Starbucks' corporate culture. The chain closed every store for half a day to teach staff to make better espresso and 10,000 store managers were invited to a conference in New Orleans where Schultz reminded them of the core values and character of the organisation. To preserve morale the firm resisted the temptation to cut the generous health benefits enjoyed by staff and they also re-emphasised their community-friendly, fair trade credentials and encouraged employees to get involved in projects at a local community level. The company also started to experiment with some very different kinds of outlet. For example it rebranded one of its US outlets as '15th Avenue Coffee and Tea' and refitted the shop with old wooden tables and pictures painted by local artists, creating an atmosphere of a local cafe rather than a corporate chain.[40] There are signs that these initiatives are beginning to work and revenues and profits are beginning to recover but whether the recovery is sustainable only time will tell.

Case questions

● How would you account for Starbucks' success in the 1990s?

● Why did Starbucks' competitive advantage prove unsustainable?

● In your opinion do the recent initiatives that Schultz has announced provide a sufficient basis on which to rebuild the company's competitive performance?

● Building on your previous answer, what would you advise Schultz to do next?

Notes

1 L. Heracleous and J. Wirtz, 'Singapore Airlines' balancing act', *Harvard Business Review* (July–August 2010): 145–9.

2 L. Heracleous and J. Wirtz (2010) op. cit.: 146.

3 J. Burton, 'Singapore Airlines sees first full-year loss', *Financial Times* (30 July 2009).

4 Richard Rumelt argues that competitive advantage lacks a clear and consistent definition ('What in the world is competitive advantage?' Policy Working Paper 2003-105, Anderson School, UCLA, August 2003).

5 The term gas-guzzler was coined in the US and refers to a car that uses fuel inefficiently.

6 K. Ferdows, M. A. Lewis and J. Machuca, 'Rapid-fire fulfillment', *Harvard Business Review* (November 2004): 104–10.

7 G. Stalk Jr, 'Time – the next source of competitive advantage', *Harvard Business Review* (July–August 1988): 41–51.

8 C. Kim and R. Mauborgne, 'Blue ocean strategy', *Harvard Business Review* (October 2004): 76–84.

9 Ibid.

10 R. Buaron, 'New game strategies', *McKinsey Quarterly Anthology* (2000): 34–6.

11 'Canon Inc.: worldwide copier strategy" Harvard Business School Case 9-384-151 (1988).

12 C. Baden-Fuller and J. M. Stopford, *Rejuvenating the Mature Business* (London: Routledge, 1992).

13 G. Hamel, 'The why, what, and how of management innovation', *Harvard Business Review* (February 2006).

14 R. P. Rumelt, 'Toward a strategic theory of the firm', in R. Lamb (Ed.), *Competitive Strategic Management* (Englewood Cliffs, NJ: Prentice Hall, 1984): 556–70.

15 See J. Cubbin and P. Geroski, 'The convergence of profits in the long run: interfirm and interindustry comparisons', *Journal of Industrial Economics* 35 (1987): 427–42; R. Jacobsen, 'The persistence of abnormal returns,' *Strategic Management Journal* 9 (1988): 415–30; and R. R. Wiggins and T. W. Ruefli, 'Schumpeter's ghost: is hypercompetition making the best of times shorter?' *Strategic Management Journal* 26 (2005): 887–911.

16 See, for example, the work of Richard D'Aveni on hypercompetition: R. D'Aveni, *Hypercompetition. Managing the Dynamics of Strategic Maneuvering* (New York: Free Press, 1994).

17 G. Stalk, 'Curveball: strategies to fool the competition', *Harvard Business Review* (September 2006): 114–22.

18 The film was based on the book by B. Traven, *The Treasure of the Sierra Madre* (New York: Knopf, 1947).

19 Monopolies and Mergers Commission, *Cat and Dog Foods* (London: Her Majesty's Stationery Office, 1977).

20 A. Brandenburger and B. Nalebuff, *Co-opetition* (New York: Doubleday, 1996): 72–80.

21 R. Schmalensee, 'Entry deterrence in the ready-to-eat breakfast cereal industry', *Bell Journal of Economics* 9 (1978): 305–27.

22 Monopolies and Mergers Commission, *Indirect Electrostatic Reprographic Equipment* (London: Her Majesty's Stationery Office, 1976): 37, 56.

23 S. A. Lippman and R. P. Rumelt, 'Uncertain imitability: an analysis of interfirm differences in efficiency under competition', *Bell Journal of Economics* 13 (1982): 418–38. See also R. Reed and R. DeFillippi, 'Causal ambiguity, barriers to imitation, and sustainable competitive advantage', *Academy of Management Review* 15 (1990): 88–102.

24 P. R. Milgrom and J. Roberts, 'Complementarities and fit: strategy, structure and organisational change in manufacturing', *Journal of Accounting and Economics* 19 (1995): 179–208.

25 M. E. Porter and N. Siggelkow, 'Contextuality within activity systems and sustainable competitive advantage', *Academy of Management Perspectives* 22 (May 2008): 34–56.

26 Ibid.

27 C. Brown and M. Reich, 'When does union–management cooperation work? A look at NUMMI and GM-Van Nuys', *California Management Review* 31 (Summer 1989): 26–44.

28 'CDOs may bring subprime-like bust for LBOs, junk debt', www.bloomberg.com (13 March 2007).

29 For an analysis of first-mover advantage, see M. Lieberman and D. Montgomery, 'First-mover advantages', *Strategic Management Journal* 9 (1988): 41–58; and M. Lieberman and D. Montgomery, 'First-mover (dis)advantages: retrospective and link with the resource-based view', *Strategic Management Journal* 19 (1998): 1111–25.

30 M. E. Porter, *Competitive Advantage* (New York: Free Press, 1985): 13.

31 Ibid.: 120.

32 On activity-based costing, see R. S. Kaplan and S. R. Anderson, 'Time-driven activity-based costing', *Harvard Business Review* (November 2004): 131–8; J. Billington, 'The ABCs of ABC: Activity-based costing and management', *Harvard Management Update* (Boston: Harvard Business School Publishing, May 1999).

33 T. Peters, *Thriving on Chaos* (New York: Knopf, 1987): 56.

34 'Cemex: cementing a global strategy', Insead Case No. 307-233-1 (2007).

35 M. E. Porter, op. cit.: 42.

36 K. Brown, 'Singapore Air to launch budget arm', *Financial Times* (25 May 2011).

37 Mintel Report on Coffee Shops, released March 2010.

38 'The HBR interview. We had to own our own mistakes. An interview with Howard Schultz', *Harvard Business Review* (July–August, 2010).

39 J. Blas, 'Arabica Coffee at 34-year peak', *Financial Times* (9 March 2011).

40 S. Johnson, 'Stealth Starbucks: Seattle-based coffee giant opening neighborhood shops in disguise', *Chicago Tribune* (17 July 2009).

5

Business strategies in different industry and sectoral contexts

Introduction and objectives

One of management's greatest challenges is to ensure that the enterprise adapts to its environment and to the changes occurring within that environment. Change in the industry environment is driven by the forces of technology, consumer need, politics, economic growth and a host of other influences. In some industries, these forces for change combine to create massive, unpredictable changes. For example, in telecommunications new digital and wireless technologies combined with regulatory changes have resulted in the telecom industry of 2011 being almost unrecognisable from that which existed 20 years previously. In other industries – food processing, house building and funeral services – change is more gradual and more predictable. Change is the result both of external forces and the competitive strategies of the firms within the industry. As we have seen, competition is a dynamic process in which firms vie for competitive advantage, only to see it eroded through imitation and innovation by rivals. The outcome is an industry environment that is being continually recreated by competition.

The purpose of this chapter is to help us to understand how managers adapt their strategies to fit their environments, how they go about predicting change and adapting their strategies to cope with change. To do this we start by exploring different industry contexts and patterns of change that can help us to predict how industries are likely to evolve over time. While recognising that every industry follows a unique development path, we will look for common drivers of change that produce similar patterns. Recognising such patterns can help us to identify and exploit opportunities for competitive advantage. We then go on to the challenges faced by managers operating in another type of context – that of the public sector and not-for-profit sectors. Again our interest lies in exploring how managers operating in these environments adapt their strategies and anticipate change.

Our starting point is the *industry life cycle*. We shall consider the extent to which industries follow a common development pattern, examine the changes in industry structure over the cycle and explore the implications for business strategy. We will then study the challenges of managing in environments where the ownership of the business is not in private hands and where profit is not necessarily the primary aim. By the time you have completed this chapter, you will be able to:

- recognise the different stages of industry development and understand the factors that drive the process of industry evolution;
- identify the key success factors associated with industries at different stages of their development and the strategies appropriate to different stages in the industry life cycle;
- recognise the particular challenges that face managers engaged in strategic decision making in public sector and not-for-profit contexts and appreciate that some of the tools and techniques of strategic analysis may need to be adapted or may be inapplicable in these contexts;
- use stakeholder analysis to gain an understanding of political priorities;
- use scenarios to explore industry and organisational futures.

Opening case The Evolution of Personal Computers

The origins of the personal computer (PC) can be traced back to the early 1970s and the development by the Intel Corporation of a microprocessor. Early machines were assembled from kits and programmed by their owners so were only of interest to knowledgeable hobbyists who enjoyed soldering and sorting out tangles of wires. Pre-assembled machines that included a basic operating system and applications software came on to the market in the mid-70s produced by companies such as Tandy, Commodore and Apple, and it was these machines that signalled the birth of the PC industry because they made microcomputers useful to a much wider customer base. Like many of today's producers, the early manufacturers did little more than assemble purchased elements, but many of the early pioneers created their own operating systems.

The potential of this newly formed market was soon recognised and new firms started to pile in. By 1981 the worldwide market was estimated to be worth about US$3000 million and there were around 150 companies producing microcomputers.[1] The first movers in the market succeeded in capturing an early lead with Apple having about 20% of the market, Tandy 15% and Commodore 7%. It is interesting to note that the initial leaders adopted significantly different strategies. Whilst Tandy chose to restrict independent firms' access to its technology, Apple chose to adopt an open architecture by releasing all the technical information necessary for independent firms to produce products that were complementary to the Apple machine.

The industry entered a second phase in the early 1980s when IBM launched its PC. IBM had previously neglected this market, focusing instead on mainframe computers and now felt the need to enter the market quickly, so it set up a 'skunk works'[2] operation in Florida. This unit functioned as a company within a company and acted outside the main IBM operation. Its independence from IBM's traditions had an important impact on the design, production and marketing of PCs. Operating in isolation from the rest ►

of the business, IBM's PC developers purchased key elements of the product – the operating system, the microprocessor, the screen, the disk drive – from third-party suppliers and adopted an open strategy which allowed third parties access to the technical details of its product so that complementary products could be developed. This strategy proved successful, the IBM PC was an immediate hit and a bandwagon effect was created. Because IBM had a good reputation as a supplier of mainframe computers, both users and writers of software anticipated that the IBM PC platform would survive and prosper and were willing to invest in the PC. The open architecture strategy meant that users of IBM machines had a wide range of applications software available to them, and the writers of software had a rapidly growing base of potential customers so the company tapped into a virtuous circle of growth.

In a short space of time IBM built a commanding share of the PC market, so much so that the IBM machine with its MS/DOS operating system became the *de facto* standard. Unfortunately for IBM, the strategy that led to its success also contained within it the seeds of the company's subsequent failure. The open strategy adopted by IBM allowed the rapid development of its product but also meant that very little of its PC was proprietary and the product was easily copied. IBM failed to profit fully from its standard-setting PCs, instead Microsoft and Intel who owned the intellectual property on their PC inputs were the major beneficiaries in terms of financial returns. Clone products proliferated and whilst consumers did not rush immediately to purchase imitative products, once the clone producers' claims of compatibility and performance had been tested and found to be true, consumers started switching to cheaper products. IBM's open strategy had, unintentionally, reduced the barriers to entry into the PC market and new entrants flooded into the market. Whilst the entrants into the PC market in the late 1970s had primarily been software and hardware specialists who provided products that complemented the early market leaders' operating systems, in the 1980s the new entrants were assemblers of full computer systems that challenged IBM directly. The nature of competition changed from differentiation, and the profits that were made in the industry tended to accrue to the industry's suppliers, who really 'owned' the PC standard, namely Microsoft who owned the operating system and Intel, who owned the microprocessor technology.

At the same time as IBM was adopting an open strategy Steve Jobs at Apple was doing exactly the opposite. Jobs chose to gain more control by producing as much of his PCs as possible in-house. Apple moved in to manufacture end-to-end computer systems including peripheral equipment such as disk drives, keyboards and monitors. Jobs justified his strategy by claiming Apple could produce 'insanely great' computer products.[3] With hindsight, this strategy had long-term benefits, but, in the short term, proved costly. Apple lost its lead position in the market by producing a highly differentiated, more expensive product that was incompatible with the IBM standard. Apple, however, managed to hold on to a core of loyal customers. It developed particular niches in the home, education and desk-top publishing markets, but to succeed in the business segment its computers needed to interconnect with the IBM/Intel (Wintel) installed base. It was a tribute to the innovative and user-friendly design of the Apple PC that the company managed to survive this period. Apple's profit margins were sufficiently high to support its research and development strategy even though its relative share of sales declined.

Ironically, the standardisation that occurred around the PC reduced the technological variety in the equipment itself but increased variety in the complementary products that went with standardised machines, particularly software. In essence the PC evolved as a general machine made versatile by adding new software functions. Whilst this versatility created enormous value for firms and end-users it also made the PC more complex, less secure, less reliable and less fit-for-use than single-purpose devices. As a result the PC increasingly has become only one of many devices adopted by users. Apple, for example, has resurrected its fortunes by bringing out devices such as the iPod, the iPhone and the iPad. Digital camera manufacturers have developed products that download direct to printers; consoles used primarily for gaming also connect to the internet. At the present time the PC is increasingly under threat as the primary platform for which software is written, as an array of other devices grow in popularity and tablet computers are starting to have an impact on low-end laptop sales.

◀ As processors have grown even smaller and more powerful and wireless and internet connections have speeded up, computing has been pushed into data centres and onto mobile devices that are not controlled by Microsoft and Intel. In addition, the growth in cloud computing[4] has resulted in new competitors, such as Amazon, trying to persuade consumers to rent rather than buy data storage space, changing the nature of end-users' PC requirements. As a consequence of these changes, the structure of the PC industry and the ways PC manufacturers compete is changing. If we imagine the computing industry as a stack of pancakes, with each pancake representing a layer of technology, for example chips, hardware, applications and so on, in the past there were obvious efficiency gains that could be realised by firms who focused on one or two layers. This seems no longer to be the case. Whilst success, in the past, appeared to be associated with vertical de-integration, in the future success is likely to depend on the ability to integrate.[5] As the landscape of the PC industry has continued to evolve so the strategies of established firms have needed to change. IBM, for example, has sold its PC business to the Chinese firm Lenovo in order to concentrate on building its service activities. Dell, Hewlett-Packard and Acer, who are estimated to account for around over 50% of world PC shipments, are rethinking their strategies[6] and diversifying into new areas of business. The future shape of this industry both in terms of who constitutes key players and how they compete depends, in large part, on how demand for PC holds up and how innovation in information technology progresses.

The industry life cycle

One of the best-known and most enduring marketing concepts is the **product life cycle**.[7] Products are born, their sales grow, they reach maturity, they go into decline and they ultimately die. If products have life cycles, so too do the industries that produce them. The **industry life cycle** is the supply-side equivalent of the product life cycle. To the extent that an industry produces multiple generations of a product, the industry life cycle is likely to be of longer duration than that of a single product.

The life cycle comprises four phases: *introduction* (or *emergence*); *growth*; *maturity*; and *decline* (see Figure 5.1). Before we examine the features of each of these stages, let us

Figure 5.1 The industry life cycle

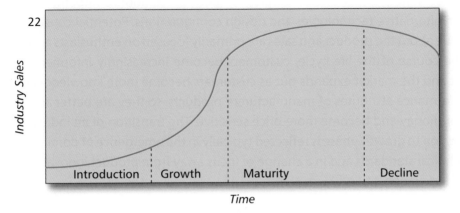

examine the forces that drive industry evolution. Two factors are fundamental: demand growth and the production and diffusion of knowledge.

Demand growth

The life cycle and the stages within it are defined primarily by changes in an industry's growth rate over time. The characteristic profile is an S-shaped growth curve.

- In the *introduction stage*, sales are small and the rate of market penetration is low because the industry's products are little known and customers are few. The novelty of the technology, small scale of production and lack of experience means high costs and low quality. Customers for new products tend to be affluent, innovation-oriented and risk-tolerant.

- The *growth stage* is characterised by accelerating market penetration as technical improvements and increased efficiency open up the mass market.

- Increasing market saturation causes the onset of the *maturity stage*. Once saturation is reached, demand is wholly for replacement.

- Finally, as the industry becomes challenged by new industries that produce technologically superior substitute products, the industry enters its *decline stage*.

The production and diffusion of knowledge

The second driver of the industry life cycle is knowledge. New knowledge in the form of product innovation is responsible for an industry's birth and the dual processes of knowledge creation and knowledge diffusion exert a major influence on industry evolution.

In the introduction stage, product technology advances rapidly. There is no dominant product technology and rival technologies compete for attention. Competition is primarily between alternative technologies and design configurations. Potential consumers often know little about the product and sales are primarily focused on enthusiasts and pioneers. Over the course of the life cycle, customers become increasingly informed about the product and the market expands but as customers become more knowledgeable about the performance attributes of manufacturers' products, so they are better able to judge value for money and become more price sensitive. The transition of an industry from its introduction to growth phase is reflected typically in the emergence of dominant designs and technical standards and in a change of focus away from product innovation towards process innovation.

Dominant designs and technical standards

A dominant design is a product architecture that defines the look, functionality and production method for the product and becomes accepted by the industry as a whole.

Dominant designs have included the following examples:

The Underwood Model 5 introduced in 1899 established the basic architecture and main features of typewriters for the 20th century: a moving carriage, the ability to see the characters being typed, a shift function or upper case and a replaceable inked ribbon.[8]

Courtesy of the Children's Museum of Indianapolis

Leica's Ur-Leica camera developed by Oskar Barnack and launched in Germany in 1924 established key features of the 35-mm camera, though it was not until

Canon began mass-producing cameras based on the Leica original that this design of 35-mm camera came to dominate still photography.

When Ray Kroc opened his first McDonald's hamburger restaurant in Illinois in 1955, he established what would soon become a dominant design for the fast-food restaurant industry: a limited menu, no waiter service, eat-in and take-out options, roadside locations and a franchise system of ownership and control.

The concepts of dominant design and **technical standard** are closely related. Dominant design refers to the overall configuration of a product or system. A technical standard is a technology or specification that is important for compatibility. A dominant design may or may not embody a technical standard. EFMPlus became the technical standards for DVDs and currently remains the dominant design for DVDs (even though it may soon be overtaken by the next generation of disks that adopt the Blu-Ray standard). Conversely, the Boeing 707 was a dominant design for large passenger jets, but did not set industry standards in aerospace technology that would dominate subsequent generations of airplanes.

Technical standards emerge where there are **network effects** – the need for users to connect in some way with one another. Network effects cause each customer to choose the same technology as everyone else to avoid being stranded. Unlike a proprietary technical standard, which is typically embodied in patents or copyrights, a firm that sets a dominant design does not normally own intellectual property in that design. Hence, except for some early-mover advantage, there is not necessarily any profit advantage from setting a dominant design. Dominant designs also exist in processes. In the flat glass industry there has been a succession of dominant process designs from glass cylinder blowing to continuous ribbon drawing to float glass.[9] Dominant designs are present too in business models. In many new markets, competition is between rival business models. In the UK internet start-up fashion retailers like Boo.com soon succumbed to competition from 'bricks 'n' clicks' retailers such as Marks & Spencer and Zara.

FROM PRODUCT TO PROCESS INNOVATION The emergence of a dominant design marks a critical juncture in an industry's evolution. Once the industry coalesces around a leading design, there is a shift from radical to incremental product innovation. This transition typically ushers in the industry's growth phase because greater standardisation reduces risks to customers that they will be left with the 'wrong technology' and encourages firms to invest in manufacturing. The shift in emphasis from design to manufacture also tends to involve increased attention being paid to process innovation as firms seek to reduce

> The emergence of a dominant design marks a critical juncture in an industry's evolution.

Figure 5.2 Product and process innovation over time

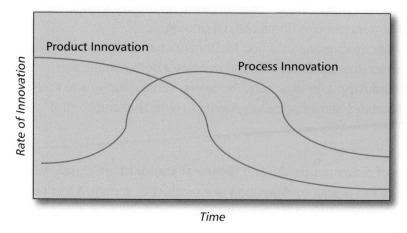

costs and increase product reliability through large-scale production methods (see Figure 5.2). The combination of process improvements, design modifications and scale economies results in falling costs and greater availability that drives rapidly increasing market penetration.

Case Insight 5.1
The life-cycle pattern in PC industry

In the opening case we saw that the PC industry has gone through a number of significant phases in a relatively short period of time. In the 1970s the industry was in its introduction stage, the term 'personal computer' had yet to be coined and the microcomputers that were on sale needed to be built from kits, and therefore were of interest only to knowledgeable enthusiasts. Different firms pioneered different operating systems and innovated in different ways. There was competition between different data storage systems (audio tapes vs. floppy disks), visual displays (TV receivers vs. dedicated monitors), operating systems (CPM vs. DOS vs. Apple II) and microprocessors. There were no dominant standards or commonly accepted 'winning' strategies. Companies like Apple, Tandy and Commodore adopted different strategies and competed on the basis of different operating systems and product configurations. Competition was primarily technology based as the early entrants into the market sought to improve the functionality and performance of their products.

The beginning of the 1980s marked the start of the industry growth phase and sales soared. Successive waves of technical improvements increased the performance of computers in terms of their power and speed but also made them easier to operate and more user-friendly. The introduction of the IBM PC based on the MS/DOS operating system and the Intelx86 series microprocessor became the dominant design for the industry. IBM's decision to adopt an open architecture together with the fact that PCs proved relatively easy to reverse engineer meant that new entrants flooded into the market with cloned products and technical knowledge was diffused rapidly. As more and more firms produced PCs based on the Wintel platform and more consumers purchased these products, the benefits to new consumers from buying a computer that was compatible with the majority of other users increased. This bandwagon effect also operated on the supply side – suppliers who produce software, peripheral equipment and other goods and services complementary with the IBM/Wintel architecture potentially had access to a larger market. Through this process IBM PCs emerged as the *de facto* standard.

By the early 1990s the market might have been viewed as reaching maturity in a number of Western economies in the sense that much of the demand became replacement demand and the rate of growth in sales of PCs in the US and other developed markets began to slow. However, continuous improvements produced multiple generations of PCs and consumers became accustomed to the need to upgrade their hardware and software on a regular basis. In addition, new markets in other parts of the world continued to develop strongly from initially low customer bases. Sources suggest that the number of PCs in use reached one billion in 2008 and looks set to reach another billion by 2014.[10] Competition during this phase focused on price with the sales price of the standard PC declining steadily over time as changes in process technology reduced the costs of production and manufacture. The production of components and sub-systems and the assembly of PCs have moved offshore to specialist contractors operating in low-cost countries, particularly China, with companies producing leading brands of PCs choosing to focus on their core competencies of product innovation, design and marketing.

How general is the life-cycle pattern?

To what extent do industries conform to this life-cycle pattern? To begin with, the duration of the life cycle varies greatly from industry to industry:

- The introduction phase of the US railroad industry extended from the building of the first railroad, the Baltimore and Ohio in 1827, to the growth phase of the 1870s. By the late 1950s, the industry was entering its decline phase.

- The introduction stage of the US car industry lasted about 25 years, from the 1890s until growth took off in 1913–15. Maturity set in during the mid-1950s followed by decline during the past decade.

- Digital audio players (MP3 players) were first introduced by SaeHan Information Systems and Diamond Multimedia during 1997–8. With the launch of Apple's iPod in 2001 the industry entered its growth phase. By 2008–9, slackening growth indicated entry into the mature phase.

The tendency over time has been for life cycles to become compressed. This is true especially in e-commerce. Businesses such as online gambling, business-to-business online auctions and online travel services have gone from initial introduction to apparent maturity within a few years. 'Competing on internet time' requires a radical rethink of strategies and management processes.[11]

> 'Competing on internet time' requires a radical rethink of strategies and management processes.

Patterns of evolution also differ. Industries supplying basic necessities such as residential construction, food processing and clothing may never enter a decline phase because it is unlikely that they become outdated and other industries may experience a rejuvenation of their life cycle. In the 1960s, the world motorcycle industry, in decline in the US and Europe, re-entered its growth phase as Japanese manufacturers pioneered the recreational use of motorcycles. The market for TV receivers has experienced multiple revivals: colour TVs, computer monitors, flat-screen TVs and, most recently, HDTVs. Similar waves of innovation have revitalised retailing (see Figure 5.3). These rejuvenations of the product life cycle are not natural phenomena – they are typically the result of companies resisting the forces of maturity through breakthrough product innovations or developing new markets.

It is also important to note that an industry is likely to be at different stages of its life cycle in different countries. Although the EU, Japanese and US car markets have entered their decline phase, markets in China, India and Russia are in their growth phases. Multinational companies can exploit such differences: developing new products and introducing them into the advanced industrial countries, then shifting attention to other growth markets once maturity sets in.

Figure 5.3 Innovation and renewal in the industry life cycle: US retailing

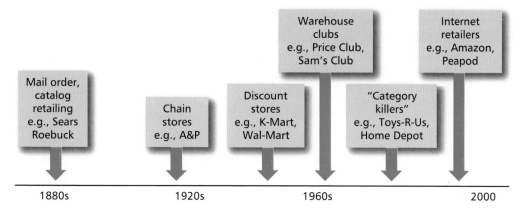

Mail order, catalog retailing e.g., Sears Roebuck

Chain stores e.g., A&P

Discount stores e.g., K-Mart, Wal-Mart

Warehouse clubs e.g., Price Club, Sam's Club

"Category killers" e.g., Toys-R-Us, Home Depot

Internet retailers e.g., Amazon, Peapod

1880s   1920s   1960s   2000

Case Insight 5.2
Does the PC industry follow the life-cycle pattern?

Whilst the PC industry has gone through clear stages of introduction, growth and maturity, evaluating whether or when sales of PCs will enter a phase of decline is more difficult. There are already signs that growth in the PC market is slowing down. The 2000s have seen the rise of new devices such as smartphones and tablet computers and the general-purpose PC has ceded ground to single-purpose devices in areas like gaming, music and e-books. Deloitte's,[12] the consulting company, predicts that in 2011 the sales of these more specialist-purpose devices will outstrip those of PCs but the PC era is far from over and currently PCs still remain the main computing platform for most households and businesses. It should be remembered that a PC manufactured in 2011 is not the same as a PC manufactured in 2001 or 1991 and product innovation continues to drive sales and rejuvenate the market at periodic intervals.

Strategy at different stages of the life cycle

Changes in demand growth and technology over the cycle have implications for industry structure, competition and the sources of competitive advantage (key success factors). Table 5.1 summarises the principal features of each stage of the industry life cycle.

Table 5.1 The evolution of industry structure and competition over the life cycle

	Introduction	Growth	Maturity	Decline
Demand	Limited to early adopters: high income, avant-garde	Rapidly increasing market penetration	Mass market, replacement/repeat buying. Customers knowledgeable and price sensitive	Obsolescence
Technology	Competing technologies. Rapid product innovation	Standardisation around dominant technology. Rapid process innovation	Well-diffused technical knowhow: quest for technological improvements	Little product or process innovation
Products	Poor quality. Wide variety of features and technologies. Frequent design changes	Design and quality improve. Emergence of dominant design	Trend to commoditisation. Attempts to differentiate by branding, quality, bundling	Commodities the norm: differentiation difficult and unprofitable
Manufacturing and distribution	Short production runs. High-skilled labour content. Specialised distribution channels	Capacity shortages Mass production. Competition for distribution	Emergence of overcapacity. Deskilling of production. Long production runs. Distributors carry fewer lines	Chronic overcapacity. Re-emergence of specialty channels
Trade	Producers and consumers in advanced countries	Exports from advanced countries to rest of world	Production shifts to newly industrialising then developing countries	Exports from countries with lowest labour costs
Competition	Few companies	Entry, mergers and exits	Shakeout. Price competition increases	Price wars, exits
Key success factors	Product innovation. Establishing credible image of firm and product	Design for manufacture. Access to distribution. Brand building. Fast product development. Process innovation	Cost efficiency through capital intensity, scale efficiency and low input costs	Low overheads. Buyer selection. Signalling commitment. Rationalising capacity

Categorising industries according to their stages of development alerts us to the type of competition likely to emerge and the strategies that are likely to be effective so it is worth examining the strategic implications of each of these phases in more detail.

The introduction phase

The number of firms in an industry increases rapidly during the early stages of an industry's life cycle. Initially an industry may be pioneered by a few firms but as the industry gains legitimacy, failure rates decline and the rate of new-firm formation increases. New entrants often have very different origins. Some are start-up companies ('*de novo*' entrants); others are established firms diversifying from related industries ('*de alio*' entrants). In the PC industry, most of the pioneering firms were *de alio* entrants. Commodore, for example, was founded in 1954 as a typewriter manufacturing company but moved into the manufacture of electronic calculators when Japanese typewriters flooded onto the US market. From calculators, Commodore moved into home computers. Similarly MITS, the makers of the popular Altair 8800 home computers, started out selling electronic calculator kits that hobbyists could assemble. Apple was, however, *de novo*.

The basis of entry is product innovation so the introduction stage typically features a wide variety of product types that reflect the diversity of technologies and designs and the lack of consensus over customer requirements. Subsequent success comes from winning the battle for technological leadership. During this phase gross margins can be high, but heavy investments in innovation and market development tend to depress return on capital.

> The introduction stage typically features a wide variety of product types that reflect the diversity of technologies and designs and the lack of consensus over customer requirements.

New industries often begin in advanced industrial countries because of the presence of affluent consumers and the availability of technical and scientific resources and, traditionally, firms have built stable demand positions in their home markets before starting to internationalise. The advent of the internet has, however, heralded the arrival of some start-ups who are 'born global'.[13] **Born global companies** are firms that, from their inception, derive significant competitive advantage from the use of resources and the sale of output in multiple countries. Companies operating in the virtual domain may be able to develop international operations quickly and cheaply. For example Eyeview is a company providing specialist advice to corporate clients on how to create effective websites. It uses video and audio materials developed in different languages to provide training sessions via the internet. Similarly, firms providing standardised products to niche markets often go global from the start. Icebreaker, a New Zealand-based company producing thermal outdoor clothing from merino wool, has been able to market its product across the globe from the outset, because its products appeal to a specific group of individuals engaged in specialist outdoor pursuits that have very similar needs and preferences.

The growth phase

As demand grows both in the domestic market and other countries a dominant design usually emerges. The key challenge then becomes scaling up. As the market expands, the firm needs to adapt its product design and manufacturing capability to large-scale production but, at the same time, to utilise increased manufacturing capability, access to distribution becomes critical. Financial resources also become important as investment requirements grow. Organisational growth also creates the need for internal administrative and strategic skills which we consider in more detail in Chapter 9.

During this phase overseas demand may be serviced initially by exports, but the drive to reduce cost and associated changes in production processes reduce the need for sophisticated labour skills and makes production attractive in newly industrialised countries. Eventually production and assembly may shift away from the advanced countries and these countries may start to import.

The maturity phase

With the maturity stage, competitive advantage is increasingly a quest for efficiency – particularly in industries that tend toward commoditisation. Cost efficiency through scale economies, low wages and low overheads become the key success factors. With the onset of maturity, the number of firms begins to fall as product standardisation and excess capacity stimulate price competition. Very often, industries go through one or more 'shakeout' phases during which the rate of firm failure increases sharply. The intensity of the shakeout depends a great deal on the capacity/demand balance and the extent of international competition.

In food retailing, airlines, motor vehicles, metals and insurance, maturity was associated with strong price competition and slender profitability. In household detergents, breakfast cereals, cosmetics and cigarettes, high seller concentration and successful maintenance of product differentiation has allowed subdued price rivalry and high profits.

In the PC industry there was a significant shakeout from the mid- to late 1990s to the early 2000s. By 1999 only 20% of the firms that began producing PCs in the previous 22 years had survived. Hewlett-Packard merged with Compaq in 2001 and in 2004 IBM exited the PC market selling its PC business to Lenovo, a large Chinese electronics firm. Whereas in 1987 there were 286 firms in the market, by 2010 six leading firms dominated – Acer, Apple, Dell, Hewlett-Packard, Lenovo and Toshiba – who between them accounted for around 60% of global sales.[14]

Once a shakeout has occurred, rates of entry and exit decline and the survival rate for incumbents increases substantially.[15] In some industries, however, increasing concentration and the focus of the leading firms on the mass market, creates a new phase of entry as new firms create niche positions in the market. An example of this is the UK brewing industry: as the mass market became dominated by a handful of national brewers, so opportunities arose for new types of brewing companies – microbreweries – to establish themselves in specialist niches.[16]

With maturity comes the commoditisation and de-skilling of production processes and production eventually shifts to developing countries where labour costs are lowest. At the beginning of the 1990s, the production of wireless handsets was concentrated in the US, Japan, Finland and Germany. By the end of the 1990s, South Korea had joined this leading group. During 2009, production in North America, Western Europe and Japan was in rapid decline as manufacturers shifted output to China, India, Brazil, Vietnam, Hungary and Romania. In the PC market the vast majority of production now takes places in China.

The decline phase

The transition from maturity to decline can be a result of technological substitution (typewriters, photographic film), changes in consumer preferences (canned food, men's suits), demographic shifts (children's toys in Europe) or foreign competition (textiles in the advanced industrialised countries). Shrinking market demand gives rise to acute strategic issues. Among the key features of declining industries are:

● excess capacity;

● lack of technical change (reflected in a lack of new product introduction and stability of process technology);

- a declining number of competitors, but some entry as new firms acquire the assets of exiting firms cheaply;

- high average age of both physical and human resources;

- aggressive price competition.

Despite the inhospitable environment offered by declining industries, research by Kathryn Harrigan has uncovered declining industries where at least some participants earned surprisingly high profits. These included electronic vacuum tubes, cigars and leather tanning. However, elsewhere – notably in prepared baby foods, rayon and meat processing – decline was accompanied by aggressive price competition, company failures and instability.[17]

What determines whether or not a declining industry becomes a competitive bloodbath? Two factors are critical: the *balance between capacity and output* and the *nature of the demand for the product*.

Achieving a balance between capacity and output is easier when the decline can be predicted and firms can plan for it rather than being taken by surprise. For example the decline in traditional photography and the rise in digital imaging was anticipated and planned for whereas the decline in cinema attendance has been much more unpredictable, with blockbuster films and investments in multiplex cinemas making the extent and character of a long-term decline more difficult to judge. Similarly in industries where capacity exits from the industry in an orderly fashion, decline can occur without trauma. Where substantial excess capacity persists, as has occurred in the steel industries of Europe, in the bakery industry, in gold mining and in long-haul bus transportation, the potential exists for destructive competition.

Key success factors and strategy

Our discussion of each of the phases of the industry life cycle has highlighted the ways in which demand, technology and industry structure change as an industry evolves with important implications for a firm's sources of competitive advantage and strategy. To summarise:

1   During the introductory stage, product innovation is the basis for initial entry and for subsequent success. Soon, however, other requirements for success emerge. In moving from the first generation of products to subsequent generations, investment requirements grow and financial resources become increasingly important. Capabilities in product development also need to be supported by capabilities in manufacturing, marketing and distribution.

2 Once the growth stage is reached, the key challenge is scaling up. As the market expands, the firm needs to adapt its product design and its manufacturing capability to large-scale production. To utilise increased manufacturing capability, access to distribution becomes critical.

3 With the maturity stage, competitive advantage is increasingly a quest for efficiency – particularly in industries that tend toward commoditisation. Cost efficiency through scale economies, low wages and low overheads become the key success factors.

4 The transition to decline intensifies pressures for cost cutting. It also requires maintaining stability by encouraging the orderly exit of industry capacity and capturing residual market demand.

Case Insight 5.3
The future shape of the PC industry

The boundaries of the PC industry are shifting rapidly as firms reshape their supply chains, their product portfolios and their relationships with related industries. Whereas, in the past, the PC industry was characterised by vertical de-integration with firms outsourcing production to contract electronics firms like Foxconn in China, some argue that the trend is now towards re-integration.[18] Even though Apple outsources production and assembly of its Mac computers, it designs its hardware and software in-house and has opened a chain of retail stores. Its development of the iPod, iPhone and iPad has taken place alongside the expansion of its digital content store, iTunes. The iTunes platform has allowed Apple to take a cut of each sale it makes through its digital storefront and by integrating its various activities it has enhanced its profitability.

Recent developments in the PC industry suggest that links between industry life cycles, industry structure and firm strategy can be complex, leading some authors to suggest that managers should focus on industry architectures rather than industry life cycles.[19] That is to say, rather than thinking primarily about the way in which the final market for a particular product or service is evolving (the industry life-cycle approach) and the implications this has for acquiring and maintaining competitive advantage, managers should be alert to the shifting vertical structures of clusters of related industries (the industry architecture approach) and consider the way they might adapt firm strategy accordingly.

Strategy in public-sector and not-for-profit contexts

We have seen how as industries evolve managers are faced with different challenges and need to pursue different strategies at different stages to achieve competitive success. The need to adapt strategy to fit the external environment doesn't apply solely to differences in industry conditions but also encompasses differences in the political and legal environments in which firms operate. Whilst the challenges faced by many public-sector and not-for-profit organisations are much the same as those confronted by their private-sector counterparts, there are also some differences that affect strategy analysis and formulation.

Defining the public and not-for-profit sectors

Defining **public-sector** and **not-for-profit organisations** is not a simple task because when we think of these organisations we normally think of a constellation of characteristics that encompasses more than formal legal designations. These characteristics help to define the strategic challenges faced by these organisations and assist us in distinguishing them from typical for-profit firms. Public-sector organisations are commonly defined in relation to ownership, funding and the interests they serve. Whilst private-sector firms are owned by their shareholders, in public-sector organisations ownership is vested in government. Owners exercise rights and control over their property so, in the case of public-sector organisations, these rights and controls rest in the hands of politicians rather than boards of directors acting on the behalf of shareholders.

Public-sector firms also differ from those in the private sector in terms of their funding, that is to say all or part of their revenue is derived from government rather than those who benefit directly from the goods or services they produce. There are some goods, labelled **public goods** by economists, that cannot be provided by markets. Examples include flood prevention systems, street lighting and national defence. Because the benefits derived from these services cannot be confined to those that pay for them and the consumption of these services by one household does not reduce their availability to others, in a free market system no household is willing to pay. Given that these services can be consumed for free if someone else pays, every household has an incentive to rely on someone else paying and this results in **market failure**. In these situations the government usually steps in to provide the service through taxation. However, the activities of public-sector organisations are by no means limited to providing public goods or correcting market failures. There are very wide variations between countries, regions and localities in the range of goods and services that are provided by the public sector and many different funding arrangements exist. For example the provision of health services is organised very differently in different countries.

Health care may be funded by general taxation, social health insurance, voluntary/ private health insurance, out-of-pocket payments or donations, and services may be provided by the state, private companies or charities. Most countries have a mix of different forms of funding and different providers but the relative weights given to the different elements in the mix vary significantly from place to place. Denmark, for example, has a universal health-care system paid largely from general taxation with municipalities delivering health-care services. Germany, in contrast, operates a mandatory health insurance system with private practices and independent, not-for-profit hospitals providing the majority of health care.

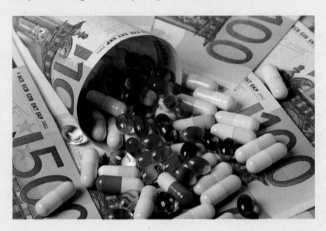

Public-sector organisations are also distinguished from private-sector organisations in terms of whose interests they serve. Those in charge of running public-sector organisations are usually required to act in the national or public interest on principles that are approved by law, typically based on achieving equity among those affected by their actions and are vested with public trust. Because they have different aims, many (but certainly not all) public-sector organisations are not required to make profits.

Whereas public-sector organisations may or may not aim to make a profit, the 'non-distribution' constraint is the defining feature of those organisations we call not-for-profits. **Not-for-profits** are organisations that do not distribute the surplus funds that may result from their operations to those in control, i.e. the organisation's directors, staff or members, instead they use such funds to pursue the organisation's goals. The easiest way to distinguish not-for-profit is through their tax and regulatory designation in that these organisations are placed in a special category for tax, legal and regulatory purposes. Not-for-profits are found principally in areas like education, health care, social services, arts and culture and religion although there are also plenty of examples of them operating in other fields, for example mutual savings societies or community shops.

> Social enterprises, like not-for-profits, do not give primacy to shareholders' interests but instead have philanthropic goals.

The notion of not-for-profit organisations also overlaps with that of a **social enterprise**. Social enterprises, like not-for-profits, do not give primacy to shareholders' interests but instead have philanthropic goals. Social enterprises achieve their goals through market-based activities and the use of business methods but may be structured as for-profit or not-for-profit entities. For example, organisations, such as cooperatives, may seek to make a profit and distribute part of their profits to those that 'own capital' but only to a limited degree. Rather than acting exclusively in the interests of shareholders and seeking to maximise profits, social enterprises give higher or equal priority to other goals, for example, integrating disadvantaged people through work, strengthening local democracy or engaging in fair trade.

Table 5.2 provides a typology of different types of organisations based on differences in ownership, interests served and funding arrangements and serves to highlight how blurred the boundaries between different sectors can be and how difficult it is to define these sectors in practice. Public-sector organisations may or may not be not-for-profits; not-for-profits may or may not be social enterprises; not-for-profits in some countries offer goods and services that are provided by public or private organisations in others. In recent years these distinctions have become even more blurred as governments in many countries have turned to private-sector management techniques to run public-sector organisations and have used private-sector firms to provide public goods and services. Firms can move from private ownership to public ownership (nationalisation) or from public ownership to private ownership (privatisation). For example, in the recent banking crisis, a number of for-profit banks like RBS and the Bank of Ireland moved from private to public or partial public ownership. Similarly many organisations that were formerly in the public sector, for example, public utilities like electricity and water have moved into private ownership.

Fortunately problems of definition do not present us with too great an obstacle because our interest is not in explaining changes in the size and scope of the public and not-for-profit sectors (interesting though this topic might be). It is in understanding the challenges that these particular contexts pose for managers engaged in strategy analysis and decision making in these sectors.

Key differences between public and private organisations that impact strategy

Whilst many of the concepts and tools that assist strategic analysis in the private sector are applicable to the public sector, there are some notable differences between the for-profit and the public and not-for-profit sectors and it is here that our focus lies. We have already emphasised the fact that the umbrella terms 'public' and 'not-for-profit' cover a

Table 5.2 Illustrative examples of different types of organisations

Organisational type	Ownership	Funding/revenue source	In whose interest?	Illustrative examples
Government department	Public	Government	Public	The Department for International Development (UK), the Department for Homeland Security (US)
State-owned enterprise	Public	Sales of goods and services and/or government	Public	Via Railways (Canada), the Australian Broadcasting Corporation (Australia)
Charity	Trustees	Donations and/or government	Those who are the focus of the organisation's mission	Oxfam, World Wildlife Fund, Save the Children
Public–private partnership	Public and private	Sales of goods and services and government	Public and private	The Global Alliance for Vaccines and Immunization, Transport for London
Social enterprise	Private or trustees	Sales of goods and services	Those who are the focus of the organisation's mission	Cafédirect (Fairtrade coffee), Elvis & Kresse (bags and accessories from waste materials), Fifteen (Jamie Oliver restaurant creating work opportunities and training for young people)
Private enterprise	Private	Sales of goods and services	Private	Tata group (India), Woolworths Holdings Ltd (South Africa), Siemens AG (Germany)

wide variety of organisations, each with its own particular characteristics, so not all of the generic differences we describe in the next section apply to every organisation. What we can say is that organisations operating in the public or not-for-profit sector are likely to be characterised by one or more distinguishing features. These features include:

1 *Multiple, potentially conflicting goals* – strategy in the public sector is not just about achieving competitive advantage although competition for resources can be of critical importance. The goals of public-sector organisations are shaped

> The goals of public-sector organisations are shaped by political considerations and, as a consequence, these organisations often have multiple, intangible and conflicting aims.

by political considerations and, as a consequence, these organisations often have multiple, intangible and conflicting aims. All organisations are faced with 'politics', competing aims and objectives and the need to take different views into account when formulating and implementing strategy. However, the primacy of shareholders' interests, in principle at least, makes it easier to prioritise and reconcile competing claims in private-sector organisations. Although all firms need to take the expectations and influence of stakeholders into consideration, this is of particular importance in public-sector contexts.

2   *Distinctive constraints and different levers* – public-sector organisations face different constraints from those of private-sector businesses. They must take into account public opinion, political factions, tax-raising capacity and so on, but they also have different tools at their disposal for achieving their aims, for example, they may be able to resort to the use of regulatory frameworks or legislation.

3   *An absence of market forces* – we have already seen that public organisations are often established to correct market failure and that some of the public sector is cut off from market forces. Strategy in the public sector just like strategy in the private sector is about the systematic use of resources and power to achieve goals (in this case public goals), but the absence of market forces means that the information and incentives provided by the price mechanism that assist in guiding resource allocation decisions are absent. Again it is worth emphasising that not all public-sector operations are insulated from market forces. Indeed many public-sector managers would argue that they face the same market pressures as their private-sector counterparts and operate in highly competitive environments.

4   *Monopoly power* – client or customer influence can be weak in situations where public organisations are monopoly suppliers of goods and services. For example, postal services are state-owned monopolies in France, India and many other countries around the world. In the US state of Virginia, liquor sales continue to be controlled by ABC stores, a retail operation controlled by the Department of Alcoholic Beverage Control. In monopolised industries, there is a danger that the supplier becomes unresponsive to its customers and inefficient and these types of complaints are often levelled at state-controlled monopolies.

5   *Less autonomy and flexibility* – public-sector organisations are subject to direct political influence and managers within these organisations may be highly constrained in the actions they can take. They may have little freedom to change the rules or to exercise personal discretion. On the other hand they may have the

opportunity to shape environments as well as responding to them. The resource-based view suggests that businesses explore their assets and capabilities, and look how they can use them to create as much value as possible. Public strategy has traditionally begun the other way round with goals. Strategies, organisational structure and projects are put in place to meet selected goals but any additional activity can be seen as a threat to focus. It is often seen as illegitimate for public-sector organisations to move into new areas of activities or for managers in these organisations to reshape their roles or the scope of their organisation's operations.

6   *Increased accountability* – whilst all businesses are accountable for their actions, public-sector organisations are subject to particular public scrutiny because organisational members are vested with public trust and are appointed to act in the public interest. As a consequence there is often a strong ethos of public service and professionalism amongst employees and emphasis on clear and transparent ethical standards.

7   *Less predictability* – not everyone would agree that public-sector organisations face more unpredictable environments than private businesses. Indeed those working in high-tech, fast-moving environments would probably see the public sector as sluggish and slow to change. Others argue that 'a week is a long time in politics' and that pressure from the media, combined with frequent changes in political leadership, make it difficult to plan for the future. Regardless of one's viewpoint on this, it seems likely that there may be differences in public- and private-sector managers' approaches to time and future value of investments.

Many of the differences outlined between the public and private sectors also apply to the not-for-profits. For example, goal conflicts often manifest themselves in not-for-profit organisations, accountability and ethical issues loom large and managers face different constraints from commercial businesses. Specific additional factors that not-for-profits may need to take into account include:

1   *The employment of volunteers* – many of the staff used to deliver services in the not-for-profit sector are volunteers. This has obvious implications for human resource management strategy. For example, it may be difficult to attract volunteers with specialist skills or to manage the performance of staff who are not being paid for their time and service. To encourage participation not-for-profits commonly engage a broad range of stakeholders in strategic decision making and place particular emphasis on creating a friendly and supportive work environment.

2   *Fundraising* – the majority of not-for-profit organisations are actively engaged in fundraising, an activity that has become increasingly competitive in recent years.[20] Most not-for-profits that fail do so because they cannot attract sufficient funding to accomplish what they set out to do.

Figure 5.4 Oster's six forces model

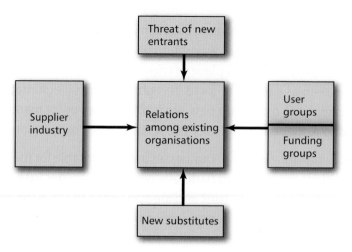

Source: S. Oster, *Strategic Management of Nonprofit Organizations* (Oxford: Oxford University Press, 1995). By permission of Oxford University Press, Inc.

Our brief review of some of the differences across sectors invites us to question whether strategic methods are universally applicable. The short answer is that good strategies take context into account and that tools need to be selected and adapted to fit the situation and issues under investigation. Models may need to be adapted to fit the circumstances, for example, Figure 5.4 shows Sharon Oster's suggested changes to Porter's five forces model that make it more applicable to the not-for-profit context. Similarly in some public-sector environments Porter's five forces of competition can provide useful insights if it is adapted appropriately, for example, by replacing the notion of buyers with that of clients or citizens or by considering new entry in terms of outsourcing or subcontracting.

Although a comprehensive review of all the ways in which strategy tools and techniques might be adapted to fit the public and not-for-profit contexts is beyond the scope of this book, two additional frameworks for analysis that are applicable across all sectors – but have particular resonance in the public and not-for-profit sectors – are considered in more detail. These are stakeholder analysis and scenario planning.

We have argued that both public and not-for-profit organisations usually have to take the views of a broader set of stakeholders into account than their private-sector counterparts, therefore stakeholder analysis can be particularly useful because it seeks to provide the organisation with a clearer insight into the individuals and groups that influence, and are influenced by, the organisation's strategy. We have also suggested that the environment in which many public and not-for-profit organisations operate can be subject to sudden and abrupt changes. In these circumstances scenario planning is a helpful technique because it provides a way for decision-makers to consider systematically the implications for strategic decision making of a number of possible futures.

Featured example 5.1 The Big Issue

The *Big Issue* was launched in 1991 by Gordon Roddick (husband of Anita Roddick who founded The Body Shop) and John Bird in response to the number of rough sleepers on the streets of London. They believed that the key to solving the problem of homelessness lay in helping people to help themselves and to give them a legitimate alternative to begging. Roddick was inspired by a newspaper called *Street News* that was sold on the streets of New York. Initially the *Big Issue* magazine was only available in London but the idea soon caught on and different regional editions were developed covering the whole of the UK. The magazine also lent its trademark to social enterprise in other parts of the world so there are now *Big Issue* operations in eight different countries and similar ventures in many more.

In order to become a *Big Issue* seller, a potential vendor must prove he or she is homeless or vulnerably housed. Vendors are put through an induction process and must sign up to a code of conduct. They are given the first five magazines for free but can buy additional copies at around half the cover price. Sellers are not compensated if they are unable to sell copies so they need to manage their finances and sales efforts carefully. The aim is to build vendors' skills, self-esteem and confidence so that they can reintegrate into mainstream society. To assist with this process The Big Issue Foundation was established as a registered charity in 1995 with the aim of tackling the underlying causes of homelessness and assisting vendors in their journey away from the streets. The main source of revenue for the Foundation is voluntary donations although it has received some small grants from government.

The *Big Issue*, however, is not without its critics and its business model has been the focus of considerable controversy. Some commentators have pointed out that whilst the Foundation itself is a charity, the magazine was started and continues to be run as a for-profit operation with John Bird and Gordon Roddick as the owners of the company's three £1 shares. Critics have questioned whether it is ethical for the magazine to charge the Foundation for its services.[21] Other criticise the fact that the magazine is run by professional journalists and that there is limited participation in the writing and production of the magazine by homeless people. In the same vein some argue that the operation is too commercial and that the *Big Issue* tries to emulate popular publications rather than concentrating on the social and political issues that affect homeless people. In addition there are complaints about the vendors themselves with members of the general public frequently expressing disquiet about the approach of certain sellers that allegedly have harassed or bullied passers-by into purchasing the magazine. Clearly the magazine evokes strong emotions in its stakeholders, who hold very different views on the magazine's contribution to the problem of homelessness.

Stakeholder analysis

Stakeholder analysis[22] is the process of identifying, understanding and prioritising the needs of key stakeholders so that the questions of how stakeholders can participate in strategy formulation and how relationships with stakeholders are best managed can be addressed. The needs and goals of stakeholders often conflict and organisations are involved in an ongoing process of balancing and managing multiple objectives and relationships. Stakeholder analysis is seen as particularly useful to managers operating in the public and not-for-profit sectors not only because it helps relationships with stakeholders to be managed more effectively but also because it helps to create an 'authorising' environment, that is to say it helps to satisfy those involved in and affected by the organisation that the management has acted fairly and equitably.

> The needs and goals of stakeholders often conflict and organisations are involved in an ongoing process of balancing and managing multiple objectives and relationships.

Bryson[23] outlines a number of key steps in stakeholder analysis:

1 Identification of the list of potential stakeholders – this stage usually involves a brainstorming session between informed parties.

2 Ranking stakeholders according to their importance and influence on the organisation.

3 Identifying the criteria that each stakeholder is likely to use to judge the organisation's performance.

4 Deciding how well the organisation is doing from its stakeholders' perspective.

5 Identifying what can be done to satisfy each stakeholder.

6 Identifying and recording longer term issues with individual stakeholders and stakeholders as a group.

To assist with this analysis Ackermann and Eden[24] suggest the use of power interest grids. These grids array stakeholders in a matrix with stakeholder interest forming one dimension and stakeholder power the other (see Figure 5.5).

Stakeholder interest refers to a particular stakeholder's political interest in an organisation or issue rather than merely their degree of inquisitiveness. Stakeholder power refers to the stakeholder's ability to affect the organisation's/issue's future. Four categories of stakeholders result. *Players* are stakeholders who have both an interest and significant power; *subjects* are stakeholders with an interest but little power; *context setters* are stakeholders with power but little direct interest; and the *crowd* make up the final box comprising those with neither interest nor power. The grid is used to identify which stakeholder interests and power bases should be taken into account but it also

Figure 5.5 Stakeholder power/interest grid

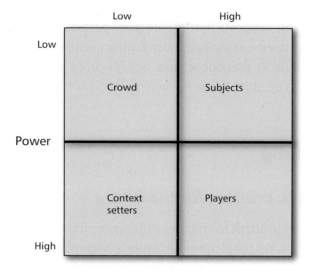

Source: C. Eden and F. Ackerman (1998). *Making Strategy: The Journey of Strategic Management* (London: Sage).

helps to identify what coalitions amongst stakeholders managers may wish to encourage or discourage.

Figure 5.6 shows the matrix redrawn to demonstrate how managers might see themselves responding to different groups in order to gain their compliance. Obviously, ensuring the acceptability of strategies to 'players' is of key importance and so relationships

Figure 5.6 Responses to stakeholders' positions within the power/interest grid

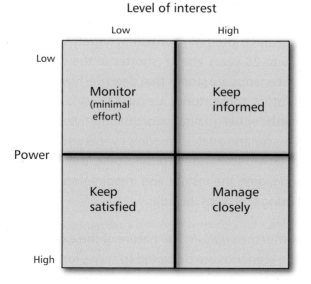

with these stakeholders need to be managed closely. In contrast stakeholders categorised as part of the crowd might be considered passive, but they do have the potential to reposition themselves by taking a more active interest therefore they need to be monitored. Bryson suggests that stakeholder participation, if properly organised, can be of positive assistance in strategy formulation, implementation and review. This is particularly important in the public and not-for-profit sectors where empowering stakeholders is often a key objective in its own right.

Scenario planning

Using scenarios to prepare for the future

An organisation's ability to adapt to changes in its environment depends on its capacity to anticipate such changes. Yet predicting the future is hazardous, if not impossible. But the inability to predict does not mean that it is not useful to think about what might happen in the future. **Scenario analysis** is a systematic way of thinking about how the future might unfold that builds on what we know about current trends and signals. Scenario analysis is not a forecasting technique, but a process for thinking and communicating about the future. Its use was pioneered by the oil company Royal Dutch Shell, who operated in an industry where the life of investment projects (up to 50 years) far exceeded the time horizon for forecasting.

> Scenarios are stories that describe how the world might look in the future; these stories are used to review and test strategic options.

Herman Kahn, who pioneered the use of scenarios defined scenarios as 'hypothetical sequences of events constructed for the purpose of focusing attention on causal process and decision points'.[25] Although there are several different ways of constructing scenarios the essence of the approach is to construct several distinct, internally consistent narratives of how the future may look 5 to 25 years ahead (shorter in the case of fast-moving sectors). Scenarios are stories that describe how the world might look in the future; these stories are used to review and test strategic options.

Scenario analysis can be either qualitative or quantitative, or involve some combination of the two. Quantitative scenario analysis models events and runs simulations to identify likely outcomes. Qualitative scenarios typically take the form of narratives and are particularly useful in engaging the insight and imagination of decision-makers. The key steps in building and using scenarios include:

● *Defining the purpose of the analysis*. The nature of the exercise depends very much on the purposes the scenarios are designed to serve, for example the main aim may be to assess risks the organisation might face in the future and to test the flexibility and robustness of current strategy in the light of these risks or it might be to consider what strategy the organisation should adopt if it wishes to achieve a particular outcome in a particular timeframe.

- *Deciding on the time horizon*. Traditionally scenarios tend to look 10–15 years ahead but there are no hard and fast rules; it mainly depends on the purpose of the analysis and the questions that the scenario exercise seeks to address.

- *Identifying key trends*. There are a number of trends and driving forces that will bring about change but they are likely to apply to all scenarios, for example the ageing population in Europe, the rise in the economic power of China and India. Trends need to be mapped and their likely impact assessed.

- *Identifying key uncertainties*. It is the uncertainties that form the basis of the alternative futures. For example uncertainty may exist with regard to the pace of a particular change or the state of the economy. Often areas of uncertainty are related, for example, higher fuel prices may be associated with political instability in oil-producing countries and higher levels of inflation in domestic economies and can be treated as a combined source. The scenario process also lends itself to consideration of large-scale disruptive change, for example, terrorist attacks or weather-related disasters.

- *Creating the scenarios and checking that they are internally consistent*. Scenarios need to be identified and described based on the way in which trends and uncertainties might come together. The descriptions of possible futures need to plausible and internally consistent. It is common to give different scenarios catchy titles as a way of emphasising the distinctiveness of different future worlds.

- *Identifying indicators that might signal which scenario is unfolding*. It is often possible to identify the events that, with the passage of time, signal that particular scenarios are becoming more likely than others.

- *Assessing the strategic implications of each scenario*. For example, using a 'what if' approach to focus on the specific questions the exercise sought to address.

As with most strategy techniques, the value of scenario analysis is not just in the results, but also in the process. Scenario analysis is a powerful tool for bringing together different ideas and insights; surfacing deeply held beliefs and assumptions; identifying possible threats and opportunities; generating and evaluating alternative strategies; encouraging more flexible thinking by managers; and building consensus. Evaluating the likely performance of different strategies under different scenarios can help identify which strategies are most robust and flexible and can ultimately assist in contingency planning.

Featured example 5.2 An example of scenario planning in local government

Work undertaken by Cairns *et al.* with a UK local government organisation, referred to as Northshire Council, provides an illustration of how scenario planning has been used in the public sector. In the early 2000s Northshire Council, like many other local councils, needed to consider the implications of the UK's central government e-initiatives for its activities. E-government initiatives were part of a government drive to 'modernise' public services by making government agencies more responsive to citizens' needs and more 'joined up' in their approach. One of the ways in which this modernisation was to be achieved was through the greater use of information and communication technologies. To better understand the possible impact of the move towards e-government on Northshire's activities the council brought in academic experts to facilitate a scenario planning workshop that was attended by decision-makers from the council, representatives from partner organisations and outside experts.

The group identified two main areas of uncertainty from which they developed four scenarios. The first area of uncertainty concerned the likely future balance of power between local and central government in decision making. The second area concerned the speed of development of new technologies, the capacity for individuals and organisations to make use of these technologies and the extent to which their use would be productive.

The four scenarios that were produced were:

- *Forward to the past* – in this scenario central government runs the show. The adoption of new technologies and resulting productivity gains are associated with a drive for economies of scale, central control or privatisation of services at a local level. This future could mark the beginning of a significant diminution in the role of local government.

- *Free enterprise* – here market forces rule and services are provided to meet the demands of those with access to and capabilities to use new technologies. Premium services are offered to those who can afford to pay for them but there is increasing exclusion of those who can either ill-afford or who are ill-equipped to use the technologies and access services online.

- *People's kailyard* – the term 'kailyard' is an old Scottish term for a cabbage patch and was selected by participants to describe a minimum level of subsistence for members of society despite vast amounts of energy expended. In this scenario there is a tendency for 'quick fixes'. New technologies are introduced in a piecemeal fashion to avoid adverse or to garner favourable publicity. However, opening up new channels of communication for citizens creates a situation where the council finds itself dealing with more complaints rather than engaging in proper consultation. If local government lacks the resources to deal effectively with issues raised because of constraints on funding the new communication technologies serve to reinforce the sense that there is a gap between reality and the potential for service effectiveness.

● *Technology serves* – here local government is able to gain funding for e-initiatives from central government and can prioritise local projects that consider the interests of all citizens including those less able to access services. New technologies allow integration from the bottom up.

Whilst accepting that there were limitations in their approach and recognising the inherent biases of organisational participants, the authors that engaged in and reported this intervention, nonetheless, argued that the scenario process was, amongst other things, valuable in encouraging divergent thinking, enabling members of the organisation to make sense of the complex environment in which they operated, revealing some plausible futures which could be unfavourable to the organisation and its current strategic intent and in invoking action-orientated responses.

Source: Cairns, G., Wright, G., Bradfield, R., van der Heijen, K. and Burt, G. (2004). Exploring e-government futures through the application of scenario planning. *Technological Forecasting and Social Change*, 71, 217–38. Reproduced by permission of Elsevier Inc.

Summary

In this chapter we have argued that some patterns are evident in the evolutionary paths that industries follow. The life-cycle model is a useful approach to exploring the impact of market maturity, technology development and knowledge dissemination on industry structure and the basis of competitive advantage. Classifying industries according to their stage of development can in itself be an insightful exercise because:

● It acts as a shortcut in strategy analysis. Categorising an industry according to its stage of development can alert us to the type of competition likely to emerge and the kinds of strategy likely to be effective.

● It encourages comparison with other industries. By highlighting similarities and differences with other industries, such comparisons can help us gain a deeper understanding of the strategic characteristics of an industry.

● It directs attention to the forces of change and direction of industry evolution, thereby helping us to anticipate and manage change.

Looking at the differences between the private, public and not-for-profit sectors is also helpful because this invites us to consider whether strategic methods are universally applicable across all sectors. The details of a strategy designed to provide home care for the elderly will clearly be very different from that designed to set up a chain of restaurants. It is, however, possible to overstate the differences. With some modest adaptations many of the same analytical tools and techniques can be used in any kind of private or public organisation. We have introduced some additional approaches – stakeholder analysis and scenario planning – which are applicable to both public, private and not-for-profit sectors but are particularly useful in contexts which are potentially politically volatile. There are, of course, limits to the use of generic techniques but by understanding where the similarities and differences between sectors lie it is more likely that appropriate context-specific strategies can be crafted.

Summary table

Learning objectives	Summary
Recognise the different stages of industry development and understand the factors that drive the process of industry evolution	We have seen that some regular patterns exist in the evolutionary paths that many industries follow. Industry life cycles typically comprise four stages; introduction, growth, maturity and decline. This evolution is driven by changes in industries' growth rates over time, changes in technology. and the creation and diffusion of knowledge over time
Identify the key success factors associated with industries at different stages of their development and the strategies appropriate to different stages in the industry life cycle	During the introduction phase the emphasis is on product innovation and marketing whereas during the growth phase the key to success is being able to scale up production efficiently and effectively. By the time a market reaches maturity price competition tends to be intense and successful strategies involve cost efficiency through mass production and low input prices. In the decline phase firms can still operate profitably if they can rationalise capacity in an orderly way, find protected market niches or innovate. The alternative is to exit at an appropriate time
Recognise the particular challenges that face managers engaged in strategic decision making in the public sector and not-for-profit contexts and	Strategy in the public-sector and not-for profit sectors differs in some significant ways from that of private-sector businesses particularly with regard to goals, constraints, accountability and flexibility. This may render certain analytical techniques inappropriate in certain circumstances, for example when considering public bodies that do

appreciate that some of the tools and techniques of strategic analysis may need to adapted or may be inapplicable in these contexts	not operate in market contexts, approaches like industry analysis are unlikely to be appropriate. However, many analytical tools can be applied across different sectoral contexts sometimes with only minor adaptations
Be able to use stakeholder analysis to gain an understanding of political priorities	Stakeholder analysis is the process of identifying, understanding and prioritising the needs of key stakeholders so that the questions of how stakeholders can participate in strategy formulation and how relationships with stakeholders are best managed can be addressed
Be able to use scenarios to explore industry and organisational futures	Scenario analysis is a systematic way of thinking about how the future might unfold that builds on what we know about current trends and signals. It can help identify which strategies are most robust and can assist in contingency planning by forcing managers to address 'what if?' questions

Further reading

Seminal reading on strategy and industry life cycle include:

Hoffer, C. (1975). Towards a contingency theory of business strategy. *Academy of Management Journal*, 18(4), 784–810.

Harrigan, K. R. and Porter, M. E (1983). End-game strategies for declining industries. *Harvard Business Review*, July–August, 111–20 is a classic explanation of the strategies available to firms in declining markets.

More recent contributions include Cusumano *et al.* who have looked at the industry life-cycle model in terms of services:

Cusumano, M., Kahl, S. and Suarez, F. (2006). Product, processes and services: a new industry lifecycle model. MIT Sloan School of Management mimeo.

There is a range of books and articles available to those who wish to explore strategy in the public sector or not-for-profit sectors in more detail. A good starting point would be:

Bovaird, T. and Loffler, E. (Eds) (2009). *Public Management and Governance* (2nd edn, chapter 6) London: Routledge.

Bryson, J. M. (2004). *Strategic Planning for Public and Nonprofit Organisations* (3rd edn). New York: John Wiley & Sons, Inc.

John Bryson also provides a nice summary of a number of stakeholder analysis techniques in:

Bryson, J. M. (2004). What to do when stakeholders matter: stakeholder identification analysis techniques. *Public Management Review*, 6(1), 21–53.

Visit your enhanced ebook at **www.foundationsofstrategy.com** for self test quiz questions

QUIZ

Self-study questions

● Consider the changes that have occurred in a comparatively new industry (e.g. wireless communication services, wireless handsets, video game consoles, online auctions, bottled water, online book retailing). To what extent has the evolution of the industry followed the pattern predicted by the industry life-cycle model? What particular features does the industry have that have influenced its pattern of evolution? At what stage of development is the industry today? How is the industry likely to evolve in the future?

● Select a product that has become a *dominant design* for its industry (e.g. the IBM PC in personal computers, McDonald's in fast food, Harvard in MBA education). What factors caused one firm's product architecture to become dominant? Why did other firms imitate this dominant design? To what extent has the dominant design evolved or been displaced?

● Select a product the market for which is declining (e.g. video rental stores, photographic film, correction fluid for typed documents, floppy disks). What advice would you give to a firm that is continuing to operate in your selected industry? Justify your advice.

● Identify the main stakeholders involved in the *Big Issue* enterprise and place them on a power/interest matrix. How might their position on the grid affect the way in which the enterprise addresses their needs and expectations?

● Consider an industry facing fundamental technology change (e.g. the recorded music industry and digital technology, computer software and open-source, newspapers and the internet, cars and alternative fuels, corporate IT services and cloud computing). Develop two alternative scenarios for the future evolution of your chosen industry. In relation to one leading player in the industry, identify the problems posed by the new technology and develop a strategy for how the company might adapt to and exploit the changes you envisage.

Visit your enhanced ebook at **www.foundationsofstrategy.com** for key term flashcards

GLOSSARY

Closing case The World Wide Fund for Nature (WWF)

In April 2011, the World Wide Fund for Nature (WWF), formerly known as the World Wildlife Fund, celebrated its 50th anniversary. Over those 50 years the WWF has grown from a small group of conservationists committed to saving wildlife to a global network, employing around 5000 people and with around 70 offices across the world.[26] Since its foundation the WWF has invested nearly US$10 billion in more than 13,000 conservation projects in over 150 countries.[27] Along the way it has changed its name, adjusted its mission and restructured its operations and, although many of the environmental challenges it faces remain the same, its approach to tackling these has altered radically. As the WWF enters its next half-century, it faces growing competition from other non-governmental agencies with similar agendas, a challenging fundraising environment and uncertainty about the best ways to achieve its mission – all of which raise questions about the way in which its strategy might need to change in the future.

A brief history of the WWF

The World Wildlife Fund (WWF) was established in 1961 by the conservationist Sir Julian Huxley, following a visit he made to East Africa. During his travels he was horrified to find that once thriving areas had become barren. On his return to the UK he wrote a series of articles for Britain's *Observer* newspaper warning that a large number of species would be extinct within 20 years if no changes were made. As a consequence of writing these campaigning articles he was approached by a number of high-profile business people and scientists and together they established the World Wildlife Fund. The initial aim of the new organisation was to conserve the world's

Credit: Reproduced by permission of the World Wide Fund for Nature

fauna, flora and natural resources. The WWF was registered as a foundation under Swiss law, governed by a board of trustees. A network of independent fundraising offices were established in various countries, for example, the World Wildlife Fund – UK, the World Wildlife Fund – Canada and the central administration office (WWF International) was set up in Switzerland. The organisation adopted the image of a panda as its logo because this image was thought to transcend different languages and cultures.

The organisation grew quickly and had particular success with campaigns focused on 'charismatic' species such as tigers, pandas and whales. Project Tiger in 1973 involved the WWF working with the Indian government to establish nature reserves for endangered Indian tigers, the 'Seas Must Live' project in 1976 set up sanctuaries for dolphins, turtles and whales and Project Rhino in 1979 sought to end rhino poaching. The 1960s was a period when environmental issues started to move from the domain of scientists into the public arena and the WWF's imaginative campaigns captured the mood of the times. During the 1970s public awareness of environmental issues continued to grow but with that awareness came more sophisticated analysis and a greater understanding of the complex links between human economic activity and the environment. The opportunistic and crisis-driven approach that WWF had adopted in its early years was increasingly viewed as outdated and an ineffective way of achieving long-term sustainable development. In 1986 the organisation changed its name from the World Wildlife Fund to the World Wide Fund for Nature[28] in order to emphasise that its remit was broader than conservation of particular species and their habitats. It expanded its mission to encompass the preservation of diversity, promotion of sustainability and reduction of wasteful consumption and pollution.[29] Although both the international and the national WWF organisations continued to make progress with projects and fundraising during the 1990s problems began to emerge that eventually resulted in the organisation reconsidering its structure and governance arrangements.

Organisational structure and governance

From the outset the WWF was structured as a network of independent national organisations with a central secretariat in Switzerland. The national organisations raised funds and ran regionally focused conservation projects. The central body, WWF International, developed policy, established priorities, coordinated the national organisations and ran international projects and campaigns. WWF International did not have the authority to enforce strategy but relied instead on the cooperation of the national bodies.

As the organisation grew in size so this structure began to creak. There were an increasing number of complaints that decision making within WWF International was slow and that procedures were becoming excessively bureaucratic. An absence of standard project initiation and reporting procedures meant that the right hand sometimes didn't know what the left hand was doing and, as a consequence, the national organisations started to 'go it alone', preferring to make their own resource allocation decisions and undertaking their own conservation projects either unilaterally or in conjunction with a small number of other national WWF organisations. An internal report was alleged to have suggested that within the organisation 'supervision was poor, reporting sporadic, financial accountability non-existent and file maintenance appalling'.[30] Although the WWF's central office argued that these claims were overstated, nonetheless, it was recognised that communication between different parts of the organisation as a whole was poor, resulting in low levels of cooperation and an unnecessary duplication of tasks and skills development. In addition the WWF's lack of transparency and accountability alienated donors who wished to know how their money was being spent.

In response to these shortcomings the WWF restructured its operations to achieve a more unified approach. A network executive team (NET) was established with a membership drawn from the national organisations and programme teams as well as from headquarters. The NET was supported by four, newly formed expert groups – Programmes, Global Partnerships, Marketing and Operations, and Network Development – and a system of key performance indicators introduced.

Continuing challenges

Over time there has been a growing recognition within the WWF that, although it has had a good deal of success in terms of its specific projects and campaigns, environmental issues such as climate change, biodiversity loss and global poverty are beyond the scope of any one organisation. Whilst they have continued to invest in acquiring land and saving particular habitats, their focus has shifted more towards lobbying, research and educational activities. The organisation has placed greater emphasis on working in partnership with others, including big business. For example in 2007 the WWF announced a US$20 million tie up with Coca-Cola to conserve water and its US national office was a major beneficiary of donations from Alcoa, the world's largest aluminium producer. These links have produced mixed reactions. Critics complain that the WWF is colluding with big business, allowing corporations to engage in 'green washing', i.e. using 'green' projects and links with organisations like the WWF to create the misleading impression that

◄ the company's policies are environmentally friendly even though they continue to pursue activities that are environmentally damaging.[31] Advocates of the policy argue that it is only by harnessing the resources of big organisations and influencing their attitudes and behaviour that progress on environmental issues will be made.

Fundraising also represents an ongoing challenge, particularly in the light of recent crises in the world economy. In 2010 the operating income of the WWF network was around €525 million with 57% coming from individual supporters, 17% from public-sector finance and 11% from corporations. Although the WWF still constitutes one of the largest independent conservation agencies in the world, there has been a significant growth in the number of non-governmental agencies addressing conservation issues and the fear is that both individual donations and government grants may diminish as a consequence of the continued economic uncertainty.[32]

The WWF is proud that it operates at many different levels dealing with specific local projects as well as lobbying national governments and speaking to supra-national agencies like the European Commission and the World Bank and sees itself as well placed to 'see the bigger picture and open doors at every level'.[33]

Case questions

● How has the WWF's strategy changed over time? What factors do you think have prompted these changes?

● Identify the International WWF's key stakeholders and map these stakeholders in terms of the power/interest grid outlined in Figure 5.5.

● Using your answer to question 2, suggest the ways in which WWF might manage its relationships with different stakeholder groups with respect to its growing engagement with big business.

● Identify some of the key trends and uncertainties facing the WWF over the next decade. Use this analysis to generate two possible future scenarios for the organisation.

Notes

1 H. Landis Gabel, *Competitive Strategies for Product Standards* (New York: McGraw-Hill, 1991).

2 The term 'skunk works' refers to a group within an organisation that has a high degree of autonomy, is unhampered by the normal corporate bureaucracy and is given the task of working on an important or secret project.

3 D. C. Wise, 'Can John Sculley clean up the mess at Apple? With Steve Jobs on the sidelines, the company will no longer go it alone', *Business Week* (29 July 1985): 70.

4 Cloud computing refers to computing services carried out on behalf of customers using hardware or software that customers do not own or operate. Software clouds are applications offered as services on the internet rather than as software packages to be purchased by individual customers.

5 *The Economist*, 'Information technology in transition: the end of Wintel' (29 July 2010).

6 *The Economist*, 'Dell and Hewlett Packard: rebooting their systems' (12 March 2011).

7 T. Levitt, 'Exploit the product life cycle', *Harvard Business Review* (November–December 1965): 81–94; G. Day, 'The product life cycle: analysis and applications', *Journal of Marketing* 45 (Autumn 1981): 60–7.

8 J. M. Utterback and F. F. Suarez, 'Patterns of industrial evolution, dominant designs and firms' survival', Sloan Working Paper #3600-93 (MIT, 1993).

9 P. Anderson and M. L. Tushman, 'Technological discontinuities and dominant designs', *Administrative Science Quarterly* 35 (1990): 604–33.

10 Deloitte. Technology, Media and Telecommunications Predictions 2011.

11 M. A. Cusumano and D. B. Yoffie, *Competing on Internet Time: Lessons from Netscape and its Battle with Microsoft* (New York: Free Press, 1998).

12 Deloitte op. cit.

13 The first use of the term 'born global' is commonly attributed to M. W. Rennie, 'Global competitiveness: born global', *McKinsey Quarterly* 4 (1993): 45–52. The concept has been developed by P. McDougall, P. Shane and B. Oviatt, 'Explaining the formation of international new ventures', *Journal of Business Venturing* 9 (1994): 469–87.

14 M. Mazzucata, 'The PC industry: new economy or early life cycle', *Review of Economic Dynamics* 5 (2002): 318–45 and http://arstechnica.com/hardware/news/2010/01. Accessed 28 February 2011.

15 High rates of entry and exit may continue well into maturity. In US manufacturing industries in any given year, it was found that 39% of larger companies were not industry participants five years earlier and 40% would not be participants five years later. See T. Dunne, M. J. Roberts and L. Samuelson, 'Patterns of firm entry and exit in US manufacturing industries', *Rand Journal of Economics* 19 (1988): 495–515.

16 G. Carroll and A. Swaminathan, 'Why the microbrewery movement? Organisational dynamics of resource partitioning in the American brewing industry', *American Journal of Sociology* 106 (2000): 715–62.

17 K. R. Harrigan, *Strategies for Declining Businesses* (Lexington, MA: D. C. Heath, 1980).

18 See, for example, *The Economist*, 'Dell and Hewlett Packard: rebooting their systems' (12 March 2010).

19 See, for example, M. Jacobides, 'Industry change through vertical disintegration: how and why markets emerged in mortgage banking', *Academy of Management Journal* 48 (2000): 465–98.

20 See, for example, S. Oster, *Strategic Management for Nonprofit Organizations* (Oxford: Oxford University Press, 1995).

21 See, for example, www.workprogramme.org.uk/20100709822/big-issue-helping-homeless.html. Accessed 28 July 2011.

22 R. Edward Freeman, *Strategic Management A Stakeholder Perspective* (London: Pitman, 1984).

23 John M, Bryson, 'What to do when stakeholders matter: stakeholder identification analysis techniques', *Public Management Review* 6 (2004): 21–53.

24 Ackermann, F and Eden, C Strategic Management of Stakeholders: Theory and Practice. *Long Range Planning* 44(3) 179–96

25 H. Kahn, *The Next 200 Years: A Scenario for America and the World* (New York: William Morrow, 1976). For a guide to the use of scenarios in strategy making, see K. van der Heijden, *Scenarios: The Art of Strategic Conversation* (Chichester: Wiley, 2005).

26 www.panda.org/who_we_are/history. Accessed 12 July 2011.

27 *WWF International Annual Review 2010*.

28 The National WWF organisations in the US and Canada retained their original titles but the rest of the organization changed its name to the World Wide Fund for Nature

29 'Towards effective conservation strategies: the application of strategic principles to increase the impact and sustainability of WWF conservation efforts', WWF Netherlands.

30 C. Wolmar, 'Wildlife fund "mission" launched amid criticism, *The Independent* (30 July 1990).

31 See, for example, R. Tieman, 'Case study: Coca-Cola and WWF hail their unlikely alliance', *Financial Times* (1 October 2010).

32 http://wwf.panda.org/who_we-are/history/wwf_conservation_1961_2006/. Accessed 30 July 2011.

33 'A message from Jim Leape: the Director General of WWF International looks back on 2010', *WWF Annual Review 2010*.

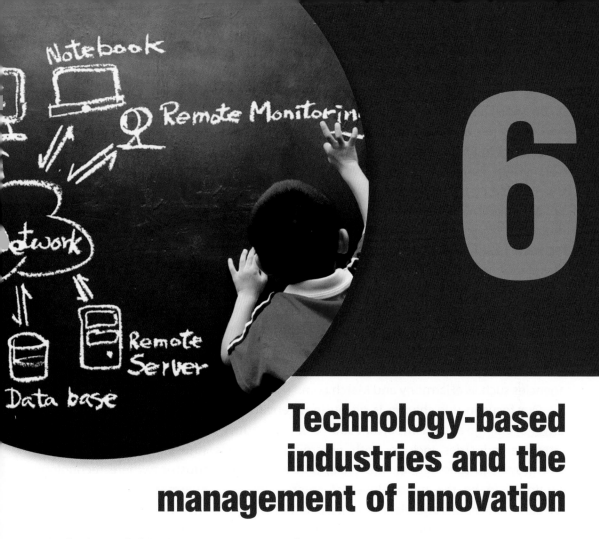

Technology-based industries and the management of innovation

Introduction and objectives

In the previous chapter we saw that technology is the primary force which creates new industries and transforms existing ones. In the past quarter century, technology-based new industries include wireless telephony, biotechnology, photovoltaic power, fibre optics, online financial services, nanotechnology and 3D printing. Industries transformed by technology include the telecom sector which has been turned upside-down by wireless technology and the internet; the pharmaceutical industry where the molecular biology revolution has made it difficult for established firms to maintain their lead; and healthcare where changes in diagnostic tools, medical equipment and surgical techniques have transformed the ways in which health services are delivered.

The impact of technology has not been limited to science-based industries. A key feature of the past decade has been the pervasive influence of digital technologies – including communication technologies and the internet. The music and book publishing industries have been reshaped and the way we organise our social lives has been transformed by social networking services like Facebook and MySpace and online dating agencies such as eHarmony and Match.com.

Our focus in this chapter is on business environments where technology is a key driver of change and an important source of competitive advantage. These technology-intensive industries include both emerging industries (those in the introductory and growth phases of their life cycle) and established industries where technology continues to be the major driver of competition (e.g. pharmaceuticals, chemicals, telecommunications and electronics). The issues we examine, however, are also relevant to a much broader range of industries where technology has the *potential* to create competitive advantage.

In this chapter our primary concern will be the use of technology as a tool of competitive strategy. How does the firm use technology to establish competitive advantage?

By the time you have completed this chapter, you will be able to:

- analyse how technology affects industry structure and competition;

- identify the factors that determine the returns to innovation and evaluate the potential for an innovation to establish competitive advantage;

- formulate strategies for exploiting innovation and managing technology, focusing in particular on:

    - the relative advantages of being a leader or a follower in innovation;

    - identifying and evaluating strategic options for exploiting innovation;

- – how to win standards battles;
- – how to manage risk.
- design the organisational conditions needed to implement such strategies successfully.

This chapter is organised as follows. First, we examine the links between technology and competition in technology-intensive industries. Second, we explore the potential for innovation to establish sustainable competitive advantage. Third, we deal with key issues in designing technology strategies, including timing (to lead or to follow), alternative strategies for exploiting an innovation, setting industry standards and managing risk. Finally, we examine the organisational conditions for the successful implementation of technology-based strategies.

VIDEO

Opening case eBook Readers

The initial introduction of eBook readers

The first commercial eBook reader (e-reader) was launched in 1997 by Softbook Press, a California start-up. Like today's e-readers the product displayed text and had a built-in modem that allowed purchasers to download content; but it was bulky, weighed about 1.4 kg and expensive (US$599), so it had few immediate advantages over paper books. Nonetheless, the market potential of this electronic device was soon recognised and many established electronics firms, for example Hewlett Packard, Sony and others, started to experiment with e-reader technologies. NuvoMedia, another Californian start-up, entered the market in 1998[1] with a slightly cheaper, smaller product, but this did not have a built-in modem and required content to be acquired using a personal computer and then transferred to the device. At the beginning of 2000 both Softbook Press and NuvoMedia were acquired by Gemstar International, a firm that provided interactive television programme technology (TV guides) to cable and satellite television providers and consumer electronics companies. This company had ambitious expansion plans to grow the eBook market.

Gemstar introduced two new products, the REB 1100 and 1200, with longer battery lives, easier-to-read screens and built-in copyright protection for digital content. The price of the readers remained reasonably high (between US$299 and US$699 depending on the model) but the company was confident it could reduce costs significantly as sales grew. To encourage take-up, Gemstar sought agreements with traditional book publishers to introduce new titles in REB format and promoted the idea of launching some titles exclusively for their readers prior to more general publication. Whilst, in public, publishers hailed the emergence of the e-reader as a welcome innovation, few actually offered their bestselling titles in the REB format. By January 2001 only 5 of the 15 titles listed in the *New York Times'* list of bestsellers were available in REB readers.[2] Unfortunately for Gemstar its core business in television technology deteriorated in 2002 and, at the same time, the company became embroiled in legal challenges with regard to some of its accounting practices. As a consequence Gemstar was not able to push ahead with its planned US$100 million marketing campaign to popularise eBooks and its e-readers and the already wary publishers became even more reluctant to release their book content in an e-format. Without Gemstar's pioneering efforts the market for eBook readers failed to take off and languished until Sony entered the market in September 2006 with its Personal Reader System (PRS 500).

The competition hots up

Sony's new e-reader utilised a display technology that made the screen easy to read even in full sunlight, used up very little battery power and was cheaper than the early eBook readers. In addition, learning from Apple's success with its iPod music player and iTunes music library, Sony realised the critical importance of having reasonably priced content available to complement its reader. The company entered into agreements with HarperCollins, Simon Schuster and Random House to publish books and sales of its e-reader began to grow. It wasn't long, however, before competition emerged. In 2007 Amazon launched the Kindle. The Kindle had two main advantages over the Sony reader; it incorporated technology that allowed users to surf the internet as well as read text and it enabled users to purchase eBooks from its newly developed online Kindle store. Many users were already familiar with ordering goods and services online and Amazon had significant capability in, and a reputation for, online book retailing. Sony responded to Amazon's entry by bringing an upgraded, less expensive version of the PRS reader onto the market and in 2008 introduced touch screen technology. Amazon, in turn, innovated with the Kindle 2, launched in February 2009 and followed up with the release of a range of Kindle 2 products later that year. In 2010 competition intensified further when Barnes & Noble entered the market with its Nook e-reader and Apple launched its iPad.

The arrival of the iPad

Apple's iPad was not strictly speaking an eBook reader; rather it was a tablet computer positioned in the market space between a laptop computer and a smartphone. The iPad offered a wider range of functions than the available e-readers because it could be used to watch videos, surf the internet, play games and view photographs as well as read books. The iPad's colour displays and backlit screen meant that it was better suited to display content with pictures, for example, comic books, newspapers and magazines, but this additional functionality also imposed some constraints like shorter battery life than rival products. The iPad was an immediate success with sales growing from 3 million in the second quarter to 7.3 million in the fourth quarter of 2010[3] and Apple established a dominant position in the tablet computer market. Other firms were, however, quick to copy and, according to *The Economist* magazine, by early 2011 there were '100 tablet devices from 60 different manufacturers scrambling for part of the tablet computer market'.[4]

Whilst the iPad was a more broadly based device than the e-reader it nonetheless provided direct competition to the lead e-reader producers like Amazon, Sony and Barnes & Noble. Having a wide range of reasonably priced digital content available for the specific reader was key to success in this market so relationships with content providers were of critical importance. Amazon's arrangements with publishers were based on a wholesale pricing model. Publishers set a recommended retail price for their eBooks and then provided Amazon with eBooks at a 50% discount so if, for example, the recommended price of an eBook was US$16 Amazon would obtain the book from the publisher at US$8. Amazon, however, reserved the right to set the actual retail price and, in order to increase demand for eBooks and its readers, choose to make a number of best-sellers loss-leaders, i.e. the company offered these titles at prices below their cost. The top publishing companies disliked this practice fearing that it was cannibalising their printed book sales and that as more consumers, attracted by these artificially low prices, turned to e-readers, their overall sales of printed books would decline further.[5] Publishers were also nervous about the ease with which digital material could be copied and were uncertain about the effectiveness of copyright protection and the prevention of piracy with regard to digitised content. Some argued that the low prices offered by Amazon meant that piracy was less likely but others felt that Amazon's growing dominance in the market was likely to squeeze margins further.

Apple, in contrast to Amazon, adopted an agency model whereby they charged publishers a 30% commission for books sold through its iBookstore and left the publishers free to set their own retail selling price. Five of the six largest US publishers (Hachette, HarperCollins, Macmillan, Penguin, Simon & Schuster) signed up with Apple immediately, with Random House agreeing to supply its titles to the iBookstore some while later. For a short time, following the launch of the iPad, the price of the same book varied significantly across platforms but both Amazon and Apple renegotiated arrangements with publishers – Amazon agreeing that publishers could set the retail price of their titles in return for a three-year contract and a best price guarantee and Apple seeking reassurances that the publishers would prohibit other retailers from selling their eBooks for less than the price listed on the iBookstore. Needless to say, these activities attracted the attention of competition authorities in both the US and Europe. For example on 1 March 2011 the Director General for Competition within the European Union announced that it had initiated unannounced inspections of the premises of companies that were active in the eBook publishing sector of several member states because they were concerned that these companies might have violated the EU laws that prohibit cartels and other restrictive business practices.[6]

The impact of e-readers on related industries

The introduction of e-readers has triggered a series of profound changes not only in the market for electronic devices but also in a range of associated industries such as publishing, smartphones and tablets computers. New entrants to the

◀ e-reader and eBook markets have come from diverse backgrounds (start-ups, established consumer electronics companies, online retailers) and the growing popularity of e-readers has triggered a series of changes in the value chains of many associated businesses. For example, Google has changed the scope of its activities and established an online bookstore.[7] Traditional booksellers like Borders have found themselves in financial difficulties and filed for bankruptcy. Even the process of getting published has changed, with authors who have found it difficult to get their work accepted by publishing houses using e-channels to attract readers.

What might, at first, have been seen as a rather straightforward product innovation continues to present a host of challenges for stakeholders in terms of business models, pricing, digital rights management, standards and regulation. The development of the e-reader was built on innovations in digital paper, touch screen, semi-conductor and battery technologies, but it has triggered a wave of further innovations in the development of interactive books,[8] new 'apps' and display technologies. It remains to be seen whether e-readers will take market share from other devices or users will download eBooks to smartphones, tablet computers, PCs or perhaps all of these devices. It is also uncertain whether the rise in popularity of eBooks marks the demise of printed books or, as some optimists hope, will stimulate an increased interest in reading across all formats. Only time will tell.

Competitive advantage in technology-intensive industries

It is the quest for competitive advantage that causes firms to invest in innovation.

The principal link between technology and competitive advantage is innovation. It is the quest for competitive advantage that causes firms to invest in innovation; it is innovation that is responsible for new industries coming into being; and it is innovation that is the main reason why some firms are able to dominate their industries. Let us begin by exploring what we mean by innovation and the conditions under which innovation generates profitability.

The innovation process

Invention is the creation of new products and processes through the development of new knowledge or from new combinations of existing knowledge. Most inventions are the result of novel applications of existing knowledge. Samuel Morse's telegraph, patented in 1840, was based on several decades of research into electromagnetism from Ben Franklin to Ørsted, Ampère and Sturgeon. Current eBook readers utilise touch screen technology that was pioneered by Dr Samuel C. Hurst in 1971.

Innovation is the initial commercialisation of invention by producing and marketing a new good or service or by using a new method of production. Once introduced, innovation diffuses: on the demand side, through customers purchasing the good or service; on the supply side, through imitation by competitors. An innovation may be the result of a single invention (most product innovations in chemicals and pharmaceuticals involve discoveries of new chemical compounds) or it may combine many inventions (the development of light emitting diodes (LEDs) involved a number of linked breakthroughs in physics and materials science). Not all invention progresses into innovation: among the patent portfolios of most technology-intensive firms are inventions that have yet to find a viable commercial application. Similarly many innovations may involve little or no new technology: eBooks have brought together a number of existing technologies such as e-ink, fingerprint resistant coatings and lithium polymer batteries; most new types of packaging – including the vast array of tamper-proof packages – involve novel design but no new technology.

Figure 6.1 shows the pattern of development from knowledge creation to invention and innovation. Historically, the lags between knowledge creation and innovation have been long, however, recently the innovation cycle has speeded up.

Figure 6.1 The development of technology: from knowledge creation to diffusion

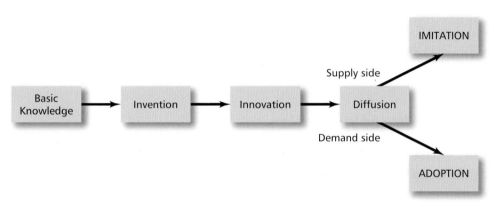

Chester F. Carlson invented xerography in 1938 by combining established knowledge about electrostatics and printing. The first patents were awarded in 1940. Xerox purchased the patent rights and launched its first office copier in 1958. By 1974, the first competitive machines were introduced by IBM, Kodak, Ricoh and Canon.

The jet engine, employing Newtonian principles of forces, was patented by Frank Whittle in 1930. The first commercial jet airliner, the De Havilland Comet, flew in 1957. Two years later, the Boeing 707 was introduced.

The mathematics of *fuzzy logic* was developed by Lotfi Zadeh at Berkeley during the 1960s. By the early 1980s, Dr Takeshi Yamakawa of the Kyushu Institute of Technology had registered patents for integrated circuits embodying fuzzy logic and in 1987 a series of fuzzy logic controllers for industrial machines was launched by Omron of Kyoto. By 1991, the world market for fuzzy logic controllers was estimated at $2 billion.[9]

MP3, the audio file compression software, was developed at the Fraunhofer Institute in Germany in 1987; by the mid-1990s, the swapping of MP3 music files had taken off in US college campuses and in 1998 the first MP3 player, Diamond Multimedia's *Rio*, was launched. Apple's iPod was introduced in 2001.

The profitability of innovation

'If a man . . . make a better mousetrap than his neighbor, though he build his house in the woods, the world will make a beaten path to his door', claimed Ralph Waldo Emerson. Yet, the inventors of new mousetraps and other gadgets too, are more likely to be found at

Figure 6.2 Appropriation of value: who gets the benefits from innovation?

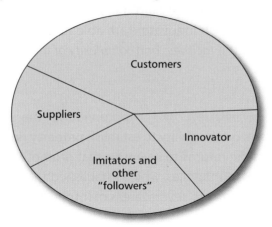

the bankruptcy courts than in the millionaires' playgrounds of the Caribbean. Certainly, innovation is no guarantor of fame and fortune, either for individuals or for companies. There is no consistent evidence that either R&D intensity or frequency of new product introductions are positively associated with profitability.[10]

The profitability of an innovation to the innovator depends on the value created by the innovation and the share of that value that the innovator is able to appropriate. The value created by an innovation is distributed among a number of different parties (see Figure 6.2). In the case of the personal computer industry (the opening case in Chapter 5), the innovators – Tandy, Commodore and Apple – earned modest profits from their innovation. The imitators – IBM, Dell, Compaq, Acer, Toshiba and a host of other later entrants – did somewhat better, but their returns were overshadowed by the huge profits earned by the suppliers to the industry: Intel in microprocessors, Seagate in disk drives, Sharp in flat-panel displays and Microsoft in operating systems. However, because of strong competition in the industry, the greatest part of the value created by the personal computer was appropriated by customers, who typically paid prices for their PCs that were far below the value that they derived.[11]

> The profitability of an innovation to the innovator depends on the value created by the innovation and the share of that value that the innovator is able to appropriate.

The term **regime of appropriability** is used to describe the conditions that influence the distribution of returns to innovation. In a strong regime of appropriability, the innovator is able to capture a substantial share of the value created: NutraSweet artificial sweetener (developed by Searle, subsequently acquired by Monsanto), Pfizer's Viagra and Pilkington's float glass process generated huge profits for their owners. In a weak regime of appropriability, other parties derive most of the value. In internet telephony (VoIP), ownership of technologies is diffused and standards are public, with the result that no players are likely to earn massive profits. Four factors are critical in determining the extent to which innovators are able to appropriate the value of their innovation: *property rights*; the *tacitness and complexity of the technology*; *lead-time*; and *complementary resources*.

PROPERTY RIGHTS IN INNOVATION Appropriating the returns to innovation depends, to a great extent, on the ability to establish property rights in the innovation. It was the desire to protect the returns to inventors that prompted the English Parliament to pass the 1623 Statute of Monopolies, which established the basis of patent law. Since then, the law has been extended to several areas of **intellectual property**, including:

- *Patents* – exclusive rights to a new and useful product, process, substance or design. Obtaining a patent requires that the invention is novel, useful and not excessively obvious. Patent law varies from country to country. In the United States, a patent is valid for 17 years (14 for a design).

- *Copyrights* – exclusive production, publication or sales rights to the creators of artistic, literary, dramatic or musical works. Examples include articles, books, drawings, maps, photographs and musical compositions.

- *Trademarks* – words, symbols or other marks used to distinguish the goods or services supplied by a firm. In the US and UK, they are registered with the Patent Office. Trademarks provide the basis for brand identification.

- *Trade secrets* – offer a modest degree of legal protection for recipes, formulae, industrial processes, customer lists and other knowledge acquired in the course of business.

The effectiveness of intellectual property law depends on the type of innovation being protected. For new chemical products (e.g. a drug or plastic), patents can provide effective protection. For products that involve new configurations of existing components or new manufacturing processes, patents may fail to prevent rivals from innovating around them. The scope of the patent law has been extended to include life forms created by biotechnology, computer software and business methods. Business method patents have generated considerable controversy – especially Amazon's patent of 'one-click-to-buy' internet purchasing.[12] While patents and copyright establish property rights, their disadvantage (from the inventor's viewpoint) is that they make information public. Hence, companies may prefer secrecy to patenting as a means of protecting innovations.

> Business method patents have generated considerable controversy.

In recent decades, companies have devoted increased attention to protecting and exploiting the economic value of their intellectual property. When Texas Instruments (TI) began exploiting its patent portfolio as a revenue source during the 1980s, the technology sector as a whole woke up to the value of its knowledge assets. During the 1990s, TI's royalty income exceeded its operating income from other sources. One outcome has been an upsurge in patenting. An average of 180,000 patents were granted by the US Patent Office in each year between 2000 and 2008 – well over double the annual rate during the 1980s.

TACITNESS AND COMPLEXITY OF THE TECHNOLOGY In the absence of effective legal protection, the extent to which an innovation can be imitated by a competitor depends on the ease with which the technology can be comprehended and replicated. This depends, first, on the extent to which the technical knowledge is codifiable. **Codifiable knowledge**, by definition, is that which can be written down. Hence, if it is not effectively protected by patents or copyright, diffusion is likely to be rapid and the competitive advantage not sustainable. Financial innovations such as mortgage-backed securities and credit default swaps embody readily codifiable knowledge that can be copied very quickly. Similarly, Coca-Cola's recipe is codifiable and, in the absence of trade secret protection, is easily copied. Intel's designs for advanced microprocessors are codified and copyable; however, the processes for manufacturing these integrated circuits are based on deeply tacit knowledge.

The second key factor is *complexity*. Every new fashion, from the Mary Quant miniskirt of 1962 to Frida Giannini's bohemian look of 2009, involves simple, easy-to-copy ideas. Airbus's A380 and Nvidia's GT212 graphics chip represent entirely different challenges for the would-be imitator.

LEAD-TIME Tacitness and complexity do not provide lasting barriers to imitation, but they do offer the innovator *time*. Innovation creates a *temporary* competitive advantage that offers a window of opportunity for the innovator to build on the initial advantage.

The innovator's **lead-time** is the time it will take followers to catch up. The challenge for the innovator is to use initial lead-time advantages to build the capabilities and market position to entrench industry leadership. Microsoft, Intel and Cisco Systems were brilliant at exploiting lead-time to build advantages in efficient manufacture, quality and market presence. Conversely, British companies are notorious for having squandered their lead-time advantage in jet planes, radars, CT scanners and genomics.

> The challenge for the innovator is to use initial lead-time advantages to build the capabilities and market position to entrench industry leadership.

Figure 6.3 Complementary resources

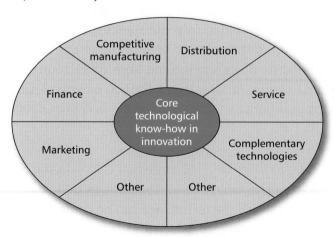

Lead-time allows a firm to move down its learning curve ahead of followers.[13] In new generations of microprocessors, Intel has traditionally been first to market, allowing it to move quickly down its experience curve, cut prices and so pressure the profit margins of its rival AMD.

COMPLEMENTARY RESOURCES   Bringing new products and processes to market requires not just invention, it also requires the diverse resources and capabilities needed to finance, produce and market the innovation. These are referred to as **complementary resources** (see Figure 6.3). Chester Carlson invented xerography, but was unable for many years to bring his product to market because he lacked the complementary resources needed to develop, manufacture, market, distribute and service his invention. Conversely, Searle (and Monsanto, its later parent company) was able to provide almost all the development, manufacturing, marketing and distribution resources needed to exploit its NutraSweet innovation. As a result, Carlson was able to appropriate only a tiny part of the value created by his invention of the plain-paper Xerox copier, while Searle/Monsanto was successful in appropriating a major part of the value created by its new artificial sweetener.

Complementary resources may be accessed through alliances with other firms – for example, biotech firms ally with large pharmaceutical companies for clinical testing, manufacture and marketing.[14] When an innovation and the complementary resources that support it are supplied by different firms, the division of value between them depends on their relative power. A key determinant of this is whether the complementary resources are *specialised* or *unspecialised*. Fuel cells may eventually displace internal combustion engines in many of the world's cars. However, the problem for the developers of fuel cells is that their success depends on car manufacturers making specialised investments in designing a whole new range of cars, oil companies providing specialised refuelling facilities, and service and repair firms investing in training and new equipment. For fuel cells to be widely adopted will require that the benefits of the innovation are shared widely with the different providers of these complementary resources.

Where complementary resources are generic, the innovator is in a much stronger position to capture value. Because Adobe Systems' Acrobat Portable Document Format (pdf) works with files created in almost any software application, Adobe is well positioned to capture most of the value created by its innovatory software product. However, one advantage of co-specialised complementary resources is that they raise barriers to imitation. Consider the threat that Linux presents to Microsoft Windows' dominance of PC operating systems. Because Intel has adapted its microprocessors to the needs of Windows and most applications software is written to run on Windows, the challenge for the Linux community is not just to develop a workable operating system, but also to encourage the development of applications software and hardware that are compatible with the Linux operating system.

Case Insight 6.1
Who will appropriate the value of eBook readers?

We have noted that the extent to which innovators are able to appropriate the value of their innovation depends on property rights, the tacitness and complexity of the technology, lead-times and complementary resources. We can use this framework to speculate on who might capture the value created by the innovations in e-readers.

Intellectual property issues loom large in this market with all the major players seeking to obtain and defend patents, enforce copyright and establish trademarks. Intellectual property rights have often been acquired through mergers and acquisitions, for example, Gemstar took over Softbook Press and NuvoMedia to gain those companies' intellectual property and, more recently, Google acquired a company called eBook Technologies in 2011 to gain access to its patents.[15] Disputes over patents have also been common, for example, in March 2009 Discovery Patent Holdings filed a suit against Amazon claiming that Amazon's Kindle violated its 'Electronic Book Security and Copyright Protection System' patent and in November of the same year Spring Design brought a suit against Barnes & Noble regarding the technology used in the Nook 3G e-reader. Whilst recognising that intellectual property rights are of tactical significance to firms operating in this market, the codified nature of the technology together with the wide range of different technologies in use and the rapid pace of innovation make it unlikely that competitors will be able to establish strong property rights with regard to e-readers. The exception here is ARM Holdings. ARM is a British company that owns and licenses semiconductor intellectual property to a network of manufacturers. ARM central processing units are estimated to be used in 90% of all e-readers and 95% of tablet computers.[16] ARM does not manufacture or sell central processing units based on its own designs but licenses the architecture to third parties.

While e-readers utilise a whole array of sophisticated technologies, innovations in this market are rapidly disseminated and easily copied by manufacturers of electronic devices. The lead-times between new product introductions in this market have been very short. For these reasons we might expect e-readers to become commodities in much the same way that PCs did. There is already evidence of strong price competition between vendors[17] which is good news for consumers but means that manufacturers' profit margins are likely to be slim. However, complementary resources, particularly the availability of a wide range of affordable eBooks, play a key role in this market. To expand the range of material available to users, many of the e-reader suppliers have made copyright-expired books available free of charge. Others have provided the opportunity for authors, who have had difficulty finding an outlet for their work through leading publishers, to distribute their books digitally, bypassing the traditional channels. This is likely to be the beginning of a series of linked changes that may ultimately lead to significant reshaping of the publishing industry, as authors, literary agents, publishing houses and others involved in the value chain adapt their business models in the face of the new technology. For example whilst the production of eBooks reduces publishers' printing costs, it also requires them to invest in technologies that convert the printed word into the specific formats used by the different e-readers and changes publishers' bargaining power with respect to suppliers and buyers.

Overall, given the current lack of standardisation in the market, it seems likely that greater profits will accrue from the sales of eBooks than e-readers but the profits from eBooks will be captured by those organisations that are have developed linkages across the value chain rather than those who focus on a narrower subset of activities. For example, Amazon has an advantage over Sony by virtue of the fact that Kindle is supported by a large online bookstore with a significant array of available titles and many customers are familiar with Amazon's 1-Click purchase facility. Similarly publishers are unlikely to capture the lion's share of the value created by eBooks because of the bargaining power established by book retailers, like Amazon, that have developed strong positions in the e-reader market.

Strategies to exploit innovation: how and when to enter

Having established some of the key factors that determine the returns to innovation, let us consider a few of the main questions concerning the formulation of strategies to manage technology and exploit innovation.

Alternative strategies to exploit innovation

How should a firm maximise the returns to its innovation? A number of alternative strategies are available. Figure 6.4 orders them according to the size of the commitment of resources and capabilities that each requires. Thus, licensing requires little involvement by the innovator in subsequent commercialisation; hence a limited investment. Internal commercialisation – possibly through creating a new enterprise or business unit – involves a much greater investment of resources and capabilities. In between, there are various opportunities for collaboration with other companies. Joint ventures and strategic alliances typically involve substantial resource sharing

Figure 6.4 Alternative strategies for exploiting innovation

	Licensing	Outsourcing certain functions	Strategic alliance	Joint venture	Internal commercialisation
Risk and return	Little investment risk but returns also limited. Risk that the licensee either lacks motivation or steals the innovation	Limits capital investment, but may create dependence on suppliers/partners	Benefits of flexibility. Risks of informal structure	Shares investment and risk. Risk of partner disagreement and culture clash	Biggest investment requirement and corresponding risks. Benefits of control
Resources requirements	Few	Permits external resources and capabilities to be accessed	Permits pooling of the resources and capabilities of more than one firm		Substantial requirements in terms of finance, production capability, marketing capability, distribution, etc.
Examples	Ericsson with its Bluetooth wireless technology; Dolby Labs with its sound reduction technology; Qualcomm and CDMA`	Microsoft's XBox was largely designed by other companies and Flextronics does the manufacturing	Ballard's strategic alliance with Daimler Chrysler to develop fuel cells	Psion created Symbian as a joint venture with Ericsson, Nokia, and Motorola to develop the Symbian mobile phone operating system	Larry Page and Sergey Brin established Google Inc. to develop and market their internet search technology

between companies. On a more limited scale, specific activities may be outsourced to other companies.

The choice of strategy mode depends on two main sets of factors: the characteristics of the innovation and the resources and capabilities of the firm.

> The extent to which a firm can establish clear property rights in an innovation critically determines the choice of strategy options.

CHARACTERISTICS OF THE INNOVATION The extent to which a firm can establish clear property rights in an innovation critically determines the choice of strategy options. Licensing is only viable where ownership in an innovation is clearly defined by patent or copyrights. Thus, in pharmaceuticals, licensing is widespread because patents are clear and defensible. Many biotech companies engage only in R&D and license their drug discoveries to large pharmaceutical companies that possess the necessary complementary resources. Royalties from licensing its sound-reduction technologies accounted for 76% of Dolby Laboratories' 2006 revenues. Conversely, Steve Jobs and Steve Wozniak, developers of the Apple I and Apple II computers, had little option other than to go into business themselves – the absence of proprietary technology ruled out licensing as an option.

The advantages of licensing are, first, that it relieves the company of the need to develop the full range of complementary resources and capabilities needed for commercialisation and, second, that it can allow the innovation to be commercialised quickly. If the lead-time offered by the innovation is short, multiple licensing can allow for a fast global rollout. The problem, however, is that the success of the innovation in the market is totally dependent on the commitment and effectiveness of the licensees. James Dyson, the British inventor of the bagless vacuum cleaner, created his own company to manufacture and market his 'dual cyclone' vacuum cleaners after failing to interest any major appliance company in a licensing deal for his technology.

RESOURCES AND CAPABILITIES OF THE FIRM   As Figure 6.4 shows, different strategies require very different resources and capabilities. Hence, the choice of how to exploit an innovation depends critically upon the resources and capabilities that the innovator brings to the party. Start-up firms possess few of the complementary resources and capabilities needed to commercialise their innovations. Inevitably they will be attracted to licensing or to accessing the resources of larger firms through outsourcing, alliances or joint ventures. In several industries we observe a sequential process of innovation where different stages are conducted by different types of firm. In biotechnology and electronics, technology is typically developed initially by a small, technology-intensive start-up, which then licenses to, or is acquired by, a larger established firm.

Conversely, large, established corporations, which can draw on their wealth of resources and capabilities, are better placed for internal commercialisation. Companies such as Sony, DuPont, Siemens, Hitachi and IBM have traditionally developed innovations internally – yet, as technologies evolve, converge and splinter, even these companies have increasingly resorted to joint ventures, strategic alliances and outsourcing arrangements to access technical capabilities outside their corporate boundaries.

Ron Adner observes that innovation increasingly requires coordinated responses by multiple companies. Innovating forms need to identify and map their innovation ecosystem, then manage the interdependencies within it. The failed introduction of HDTV can be attributed to inadequate coordination among TV manufacturers, production studios and broadcasters.[18] The initial slow take-up of e-readers could also be attributed to the lack of a coordinated response between device manufacturers and publishers.

TIMING INNOVATION: TO LEAD OR TO FOLLOW?   To gain competitive advantage in emerging and technologically intensive industries, is it best to be a leader or a follower in innovation? As Table 6.1 shows, the evidence is mixed: in some products the leader has been the first to grab the prize, in others the leader has succumbed to the risks and costs of pioneering. Optimal timing of entry into an emerging industry and the introduction of

Table 6.1 Leaders, followers, and success in emerging industries

Product	Innovator	Follower	The winner
Jet airliner	De Havilland (Comet)	Boeing (707)	Follower
Float glass	Pilkington	Corning	Leader
X-ray scanner	EMI	General Electric	Follower
Office PC	Xerox	IBM	Follower
VCRs	Ampex/Sony	Matsushita	Follower
Instant camera	Polaroid	Kodak	Leader
Pocket calculator	Bowmar	Texas Instruments	Follower
Microwave oven	Raytheon	Samsung	Follower
Fiber-optic cable	Corning	Many companies	Leader
Video games player	Atari	Nintendo/Sony	Followers
Disposable diaper	Procter & Gamble	Kimberley-Clark	Leader
Ink jet printer	IBM and Siemens	Hewlett Packard	Follower
Web browser	Netscape	Microsoft	Follower
MP3 music players	Diamond Multimedia	Apple (iPod)	Follower
Operating systems for mobile phones	Symbian	Microsoft	Leader
Laser printer	Xerox, IBM	Canon	Follower
Flash memory	Toshiba	Samsung, Intel	Followers
E-book reader	Sony (Digital Reader)	Amazon (Kindle)	Follower

Source: Based in Part on D. Teece, *the Competitive Challenge: Strategies for Industrial Innovation and Renewal* (Cambridge: Ballinger, 1987): 186–8.

new technology are complex issues. The advantage of being an early mover depends on the following factors:

1 *The extent to which innovation can be protected by property rights or lead-time advantages*. If an innovation is appropriable through a patent, copyright or lead-time advantage, there is advantage in being an early mover. This is especially the case where patent protection is important, as in pharmaceuticals. Notable patent

races include that between Alexander Graham Bell and Elisha Gray to patent the telephone (Bell got to the Patent Office a few hours before Gray),[19] and Celera Inc and the National Institutes of Health to patent the sequence of the human genome.[20]

2 *The importance of complementary resources.* The more important are complementary resources in exploiting an innovation, the greater the costs and risks of pioneering. Several firms – from Clive Sinclair with a battery-driven car to General Motors with a fuel-cell car – have already failed in their attempts to develop and market an electric car. The problem for the pioneer is that the development costs are huge because of the need to orchestrate multiple technologies and establish self-sufficiency across a range of business functions. Followers are also favoured by the fact that, as an industry develops, specialist firms emerge as suppliers of complementary resources. Thus, in pioneering the development of the British frozen foods industry, Unilever's Bird's Eye subsidiary had to set up an entire chain of cold stores

and frozen distribution facilities. Later entrants were able to rely on the services of public cold stores and refrigerated trucking companies.

3 *The potential to establish a standard.* As we shall see later in this chapter, some markets converge toward a technical standard. The greater the importance of technical standards, the greater the advantages of being an early mover in order to influence those standards and gain the market momentum needed to establish leadership. Once a standard has been set, displacing it becomes exceptionally difficult. IBM had little success with its OS/2 operating system against the entrenched position of Microsoft Windows. Linux has succeeded in taking market share from Windows, however, the main reason is that Linux is free!

Optimal timing depends also on the resources and capabilities that the individual firm has at its disposal. Different companies have different strategic windows – periods in time when their resources and capabilities are aligned with the opportunities available in the market. A small, technology-based firm may have no choice but to pioneer innovation: its opportunity is to grab first-mover advantage and then develop the necessary complementary resources before more powerful rivals appear. For the large, established firm with financial resources and strong production, marketing and distribution capabilities, the strategic window is likely to be both longer and later. The risks of pioneering are greater for an established firm with a reputation and brands to protect, while to exploit its complementary resources effectively typically requires a more developed market. Consider the following examples.

In personal computers, Apple was a pioneer, IBM a follower. The timing of entry was probably optimal for each. Apple's resources were its vision and its technology: only by pioneering could it hope to become a leading player. IBM had enormous strengths in manufacturing, distribution and reputation. It could build competitive advantage even without a clear technological advantage. The key for IBM was to delay its entry until the time when the market had developed to the point where IBM's strengths could have their maximum impact.

In the browser war between Netscape and Microsoft, Microsoft had the luxury of being able to follow the pioneer, Netscape. Microsoft's huge product development, marketing and distribution capabilities and – most important – its vast installed base of the Windows operating system allowed it to overhaul Netscape's initial lead.

Although General Electric entered the market for CT scanners some four years after EMI, GE was able to overtake EMI within a few years because of its ability to apply vast technological, manufacturing, sales and customer service capabilities within the field of medical electronics.

> The most effective follower strategies are those that initiate a new product's transition from niche market to mass market.

The most effective follower strategies are those that initiate a new product's transition from niche market to mass market. According to Markides and Geroski, successful first movers pioneer new products that embody new technologies and new functionality.[21] The opportunity for the fast-second entrant is to grow the niche market into a mass market by lowering cost and increasing quality. In the opening case we saw that Amazon's Kindle fulfilled this function and created momentum in the e-reader market. Timing is critical. Don Sull argues a successful follower strategy requires 'active waiting': a company needs to monitor market developments and assemble resources and capabilities while it prepares for large-scale market entry.[22]

Case Insight 6.2
How and when to enter the e-reader market

The opening case highlights the fact that lead innovators do not always gain competitive advantage in technologically intensive industries. Firms like Softbook Press, NuvoMedia and Gemstar found it difficult to establish a sustainable advantage even though they patented many of their ideas. It proved relatively easy for followers to circumvent these property rights and these early pioneers lacked the complementary resources, particularly the digital content, needed to gain critical mass quickly. Sony reinvigorated the market but it was Amazon as a fast follower that managed to transform what hitherto had been a niche market to one with more mass appeal. It is a matter of debate, whether in this context, Apple with its iPad was a follower or a leader. On the one hand, when Apple initially launched its iPad it positioned the product as an e-reader but the device had a much broader functionality than the e-readers on the market at that time and Apple is now referred to by many commentators as the first mover in tablet computing.[23]

Managing risks

Emerging industries are risky. There are two main sources of uncertainty:

- *Technological uncertainty* arises from the unpredictability of technological evolution and the complex dynamics through which technical standards and dominant designs are selected. Hindsight is always 20/20, but before the event it is difficult to predict how technologies and the industries that deploy them will evolve.

- *Market uncertainty* relates to the size and growth rates of the markets for new products. When Xerox introduced its first plain-paper copier in 1959, Apple its first personal computer in 1977, or Sony its Walkman in 1979, none had any idea of the size of the potential market. Forecasting

> When Xerox introduced its first plain-paper copier in 1959, Apple its first personal computer in 1977, or Sony its Walkman in 1979, none had any idea of the size of the potential market.

demand for new products is hazardous since all forecasting is based on some form of extrapolation or modelling based on past data. One approach is to use analogies.[24] Another is to draw on the combined insight and experience of a panel of experts.

If reliable forecasting is impossible, the keys to managing risk are alertness and responsiveness to emerging trends together with limiting vulnerability to mistakes through avoiding large-scale commitments. Useful strategies for limiting risk include:

- *Cooperating with lead users.* During the early phases of industry development, careful monitoring of and response to market trends and customer requirements

is essential to avoid major errors in technology and design. Von Hippel argues that lead users provide a source of leading market indicators, they can assist in developing new products and processes and offer an early cash flow to fund development expenditures.[25] In computer software, 'beta versions' are released to computer enthusiasts for testing. Nike has two sets of lead users: professional athletes who are trendsetters for athletic footwear and gang members and hip-hop artists who are at the leading edge of urban fashion trends. In communications and aerospace, government defence contracts play a crucial role in developing new technologies.[26]

- *Limiting risk exposure.* The financial risks of emerging industries can be mitigated by financial and operational practices that minimise a firm's exposure to adversity. By avoiding debt and keeping fixed costs low, a firm can lower its financial and operational gearing. Outsourcing and strategic alliance can also hold down capital investment and
fixed costs.

- *Flexibility.* Uncertainty necessitates rapid responses to unpredicted events. Achieving such flexibility means keeping options open and delaying commitment to a specific technology until its potential becomes clear. Large, well-resourced companies have the luxury of pursuing multiple strategic options.

Case Insight 6.3
Managing risks in the eBook market

Firms in the e-reader market face both technological and market uncertainty. On the technology side it is not clear what screen and power technologies will dominate; on the market side it remains to be seen how many consumers will decide to move away from the traditional, paper books and if they do, whether they will prefer to read the digital version on dedicated use (e-reader) or multiple use (e-tablet) devices. Google, as a late mover into the eBook market with the launch of its online book store, Google Editions, in 2011 has kept its options open. Google's digital books are stored on the cloud[27] and can, therefore, be accessed via the web using computers, smartphones or tablets. It also allows books to be downloaded in a variety of different formats to different readers. In line with its 'open' approach it is also intending to enter a series of partnership agreements with book retailers WH Smith and Blackwell to build a large digital library.

Competing for standards

In the previous chapter, we noted that the establishment of standards is a key event in industry evolution. The emergence of the digital, networked economy has made standards increasingly important and companies that own and influence industry standards are capable of earning returns that are unmatched by any other type of competitive advantage. The shareholder value generated by Microsoft and Intel from the 'Wintel' PC standard, by Qualcomm from its CDMA digital wireless communications technology and Cisco from its leadership role in setting internet protocol standards are examples of this potential. Table 6.2 lists several companies whose success is closely associated with their control of standards within a particular product category.

> Companies that own and influence industry standards are capable of earning returns that are unmatched by any other type of competitive advantage.

Types of standard

A **standard** is a format, an interface, or a system that allows interoperability. It is adherence to standards that allows us to browse millions of different web pages, that

Table 6.2 Examples of companies that own de facto industry standards

Company	Product category	Standard
Microsoft	PC operating systems	Windows
Intel	PC microprocessors	x86 series
Matsushita	Videocassette recorders	VHS system
Sony/Philips	Compact disks	CD-ROM format
ARM (Holdings)	Microprocessors for mobile devices	ARM architecture
Sun Microsystems	Programming language for web apps	Java
Rockwell and 3Com	56K modems	V90
Qualcomm	Digital cellular wireless communication	CDMA
Adobe Systems	Common file format for creating and viewing documents	Acrobat Portable Document Format
Bosch	Antilock braking systems	ABS and TCS (Traction Control System)
Symbian	Operating systems for mobile phones	Symbian OS
Sony	High definition DVD	Blu-ray

ensure the light bulbs made by any manufacturer will fit any manufacturer's lamps and that keep the traffic moving in Los Angeles (most of the time). Standards can be *public* or *private*.

● Public (or *open*) standards are those that are available to all either free or for a nominal charge. Typically they do not involve any privately owned intellectual property or the IP owners make access free (e.g. Linux). Public standards are set by public bodies and industry associations. Thus, the GSM mobile phone standard was set by the European Telecom Standards Institute. Internet protocols – standards governing internet addressing and routing – are mostly public. They are governed by several international bodies, including the Internet Engineering Task Force.

● Private (*proprietary*) standards are those where the technologies and designs are owned by companies or individuals. If I own the technology that becomes a standard, I can embody the technology in a product that others buy (Microsoft Windows) or license the technology to others who wish to use it (Qualcomm's CDMA).

Standards can also be classified according to who sets them. *Mandatory standards* are set by government and have the force of law behind them. They include standards relating to car safety and construction specifications and to TV broadcasting. *De facto standards* emerge through voluntary adoption by producers and users. Table 6.2 gives examples.

A problem with effective standards is that they may take a long time to emerge, resulting in duplication of investments and delayed development of the market. It was 40 years before a standard railroad gauge was agreed in the US.[28] The delayed emergence of a standard may kill a technology altogether. The failure of quadraphonic sound to displace stereophonic sound during the 1970s resulted from incompatible technical standards which inhibited audio manufacturers, record companies and consumers from investing in the technology.[29]

Why standards appear: network externalities

Standards emerge in markets that are subject to **network externalities**. A network externality exists whenever the value of a product to an individual customer depends on the number of other users of that product. The classic example of network externality is the telephone. Since there is little satisfaction to be gained from talking to oneself on the telephone, the value of a telephone to each user depends on the number of other users connected to the same telephone system. This is different from most products. When one of the authors pours himself a glass of Glenlivet after teaching a couple of exhausting classes, his enjoyment is independent of how many other people in the world are also drinking Glenlivet. Indeed, some products may have *negative* network externalities – the value of the product is less if many other people purchase the same product. If a professor spends £3000 on an Armani dress and finds that another female colleague at the faculty Christmas party is wearing the same garment, her satisfaction is significantly reduced.

Network externalities do not require everyone to use the same product or even the same technology, but rather that the different products are *compatible* with one another through some form of common interface. In the case of wireless telephone service, it does not matter (as far as network access is concerned) whether the customer purchases service from Orange or T-Mobile because compatibility between each network allows connectivity. Similarly with railways, if a company is transporting coal from a mine to a power station, their choice of rail company is not critical, as unlike in the 1800s, the whole railway now uses a standard gauge.

> Network externalities do not require everyone to use the same product or even the same technology, but rather that the different products are *compatible* with one another through some form of common interface.

Network externalities arise from several sources:

- *Products where users are linked to a network.* Telephones, railways and email instant messaging groups are networks where users are linked together. Applications software, whether spreadsheet programs or video games, also link users – they can share files and play games interactively. User-level externalities may also arise through social identification. You might watch CSI or the Oscar ceremony on TV not because you enjoy them, but so that you have something to talk to colleagues about at work or at university.[30]

- *Availability of complementary products and services.* Where products are consumed as systems, the availability of complementary products and services depends on the number of customers for that system. Apple's key problem in the computer market is that, because the Macintosh accounts for only 9% of the installed base of personal computers, few leading software firms are writing Mac-based applications. You may choose to drive a Ford Focus rather than a Ferrari Testarossa because you know that, should you break down 200 miles from the nearest town, spare parts and a repair service will be more readily available.

- *Economising on switching costs.* By purchasing the product or system that is most widely used, there is less chance that I shall have to bear the costs of switching. By using Microsoft Office rather than Apple iWork, it is more likely that we will avoid the costs of retraining and file conversion when we become visiting professors at other universities.

The implication of network externalities is that they create **positive feedback**. Once a technology or system gains market leadership, it attracts a growing proportion of new buyers. Conversely, once market leadership is lost, a downward spiral is likely. This process is called **tipping**: once a certain threshold is reached, cumulative forces become unstoppable.[31] The result is a tendency toward a *winner-takes-all* market. The markets subject to significant network externalities tend to be dominated by a single supplier (Microsoft in PC operating systems and office applications, eBay in internet auctions).

Once established, technical and design standards tend to be highly resilient. Standards are difficult to displace due to learning effects and collective lock-in. Learning effects cause the dominant technology and design to be continually improved and refined. Even where the existing standard is inherently inferior, switching to a superior technology may not occur because of collective lock-in. The classic case is the QWERTY typewriter layout. Its 1873 design was based on the need to *slow* the speed of typing to prevent typewriter keys from jamming. Although the jamming problem was soon solved, the QWERTY layout has persisted, despite the patenting in 1932 of the more ergonomic Dvorak Simplified Keyboard (DSK).[32]

Winning standards wars

In markets subject to network externalities, control over standards is the primary basis for competitive advantage. Sony and Apple are unusual in that they lost their standards wars (in VCRs and personal computers, respectively) but returned as winners in other markets. Most of the losers in standards wars – Lotus in spreadsheet software, Netscape in browsers, WordPerfect in word processing software – become mere footnotes in the history of technology. What can we learn from these and other standards wars about designing a winning strategy in markets subject to network externalities?

The first key issue is to determine whether we are competing in a market that will converge around a single technical standard. This requires a careful analysis of the presence and sources of network externalities.

The second strategic issue in standards setting is recognising the role of positive feedback: the technology that can establish early leadership will rapidly gain momentum. Building a 'bigger bandwagon', according to Shapiro and Varian,[33] requires the following:

- *Before you go to war, assemble allies.* You'll need the support of consumers, suppliers of complements, even your competitors. Not even the strongest companies can afford to go it alone in a standards war.

- *Pre-empt the market.* Enter early, achieve fast-cycle product development, make early deals with key customers and adopt penetration pricing.

- *Manage expectations.* The key to managing positive feedback is to convince customers, suppliers and the producers of complementary goods that you will emerge as the victor. These expectations become a self-fulfilling prophecy. The massive pre-launch promotion and publicity built up by Sony prior to the American and European launch of PlayStation 2 in October 2000 was an effort to convince consumers, retailers and game developers that the product would be the blockbuster consumer electronics product of the new decade, thereby upsetting Sega and Nintendo's efforts to establish their rival systems.

> The key to managing positive feedback is to convince customers, suppliers and the producers of complementary goods that you will emerge as the victor.

The lesson that has emerged from the classic standards battles of the past is that in order to create initial leadership and maximise positive feedback effects, a company must share the value created by the technology with other parties (customers, competitors, complementors and suppliers). If a company attempts to appropriate too great a share of the value created, it may well fail to build a big enough bandwagon to gain market leadership. Thus, recent standards battles involve broad alliances, where the owner enlists the support of complementors and would-be competitors. In the 2006–8 struggle between Sony (Blu-ray) and Toshiba (HD-DVD) each camp recruited movie studios, software firms and producers of computers and consumer electronics using various inducements – including direct cash payments. The defection of Warner Brothers to the Sony camp was critical to the market tipping suddenly in Sony's favour. However, it appears that all the financial gains from owning the winner DVD standard were dissipated by the costs of the war.[34]

Achieving compatibility with existing products is a critical issue in standards battles. Advantage typically goes to the competitor that adopts an **evolutionary strategy** (i.e. offers backward compatibility) rather than one that adopts a **revolutionary strategy**.[35] Microsoft Windows won the PC war against the Apple Macintosh for many reasons. Both companies offered an operating system with a graphical user interface. However, while Windows was designed for compatibility with the DOS operating system, the Apple Mac was incompatible both with DOS and the Apple II. Similarly, a key advantage of the Sony PlayStation 2 over the Sega Dreamcast and Nintendo Cube was its compatibility with the PlayStation 1.

What are the key resources needed to win a standards war? Shapiro and Varian emphasise the following:

- control over an installed base of customers;

- owning intellectual property rights in the new technology;

- the ability to innovate in order to extend and adapt the initial technological advance;

- first-mover advantage;

- strength in complements (e.g. Intel has preserved its standard in microprocessors by promoting standards in buses, chipsets, graphics controllers and interfaces between motherboards and CPUs);

- reputation and brand name.[36]

As companies become more familiar with the dynamics of standards competition, they are launching their strategic initiatives earlier – long before product release dates. As a result, standards wars are increasingly about the management of expectations. Companies are also more alert to the emergence of tipping points. As a result, standards wars are being resolved quicker: in high definition DVDs a mere 19 months elapsed between Toshiba's launch of its HD-DVD and its withdrawal announcement.

Case Insight 6.4
Winning standards battles

As anyone who has tried to download an eBook will know, compatibility issues remain a source of frustration for consumers wishing to download digital content to their e-readers and for publishers who are required to provide content in a range of different formats. The majority of e-readers are designed to work with their own proprietary eBook formats and as e-readers have gained in popularity so new formats have emerged and proliferated. The lack of standardisation is reflected in the plethora of different file extensions associated with digital text, for example Sony initially used the format .lrx, (moving later to ePub) whilst Amazon uses .azw and iPad's is supported by the iBooks app. In addition to the proprietary e-reader formats, software has been developed by major software companies that is not specific to particular devices, for example Adobe's .pdf format. Nucci[37] described the situation of the e-reader market as follows: 'imagine having to decide which CD player to buy based not only on features and price but also on what music you'd be able to play on it. Music labels would publish music in one or more formats and pay commissions to the CD player manufacturers based on the sales of each CD issued in its format. If you didn't own the device(s) that supported discs by your favourite artist you'd be out of luck'.

Whilst the major players have recognised the problem, a common format has yet to emerge either *de facto* or by agreement. The International Digital Publishing Forum (www.idpf.org), a trade and standards association for digital publishing, has developed and maintained a voluntary standard called EPub. Whilst a number of reading devices support EPub in addition to their own proprietary formats, there has been no large-scale convergence towards this standard. Instead there have been numerous 'apps' developed for the market that can be downloaded free of charge which allow readers to convert content from one format to another. The existence of these 'converters' may mean that a standard format is slow to emerge or that the industry will continue to support a variety of different standards.

Creating the conditions for innovation

Our analysis so far has taught us about the potential for generating competitive advantage from innovation and about the design of technology-based strategies, but has said little about the conditions under which innovation is achieved. The danger is that strategic analysis can tell us a great deal about making money out of innovation, but this isn't much use if we cannot generate innovation in the first place. While innovation requires certain resources – people, facilities, information and time – there is no predetermined relationship between R&D input and innovation output.[38] Clearly the productivity of R&D depends heavily on the organisational conditions that foster innovation. Hence, the crucial challenge facing firms in emerging and technology-based industries is to create the conditions conducive to innovation.

> While invention depends on creativity, innovation requires collaboration and cross-functional integration.

To address this question, we must return to the critical distinction between invention and innovation. While these activities are complementary, they require different resources and different organisational conditions. While invention depends on creativity, innovation requires collaboration and cross-functional integration.

Managing creativity

Invention is an act of creativity requiring knowledge and imagination. The creativity that drives invention is typically an individual act that establishes a meaningful relationship between concepts or objects that had not previously been related. This reconceptualising can be triggered by accidents: an apple falling on Isaac Newton's head or James Watt observing a kettle boiling. Creativity is associated with particular personality traits. Creative people tend to be curious, imaginative, adventurous, assertive, playful, self-confident, risk taking, reflective and uninhibited.[39]

Individual creativity also depends on the organisational environment in which people work – this is as true for the researchers and engineers at Amgen and Google as it was for the painters and sculptors of the Florentine and Venetian schools. Few great works of art or outstanding inventions are the products of solitary geniuses. Creativity is stimulated by human interaction: the productivity of R&D laboratories depends critically on the communication networks that the engineers and scientists establish.[40] An important catalyst of interaction is *play*, which creates an environment of enquiry, liberates thought from conventional constraints and provides the opportunity to establish new relationships by rearranging ideas and structures at a safe distance from reality. The essence of play is that it permits unconstrained forms of experimentation.[41] The potential for low-cost experimentation has expanded vastly thanks to advances in

Featured example 6.1 Using 3D printing to stimulate creativity

Engineers and designers have been using 3D printers for more than a decade to create prototypes and designs for new products but recent innovations are making these technologies cheaper to use and more widely available. 3D printing is much like printing a document from a computer file but instead of ink the printer deposits successive layers of thin material onto a tray and gradually builds a solid object by fusing the deposited material with a laser or electronic beam. These printers can now work with a wide range of materials including industrial grade plastics and metals which can be used to make objects quickly and cheaply. This technology is being used by firms in sectors as diverse as aerospace, jewellery, orthodontics, mobile phones and football boots. Perhaps one of the most exciting aspects of the technology, however, is the possibilities it opens up to experiment and play with ideas. A would-be entrepreneur could run off one or two prototypes to see if her ideas work and could adjust the design based on feedback.[43]

computer modelling and simulation that permit prototyping and market research to be undertaken speedily and virtually.[42]

ORGANISING FOR CREATIVITY Creativity requires management systems that are quite different from those appropriate for efficiency. In particular, creatively oriented people tend to be responsive to distinctive types of incentive. They desire to work in an egalitarian culture with enough space and resources to provide the opportunity to be spontaneous, experience freedom and have fun in the performance of a task that, they feel, makes a difference to the strategic performance of the firm. Praise, recognition and opportunities for education and professional growth are also more important than assuming managerial responsibilities.[44] Nurturing the drive to create may require a degree of freedom and flexibility that conflicts with conventional HR practices. At Google, engineers have considerable discretion as to which project to join.

Organisational environments conducive to creativity tend to be both nurturing and competitive. Creativity requires a work context that is secure but not cosy. Dorothy Leonard points to the merits of **creative abrasion** within innovative teams – fostering innovation through the interaction of different personalities and perspectives. Managers must resist the temptation to clone in favour of embracing diversity of cognitive and

Table 6.3 The characteristics of 'operating' and 'innovating' organizations

	Operating organization	Innovating organization
Structure	Bureaucratic. Specialization and division of labor. Hierarchical control. Defined organizational boundaries.	Flat organization without hierarchical control. Task-oriented project teams. Fuzzy organizational boundaries.
Processes	Emphasis on eliminating variation (e.g. six-sigma). Top-down control. Tight financial controls.	Emphasis on enhancing variation. Loose controls to foster idea generation. Flexible strategic planning and financial control.
Reward systems	Financial compensation, promotion up the hierarchy, power, and status symbols.	Autonomy, recognition, equity participation in new ventures
People	Recruitment and selection based on the needs of the organization structure for specific skills: functional and staff specialists, general managers, and operatives.	Key need is for idea generators that combine required technical knowledge with creative personality traits. Managers must act as sponsors and orchestrators.

Source: Based on J. K. Galbraith and R. K. Kazanjian, *Strategy Implementation: Structure, Systems and Processes,* 2nd Edn (St. Paul, Mn: West, 1986).

behavioural characteristics within work groups – creating *'whole brain teams.'*[45] Exploiting diversity may require constructive conflict. Microsoft's development team meetings are renowned for open criticism and intense disagreement. Such conflict can spur progress towards better solutions.

Table 6.3 contrasts some characteristics of innovative organisations compared with those designed for operational efficiency.

From invention to innovation: the challenge of integration

BALANCING CREATIVITY AND COMMERCIAL DIRECTION For creativity to create value – both for the company and for society – it must be directed and harnessed. Balancing creative freedom with discipline and integration is a key issue of companies such as Apple and Google, who position themselves on the leading edge of innovation. The problem is especially acute in media companies: 'The two cultures – of the ponytail and the suit – are a world apart and combustible together.'[46] Many creative companies have been formed by frustrated innovators leaving established companies. Disney's 2006 acquisition of Pixar was motivated by its desire to reinvigorate its animated movies. Yet Pixar's John Lasseter, who was appointed creative head of Disney's animation studio, had been fired from Disney 20 years earlier for his advocacy of computer animation![47] Conversely, HBO's remarkable run of successful TV series between 1999 and 2007 (*The*

Featured example 6.2 Being creative in orthodontics

In 2001 Chishti and Wirth, two Stanford University MBA graduates, came up with a new system for realigning teeth. Their Invisalign system involved patients wearing a series of clear plastic retainers rather than metal braces to realign teeth. The original idea came from Chishti who had undergone conventional orthodontic treatment and found metal braces to be both unattractive and uncomfortable. The orthodontist takes dental impressions and X-rays and sends them to the Invisalign company who through the use of 3D computer modelling creates sets of retainers that move teeth to the final position recommended by the orthodontist. This technique has proved very popular, particularly with adults who want to avoid the look of metal braces. The system does, however, have strategic implications because the technology, in part, substitutes capital (computer systems operated by staff who do not require training in dentistry) for skilled labour (orthodontists) and changes the cost structure of this business.

Sopranos, Sex in the City, The Wire and *Six Feet Under*) reveals a remarkable ability to mesh creativity with commercial acuity.

> The critical linkage between creative flair and commercial success is market need.

The critical linkage between creative flair and commercial success is market need. Few important inventions have been the result of spontaneous creation by technologists; almost all have resulted from grappling with practical problems.

The old adage that 'necessity is the mother of invention' explains why customers are such fertile sources of innovation – they are most acutely involved with matching existing products and services to their needs.[48] Involving customers in the innovation process is an initial stage in the move towards open innovation (described in more detail below).

ORGANISATIONAL APPROACHES TO THE MANAGEMENT OF INNOVATION

Creative activities require different organisational structures and management systems than operational activities. Yet, the commercialisation of new technology – developing and introducing new products and implementing new processes – requires the integration of creativity and technological expertise with capabilities in production, marketing, finance, distribution and customer support. Achieving such integration is difficult. Tension between the operating and the innovating parts of organisations is inevitable. Innovation upsets established routines and threatens the status quo. The more stable the operating and administrative side of the organisation, the greater the resistance to innovation. A classic example was the opposition by the US naval establishment to continuous-aim firing, a process that offered huge improvements in gunnery accuracy.[49]

As innovation has become an increasing priority for established corporations, so chief executives have sought to emulate the flexibility, creativity and entrepreneurial spirit of technology-based start-ups. Organisational initiatives aimed at stimulating new product development and the exploitation of new technologies include the following:

- *Cross-functional product development teams.* Cross-functional product development teams have proven to be highly effective mechanisms for integrating creativity with functional effectiveness. Conventional approaches to new product development involved a sequential process that began in the corporate research lab then went 'over the wall' to engineering, manufacturing, finance and so on. Japanese companies pioneered autonomous product development teams staffed by specialists seconded from different departments with leadership from a 'heavyweight' team manager who was able to protect the team from undue corporate influence.[50] Such teams have proven effective in deploying a broad range of specialist knowledge and, most importantly, integrating that knowledge flexibility quickly – e.g. through rapid prototyping and concurrent engineering.[51]

- *Product champions* provide a means, first, for incorporating individual creativity within organisational processes and, second, for linking invention to subsequent commercialisation. The key is to permit individuals who are sources of creative ideas to lead the teams which develop those ideas – but also to allow this leadership to continue through into the commercialisation phases. Companies that are consistently successful in innovation have the ability to design organisational processes that capture, direct and exploit individuals' drive for achievement and success and their commitment to their innovations. The rationale for creating product champions is that these committed individuals can overcome resistance to change within the organisation and generate enthusiasm that attracts involvement of others and forges cross-functional integration. Schön's study of 15 major innovations concluded that: 'the new idea either finds a champion or dies'.[52] A British study of 43 matched pairs of successful and unsuccessful innovations similarly concluded that a key factor distinguishing successful innovation was the presence of a 'business innovator' to exert entrepreneurial leadership.[53] 3M Corporation has a long tradition of using product champions to develop new product ideas and grow them into new businesses.

> Companies that are consistently successful in innovation have the ability to design organisational processes that capture, direct and exploit individuals' drive for achievement and success and their commitment to their innovations.

Featured example 6.3 Innovation at 3M – the role of the product champion

Start little and build

We don't look to the president or the vice president for R&D to say, all right, on Monday morning 3M is going to get into such-and-such a business. Rather, we prefer to see someone in one of our laboratories, or marketing or manufacturing units bring forward a new idea that he's been thinking about. Then, when he can convince people around him, including his supervisor, that he's got something interesting, we'll make him what we call a 'project manager' with a small budget of money and talent and let him run with it. Throughout all our 60 years of history here, that has been the mark of success. Did you develop a new business? The incentive? Money, of course. But that's not the key. The key . . . is becoming the general manager of a new business . . . having such a hot project that management just has to become involved whether it wants to or not (Bob Adams, vice-president for R&D, 3M Corporation).

Scotchlite

Someone asked the question, 'Why didn't 3M make glass beads, because glass beads were going to find increasing use on the highways?' . . . I had done a little working in the mineral department on trying to color glass beads and had learned a little about their reflecting properties. And, as a little extra-curricular activity, I'd been trying to make luminous house numbers.

Well, this question and my free-time lab project combined to stimulate me to search out where glass beads were being used on the highway. We found a place where beads had been sprinkled on the highway and we saw that they did provide a more visible line at night . . . From there, it was only natural for us to conclude that, since we were a coating company and probably knew more than anyone else about putting particles onto a web, we ought to be able to coat glass beads very accurately on a piece of paper.

So, that's what we did. The first reflective tape we made was simply a double-coated tape – glass beads sprinkled on one side and an adhesive on the other. We took some out here in St. Paul and, with the cooperation of the highway department, put some down. After the first frost came and then a thaw, we found we didn't know as much about adhesives under all weather conditions as we thought . . .

We looked around inside the company for skills in related areas. We tapped knowledge that existed in our sandpaper business on how to make waterproof sandpaper. We drew on the expertise of our roofing people who knew something about exposure. We reached into our adhesive and tape division to see how we could make the tape stick to the highway better.

The resulting product became known as 'Scotchlite'. Its principal application was in reflective signs; only later did 3M develop the market for highway marking. The originator of the product, Harry Heltzer, interested the head of the New Products Division in the product and he encouraged Heltzer to go out and sell it. Scotchlite was a success and Heltzer became the general manager of the division set up to produce and market it.

Source: 'The technical strategy of 3M: start more little businesses and more little businesses', *Innovation* no. 5 (1969).

- *Buying innovation.* Recognition that small, technology-intensive start-ups have advantages in the early stages of the innovation process, while large corporations have superior capabilities, has encouraged large companies to enhance their technological performance by acquiring innovation from other firms. Such acquisition may involve licensing, outright purchase of patents or acquiring the whole company. In biotechnology, pharmaceutical companies have pioneered this outsourcing of innovation. In addition to licensing drug patents, signing marketing agreements and acquiring specialist biotech firms (these include Genentech by Roche in 2009, ICOS by Eli Lily in 2007, Chiron by Novartis in 2006, Scious by Johnson & Johnson in 2003), pharmaceutical companies have formed research alliances with biotech specialists.[54] In our opening case we noted a number of similar moves in the e-reader market, for example, with Google's acquisition of eBook Technologies. Similarly Amazon's has acquired Mobipocket.com, a French software company that produces publishing and reading tools for handheld devices.[55]

- *Open innovation.* The shift from vertically integrated systems of innovation where companies develop their own technologies in-house, then exploit them internally, to more market-based systems where companies buy in technology while also licensing out their own technologies, has given way to ideas of **open innovation**. As innovation increasingly requires the integration of multiple technologies often from traditionally separate scientific areas, so firms have been forced to look wider in their sourcing technology and in sharing knowhow and ideas. Evidence

Featured example 6.4 Procter & Gamble's open innovation initiative

In 2000 it became clear that P&G's internally focused approach to innovation and new product develop was incapable of delivering the growth targets that the company had set itself. Despite a research staff numbering 7500 P&G estimated that for every one of its own research scientists there were probably 200 outside the company with the potential to contribute to P&G's development efforts. When CEO A. G. Laffey challenged the company to acquire 50% of its innovations from outside the company, the quest for a new innovation model began.

P&G's *Connect and Develop* innovation model seeks to 'identify promising ideas throughout the world and apply our own R&D, manufacturing, marketing and purchasing capabilities to them to create better and cheaper products, faster'.

The starting point is to identify what P&G is looking for. The approach was to avoid 'blue sky' innovation and seek ideas that had already been successfully embodied in a product, a prototype or a technology. To focus the search, each business was asked to identify its top 10 customer needs. These included: 'reduce wrinkles, improve skin texture and tone . . . softer paper products with higher wet strength'. These needs were then translated into specific technical requirements, e.g. biotechnology solutions that permit detergents to perform well at low temperatures. Priorities are then reordered by identifying initiatives which fit with existing areas of brand strength ('adjacencies') and those which permit strengthening of P&G's strategically important areas of technology ('technology game boards').

P&G's innovation network comprises a number of organisations:

- Within P&G, 70 *technology entrepreneurs* are responsible for developing external contacts and exploring for innovation in particular localities and with a focus around a particular product or technology area.

- *Suppliers.* P&G has an IT platform that allows it to share technology briefs with its suppliers. This is complemented by regular meetings between senior P&G executives and senior executives at individual suppliers which explore mutual development opportunities.

- *Technology brokers.* P&G is a member (in some cases a founder member) of serial prominent technology brokering networks. These include *NineSigma* which links companies with universities, private labs, government bodies, consultants and other potential solutions providers; *Innocentive* which brokers solutions to science-based problems; *YourEncore* a network of retired scientists and engineers; and *Yet2.com* an online marketplace for intellectual capital.

These networks generate an enormous flow of suggestions and proposals that are initially screened and disseminated through P&G's *Eureka* online catalogue. It is then up to executives within the business groups to identify interesting proposals, to pursue these with the external provider through P&G's External Business Development group and to then move the initiative into their own product development process.

By 2005, 35% of P&G's new product launches had their origins outside the company. Some of P&G's most successful new products – including Swiffer cleaning cloths, Olay Regeneration and Crest Spinbrush – had been initiated by outsiders.

Source: L. Huston and N. Sakkab, 'Connect and develop: inside Procter & Gamble's new model for innovation', *Harvard Business Review* (March 2006): 58–66. Reproduced by permission of Harvard Business Publishing.

that external linkages promote innovation has reinforced firms' desire to seek technological knowledge from beyond their own borders.[56] Open innovation requires creating a network of collaborative relationships that comprises licensing deals, component outsourcing, joint research, collaborative product development and informal problem solving and exchanges of ideas. The following example outlines Procter & Gamble's approach to open innovation.

● *Corporate incubators* are business developments established to fund and nurture new businesses, based upon technologies that have been developed internally, but have limited applications within a company's established businesses. **Corporate incubators** became very popular during the IT boom at the end of the 1990s when companies saw the potential to generate substantial value from establishing then spinning off new tech-based ventures.[57] Despite a sound strategic and organisational logic, few major companies have achieved sustained success from the incubator units that they established and among the successful ones, many have been sold to venture capital firms. A key problem, according to Gary Hamel is that: 'Many corporate incubators became orphanages for unloved ideas that had no internal support or in-house sponsorship'.[58] Despite their uneven track record, several leading companies have experienced considerable success in introducing company-wide processes for developing new businesses based upon internally generated innovations. The below example outlines the approaches of IBM and Cisco Systems.

Featured example 6.5 Incubating innovation at IBM and Cisco systems

IBM uses *Innovation Jam* – a massive online brainstorming process – to generate, select and develop new business ideas. The 2006 Jam was based upon an initial identification of 25 technology clusters grouped into six broad categories. Websites were built for each technology cluster and for a 72-hour period IBM employees, their families and friends, suppliers and customers from all around the world were invited to contribute ideas for innovations based on these technologies. The 150,000 participants generated vast and diverse sets of suggestions that were subject to text-mining software and review by 50 senior executives and technical specialists who worked in nine separate teams to identify promising ideas. The next phase of the Jam subjected the selected innovation ideas to comments and review by the online community. This was followed by a further review process in which the 10 best proposals were selected and a budget of $100 million was allocated to their development. The selected business included a real-time foreign language translation service, smart healthcare payment systems, IT applications to environmental projects and 3D internet. The new businesses were begun as incubator projects and were then transferred to one or other of IBM's business groups. As well as divisional links, the new ventures were also subject to monthly review by IBM's corporate top management.

Cisco Systems created its *Emerging Technology Business Group* with the goal of creating 20 new ventures by 2012. Within 18 months, 400 ideas for new businesses had been posted on the Cisco wiki and the Emerging Technology Business Group had begun developing several of these suggestions including *TelePresence*, a video surveillance security system and an IP interoperability and collaboration systems server for emergency services. By 2008, *TelePresence* was established as a regular business group. Like IBM's *Innovation Jam,* a key feature of Cisco's incubator model is its close linkage with the rest of the company: the emerging technology group is part of Cisco's R&D organisation and is subject to close involvement by Cisco's senior management – including CEO John Chambers.

Sources: O. M. Bjelland and R.C. Wood, 'An inside view of IBM's Innovation Jam', *MIT Sloan Management Review* (Fall 2008): 32–43. Tom Sanders, 'Cisco reinvents the corporate incubator' (27 July 2007), www.vnunet.com/vnunet/news/2194961/cisco-reinvents-corporate.

Summary

In emerging and technology-based industries, nurturing and exploiting innovation is the fundamental source of competitive advantage and the focus of strategy formulation. Yet the basic tools of strategy analysis are the same as those that we have already encountered in this book. The fundamental strategic issues we are concerned with are the drivers of competition in these markets, in resources and capabilities through which a firm can establish competitive advantage and the design of structures and systems to implement strategy.

Yet, the unpredictability and instability of these industries mean that strategic decisions in technology-driven industries have a very special character. The remarkable dynamics of these industries mean that difference between massive value creation and ignominious failure may be the result of small errors of timing or technological choices.

It is in these industries that traditional approaches to strategy based upon forecasting and detailed planning are so obviously inadequate. The combination of speed and unpredictability of change means that effective strategies are those which combine clarity of vision with flexibility and responsiveness. The companies that have succeeded in emerging and technology-based industries are those which recognised most clearly the strategic characteristics of their industries and adapted most effectively to them. In industries that have been turned upside-down by technological change – whether telecommunications equipment, medical imaging, information storage or sports equipment – it is companies that have understood the sources of competitive advantage and assembled the resources and capabilities needed to exploit them that have emerged as winners.

We hope to have persuaded you that, despite the turbulence and uncertainty of these industries, there are analytic principles that can guide us towards strategies which, although they do not guarantee us success, certainly improve the odds. For example, our learning has included:

- evaluating an innovation's potential to generate profit;
- assessing the relative merits of licensing, alliances, joint ventures and internal development as alternative strategies for exploiting an innovation;
- identifying the factors that determine the comparative advantages of being a leader or a follower in innovation.

This chapter also pointed to the central importance of strategy implementation in determining success, a theme we return to in Chapter 9. The key to successful innovation is not resource allocation decisions, but creating the structure, integration mechanisms and organisational climate conducive to innovation. Strategies aimed at the exploitation of innovation, choices of whether to be a leader or a follower and the management of risk must take careful account of organisational characteristics.

Technology-based industries also reveal some of the dilemmas that are a critical feature of strategic management in complex organisations and complex business environments. For example, technology-based industries are unpredictable, yet some investments in technology have time horizons of a decade or more. Successful strategies must be responsive to changing market conditions, but successful strategies also require long-term commitment. The fundamental dilemma is that innovation is an unpredictable process that requires creating a nurturing organisational context, whereas strategy is about resource-allocation decisions. How can a company create the conditions for nurturing innovation while planning the course of its development? John Scully, a former CEO of Apple, observed: 'Management and creativity might even be considered antithetical [mutually contrasting] states. While management demands consensus, control, certainty and the status quo, creativity thrives on the opposite: instinct, uncertainty, freedom and iconoclasm'.[59]

Fortunately, the experiences of companies such as 3M, Cisco Systems, Google and Nintendo point to solutions to these dilemmas. The need for innovation to reconcile individual creativity with coordination points towards the advantages of cross-functional team-based approaches over the isolation of R&D in a separate 'creative' environment. Moreover, the need to reconcile innovation with efficiency points towards the advantage of parallel organisational structures where, in addition to the 'formal' structure geared to the needs of existing businesses and products, an informal structure exists, which is the source of new products and businesses. The role of top management in balancing creativity with order and innovation with efficiency becomes critical – such reconciliation requires senior executives who are not necessarily experts in technology, but certainly literate in it to the point of appreciating its strategic implications.

The increasing pace of technological change and intensifying international competition suggests that the advanced, industrialised countries will be forced to rely increasingly on their technological capabilities as the basis for international competitiveness. Strategies for promoting innovation and managing technology will become more important in the future.

Summary table

Learning Objectives	Summary
Analyse how technology affects industry structure and competition	Technological change often changes industry dynamics, altering amongst other things cost structures, models of revenue generation, rivalry, entry barriers and the relative bargaining strength of buyers and suppliers. Firms that succeed in technologically intensive industries recognise the strategic characteristic of their markets and adapt effectively

Identify the factors that determine the returns to innovation and evaluate the potential for an innovation to establish competitive advantage	Four factors are critical in determining the extent to which innovators are able to appropriate the value of their innovation: property rights, the tacitness and complexity of the technology, lead-time and complementary resources
Formulate strategies for exploiting innovation and managing technology, focusing in particular on: – the relative advantages of being a leader or a follower in innovation – identifying and evaluating strategic options for exploiting innovation – how to win standards battles – how to manage risk	The choice of strategy to exploit innovation depends on the characteristics of the innovation and the resources and capabilities of the firm. Deciding on the optimal strategy is complex but we have reviewed a range of analytical principles that improve the chances of success
Design the organisational conditions needed to implement such strategies successfully	Organising for innovation requires different organisational structures and management systems than mainstream operational activities. We have considered a range of approaches and practices that enhance creativity and the likelihood of innovation success

Further reading

David Teece's 1986 article – 'Profiting from technological innovation', *Research Policy* 15(6) 285–305 – remains a seminal work in this area and he has followed this more recently with an article written with Gary Pisano:

> Pisano, G. and Teece, D. (2007). How to capture value from innovation: shaping intellectual property and industry architecture. *California Management Review*, 50(1): 278–96.

Shapiro and Varian provide an excellent exposition of the strategic issues surrounding the establishment of standards and the routes to success in standards wars in:

> Shapiro, C. and Varian, H. (1999). The art of standards wars. *California Management Review*, 41(2), 8–32.

In an article published in 2008 Teresa Amabile and Mukti Khaire report on a two-day colloquium held at Harvard Business School with invited leaders from businesses whose success depends on creativity and scholars specialising in the study of creativity. Their conclusions from this event are written up in the following article:

> Amabile, T. and Khaire, M. (2008). Creativity and the role of the leader. *Harvard Business Review*, October, 101–9.

Visit your enhanced ebook at **www.foundationsofstrategy.com** for self test quiz questions

QUIZ

Self-study questions

1   Trevor Baylis, a British inventor, submitted a patent application in November 1992 for a wind-up radio for use in Africa in areas where there was no electricity supply and people were too poor to afford batteries. He was excited by the prospects for radio broadcasts as a means of disseminating health education in areas of Africa devastated by AIDS. After appearances on British and South African TV, Baylis attracted a number of entrepreneurs and companies interested in manufacturing and marketing his clockwork radio. However, Bayliss was concerned by the fact that his patent provided only limited protection for his invention: most of the main components – a clockwork generator and transistor radio – were long-established technologies. What advice would you offer Baylis as to how he can best protect and exploit his invention?

2   There have been several efforts to develop 3D printers suitable for desk-top use by individual households. What are the main risks facing a start-up company intending to develop such a product?

3   From the evidence presented in Table 6.1 what conclusions can you draw regarding the factors that determine whether leaders or followers win out in the markets for new products?

4   In the battle for dominance of the e-reader market, Amazon with Kindle 2 was ahead of Sony with its Reader Digital Book. Kindle 2 had the biggest number of recent titles available, but Sony had a huge number of out-of-copyright titles. What are the sources of network externalities in this market? Will eBook readers become a winner-take-all market? Why has Amazon been able to gain a lead over Sony (and Samsung)? What can Sony do to fight back?

Visit your enhanced ebook at **www.foundationsofstrategy.com** for key term flashcards

GLOSSARY

Closing case Nespresso

Nespresso is the brand name of a coffee brewing system developed in the late 1970s by Nestlé, the multinational food company founded and headquartered in Switzerland. Nespresso allows consumers to brew high-quality coffee at the push of a button by placing hermetically sealed, aluminium covered, coffee capsules into a specially designed machine. Whilst the idea sounds simple, the technology behind Nespresso is, in fact, complex because it requires air and water to be passed through ground coffee at the right temperature and pressure. At the time of its development Nespresso constituted a major departure for Nestlé from its core

operations that were based on the large-scale production and mass marketing of food products. In the late 1970s Nestlé's presence in the coffee market centred on instant coffees with products like Nescafé accounting for 80% of its revenue from coffee sales.

The early development

The original technology underpinning Nespresso was developed by the Battelle Institute, an independent research organisation based in Geneva[60] but Nestlé acquired the rights to develop the idea commercially in 1974 and reportedly went on to file more than 70 patents on the product.[61] Camillo Pagano, who was at that time the senior executive in charge, felt that the product had potential. Overall sales in the coffee market were sluggish but the gourmet coffee market was beginning to expand. Nestlé also wished to strengthen its position in the restaurant market and Nespresso was positioned initially as a product for that market. Many of Pagano's colleagues were sceptical about the innovation, questioning whether Nespresso could be commercialised and the amount of time and effort that would be taken up in launching a niche product that appeared to have a poor fit with Nestlé's mainstream operations. Pagano felt that in order to flourish the Nespresso project needed to be taken outside Nestlé's day-to-day operations so, in 1984, he established Nespresso as a separate company (100% owned by Nestlé) which was free to develop its own marketing, operations and personnel policies.

Nespresso developed its system in conjunction with a number of partners; it collaborated with a Swiss company to improve the design of the machines. It licensed the manufacture of the machines to Turmix, a Swiss domestic appliance manufacturer; it partnered with Sobal, a distributor, who bought the machines from Turmix and the coffee capsules from Nespresso and sold the product to end-users. The Nespresso system was launched in 1986 in Italy, Switzerland and Japan but the product flopped. By the end of 1987 only half the machines that had been manufactured had been sold and without sales of machines there could be no sales of the specially designed capsules. It looked very likely that Nestlé headquarters would kill off the project but it was decided to give it a further chance by bringing in an outsider to see if a turnaround could be effected. The person selected for this role was Jean-Paul Gaillard,[62] a former executive with Philip Morris, the tobacco company.

The turnaround

Rupert Gasser, head of research at Nestlé, described Gaillard as 'ambitious and strong headed. He wanted to do something outstanding. Lang [Gaillard] had personality; he was a force. And importantly, he did not carry all the trappings of the company history'.[63] Gaillard made a number of changes the most important of which were:

● Changing the customer focus: Gaillard reasoned that the Nespresso system was more suited to the household than the restaurant market. Although his intuition was not supported by explicit market research, market trends in the late 1980s pointed in that direction. Gaillard's strategy was to target high-income households and, in line with that strategy, he sought to ensure that the coffee machines were retailed through high-end stores.

● Establishing a direct channel to the end-users through the establishment of Nespresso Clubs: selling Nespresso coffee capsules through supermarkets did not fit well with the exclusive brand image Gaillard wished to create and he is credited with the idea of establishing the Nespresso Club. When households bought a machine they automatically became members of the Club that offered around-the-clock ordering of coffee capsules, prompt delivery of orders and advice on coffee making and machine maintenance. The Club

◄ had the additional advantage of providing the company with up-to-date customer information.

● Positioning the brand at the top end of the market: the company developed partnerships with household appliances makers like Alessi, Krups, Magimix and Philips to produce well-designed machines sold through upmarket retail outlets. Although the machines carried the appliance makers' labels manufacture was mainly outsourced to a Swiss coffee appliance maker with manufacturing capacity in China.

Sales took off and by the time Gaillard left Nespresso to take up a job in another part of Nestlé, there were 220,000 club members and the Nespresso system was sold across Europe.

More recent challenges

Since Gaillard's departure, Nespresso top management has comprised long-serving Nestlé managers rather than outside recruits. Since 1997 the operation has grown significantly and the company has extended both its market scope and its product range. It has expanded geographically and now operates in Europe, Scandinavia, the Americas, Africa and Asia; in addition, Nespresso has extended its target market into small offices and businesses. The range of machines has been increased to offer a number of sophisticated design options and the company has opened a number of retail outlets – Nespresso boutiques – that sell coffee-related paraphernalia as well as the Nespresso system. Whilst the company initially relied on word of mouth to reach its target audience, it launched a long running and successful television advertising campaign featuring George Clooney to further promote the product. Table 6.4 indicates the company's rapid growth in recent years.

Table 6.4 Key indicators of Nespresso's growth 2000–9

Category	2000	2009
Turnover in CHF	210 million	2.7 billion
Global Club community membership	600,000	8 million
Global boutique network	1	191
Employees	331	4500

Source: Giradot, R., www.nestle.com/common/NestleDocuments/Documents/Library/Presentations/ Investor_Events/Investor-Seminar-2010/Nestle-Nespresso. Accessed 21 March 2011.

However, as might be expected, competition has also increased. Competition has taken two main forms; firstly from companies like Tassimo and Senseo who offer a similar product but with different coffee extraction methods that do not violate Nespresso's patents; secondly from companies like the Ethical Coffee Company (established by a former Nespresso manager) that offer substitute capsules that fit Nespresso machines. Many of the direct competitors have chosen to occupy middle market positions offering coffee capsules and machines at a significantly lower price than Nespresso. The providers of the substitute capsules have also made much of the high cost of Nespresso coffee, suggesting they offer better value for money. They also highlight the fact that their compatible capsules can be fully recycled because, despite Nespresso's commitment to recycling, the company has long been criticised by environmental campaigners for its single use aluminium containers.

With competition intensifying and some of its original patents due to expire in 2012,[64] Nespresso is faced with a number of dilemmas with regard to future direction. Can it sustain rapid growth in the current economic climate and retain its exclusive image? Should it move down market to reach a larger target market and to compete directly with middle market rivals? Should the company be re-integrated with the mainstream Nestlé organisation to stimulate further innovation?

Case questions

- What insights into the innovation process can be gained from this case?

- It can be argued that the Nespresso innovation took more than 20 years to come to fruition. How would you account for the slow commercialisation of this product?

- Do you think that Nespresso has a sustainable competitive advantage? What suggestions would you make to Nespresso's management regarding future strategy?

Notes

1 K. Cool, P. Paranika and T. Cool, 'iPad vs. Kindle: e-Books in the US in 2010', INSEAD Case Study (2011)

2 Cool *et al.*, op. cit.: 2.

3 Chris Foresman, 'Apple way ahead of tablet competitors', *Wired* (11 March 2011).

4 *The Economist*, 'The difference engine: send in the clones' (11 March 2011).

5 See, for example, G. A. Fowler, 'Price cuts electrify the e-reader market', *Wall Street Journal* (22 June 2010).

6 www.reuters.com/article/2011/03/02/eu-media-antitrust-idUSLDE7210OT20110302. Accessed 14 March 2011.

7 T. Bradshaw, 'Google launches on-line bookstore', *Financial Times* (6 December 2010).

8 See, for example, www.time.com/time/business/article/0,8599,1929387,00.html. Accessed 14 July 2011.

9 *The Economist*, 'The logic that dares not speak its name,' (16 April 1994): 89–91.

10 In the US, the return to R&D spending was estimated at between 3.7% and 5.5%. See M. Warusawitharana, 'Research and development, profits and firm value: a structural estimation', Discussion Paper (Washington, DC: Federal Reserve Board, September 2008).

11 The excess of the benefit received by the consumer over the price they paid is called *consumer surplus*. See: D. Besanko, D. Dranove and M. Shanley, *Economics of Strategy* (New York: Wiley, 1996): 442–3.

12 *The Economist*, 'Knowledge monopolies: patent wars', *Economist* (8 April 2000): 95–9.

13 F. T. Rothermael, 'incumbent advantage through exploiting complementary assets via interfirm cooperation', *Strategic Management Journal* 22 (2001): 687–99.

14 R. C. Levin, A. K. Klevorick, R. R. Nelson and S. G. Winter, 'Appropriating the returns from industrial research and development,' *Brookings Papers on Economic Activity* 3 (1987).

15 'Why Google acquired eBook technologies', http://mashable.com/2011/01/13/why-google-acquired-ebook-technologies/. Accessed 1 August 2011.

16 Matt Phillips, 'Tablet glut won't matter for ARM Holdings analyst says', *Wall Street Journal* (11 March 2011).

17 'Kindle vs. Nook Price War', www.suite101.com/content/kindle-vs-nook-price-war-reactions-offer-reasons-and-predictions. Accessed 1 August 2011.

18 R. Adner, 'Match your innovation strategy to your innovation ecosystem', *Harvard Business Review* (April 2006): 17–37.

19 S. Shulman, *The Telephone Gambit* (Norton, 2008).

20 'The Human genome race,' *Scientific American* (24 April 2000).

21 C. Markides and P. A. Geroski, *Fast Second* (San Francisco: Jossey-Bass, 2005).

22 D. Sull, 'Strategy as active waiting', *Harvard Business Review* (September 2005): 120–9.

23 See, for example, C. Beaumont, 'Apple launches iPad tablet computer', *The Telegraph* (27 January 2010).

24 For example, data on penetration rates for electric toothbrushes and CD players were used to forecast the market demand for HD TVs in the United States (B. L. Bayus, 'High-definition television: assessing demand forecasts for the next generation consumer durable', *Management Science* 39 (1993): 1319–33).

25 E. Von Hippel, 'Lead users: a source of novel product concepts,' *Management Science* 32 (July 1986).

26 In electronic instruments, customers' ideas initiated most of the successful new products introduced by manufacturers. See E. Von Hippel, 'Users as innovators', *Technology Review* 5 (1976): 212–39.

27 The cloud refers to the internet and, in this instance, refers to retrieving data or digital content from an internet source rather than storing it on the drive of a local computer.

28 A. Friedlander, *The Growth of Railroads* (Arlington, VA: CNRI, 1995).

29 S. Postrel, 'Competing networks and proprietary standards: the case of quadraphonic sound,' *Journal of Industrial Economics* 24 (December 1990): 169–86.

30 S. J. Liebowitz and S. E. Margolis ('Network externality: an uncommon tragedy', *Journal of Economic Perspectives* 8, Spring 1994: 133–50) refer to these user-to-user externalities as *direct externalities*.

31 M. Gladwell, *The Tipping Point* (Boston: Little Brown, 2000).

32 P. David, 'Clio and the economics of QWERTY,' *American Economic Review* 75 (May 1985): 332–7; S. J. Gould, 'The panda's thumb of technology,' *Natural History* 96 (1986). For an alternative view see S. J. Leibowitz and S. Margolis, 'The fable of the keys', *Journal of Law and Economics* 33 (1990): 1–26.

33 C. Shapiro and H. R. Varian, 'The art of standards wars', *California Management Review* 41 (Winter 1999): 8–32.

34 R. M. Grant 'The DVD war of 2006–8: Blu-ray vs. HD-DVD', *Contemporary Strategic Analysis* (Chichester: John Wiley & Sons, 2009): 7th edn: 692–7.

35 Shapiro and Varian, 'The art of standards wars', op. cit.: 15–16.

36 Ibid.: 16–18.

37 C. Nucci, 'E-book dilemma : potboiler of the digital age', *TechWeb* (5 February). http://conent.techweb.com/wire/story/TWB20000092850002. Accessed 11 February 2011.

38 S. Ahn, 'Firm dynamics and productivity growth: a review of micro evidence from OECD countries', Economics Department Working Paper 297 (OECD, 2001).

39 J. M. George, 'Creativity in organisations', *Academy of Management Annals* 1 (2007): 439–77.

40 M. L. Tushman, 'Managing communication networks in R&D laboratories', *Sloan Management Review* (Winter 1979): 37–49.

41 D. Dougherty and C. H. Takacs, 'Team play: heedful interrelating as the boundary for innovation', *Long Range Planning* 37 (December 2004): 569–90.

42 S. Thomke, 'Enlightened experimentation: the new imperative for innovation', *Harvard Business Review* (February 2001): 66–75.

43 *The Economist*, 'The printed world' (12 February 2011): 75–7.

44 R. Florida and J. Goodnight, 'Managing for creativity', *Harvard Business Review* (July–August 2005).

45 D. Leonard and S. Straus, 'Putting your company's whole brain to work', *Harvard Business Review* (July–August 1997): 111–21; D. Leonard and P. Swap, *When Sparks Fly: Igniting Creativity in Groups* (Boston: Harvard Business School Press, 1999).

46 *The Economist* 'How to manage a dream factory' (16 January 2003).

47 'Lunch with the FT: John Lasseter', *Financial Times* (17 January 2009).

48 E. Von Hippel, *The Sources of Innovation* (New York: Oxford University Press, 1988), provides strong evidence of the dominant role of users in the innovation process.

49 E. Morrison, 'Gunfire at sea: a case study of innovation', in M. Tushman and W. L. Moore (Eds), *Readings in the Management of Innovation* (Cambridge, MA: Ballinger, 1988): 165–78.

50 K. Clark and T. Fujimoto, *Product Development Performance: Strategy, Organisation and Management in the World Car Industry* (Boston: Harvard Business School Press, 1991).

51 K. Imai, I. Nonaka and H. Takeuchi, 'Managing the new product development process: how Japanese companies learn and unlearn', in K. Clark, R. Hayes and C. Lorenz (Eds), *The Uneasy Alliance* (Boston: Harvard Business School Press, 1985).

52 D. A. Schön, 'Champions for radical new inventions', *Harvard Business Review* (March–April, 1963): 84.

53 R. Rothwell *et al.*, 'SAPPHO updated – Project SAPPHO Phase II', *Research Policy* 3 (1974): 258–91.

54 G. P. Pisano, *Science Business: The Promise, the Reality and the Future of Biotech* (Boston: Harvard Business School Press, 2006).

55 www.drmwatch.com/drmtech/article.php/3499386. Accessed 1 August 2011.

56 A. Arora, A. Fosfur and A. Gambardella, *Markets for Technology* (Cambridge, MA: MIT Press, 2001); S. Breschi and F. Malerba, *Clusters, Networks and Innovation* (Oxford: Oxford University Press, 2005).

57 M. T. Hansen, H. W. Chesborough, N. Nohria and D. N. Sull, 'Networked incubators: hothouse of the new economy,' *Harvard Business Review* (September–October, 2000): 74–88; 'How to make the most of a brilliant idea,' *Financial Times* (6 December 2000): 21.

58 'Nurturing creativity: putting passions to work', *Shell World* (Royal Dutch Shell, 14 September 2007): 1–12.

59 J. Sculley, *Odyssey: Pepsi to Apple. A Journey of Adventure, Ideas and the Future* (New York: Harper & Row, 1987).

60 J. Miller, *Innovation and Renovation: The Nespresso Story*, Case 543 (Lausanne: IMD: 2003).

61 Nespresso. Wikipedia [online]. Last updated 13 March 2011, http://en.wikipedia/wiki/nespresso. Accessed 21 March 2011.

62 Jean-Paul Gaillard is referred to as Yannick Lang in the IMD case, see P. Silberzahn, Nespresso: victim of low-end disruption? *The Management of Innovation* [blog] (13 April 2010), http://philippesilberzahneng.wordpress.com/tag/jean-paul-gaillard/. Accessed 21 March 2011.

63 IMD case study (2003) op. cit.: 6.

64 Nespresso (2011) Wikipedia op. cit.

Corporate strategy

Introduction and objectives

In Chapter 1 we introduced the distinction between corporate and business strategy. Corporate strategy is concerned with *where* a firm competes whereas business strategy is concerned with *how* a firm competes in a particular area of business. The major part of this book so far has been about business strategy but in the next two chapters we turn our attention to corporate strategy and the scope of the firm's activities. When we refer to the scope of the firm we are directing our attention to the range of product/market activities the firm undertakes. This includes the firm's:

- *Product scope* – how specialised the firm is in terms of the range of products it supplies. Coca-Cola (soft drinks), Gap (fashion retailing) and SAP (software) are specialised companies: each is engaged in a single industry sector. Sony Corporation, General Electric and Tata Group are diversified companies: each spans multiple industries. In our opening case we will see that Tesco, a grocery retailer, has extended the range of its activities into retail banking and telecommunication services.

- *Vertical scope* – the range of vertically linked activities the firm encompasses. Most oil companies such as Shell and Exxon are active along the whole supply chain. They prospect for new oil deposits, drill and extract crude oil, transport it through pipelines and specialised shipping, refine it and distribute it through their retail outlets. Nike is much more vertically specialised: it design and markets footwear and apparel, but outsources most activities in its value chain, including manufacturing, distribution and retailing. In our opening case we will see that although Tesco has developed long-term relationships with its suppliers, it rarely undertakes food processing or product manufacture.

- *Geographical scope* – the geographical spread of activities for the firm. In the advertising business, Saatchi & Saatchi is a global company operating in 80 countries whereas StrawberryFrog is an independent agency with offices in three main centres: Amsterdam, New York and Sao Paulo. In the case of Tesco, whilst the UK still dominates its sales of groceries, 65% of its selling space is now outside the UK.[1]

In this chapter we consider the factors that influence the scope of the firm's activities and the key challenges managers face in developing and implementing corporate strategy. We begin by considering the overall scope of the firm and introduce a number of important analytical concepts that help us to understand what shapes firm boundaries. We devote the remainder of the chapter to consideration of the rationale for operating multiple businesses and the costs and benefits to firms of extending vertical and product scope. The strategic issues associated with a firm's geographical scope are discussed in Chapter 8.

By the end of this chapter, you will:

- be familiar with the concepts of economies of scope, transaction costs and the costs of managing complexity, and understand how these ideas help to explain firm boundaries and the shifts in firm boundaries over time;

- understand the rationale behind multi-business activity and the potential benefits and costs of extending the horizontal or vertical scope of a firm;

- be able to evaluate the advantages and disadvantages of changing a firm's scope and the different ways of exploiting opportunities for value creation;

- appreciate the trends in diversification and vertical integration over time;

- be familiar with the techniques of portfolio analysis and be able to apply these to corporate strategic decisions.

VIDEO

Opening case Tesco Bank: from Food to Finance

Tesco is a global grocery and general merchandise retailer headquartered in London. In 2010 it reported sales revenues (excluding value added tax) in excess of £56 billion, up around 9% on the previous year and profit before tax in excess of £3 billion.[2] By 2011 Tesco was the third largest retailer in the world by turnover, behind Wal-Mart in first place and Carrefour in second,[3] employing more than 472,000 people worldwide and with 4811 stores in 14 different countries.

A brief history

The company was founded by Jack Cohen, the son of a Polish shopkeeper, in 1919. Jack started with a market stall in the East End of London in 1919 and adopted the name Tesco when he had labels made up for a shipment of tea he had bought from the supplier T. E. Stockwell. He used the first three letters from the supplier's name (TES) and the first two from his surname (CO).[4] In the 1950s and 1960s the company grew primarily through acquisitions and successfully pursued a strategy of 'piling it high and selling it cheap'. But, as consumers grew more sophisticated and demanded higher quality and greater choice results slipped. Jack stepped down in 1973 and handed control to Leslie Porter (chairman and Jack's son-in-law) and Ian MacLaurin (managing director). The new management team abandoned the low price, middling quality approach because they felt it had resulted in the company having a downmarket image. MacLaurin introduced new store formats including Tesco Extra (out-of-town hypermarkets) and Tesco Express (neighbourhood convenience stores) and also invested heavily in new systems and technology. Through skilful pricing and positioning, MacLaurin succeeded in broadening the supermarket's appeal to a wide range of market segments and also expanded the company through acquisition.

Tesco became the first UK supermarket to introduce loyalty cards. Its 'Clubcard' offered customers points for every pound spent and proved very popular, despite criticisms that each point was of low monetary value.[5] The loyalty card provided Tesco with valuable information about its customer base because shoppers signing up for the card provided personal details including their age, gender and postcode, and when customers used the card, purchase information was uploaded to the Tesco database. This data allowed Tesco to segment its customer base more accurately and to target promotions and cross-selling initiatives in a more focused way.

When MacLaurin retired and Terry Leahy took over as chief executive officer in 1997, the company was in good shape. Leahy, recognising that the company was reaching the limits of growth in the highly competitive UK grocery market, continued to broaden Tesco's scope. The company had already diversified into areas such as discount clothing, consumer electronics and DVDs and had also moved into online grocery deliveries. The company added online non-food retailing to its portfolio in 1998 via a profit-sharing joint venture with Grattan, a mail-order company. Tesco passed online, non-food orders from its customers to Grattan, who fulfilled them. The joint venture lasted until 2006 when Tesco decided to go it alone and launch Tesco Direct. It was agreed by senior management that the Tesco Direct offering needed to be supported by the publication of a printed catalogue. Producing this catalogue posed a serious challenge for the company in that it had no capability in high-quality photographic publishing. On the surface, at least, the obvious choice was to outsource this activity. Tesco, however, decided to build its capability in-house. The head of Tesco Direct argued: 'If you're going to sell something over the Internet and through a catalogue you absolutely have to own the photography and the design. It's not like in a store where people can simply touch and look at goods. Owning the publishing facility was an absolutely crucial strategic capability we needed to develop.'[6]

Diversification into personal financial services

Alongside these other developments Tesco's also launched Tesco Personal Finance in 1997 as a 50-50 banking joint venture with the Royal Bank of Scotland (RBS). The company offered a range of simple, easy-to-understand products that included credit cards, savings accounts and several types of insurance. Financial services were attractive to Tesco for a number of reasons. Firstly the sheer size of the potential market that could be tapped made the prospect interesting. Tesco already had a large established customer base and a deep knowledge of its customers through its Clubcard database. By combining in-store offers, particularly on non-food items, with financing options, the company could extend its reach. Secondly Tesco was in a strong position in terms of its financial and physical assets. The resources of the company meant that it was able to meet the capital requirement necessary for the award of a banking licence[7] and its large numbers of stores obviated the need to establish a branch network. In addition, customers were already familiar with using supermarkets for simple financial transactions, for example, withdrawing cash at supermarket check-outs rather than ATMs. Finally the company felt that by extending its retailing capabilities into the financial services sector it could release the potential for synergy and innovation, for example, simple, financial products could be purchased as a standard pack from the supermarket shelf and swiped through the checkout or Clubcard points could be offered to those using Tesco financial services.

Tesco plans to develop into a full-scale bank were given an unanticipated boost by the financial crisis. In 2008 Tesco acquired RBS's share in Tesco Personal Finance and the newly branded Tesco Bank become a wholly owned subsidiary of Tesco. In addition, consumers became disillusioned with mainstream banks and were thought likely to switch to alternative financial service providers. Tesco seized this opportunity to announce its plan to move further into retail banking by offering current accounts, mortgages and loans to small businesses. With this aim it launched pilot schemes to introduce bank branches in a few key stores.

The fact that three years further on, Tesco seems to be pulling back from this ambitious plan is an indication of some of the serious challenges the organisation faces in making this move.[8] The core competencies of store retailers are different from those bankers and to be successful Tesco needs not only to develop its capabilities in capital and liquidity management but also to invest heavily in information systems and processes. Whilst financial services seem to offer attractive opportunities for profit, Tesco's share of the market is currently very small and, when it comes to current accounts, customers are notoriously reluctant to switch between providers even if they are dissatisfied with the service their current bank offers. Felsted[9] suggests that consumer trust in firms like Tesco might be overstated and that the lack of trust in banks actually goes across to large companies in general and that banks just happen to be a recent special case. She suggests that 'if store groups begin behaving like banks – repossessing houses at the most extreme for example – customers may come to view them with disdain'.

Despite the challenges Tesco bank has performed well, reporting the number of customer accounts across all products to be 6.2 million and its trading profits up around 13% on the previous year to £250 million for the financial year 2009/10. It remains to be seen how far Tesco will extend its product portfolio in financial services but its strengths will lie in developing a new approach rather than mimicking traditional banks.

The scope of the firm

Deciding 'What business are we in?' is the starting point of strategy and the basis for defining the firm's identity. Corporate strategic decisions encompass both the breadth of the firm's product range (product scope) and the extent of its involvement in the industry value chain (vertical scope). In their statements of vision and mission, some companies define their businesses broadly. Shell's objective is 'to engage efficiently, responsibly and profitably in oil, oil products, gas, chemicals and other selected businesses'. Other companies define their businesses more narrowly: McDonald's vision is 'to be the world's best quick-service restaurant chain'; Caterpillar will 'be leader in providing the best value in machines, engines and support services for companies dedicated to building the world's infrastructure and developing and transporting its resources'. Some companies focus exclusively on a narrow part of the supply chain; others extend their reach across many supply chain activities. For example in the travel market some tour operators like Kuoni focus exclusively on coordinating tour and travel arrangements for holiday-makers whereas other companies, such as First Choice, have extended their activities and have their own airline.

> Corporate strategic decisions encompass both the breadth of the firm's product range (product scope) and the extent of its involvement in the industry value chain (vertical scope).

The scope of a firm's business is likely to change over time. The dominant trend of the past two decades has been 'refocusing on core businesses'. Philip Morris Companies, Inc (now renamed Altria Group, Inc) sold off 7-Up, Miller Brewing and Kraft Foods and became a specialist tobacco company. Most diversified industrial groups – US and

European conglomerates – ITT, Hanson, Gulf & Western, Cendant, Vivendi Universal and Tyco – have broken up altogether.

Some companies have moved in the opposite direction. Microsoft, once a supplier of operating systems, expanded into application and networking software, information services, entertainment systems and video games consoles. Google is no longer simply a search engine company, it supplies a wide array of information products, advertising management services, an internet browser (Chrome), an operating system for mobile phones (Android) and a wide array of applications software. In our opening case we have seen how Tesco, once a UK chain of supermarkets selling groceries and household products, has diversified into a variety of goods and services as well as expanding internationally.

Similar trends are evident with respect to the vertical reach of business organisations. In the past **vertical integration** was seen as highly beneficial and a way of improving coordination and reducing risk. More recently the trend has been towards outsourcing and de-integration. In the pharmaceutical industry, for example, firms were traditionally highly vertically integrated and involved in all stages of the production process from basic research on drug formulation through the manufacture of the active chemical ingredients to packaging and marketing of the product. From the 1980s onwards the industry started to de-integrate with pharmaceutical companies initially outsourcing chemical manufacture, then product formulation and more recently clinical trials and some basic research.

Case Insight 7.1
The scope of Tesco's activities

In its 2010 Annual General Report Tesco declares it 'has a well-established and consistent strategy for growth. The rationale for the strategy is to broaden the scope of the business to enable it to deliver strong, sustainable, long-term growth by following customers into large expanding markets – such as financial services, non-food and telecoms – and new markets abroad, initially Central Europe and Asia and more recently America'.[10]

With regard to its product scope, as well as extending the range of non-food products it retails in its stores, Tesco has also moved into retailing services which include Tesco Bank (provision of financial services), Tesco.com (provision of online retailing services such as Tesco Direct), Tesco Telecoms (the provision of mobile phone and broadband services) and dunnhumby (the provision of market research and data analysis services to other companies). Whilst the core of Tesco's business still remains in UK retail stores, sales of retailing services now account for around 6% of group sales.

In terms of its vertical scope Tesco operates warehouses and distribution centres in addition to its retail stores but has stopped short of its rival Morrison's that has integrated backwards into meat and food production, owning its own abattoirs and fresh food processing plants. Tesco has, however, acquired a controlling interest (83% of the shares) in the market research and data analysis company, dunnhumby, that processes the information generated by consumers' Clubcard activities.

Tesco has also placed a great deal of emphasis on widening its geographical scope. In 2010 the company reported that 65% of its store selling space was now outside the UK and that 31% of its revenue was generated by its overseas operations.

Key concepts for analysing firm scope

Firms extend (or reduce) their scope because they perceive this to be in the organisation's best interest. In the case of for-profit firms, it is reasonable to assume that changes in firm boundaries are designed to create value for shareholders either by increasing revenue or reducing costs (hopefully both). In this section we introduce three concepts that are key to analysing corporate strategic decisions and shifts in the scope of firms' activities over time – economies of scope, transaction costs and the costs of corporate complexity. These concepts provide important insights into value creation and destruction in multi-business firms and shed light on what have proved to be hot topics in corporate strategy in recent times.

Economies of scope

Whilst most students are familiar with the notion of **economies of scale**, the equally important notion of **economies of scope** is often less well understood. Whereas economies of scale refer to the reductions in average costs that result from an increase in the output of a single product, economies of scope are cost economies from increasing the output of multiple products.[11] Economies of scope exist when using a resource across multiple activities uses less of that resource than when the activities are carried out independently. The existence of economies of scope creates the potential for multi-business firms to gain cost advantages over more

> Whereas economies of scale refer to the reductions in average costs that result from an increase in the output of a single product, economies of scope are cost economies from increasing the output of multiple products.

specialised businesses. The nature of economies of scope varies between different types of resources and capabilities.

Tangible resources – such as distribution networks, information technology systems, sales forces and research laboratories – offer economies of scope by eliminating duplication between businesses through creating a single shared facility. The greater the fixed costs of these items, the greater the associated economies of scope are likely to be. Entry by cable TV companies into telephone services and telephone companies into cable TV are motivated by the desire to spread the costs of networks and billing systems over as great a volume of business as possible. Common resources such as customer databases, customer service centres and billing systems have encouraged British Gas, a former publicly owned gas utility, to diversify into supplying electricity, fixed-line and mobile telephone services, broadband internet connections, home security systems, home insurance and home appliance repair.

Economies of scope also arise from the centralised provision of administrative and support services to the different businesses of the corporation. Within diversified companies, accounting, legal services, government relations and information technology tend to be centralised – often through **shared service organisations** that supply common administrative and technical services to the operating businesses. Similar economies arise from centralising research activities in a corporate R&D lab.

Intangible resources such as brands, corporate reputation and technology offer economies of scope from the ability to extend them to additional businesses at low marginal cost.[12] Exploiting a strong brand across additional products is called **brand extension**. Starbucks has extended its brand to ice cream, packaged cold drinks, home espresso machines, audio CDs and books.

Organisational capabilities are also subject to economies of scope. These economies result from the ability to transfer capabilities between businesses within the diversified company. For example, once developed, an organisational capability can typically be replicated in a new business at a fraction of the cost of the initial creation.

LVMH is the world's biggest and most diversified supplier of branded luxury goods. Its distinctive capability is the management of luxury brands. This capability comprises market analysis, advertising, promotion, retail management and quality assurance. These capabilities are deployed across Louis Vuitton (accessories and leather goods); Hennessey (cognac); Moet et Chandon, Dom Perignon, Veuve Clicquot and Krug (champagne); Celine, Givenchy, Kenzo, Dior, Guerlain and Donna Karan (fashion clothing and perfumes); TAG Heuer and Chaumet (watches); Sephora and La Samaritaine (retailing); and some 25 other branded businesses.

Sharp Corporation – originally established to manufacture metal products and the Ever Sharp Pencil – developed capabilities in the miniaturisation of electronic products that it has deployed to develop and introduce a stream of innovative products, beginning with the world's first transistor calculator (1964), the first LCD pocket calculator (1973), LCD colour TVs, PDAs, internet viewcams, ultraportable notebook computers and 3G mobile telephones.

Some of the most important capabilities in influencing the performance of multi-business corporations are general management capabilities. General Electric possesses strong technological and operational capabilities at business level and it is good at sharing these capabilities between businesses (e.g. turbine knowhow between jet engines and electrical generating equipment). However, its core capabilities are in general management and these reside primarily at the corporate level. These include its ability to motivate and develop its managers, its outstanding strategic and financial management that reconciles decentralised decision making with strong centralised control, and its international management capability. Similar observations could be made about 3M. While 3M's capabilities in technical knowhow, new product development and international marketing reside within the individual businesses, it is the corporate management capabilities and the systems through which they are exercised that maintain, nourish, coordinate and upgrade these competitive advantages.[13]

Case Insight 7.2
Economies of scope at Tesco

In the opening case we saw that Tesco has diversified into areas that have allowed it to make shared use of both its tangible and non-tangible resources. Its network of retail stores has provided the platform for diversification into non-food retailing but has also created the opportunity for entry into full-scale retail banking by removing the need for the company to establish a costly branch network. The database that Tesco has built up from information generated by its Clubcard holders provides the company with the means of 'following its customers into new markets'. In the case of banking new entry is difficult because customers want to deal with institutions they trust and trust is hard to establish and slow to build. Tesco's brand name and established reputation transfers from one line of business to another, although equally there is a risk that problems in one area of business can be detrimental to the company's image in others. The company's organisational capabilities also create the potential for exploiting economies of scope. For example Tesco's capability in market analytics and information processing, via dunnhumby, has allowed the company to enter the retailing services market, supplying information processing and analysis services to other companies. More recently[14] Tesco has announced its decision to engage in a number of house-building projects. Whilst this may, at first sight, seem surprising, when we consider the expertise and capabilities the company has developed in managing the land and property for its retail stores, this move is easier to understand.

Whilst the existence of economies of scope goes some way to explaining why firms often seek to extend the scope of their activities, it does not provide a complete explanation of decisions to engage in multi-business operations. Firms do not need to actively engage in different activities to exploit the benefits of scope. Economies of scope can be exploited simply by selling or licensing the use of the resource or capability to another company. For example, Starbucks' extension of its brand and trademark to other products has been achieved primarily through licensing: Pepsi produces and distributes Starbucks' Frappuccino; Unilever produces Tazo Tea beverages, Dreyer's produces Starbucks' ice cream. Even tangible resources can be shared across different businesses through market transactions. Airport and railway station operators exploit economies of scope in their facilities not by diversifying into catering and retailing, but by leasing out space to specialist retailers and restaurants. As our opening case illustrates Tesco has decided to exploit its retail store assets by diversifying into new lines of business but it could have chosen to lease space to third parties, for example, entering agreements with established clothing retailers rather than offering its own range of discount clothing. To explain why firms sometimes choose to internalise activities and sometimes to exploit them externally through market contracts, we turn to the second of our key concepts – transaction costs.

> Economies of scope can be exploited simply by selling or licensing the use of the resource or capability to another company.

Transaction costs

Although the capitalist economy is frequently referred to as a 'market economy', in fact, it comprises two forms of economic organisation. One is the **market mechanism**, where individuals and firms, guided by market prices, make independent decisions to buy and sell goods and services. The other is the **administrative mechanism** of firms, where decisions concerning production and resource allocation are made by managers and imposed through hierarchies. The market mechanism was characterised by Adam Smith, the 18th-century Scottish economist, as the 'invisible hand' because its coordinating role does not require conscious planning. Alfred Chandler has referred to the administrative mechanism of firms as the 'visible hand' because coordination involved active planning.[15]

Firms and markets may be viewed as alternative forms for organising production. Firms are distinguished by the fact that they comprise a number of individuals bound by employment contracts with a central contracting authority. But firms are not essential for organising production. If you wished to install a new kitchen, you could engage a specialist firm that employs its own workers but alternatively you could get the job done by contracting with a number of self-employed tradespeople, negotiating directly, for example, with a general builder, a plumber, an electrician, a joiner and a painter to complete the project. Although the job involves the coordinated activity of several individuals, these self-employed specialists are not linked by employment relations but by a series of market contracts.

As this example shows, firms and markets coexist, but their relative roles vary. If we compare the mainframe computer industry with the personal computer (PC) industry, the administrative mechanisms of firms predominate in the former, markets are more important in the latter. Thus, in mainframes, the dominant supplier, IBM (smaller players include Fujitsu, Honeywell-Bull and Unisys) is highly vertically integrated. It produces many of its own components (e.g. microprocessors), develops its own operating and applications software and undertakes distribution, marketing and customer support. PCs involve a network of firms linked by market contracts: design and marketing is undertaken by firms such as HP, Acer and Lenovo. Components are produced by firms such as Intel, Seagate and Samsung. Assembly is outsourced to contract manufacturers such as Asustek and Quanta Computer. Customer support is also outsourced to specialist suppliers – often located in India or Eastern Europe.

What determines which particular activity is undertaken within a firm or through arm's length market contracts? Ronald Coase's answer was relative cost.[16] Markets are not costless: making a purchase or sale involves search costs, the costs of negotiating and drawing up a contract, the costs of monitoring to ensure that the other party's side of the contract is being fulfilled and the enforcement costs of arbitration or litigation should a dispute arise. All these costs are types of **transaction costs**.[17] If the transaction costs associated with organising across markets are greater than the administrative costs of organising within firms, we can expect the coordination of productive activity to be internalised within firms.

This situation is illustrated in Figure 7.1. With regard to vertical scope, which is more efficient: three independent companies – one producing steel, the next rolling the steel into sheet and the third producing steel cans – or having all three stages of production within a single company? In the case of geographical scope, which is more efficient: three independent companies producing cans in the US, UK and Italy; or a single multinational company owning and operating the can-making plants in all three countries? In the case of product scope, should metal cans, plastic packaging and domestic appliances be produced by three separate companies, or are there efficiencies to be gained by merging all three into a single company?

The answers to these questions have changed over time. During most of the 20th century, companies grew in size and scope, absorbing transactions that had previously taken place across markets. A major factor encouraging firms to extend their boundaries was the fall in the administrative costs of firms relative to the transaction costs of markets. Technology was a major source of falling administrative costs.

Figure 7.1 The scope of the firm: specialisation versus integration

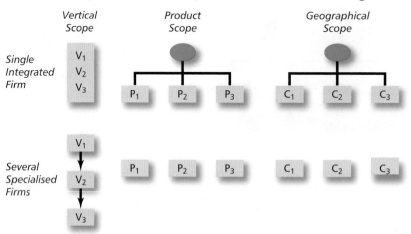

In the integrated firm there is an administrative interface between the different vertical units (V), product units (P), and country units (C). Where there is specialisation, each unit is a separate firm linked by market interfaces.

The telegraph, telephone and computer significantly enhanced coordination and decision making within firms. Changes in the principles and techniques of management have greatly expanded the organisational and decision-making effectiveness of managers and made it easier for firms to manage across distance and between different businesses. Through the development of ideas such as scientific management in the early 20th century,[18] the multidivisional corporation in the 1920s and techniques of investment appraisal from the 1930s onwards, the 20th century has seen massive advances in managerial capacity. By the 1960s, the increasing dominance of the economy by a few giant corporations encouraged the economist J. K. Galbraith to declare that *market economy* had been replaced by a *corporate economy*.[19]

Yet, during the 1980s and 1990s, the trend towards increased corporate scope was reversed. Although large companies continued to expand internationally, the dominant trends of the past three decades were 'downsizing' and 'refocusing', as large industrial companies reduced both their product scope through focusing on their core businesses and their vertical scope through outsourcing.

> The dominant trends of the past three decades were 'downsizing' and 'refocusing', as large industrial companies reduced both their product scope through focusing on their core businesses and their vertical scope through outsourcing.

During this period several factors contributed to markets increasing their efficiency relative to firms' administrative processes. Increased turbulence of the business environment – especially during the 21st century – has raised the costs of administration within large, complex firms as traditional management systems have struggled to become more flexible and responsive. Secondly, developments in information and communications technology (ICT) have favoured small firms linked by market. While the mainframes of the 1970s reinforced the advantages of giant corporations, the PC, internet and mobile communications have put small firms at the leading edge and revolutionised market efficiency.

Case Insight 7.3
Transaction costs at Tesco

Grocery retailers like Tesco transact with a large range of suppliers. If we take as an example the supply chain arrangements that support Tesco's provision of fresh fruit and vegetables to its stores, we can identify the source of many different types of transaction cost. In order to ensure that its stores receive regular supplies of good quality fresh fruit and vegetables Tesco has to:

- search for potential sellers and acquire relevant information on their behaviour and circumstances. The retailer needs to ascertain which farmers or agricultural businesses can supply them with sufficient quantity of particular fruit or vegetables and whether these farmers' business practices ensure that their produce is consistently of appropriate quality;
- bargain with selected suppliers to establish prices, quality standards, delivery and other detailed aspects of the proposed supply arrangements;
- draw up a legal contract;
- monitor the supplier to make sure that what is delivered meets the terms of the agreement;
- enforce the contract and seek damages if the chosen supplier reneges on part of the contract.

All of this takes time, requires specialist expertise and knowledge and is costly. The transport arrangements for perishable produce are also of critical importance to the condition in which fresh products are received in store so Tesco needs to go through the same kind of processes and incur another set of transaction costs with respect to delivery and logistics.

Tesco, faced with a competitive retail environment, naturally wishes to keep its costs down and will seek to organise its supply arrangements in the most cost-efficient manner it can. It could, for example, buy its fruit and vegetables on spot markets or it could own and operate its own farms. Both options have some advantages and drawbacks. A spot market transaction is a short-term exchange based on market prices with no prior agreements between the parties. The problem for supermarkets like Tesco is that the prices and quality of produce offered on spot markets fluctuate and, whilst such markets are useful for coping with unanticipated shortfalls, they don't offer a sufficiently reliable and predictable basis for long-term supply. Integrating backwards into farming is also likely to be unattractive to Tesco since this would require major capital investment, involve the firm in significant administrative cost and would draw the company away from its core capabilities in retailing. Most supermarkets, Tesco included, prefer to operate in the middle ground, i.e. neither fully vertically integrated nor wholly reliant on the market, instead it opts for long-term contractual relationships with a small number of trusted suppliers. We explore this 'middle ground' of alternative types of vertical relationships later in this chapter.

Even though vertical integration reduces or eliminates certain transaction costs, this doesn't mean that incorporating different areas of business within the firm boundaries is necessarily an efficient solution. Internalising business transactions imposes its own costs which brings us to our third key concept – the costs of corporate complexity.

The costs of corporate complexity

If a firm extends the scope of its operations by engaging directly in additional business activities, it may benefit from economies of scope and it may avoid the transaction costs of using the market but it does so by incurring additional management costs. The size of these management costs is important because they can outweigh the potential cost savings. Engaging in more arenas of business involves greater **organisational complexity** as managing different businesses usually requires different organisational capabilities. Even large technology-based companies like Xerox, Kodak and Phillips cannot maintain IT capabilities that match those of IT specialist services such as EDS, IBM and Accenture. Managing strategically diverse businesses does not just involve building and sustaining different capabilities but can also require different strategic planning systems, different approaches to the control of human resource management and different top management styles and skill. The extent to which an increase in the scope of the firm adds to its complexity and administrative costs depends, in large part, on the linkages that exist between the firm's multiple businesses.

Case Insight 7.4
The costs of corporate complexity at Tesco

Diversification into non-food products primarily utilises Tesco's existing skills in purchasing, merchandising and the development of private labels – the company introduced its own label, F&F, for discount clothes. The move into financial services, however, represents a bigger stretch, requiring the company to develop new competencies in capital and liquidity management and to deal with a very different regulatory environment. Tesco sought to minimise the risk and reduce the costs of complexity by entering the market initially through a joint venture with the Royal Bank of Scotland and offering a limited range of straightforward financial products. Whilst the company has a declared intention to move into full-scale retail banking, the fact that several years after buying out RBS it has yet to offer current accounts and mortgages is perhaps indicative of the fact that Tesco's recognises the organisational challenge that such a move represents.

The three concepts we have introduced – economies of scope, transaction costs and costs of managing complexity – provide important insights into corporate strategic decisions and we next use these ideas to explore strategic decisions with regard to product scope (diversification) and vertical scope (vertical integration) in more detail.

Diversification

Defining diversification

Diversification refers to the expansion of an existing firm into another product line or field of operation. Diversification may be related or unrelated. Unrelated diversification takes place when the additional product line is very different from the firm's core business, for example a food-processing firm starts to manufacture medical devices. Unrelated diversification is sometimes also referred to as conglomerate diversification. Related diversification occurs when a firm expands into a similar field of operation, for example a car manufacturer extends its product range to trucks or buses. This kind of diversification is sometimes referred to as concentric diversification.

The distinction between related and unrelated diversification is, however, not as straightforward as it might at first seem because it depends on the notion of relatedness.

In our illustrative example we classified a car manufacturer diversifying into the truck market as related diversification because cars and trucks use similar manufacturing processes. In so doing we are defining relatedness at an operational level but this is not the only, or necessarily the most useful, way of viewing relatedness.

As we saw when we discussed the resource-based view in Chapter 3 and the notion of economies of scope at the start of this chapter, some of the most important sources of value creation are derived from a firm's ability to apply common management capabilities, strategic management systems and resource allocation processes to different businesses. Whilst at first glance food processing and the manufacture of medical devices appear to be very different, unrelated businesses, closer investigation might reveal that they involve similar management skills, for example, managing sterile environments or establishing very high standards of quality control in relation to health and safety standards.

Whereas the opportunities for economies of scope derived from exploiting joint inputs may be relatively easy to identify at an operational level, strategic relatedness is more elusive. Richard Branson's Virgin Group covers a huge array of businesses from airlines to music stores yet they share certain strategic similarities: almost all are start-up companies that benefit from Branson's entrepreneurial zeal and expertise; almost all sell to final consumers and are in sectors that offer opportunities for innovative approaches to differentiation. Classifying diversification as related or unrelated requires an understanding of the overall strategic approach of the company and recognition of its corporate-level management capabilities.

Diversification is also often classified in relation to its direction. **Horizontal diversification** involves the firm moving into the same stage of production whereas **vertical diversification** occurs when a firm undertakes successive stages in the production of a good or service. Since the issues relating to vertical diversification are somewhat different from those raised by other extensions to product scope we explore vertical integration as a topic in its own right later in the chapter.

The benefits and costs of diversification

Diversification is perceived as beneficial if it helps a firm to achieve its objectives. Our main focus is on for-profit firms so we concentrate on the ways in which diversification can assist firms to improve profitability, but it is important to recognise that diversification can be undertaken for motives that are not necessarily consistent with the creation of shareholder value. It is also worth noting that for many organisations operating in the public and not-for-profit sectors the options for diversification may be very restricted either because the scope of the organisation's activities is limited by statute or because the organisation's mission is very focused. The most commonly cited motives for diversification are growth, risk reduction and value creation. Whereas value creation is a necessary, but not sufficient, condition for enhanced profitability, diversification to achieve growth or risk reduction is not always in shareholders' interests.

> In the absence of diversification firms are prisoners of their industry.

GROWTH In the absence of diversification firms are prisoners of their industry. For firms in stagnant or declining industries this is a daunting prospect – especially for top management. The urge to achieve corporate growth which outstrips that of a firm's primary industry is an appealing prospect for managers. Companies in low-growth, cash flow-rich industries such as tobacco and oil have been especially susceptible to the temptations of diversification. During the 1980s, Exxon diversified into copper and coal mining, electric motors and computers and office equipment; RJR Nabisco transformed itself from a tobacco company into a diversified consumer products company. In both cases diversification was highly destructive of shareholder value. Shareholders are quite happy to invest in companies in low growth, even declining industries, so long as these companies throw off plenty of cash flow which shareholders can invest in promising growth companies.

RISK REDUCTION The rationale for diversifying to reduce risk is captured by the familiar advice 'don't put all your eggs in one basket'. If the cash flows of different businesses are imperfectly correlated, then bringing them together under common ownership results in more stable profit earnings. But does such risk reduction create value for shareholders? Shareholders can diversify risk by holding diversified portfolios of shares rather than shares in diversified companies and portfolio diversification by individual shareholders is typically cheaper than business diversification by companies. Not only do acquiring firms incur the heavy costs of using investment banks and legal advisers, they must also pay an acquisition premium to gain control of an independent company. The primary beneficiaries of risk reduction through diversification tend to be managers: stable profits are likely to mean job security.

VALUE CREATION The primary source of value creation from diversification is exploiting linkages between different businesses. We have already discussed how both operational and strategic links between businesses give rise to economies of scope but have also seen that economies of scope can be exploited through means other than diversification, for example simply selling or licensing the use of the resource or capabilities to other companies. This raises the question of whether economies of scope are better exploited internally within the firm through diversification, or externally through market contracts with independent companies. Our earlier discussion of transaction costs tells us that the key issue is relative efficiency: what are the transaction costs of market contracts, as compared with the administrative costs of diversified activities?

EXPLOITING ECONOMIES OF SCOPE Finding the most efficient way of exploiting potential economies of scope is complex as the following examples illustrate.

> In the case of the Walt Disney Company, it licenses Donald Duck trademarks to Florida's Natural Growers rather than set up its own orange juice company; it owns and operates its US theme parks, but licenses its trademarks and technology to the Oriental Land Company which owns and operates Tokyo Disneyland.
>
> Both Mars and Cadbury used their confectionary brands to enter the European ice cream market. Cadbury decided to license its brands to Nestlé; Mars entered the business itself setting up production and distribution facilities to compete with market leaders, Unilever and Nestlé. The result was that Cadbury made significant profits from its licences, whereas Mars experienced years of losses or low returns on its entry costs.

In all of these examples it is the company's reputation as signified by its brand name or trademark that is the key resource linking the businesses. If the resource that forms the basis for potential economies of scope can be traded or licensed out for anything close to its real value, as in the case of the Donald Duck trademark or the confectionery brands, then it is not necessary to enter another business in order to capture the extra profitability. Cadbury captured more profitability by not entering the ice cream business. If, on the other hand, the resource is one that cannot easily be traded, such as general management capabilities, then it will be necessary to enter the new business in order to create the extra profitability. There is little scope for 3M to deploy its new product development capabilities other than within its own business. Similarly, for Apple, the only way for it to exploit its capabilities in user-friendly design is to diversify outside of its core computer business. Virgin has a separate licensing company but only licenses its brand to companies within the Virgin group. So why doesn't Virgin license its brand to companies it does not own? The answer presumably is that the brand is part of a package of benefits that Virgin offers, some of which could not be traded or licensed. For example, Virgin has developed special marketing skills around its brand, often using the brand and Richard Branson to gain press comment in place of expensive advertising.

INTERNAL CAPITAL MARKETS The diversified firm represents an **internal capital market**: the corporate allocating of capital between the different businesses through the capital expenditure budget. Which is more efficient, the internal capital markets of diversified companies or the external capital market? Diversified companies have two key advantages:

- By maintaining a balanced portfolio of cash-generating and cash-using businesses, diversified firms can avoid the costs of using the external capital market, including the margin between borrowing and lending rates and the heavy costs of issuing new debt and equity.

● Diversified companies have better access to information on the financial prospects of their different businesses than that typically available to external financiers.[20]

Against these advantages is the critical disadvantage that investment allocation within the diversified companies is a politicised process in which strategic and financial considerations are subordinated by turf battles and ego building. Evidence suggests that diversified firms sometimes cross-subsidise poorly performing divisions and are reluctant to transfer cash flows to the divisions with the best prospects.[21] However, the efficiency of capital allocation varies greatly across companies.

INTERNAL LABOUR MARKETS Efficiencies also arise from the ability of diversified companies to transfer employees – especially managers and technical specialists – between their divisions and to rely less on hiring and firing. As companies develop and encounter new circumstances, so different management skills are required. The costs associated with hiring include advertising, the time spent in interviewing and selection and the costs of 'head-hunting' agencies. The costs of dismissing employees can be very high where severance payments must be offered. A diversified corporation has a pool of employees and can respond to the specific needs of any one business through transfer from elsewhere within the corporation.

> A diversified corporation has a pool of employees and can respond to the specific needs of any one business through transfer from elsewhere within the corporation.

The broader set of opportunities available in the diversified corporation as a result of internal transfer may also result in attracting a higher calibre of employee. Graduating students compete intensely for entry-level positions with diversified corporations such as Siemens, General Electric, Unilever and Nestlé in the belief that these companies can offer richer career development than more specialised companies.

The informational advantages of diversified firms are especially important in relation to internal labour markets. A key problem of hiring from the external labour market is limited information. A CV, references and a day of interviews are poor indicators of how a new hire will perform in a particular job. The diversified firm that is engaged in transferring employees between different positions and different internal units can build detailed information on the competencies and characteristics of its employees. This informational advantage exists not only for individual employees but also for groups of individuals working together as teams. Hence, in exploiting a new business opportunity an established firm is at an advantage over the new firm which must assemble its team from scratch.

When does diversification create value?

If we make the assumption that corporate strategy should be directed towards the interests of shareholders, what are the implications for diversification strategy? Michael Porter proposes three 'essential tests' to be applied in deciding whether diversification will truly create shareholder value:

- *The attractiveness test.* The industries chosen for diversification must be structurally attractive or capable of being made attractive.

- *The cost-of-entry test.* The cost of entry must not capitalise all the future profits.

- *The better-off test.* Either the new unit must gain competitive advantage from its link with the corporation, or vice versa.[22]

THE ATTRACTIVENESS AND COST-OF-ENTRY TESTS A key feature of Porter's 'essential tests' is that industry attractiveness is insufficient on its own. Although diversification allows a firm to access more attractive investment opportunities than are available in its own industry, it faces the challenge of entering the new industry. The second test, *cost of entry*, recognises that, for outsiders, the cost of entry may counteract the attractiveness of the industry. Pharmaceuticals, corporate legal services and defence contracting offer above-average profitability precisely because they are protected by barriers to entry. Firms seeking to enter these industries have a choice. They may acquire an established player, in which case the acquisition price will almost certainly fully capitalise the target firm's profit prospects (especially given the need to pay an acquisition premium over the market price of the target).[23] Alternatively, entry may occur through establishing a new corporate venture. In this case, the diversifying firm must directly confront the barriers to entry protecting that industry.[24]

THE BETTER-OFF TEST This addresses the basic issue of competitive advantage: if two businesses producing different products are brought together under the ownership and control of a single enterprise, is there any reason why they should become any more profitable? We have already identified the circumstances where operating multiple businesses creates value: the first is economies of scope where firms share resources and capabilities, the second is the presence of transaction costs which makes diversification (i.e. directly investing in another business) more profitable than merely licensing the shared resource or capability.

In most diversification decisions, it is the better-off test that dominates. Industry attractiveness cannot be relied on as an ongoing source of superior profitability. Moreover, the attractiveness test and the cost-of-entry test can cancel each

> In most diversification decisions, it is the better-off test that dominates.

other since industries tend to be attractive because they are difficult to enter. Indeed, the reverse is often true. It can make sense for a company to enter an unattractive industry so long as the cost of entry is sufficiently discounted and the better-off test is met. This is a strategy often used by companies acquiring businesses in a fragmented industry. The hairdressing industry, for example, is structurally unattractive – there are low barriers to entry. But, if the acquiring company can create a brand or has a proprietary range of hairdressing products, it may still make sense to diversify into the hairdressing business because the cost of entry is low and the acquired businesses can be improved.

Case Insight 7.5
Assessing the pros and cons for Tesco of entry into the financial services market

To evaluate whether Tesco's decision to enter full-scale retail banking is in its shareholders' interest, Michael Porter proposes three essential tests.

The attractiveness test invites us to ask whether the retail financial services market is attractive or capable of being made attractive. For many years retail banking in the UK has been dominated by a few large players, such as RBS, Barclays, Lloyds. Until 2008 British banks were argued to be the envy of Europe for their high returns on equity which were thought to be around 20% compared to levels of 12% elsewhere.[25] However, the financial collapse and the subsequent 'credit crunch' severely dented industry prospects. Bad debts and the increased cost and difficulty of obtaining wholesale funds reduced profitability and contributed to a number of banks being rescued by the government. In addition, the high levels of competition between existing players, the recent entry of

new ambitious new players like Santander and Metro Bank and the well-documented reluctance of UK bank customers to switch their current accounts all combine to reduce the attractiveness of the market.

Tesco recognises that particular segments of the retail banking market have become unattractive.

Andrew Higginson, the CEO of Tesco speaking in 2009 about the company's earlier decision to hold back on its entry into retail banking, suggested this was a positive decision not an accident. He argued: 'we couldn't see a way of making money and didn't know how the banks were doing so. We were happy to leave it alone.'[26] On the other hand financial turmoil has also created the opportunity for Tesco to make the most of its trusted brand and customer relationships at a time when the status of high street banks has been diminished.

The cost of entry test requires that the future profits are not negated by the cost of gaining a position in the market. Two of the most significant costs of entry into retail banking are the costs of setting up a branch network and of establishing an appropriate IT infrastructure. Tesco, like a number of other retail chains, can use its existing stores as the basis for banking operations. Whilst it already has a good capital base and a sophisticated IT system in place, the company has been required to make significant further IT investments following its purchase of the RBS interests in Tesco bank.[27]

The better-off test requires that the new business provides the parent company with a competitive advantage. Tesco has a number of resources and capabilities that can be extended to retail financial services and benefits from an absence of some of the legacies that constrain established banks. Tesco stores are open for longer hours than bank branches, are located in places that provide free parking and allow customers to combine banking with weekly shopping. Simple savings products and general insurance have characteristics that lend themselves to 'off-the-shelf' retailing and Tesco already has a large internet operation. The company has strong capabilities in building and integrating IT systems and in customer relationship management as well as a significant presence in markets such as Eastern Europe and Asia that currently lack mature retail banking services. Given the potential that exists for exploiting economies of scope, Tesco sees retail banking as offering significant value creation opportunities for its shareholders.

Diversification and performance

Empirical research into diversification has concentrated on two major issues: first, how do diversified firms perform relative to specialised firms and, second, does related diversification outperform unrelated diversification?

Despite many empirical studies over the past four decades, consistent, systematic relationships between diversification and performance are lacking. Beyond a certain threshold, high levels of diversification appear to be associated with lower profitability – probably because of the organisational complexity that diversification creates. Among British companies, diversification was associated with increased profitability up to a point, after which further diversification was accompanied by declining profitability.[28] Several other studies have detected a similar curvilinear relationship between diversification and profitability.[29] McKinsey & Company also point to the benefits of moderate diversification – 'a strategic sweet spot between focus and broader diversification'. Diversification, they argue, makes most sense when a company has exhausted growth opportunities in its existing markets and can match its existing capabilities to emerging external opportunities.[30]

A key problem is distinguishing *association* from *causation*. If moderately diversified companies are generally more profitable than specialised firms, is it because diversification increases profitability or because profitable firms channel their cash flows into diversifying investments?

The performance effects of diversification depend on the mode of diversification. Mergers and acquisitions involving companies in different industries appear to perform especially poorly.[31]

More consistent evidence concerns the performance results of refocusing initiatives by North American and European companies: when companies divest diversified businesses and concentrate more on their core businesses, the result is typically increased profitability and higher stock market valuation.[32] These findings may reflect a changing relationship between diversification and profitability over time: growing turbulence of the business environment may have increased the costs of managing diversified corporations.

Related and unrelated diversification

Given the importance of economies of scope in shared resources and capabilities, it seems likely that diversification into *related* industries should be more profitable than diversification into *unrelated* industries. Yet the findings of empirical research have been inconsistent. Initial findings that appeared to show that closely related diversification was more profitable than unrelated diversification[33] were contradicted by some subsequent studies.[34] Several factors may be confusing the relationship. First, related diversification offers greater potential benefits than unrelated diversification, but managing these linkages also creates greater management complexity. Second, the distinction between 'related' and 'unrelated' diversification is not always clear – it may depend upon the strategy and characteristics of individual firms. Champagne and luggage are not obviously related products, but LVMH applies similar brand management capabilities to them both.

Recent trends in diversification

When considering 'The Scope of the Firm' early in this chapter, we observed that, since the 1980s, the trend towards diversification has reversed and diversified companies have been refocusing their business portfolios through divesting non-core businesses. Equally significant, *conglomerate firms* – highly diversified companies created from multiple, unrelated acquisitions – have almost disappeared as a distinctive corporate form. In the UK, Hanson split into eight separate companies including Imperial Tobacco and BTR became a specialised engineering company. In the US, similar dismemberment occurred at ITT, Textron and Allied Signal. The divestment trend among large US companies meant that between 1980 and 1990, the average index of diversification for the Fortune 500 declined from 1.00 to 0.67.[35]

Outside of North America and Western Europe and the mature industrialised countries, the situation is very different. Highly diversified business groups dominate the industrial sectors of many emerging countries: Tata Group and Reliance in India, Charoen Pokphand (CP) in Thailand, Astra in Indonesia, Sime Darby in Malaysia, Grupo Alfa and Grupo Carso in Mexico. One reason for the continued dominance of large conglomerates in emerging market countries may be higher transaction costs associated with their less sophisticated markets for finance, information and labour that offer diversified companies advantages over their specialised competitors.[36]

There are also signs that diversification may be making a comeback in the advanced industrial nations. In the technology sector, digitisation is tending to break down conventional market boundaries. Simultaneously, complementarities are becoming more important between different products. Apple's diversification from personal computers into MP3 players, content download services, smartphones and tablet computers reflects increasing linkages between them. Similarly, Google has diversified from its core search engine into a bewildering variety of search and software products – including an operating system for mobile devises (Android) and an internet browser (Chrome). As the rate at which technologies and products become obsolete increases and competitive advantage in core businesses erodes, so firms are finding it desirable to create (or acquire) 'growth options' in other industries.

> As the rate at which technologies and products become obsolete increases and competitive advantage in core businesses erodes, so firms are finding it desirable to create (or acquire) 'growth options' in other industries.

Vertical integration

Defining vertical integration

Vertical integration refers to a firm's ownership of vertically related activities. The greater the extent to which a firm's ownership extends over successive stages of the value chain for its product, the greater its degree of vertical integration. The extent of vertical integration is indicated by the *ratio of a firm's value added to its sales revenue*: the more a firm makes rather than buys, the lower are its costs of bought-in goods and services relative to its final sales revenue.

Vertical integration can be either *backward*, where the firm acquires ownership and control over the production of its own inputs, or *forward*, where the firm acquires ownership and control of activities previously undertaken by its customers.

Vertical integration may be *full* or *partial*. Some Australian wineries are fully integrated: they produce wine only from the grapes they grow and sell it all directly to final customers. Most are partially integrated: their home-grown grapes are supplemented with purchased grapes and they sell some wine through their own tasting rooms with independent distributors taking the rest.

The benefits and costs of vertical integration

Strategies towards vertical integration have been subject to shifting fashions. For most of the 20th century, the prevailing wisdom was that vertical integration was generally beneficial because it allowed superior coordination and reduced risk. During the past 25 years there has been a profound change of opinion: outsourcing, it is claimed, enhances flexibility and allows firms to focus on their 'core competencies'. Moreover, many of the coordination benefits traditionally associated with vertical integration can be achieved through collaboration between vertically related companies.

> The vertical integration of software devices and content is viewed as a critical advantage in the face of rapid technological change in a number of high-tech industries.

However, as in other areas of management, fashion is fickle. As we saw in the opening case to Chapter 5 on the evolution of the computer industry and Chapter 6 on e-readers, the vertical integration of software devices and content is viewed as a critical advantage in the face of rapid technological change in a number of high-tech industries. Our task is to go beyond fads and fashions to uncover the factors that determine whether vertical integration enhances or weakens performance. On the positive side, vertical integration can produce cost savings due to the physical integration of processes, eliminate certain transaction costs and facilitate transaction-specific investments. On the negative side, vertical integration may restrict a firm's ability to benefit from scale economies and may reduce flexibility and increase risk.

Technical economies from the physical integration of processes

Analysis of the benefits of vertical integration has traditionally emphasised the technical economies of vertical integration: cost savings that arise from the physical integration of processes. Thus, most steel sheet is produced by integrated producers in plants that first produce steel, then roll the hot steel into sheet. Linking the two stages of production at a single location reduces transportation and energy costs. Similar technical economies arise in pulp and paper production and from linking oil refining with petrochemical production.

However, although these considerations explain the need for the co-location of plants, they do not explain why vertical integration in terms of **common ownership** is necessary. Why can't steel and steel strip production or pulp and paper production be undertaken by separate firms which own physically integrated plants? To answer this question, we must look beyond technical economies and consider the implications of linked processes for transaction costs – a concept that we introduced earlier.

Transaction costs in vertical exchanges

Consider the value chain for steel cans, which extends from mining iron ore to delivering cans to food-processing companies (see Figure 7.2). Between the production of steel and steel strip, most production is vertically integrated. Between the production of steel strip and steel cans, there is very little vertical integration: can producers such as Crown Holdings and Ball Corporation are specialist packaging companies that purchase steel strip from steel companies on contracts.[37]

The predominance of market contracts between steel strip production and can production is the result of low transaction costs in the market for steel strip: there are many buyers and sellers, information is readily available and the switching costs for buyers and suppliers are low. The same is true for many other commodity products: few jewellery companies own gold mines; few flour-milling companies own wheat farms.

To understand why vertical integration predominates across steel production and steel strip production, let us see what would happen if the two stages were owned by

Figure 7.2 The value chain for steel cans

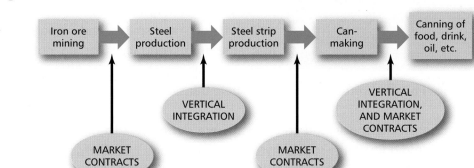

separate companies. Because there are technical economies from hot-rolling steel as soon as it is poured from the furnace, steel makers and strip producers must invest in integrated facilities. A competitive market between the two stages is impossible; each steel strip producer is tied to its adjacent steel producer. In other words, the market becomes a series of **bilateral monopolies**.

Why are these relationships between steel producers and strip producers problematic? To begin with, where a single supplier negotiates with a single buyer, there is no market price: it all depends on relative bargaining power. Such bargaining is likely to be costly: the mutual dependency of the two parties is likely to give rise to opportunism and strategic misrepresentation as each company seeks to both enhance and exploit its bargaining power at the expense of the other. Hence, once we move from a competitive market situation to one where individual buyers and sellers are locked together in close bilateral relationships, the efficiencies of the market system are lost.

The culprits in this situation are transaction-specific investments. When a can-maker buys steel strip, neither the steel strip producer nor the can-maker needs to invest in equipment or technology that is specific to the needs of the other party. In the case of the steel producer and the steel roller, each company's plant is built to match the other party's plant. Once built, the plant's value depends upon the availability of the other party's complementary facilities – each seller is tied to a single buyer, which gives each the opportunity to 'hold up' the other.

Thus, transaction-specific investments result in transaction costs arising from the difficulties of framing a comprehensive contract and the risks of disputes and opportunism that arise from contracts that do not cover every possible eventuality. Empirical research confirms the likelihood of vertical integration where transaction-specific investments are required:[38]

Among automakers, specialised components are more likely to be manufactured in-house than commodity items such as tyres and spark plugs.[39] Similarly, in aerospace, company-specific components are more likely to be produced in-house rather than purchased externally.[40]

In semiconductors some companies, like Intel and ST Microelectronics, are integrated across design and fabrication; others are specialists in either chip design (e.g. ARM) or in fabrication. The more technically complex the integrated circuit and hence the greater the need for the designer and fabricator to invest in technical collaboration and adapt processes to the needs of the other, the better the relative performance of integrated producers.[41]

The problem of hold up could be eliminated by contracts that fully specify prices, quality, quantities and other terms of supply under all possible circumstances. The problem is uncertainty about the future – it is impossible to anticipate all eventualities during the contract period – contracts are inevitably incomplete.

DIFFERENCES IN OPTIMAL SCALE BETWEEN DIFFERENT STAGES OF PRODUC-TION Suppose that FedEx requires delivery vans that are designed and manufactured to meet its particular needs. To the extent that the van manufacturer must make transaction-specific investments, there is an incentive for FedEx to avoid the ensuing transaction costs by building its own vehicles. Would this be an efficient solution? Almost certainly not: the transaction costs avoided by FedEx are likely to be trivial compared with the inefficiencies incurred in manufacturing its own vans. FedEx purchases over 40,000 trucks and vans each year, well below the 200,000 minimum efficient scale of an assembly plant. (Ford produced two million commercial vehicles in 2005.)

The same logic explains why specialist brewers such as Adnams of Suffolk, England or Leffe of Belgium are not backward integrated into cans and bottles like Anheuser-Busch InBev or SAB-Miller – they simply do not possess the scale needed for efficiency in bottle and can manufacture.

THE INCENTIVE PROBLEM Vertical integration changes the incentives between vertically related businesses. Where a market interface exists between a buyer and a seller, profit incentives ensure that the buyer is motivated to secure the best possible deal and the seller is motivated to pursue efficiency and service in order to attract and retain the buyer – these are termed *high-powered incentives*. With vertical integration, internal supplier–customer relationships are subject to *low-powered incentives* – if Shell's tanker fleet is inefficient, employees will lose their bonuses and the head of shipping may be fired. However, these consequences tend to be slow and undramatic. Most of us who have worked in large organisations have found that external contractors are often more responsive to our requests than internal service providers.

One approach to creating stronger performance incentives within vertically integrated companies is to open internal divisions to external competition. Many large corporations have created *shared service organisations* where internal suppliers of corporate services such as IT, training and engineering compete with external suppliers of the same services to serve internal operating divisions.

FLEXIBILITY Both vertical integration and market transactions can claim advantage with regard to different types of flexibility. Where the required flexibility is rapid responsiveness to uncertain demand, there may be advantages in market transactions. The lack of vertical integration in the construction industry reflects, in part, the need for flexibility in adjusting both to cyclical patterns of demand and to the different requirements of each project. Vertical integration may also be disadvantageous in responding quickly to new product development opportunities that require new combinations of technical capabilities. Some of the most successful new electronic products of recent years – Apple's iPod, Microsoft's Xbox, Dell's range of notebook computers – have been produced by contract manufacturers. Extensive outsourcing has been a key feature of fast-cycle product development throughout the electronics sector.

> Extensive outsourcing has been a key feature of fast-cycle product development throughout the electronics sector.

Yet, where system-wide flexibility is required, vertical integration may allow for speed and coordination in achieving simultaneous adjustment throughout the vertical chain. The value chain for T-shirts typically involves specialist companies that undertake knitting, cut-and-sew operations, printing and retailing. Yet, American Apparel operates a tightly coordinated integrated chain that extends from its Los Angeles design and manufacturing centre to its 160 retail stores across 10 countries. This vertical integration allows a super-fast, highly responsive, design-to-distribution cycle.

COMPOUNDING RISK To the extent that vertical integration ties a company to its internal suppliers, vertical integration represents a compounding of risk insofar as problems at any one stage of production threaten production and profitability at all other stages. When union workers at a GM brake plant went on strike in 1998, GM's 24 US assembly plants were quickly brought to a halt. If Disney animation studios fail to produce blockbuster animation movies with new characters, then the knock-on effects are felt through DVD sales, merchandise sales in Disney Stores and lack of new attractions at Disney theme parks.

Assessing the pros and cons of vertical integration

Vertical integration, as we have seen, is neither good nor bad. As with most questions of strategy: it all depends. The value of our analysis is that we are now able to identify the factors that determine the relative advantages of the market transactions versus internalisation within the firm. Table 7.1 summarises some of the key criteria. However, our analysis is not yet complete, we must consider some additional factors that influence the choice of vertical strategy – in particular, the fact that vertical relationships are not limited to the simple choice of make or buy.

Designing vertical relationships

Our discussion so far has compared vertical integration with arm's-length market contracts. In practice, there are a variety of relationships through which buyers and sellers can interact and coordinate their interests. Figure 7.3 shows a number of different types of relationship between buyers and sellers. These relationships may be classified in relation to two characteristics. First, the extent to which the buyer and seller commit resources to the relationship: arm's-length, spot contracts involve no resource commitment beyond the single deal; vertical integration typically involves a substantial investment. Second, the formality of the relationship: long-term contracts and franchises are formalised by the complex written agreements they entail; spot contracts may involve little or no documentation, but are bound by the formalities of common law; collaborative agreements between buyers and sellers are usually informal, while the formality of vertical integration is at the discretion of the firm's management.

Different types of vertical relationship

These different types of vertical relationship offer different combinations of advantages and disadvantages. For example:

● *Long-term contracts.* Market transactions can be either **spot contracts** – buying a cargo of crude oil on the Rotterdam petroleum market – or **long-term contracts** that involve a series of transactions over a period of time and specify the terms of sales and the responsibilities of each party. Spot transactions work well under competitive conditions (many buyers and sellers and a standard product) where there is no need

Figure 7.3 Different types of vertical relationship

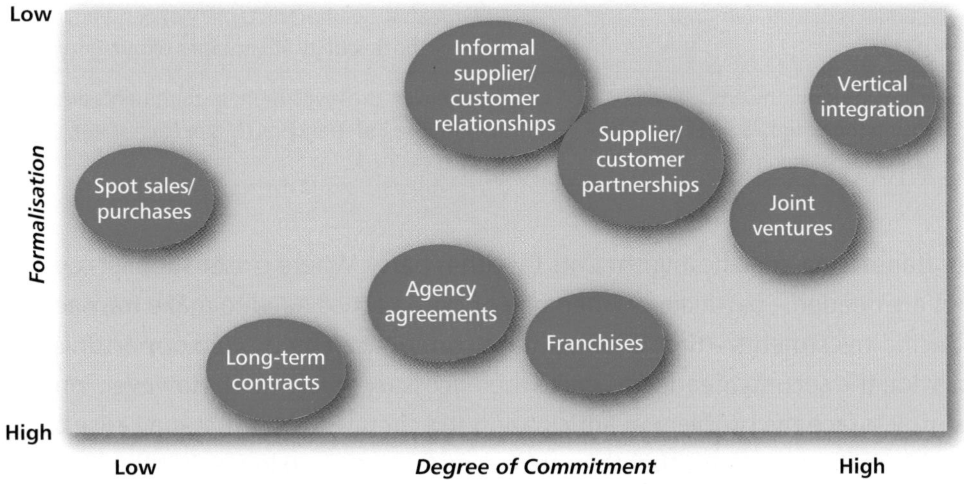

Table 7.1 Vertical integration (VI) versus outsourcing: some key considerations

Characteristics of the vertical relationship	Implication
How many firms are there in the vertically adjacent activity?	The fewer the number of firms, the greater are the transaction costs and bigger the advantages of VI
Do transaction-specific investments need to be made by either party?	Transaction-specific investments increase the advantages of VI
How evenly distributed is information between the vertical stages?	The greater the information asymmetries, the more likely is opportunistic behaviour and the greater the advantages of VI
Are market transactions in intermediate products subject to taxes or regulations?	Taxes and regulations are a cost of market contracts that can be avoided by VI
How uncertain are the circumstances of the transactions over the period of the relationship?	The greater the uncertainties concerning costs, technologies and demand, the greater the difficulty of writing contracts and the greater the advantages of VI
Are two stages similar in terms of the optimal scale of operation?	The greater the dissimilarity, the greater the advantages of market contracts as compared with VI
Are the two stages strategically similar (e.g., similar key success factors, common resources/capabilities)?	The greater the strategic similarity, the greater the advantages of VI over outsourcing
How great is the need for continual investment in upgrading and extending capabilities within individual activities?	The greater the need to invest in capability development, the greater the advantages of outsourcing over VI
How great is the need for entrepreneurial flexibility and drive in the separate vertical activities?	The greater the need for entrepreneurship and flexibility, the greater the advantages of high-powered incentives provided by market contracts and the greater the administrative disadvantages of VI
How uncertain is market demand?	The greater the unpredictability of demand, the greater the flexibility advantages of outsourcing
Does vertical integration compound risk, exposing the entire value chain risks affecting individual stages?	The heavier the investment requirements and the greater the independent risks at each stage, the more risky is VI

for transaction-specific investments by either party. Where closer supplier–customer ties are needed – particularly when one or both parties need to make transaction-specific investments – then a longer term contract can help avoid opportunism and provide the security needed to make the necessary investment. However, long-term contracts face the problem of anticipating the circumstances that may arise during the life of the contract: either they are too restrictive, or so loose that they give rise to opportunism and conflicting interpretation. Long-term contracts often include provisions for the arbitration of contract disputes.

● *Vendor partnerships.* The greater the difficulties of specifying complete contracts for long-term supplier–customer deals, the greater the advantage of vertical relationships being based on trust and mutual understanding. Such relationships can provide the security needed for transaction-specific investments, the flexibility to meet changing circumstances and the incentives to avoid opportunism. Such arrangements may be entirely **relational contracts** with no written contract at all. The model for vendor partnerships has been the close collaborative relationships that many Japanese companies have with their suppliers. Japanese automakers have been much less backward integrated than their US or European counterparts, but have also achieved close collaboration with component makers in technology, design, quality and production scheduling.[42]

● *Franchising.* A **franchise** is a contractual agreement between the owner of a business system and trademark (the franchiser) that permits the franchisee to produce and market the franchiser's product or service in a specified area. Franchising brings together the brand, marketing capabilities and business systems of the large corporation with the entrepreneurship and local knowledge of small firms. The franchising systems of companies such as McDonald's, Hilton Hotels and 7-Eleven convenience stores facilitate the close coordination and investment in transaction-specific assets that vertical integration permits with the high-powered incentives, flexibility and cooperation between strategically dissimilar businesses that market contracts make possible.

Recent trends in vertical integration

The main feature of recent years has been a growing diversity of hybrid vertical relationships that have attempted to reconcile the flexibility and incentives of market transactions with the close collaboration provided by vertical integration. Although collaborative vertical relationships are viewed as a recent phenomenon – associated with microelectronics, biotechnology and other hi-tech sectors – local groupings of vertically collaborating firms are a long-time feature of the craft industries of Europe. This is especially true of northern Italy – both in traditional sectors such as textiles[43] and newer sectors such as packaging equipment[44] and motorcycles.[45]

The supplier networks of Japanese manufacturers with their knowledge sharing and collaborative new product development have become models for many large American and European companies.[46] There has been a massive shift from arm's-length

> There has been a massive shift from arm's-length supplier relationships to long-term collaboration with fewer suppliers.

supplier relationships to long-term collaboration with fewer suppliers. In many instances, competitive tendering and multiple sourcing have been replaced by single-supplier arrangements. Vendor relationships frequently involve supplier certification and quality management programmes and technical collaboration.

At the same time enthusiasm for exploiting lower labour costs in emerging countries has intensified outsourcing among companies in North America, Europe and Japan.[47] In the electronics sector, companies such as Nokia, Hewlett Packard and Sony have outsourced manufacturing to China and services (including call centres and software development) to India.

The mutual dependence that results from close, long-term supplier–buyer relationships creates vulnerability for both parties. While trust may alleviate some of the risks of opportunism, companies can also reinforce their vertical relationships and discourage opportunism through equity stakes and profit-sharing arrangements. For example: Commonwealth Bank of Australia took an equity stake in its IT supplier, EDS Australia; pharmaceutical companies often acquire equity stakes in the biotech companies that undertake much of their R&D; and oil field services companies are increasingly equity partners in upstream projects.

However, in this world of closer vertical relationships, some trends have been in the opposite direction. The internet has radically reduced the transaction costs of markets – particularly in pruning search costs and facilitating electronic payments. The result has been a revival in arm's-length competitive contracting through business-to-business e-commerce hubs such as Covisint (car parts), Elemica (chemicals) and Rock and Dirt (construction equipment).[48]

> Increasingly, outsourcing involves not just individual components and services, but whole chunks of the value chain.

The scope of outsourcing has extended from basic components to a wide range of business services including payroll, IT, training and customer service and support. Increasingly, outsourcing involves not just individual components and services, but whole chunks of the value chain. In electronics, the design and manufacture of entire products are often outsourced to contract manufacturers such as Hon Hai Precision Industry Co Ltd, which makes Apple iPods, Nokia phones and Sony's PlayStation.

Extreme levels of outsourcing have given rise to the concept of the **virtual corporation**: a firm whose primary function is to coordinate the activities of a network of suppliers and downstream partners.[49] In this organisational form, the hub company has the role of *systems integrator*. The critical issue is whether a company that outsources most functions can retain the **architectural capabilities** needed to manage the **component capabilities** of the various partners and contractors. The risk is that the virtual corporation may degenerate into a 'hollow corporation', where it loses the capability to evolve and adapt to changing circumstances.[50] If, as Prahalad and Hamel argue, core competencies are embodied in 'core products' then the more these core products are outsourced, the greater is the potential for the erosion of core competence.[51] Andrea Prencipe's research into aero engines points to the complementarity between architectural capabilities and component capabilities. Thus, even when the aero engine manufacturers outsource key components, they typically maintain R&D into those component technologies.[52] The problems experienced by Boeing in managing the outsourced network model it adopted for its 787 Dreamliner point to the complexity of the system integrator role.[53]

Case Insight 7.6
Should Tesco own and operate its own fleet of lorries?

Table 7.2 outlines some of the key considerations for Tesco with regard to outsourcing transport. The analysis reveals that in terms of its main food retailing business there are advantages to Tesco in operating its own transport fleet although it is possible to conceive of circumstances where work will be contracted out or undertaken in partnership with other specialist logistics firms.

Table 7.2 Key considerations in outsourcing transport for Tesco

Characteristics of the vertical relationship	Implication
How many firms are there in the vertically adjacent activity?	There are a large number of logistics firms that own and operate their own fleets of vehicles, but very few would have the scale of operation necessary to service Tesco's requirements. The fewer the firms that could realistically supply Tesco's transport requirements, the higher the transaction costs and the bigger the advantage to Tesco of operating its own fleet
Do transaction-specific investments need to be made by either party?	Yes. Supplying produce to Tesco stores requires specific investment in particular types of transport vehicle, e.g. refrigerated lorries, but, more importantly, requires investment in highly specific information systems and tracking technologies. Transaction-specific investments increase the advantages of Tesco retaining transport in-house
How evenly distributed is information between the vertical stages?	Tesco has total access to customer and store data which would be difficult and costly to share with third parties. Keeping logistics in-house is less risky for Tesco

▶

How uncertain are the circumstances of the transactions over the period of the relationship?	Whilst there is a certain degree of predictability in demand for grocery products, changes in the weather, the promotional activities of major food producers and even television cookery programmes by chefs like Jamie Oliver can affect the distribution requirements of Tesco stores. There are also uncertainties concerning fuel prices and sources of supply. The greater the uncertainties concerning costs, technologies and demand, the greater the difficulty of writing contracts and the greater the advantages of VI
Are two stages similar in terms of the optimal scale of operation?	A whole host of detailed factors need to be taken into consideration in trying to optimise the size of the fleet needed to distribute goods to Tesco stores in the most effective manner. This would also be the case in trying to optimise the loading and delivery routes of specific vehicles. Tesco's operation in most countries is so large that deliveries require multiple vehicles and scale issues do not loom large. However, there might be some advantage in contracting out certain parts of the logistics operations if scale advantages exist – e.g. if Tesco needs specialist vehicles to deliver perishable food in countries where they have very few stores
Are the two stages strategically similar (e.g., similar key success factors, common resources/ capabilities)?	Logistics and the replenishment of stocks at stores are critical to retail performance. Transport and logistics are strategically dissimilar from retailing in that they require different resources and capabilities. But many large food retailers see retaining competence in distribution and logistics to be very important
How great is the need for continual investment in upgrading and extending capabilities within individual activities?	The greater the need to invest in capability development, the greater the advantages of outsourcing over VI. Whilst, as in most businesses, there is a need to invest in capability development as new technologies develop, the capability investment requirements in this business are modest
How great is the need for entrepreneurial flexibility and drive in the separate vertical activities?	The greater the need for entrepreneurship and flexibility, the greater the advantages of high-powered incentives provided by market contracts and the greater the administrative disadvantages of VI. There is little need for entrepreneurial flexibility in this part of the distribution business
How uncertain is market demand?	The greater the unpredictability of demand, the greater the flexibility advantages of outsourcing. Although consumer tastes change over time, there is a great deal of stability with regard to regular purchases of food products. We have, nonetheless, pointed to sources of uncertainty in demand for certain products, in certain stores at certain times. It is relatively easy to contract for additional lorry space from outside haulage companies should the need arise

Does vertical integration compound risk, exposing the entire value chain to risks affecting individual stages?	The heavier the investment requirements and the greater the independent risks at each stage, the more risky is VI. The investment requirement in distribution is likely to be modest relative to Tesco's total asset base

Managing the corporate portfolio

If opportunities exist to create value through diversification or vertical integration, then managers are confronted by another question: 'how do we manage a multi-business firm in ways that generate as much value as possible?' Portfolio planning models can be a helpful way of starting to address this question.

Portfolio planning: the GE/McKinsey matrix

The basic idea of a portfolio planning model is to represent graphically the individual businesses of a multi-business company in terms of key strategic variables that determine their potential for profit. These strategic variables typically relate to the attractiveness of their market and their competitive advantage within that market. This analysis can guide:

- allocating resources between the businesses on the basis of each business's market attractiveness and competitive position;

- formulating business unit strategy – by comparing the strategic positioning of different businesses, opportunities for repositioning (including divestment) can be identified;

- analysing portfolio balance – a single display of all the company's businesses permits assessment of the overall balance of the portfolio in terms of *cash flow generation* and *growth prospects*;

- setting performance targets on the basis of each business's market attractiveness and its competitive position.

In the GE/McKinsey matrix (see Figure 7.4) the industry attractiveness axis combines: market size, market growth rate, market profitability (return on sales over three years); cyclicality, 'inflation recovery' (potential to increase productivity and product prices) and international potential (ratio of foreign to domestic sales). Business unit competitive advantage combines: market share; return on sales relative to competitors; and relative position with regard to quality, technology, manufacturing, distribution, marketing and cost.[54] The strategy implications are shown by three regions of Figure 7.4.

Figure 7.4 The GE/McKinsey portfolio planning matrix

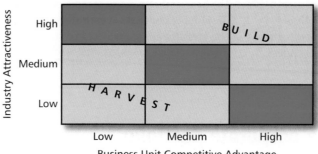

Portfolio planning: BCG's growth–share matrix

The Boston Consulting Group's growth–share matrix also uses industry attractiveness and competitive position to compare the strategic positions of different businesses. However, it uses a single indicator as a proxy for each of these dimensions: industry attractiveness is measured by *rate of market growth*, competitive advantage by *relative market share* (the business unit's market share relative to that of its largest competitor). The four quadrants of the BCG matrix predict patterns of profits and cash flow and indicate strategies to be adopted (see Figure 7.5).[55]

The simplicity of the BCG matrix is both its limitation and its usefulness. It can be prepared very easily and offers a clear picture of a firm's business portfolio in relation to some important strategic characteristics. But the simplicity also masks some problems, for example with respect to market definition. For example, in the BCG matrix, is BMW's car business a 'dog' because it holds less than 2% of the world car market, or a 'cash cow' because it is market leader in the luxury car segment? An even greater problem is the implicit assumption that every business in the portfolio is independent – a direct denial of the basic rationale for the multi-business corporation: the synergistic linkages between businesses.[56]

Portfolio planning: the Ashridge portfolio display

The Ashridge portfolio display is based upon Goold, Campbell and Alexander's parenting advantage framework.[57] It takes account of the fact that the value-creating potential of a business within a company's business portfolio depends, not just upon the characteristics of the business (as assumed by the McKinsey and BCG matrices), but also on the characteristics of the parent. The focus, therefore, is on the *fit* between a business and its parent company. The horizontal axis of Figure 7.6 shows the parent's potential for creating additional profit within the business, e.g. from applying corporate-level management capabilities to the business, from sharing resources and capabilities with other businesses, from economising on transaction costs and so on. The vertical axis measures the potential for value destruction by the parent – these result both from

Figure 7.5 The BCG growth–share matrix

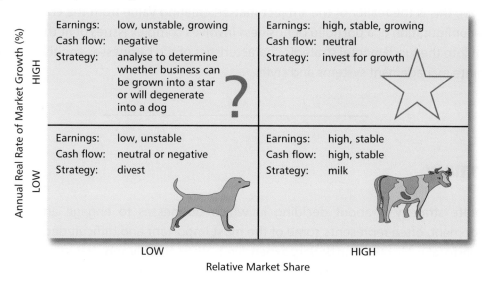

the costs of corporate overhead and mismatch between the management needs of the business and the management systems and style of the parent. These might include bureaucratic rigidity, incompatibility with top management mindset, politicisation of decision making and risks of inappropriate strategic guidance.

The need for assessment of complex issues of fit between the business and the parent and the fact that these assessments inevitably require subjective judgements, mean

Figure 7.6 Ashridge portfolio display: the potential for patenting advantage

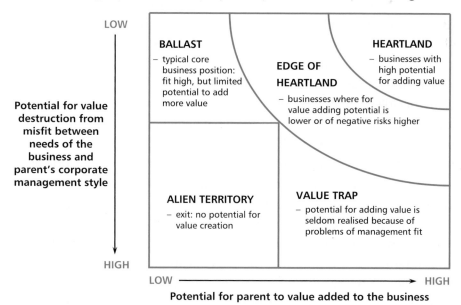

Source: Ashridge Strategic Management Centre

that the Ashridge display is more difficult to use than the GE/McKinsey or BCG matrices. However, this is the reality of the subject matter: creating value from the configuration and reconfiguration of a portfolio of business involves complex issues of fit that requires insight into the fundamental strategic characteristics of the businesses and the nature of corporate management systems and style.

_____

Summary

Corporate strategy is about deciding in which businesses to engage and, for top management, often represents some of the most important and difficult decisions they are likely to take. Mistakes can be very expensive, both financially and strategically, and the business press is littered with examples of large companies who have made such errors. Nevertheless, for firms to prosper in the long term, they must change and inevitably this involves redefining the business in which they operate. Whenever we look at firms that have long histories, we see that they have changed their product lines, acquired new resources and developed new capabilities in line with market opportunities.

Long-term adaptation to market conditions through diversification is likely to be much more successful if it is based on sound strategic analysis. First the objectives of diversification need to be clear and, although some top managers might be tempted to use diversification as a means of growing their own empire, such empires are unlikely to endure unless they are based on genuine value creation. In the late 1980s diversification decisions were often based on vague notions of synergy that involved identifying linkages (sometimes rather tenuous) between industries. We are now able to be much more precise about the need for economies of scope in resources and capabilities and economies of internalisation[58] if diversification is to add value.

Similarly deciding what parts of the value chain to engage in requires systematic thought. Managers not only need to decide what activities they will undertake internally and what they will outsource but also how to best organise their arrangements with external and internal buyers and suppliers. Possible arrangements include arm's-length contracts, long-term agreements and strategic alliances. To decide what constitutes the best option, each firm needs to evaluate its strategic needs, its resources and capabilities at different stages of the value chain, the relative attractiveness of different parts of the value chain and the characteristics of the transactions involved.

Having determined the potential for diversification or vertical integration to add value, the challenge is then how to manage the multi-business firm to extract this potential value. Portfolio planning models can aid managers to make sense of the complexity and to start to develop a degree of consistency in the firm's activities to produce coherence and fit.

Summary table

Learning Objectives	Summary
Be familiar with the concepts of economies of scope, transaction costs and the costs of managing complexity and understand how these ideas help to explain firm boundaries and the shifts in firm boundaries over time	Economies of scope provide cost savings from sharing and transferring resources and capabilities but those cost savings can be achieved by simply selling or licensing the use of resources and capabilities to other companies. Entering into market contracts results in firms incurring transaction costs. On the other hand internalising transactions involves the firm in administrative costs. We would expect profit-seeking firms to seek the least-cost options and for the boundaries of the firm to reflect this. Over time firm boundaries change because the transaction costs of market contracts and the administrative costs of diversified activities change relative to each other
Understand the rationale behind multi-business activity and the potential benefits and costs of extending the horizontal or vertical scope of a firm	We have primarily looked at the ways in which extensions to product and vertical scope can create (or destroy) value by reducing (or increasing) costs and by creating (or destroying) competitive advantage but we also noted that managers sometimes act in their own self-interest rather than that of shareholders. Managers may pursue multiple business activities for reasons of growth or risk reduction rather than profit
Be able to evaluate the pros and cons of changing a firm's scope and different ways of exploiting opportunities for value creation	Porter suggests that there are three essential tests to be applied to diversification: the attractiveness test; the cost-of-entry test; and the better-off test
Appreciate recent trends in diversification and vertical integration over time	In recent years the dominant trend in terms of product scope has been refocusing on the core business. Many large diversified conglomerates have been broken up. The picture with regard to vertical scope has been more complex with a trend towards more hybrid collaborative arrangements
Be familiar with the techniques of portfolio analysis and be able to apply these to corporate strategic decisions	Three portfolio approaches have been outlined – the GE/McKinsey matrix, the BCG matrix and the Ashridge portfolio display. All three approaches assist managers to make sense of complex multi-business activities but all require some element of subjective judgement and insight into the fundamental strategic characteristics of the businesses

Further reading

One of the classic readings on corporate strategy is:

> Porter, M. (1987). From competitive advantage to corporate strategy. *Harvard Business Review*, 65(3), 43–59.

The paper by Constantinos Markides also provides a nice introduction to the diversification debate:

> Markides, C. (1997). To diversify or not to diversify? *Harvard Business Review*, Nov/Dec, 93–9.

A recent article by Jérôme Barthélemy looks at outsourcing versus vertical integration in the case of the Disney-Pixar relationship:

> Barthélemy, J. (2011) The Disney-Pixar relationship dynamics: lessons for outsourcing and vertical integration. *Organizational Dynamics*, 40, 43–8.

In a recent blog Professor Rita McGrath of Harvard Business School argues that vertical integration is making a comeback. The blog 'Why vertical integration is making a comeback' can be found on:

> http://blogs.hbr.org/mcgrath/2009/12/vertical-integration-can-work.html. Accessed 1 May 2011.

With respect to portfolio planning techniques the critique offered by Malcolm Coate provides a summary of the limitations of the approach:

> Coate, M. (1983). Pitfalls in portfolio planning. *Long Range Planning*, 16(3), 47–56.

QUIZ

Visit your enhanced ebook at **www.foundationsofstrategy.com** for self test quiz questions

Self-study questions

1   It has been argued that the developments in information and communication technology (e.g. telephone and computer) during most of the 20th century tended to lower the costs of administration within the firm relative to the costs of market transactions, thereby increasing the size and scope of firms. What about the internet? How has this influenced the efficiency of large integrated firms relative to small, specialised firms coordinated by markets?

2 Minor International plc (MINT) is a large Thai conglomerate that owns and operates over 70 hotel and resorts, runs a range of fast food outlets and is one of Thailand's largest distributors of fashion and cosmetics brands. What are the main advantages and advantages for MINT of engaging in such a wide portfolio of activities?

3 A large proportion of major corporations outsource their IT function to specialist suppliers of IT services such as IBM, EDS (now owned by Hewlett Packard), Accenture and Cap Gemini. What transaction costs are incurred by these outsourcing arrangements and why do they arise? What are the offsetting benefits from IT outsourcing?

4 Electro, a multinational electronics company, operates in four broad product markets. It produces personal computers, printers and scanners, server computers (basic infrastructure for corporate IT) and also provides IT services. Its position in each of these markets is as follows:

- The company is currently the leading manufacturer of personal computers with a market share of 20% of the global market. It is, however, facing strong competition from rival manufacturers whose cost bases appear to be lower than Electro's.

- The company's printer and scanning business has been long been regarded by the company as its crown jewel. The profits made by this unit are regularly used to subsidise other parts of the business.

- The company is the third largest supplier of server computers but in recent years it has lost ground to other established competitors.

- IT services represents a new venture for the company and it has met with some initial success in this market. Its current capabilities in this area are, however, limited and it will need to invest heavily and recruit more specialist staff if it wishes to build this part of the business.

Use a portfolio planning model of your choice to analyse Electro's position. What challenges do you face in trying to apply your selected model? What additional information would you need to make a proper evaluation? What advice might you be able to offer Electro on managing its portfolio? What are the limitations of the portfolio approach you have selected?

GLOSSARY

Visit your enhanced ebook at **www.foundationsofstrategy.com** for key term flashcards

VIDEO

Closing case Diversification at Disney

Introduction

The Walt Disney Company, founded by Walt and Roy Disney, started life as The Disney Brothers Cartoon Studio producing the cartoon series which brought the world such memorable characters as Mickey Mouse and Donald Duck. Having achieved success with short films, the Disney Studio quickly moved into the production of feature-length animated films including *Snow White and the*

Credit: Getty Images

Seven Dwarves, *Pinocchio* and *Fantasia*. The brothers were introduced early in the company's existence to opportunities for diversification when a businessman who wanted to use the image of Mickey Mouse to promote sales of a drawing tablet for children approached them. The establishment of the Mickey Mouse Club for fans soon after this encounter suggests that the Disney brothers recognised immediately the potential for selling toys, books and other products linked to their animated characters. Today the company's retail activities include clothing, home decor, books and magazines, food and drink and stationery products, much of which is sold through the company's retail outlets, Disney Stores. To understand how a small animation studio has grown to become a highly diversified, international media and entertainment company with revenues in excess of US$38 billion,[59] we need to unpick Disney's portfolio of activities in more detail.

The firm's business activities

The Walt Disney Company groups its activities into five main areas – Media Networks, Parks and Resorts, Studio Entertainment, Consumer Products, and Interactive Media – but beneath these five titles lies a multiplicity of different business activities.

Table 7.3 indicates the size of these different parts of the business by revenue in 2010.

Table 7.3 Disney's revenue 2009/10

Business group	Revenue US$ million	Revenue as % of the total
Media Networks	17,162	46
Parks and Resorts	10,761	28
Studio Entertainment	6,701	18
Consumer Products	2,678	7
Interactive Media	761	1
Total	38,063	100

Extending product scope

Amongst the first areas of business developed by Disney outside its animation and merchandising base were theme parks. The company opened Disneyland in California in 1955 and went on to establish the Walt Disney World Resort in Orlando, Florida in 1971. Disneyland resorts were subsequently developed in Tokyo (Japan in 1983), Paris (France in 1993), Hong Kong in 2005 and most recently Shanghai (China, currently under construction). The theme parks were a natural extension of Disney's core business because the themes and characters that appeared in its films provided the basis for the rides and fantasy settings. A virtuous circle was created whereby the films promoted the parks and the parks promoted the films. Over time the development of the theme parks took Disney into a new area. Visitors to the theme parks needed accommodation so Disney built and ran hotels; Disney became skilful in managing travel arrangements and the tourist experience and subsequently founded the Disney Vacation Club and the Disney Cruise Line; Disney planned and built retail, entertainment and dining complexes, which led to the establishment of the Disney Development Company.

Perhaps one of the most surprising extensions to Disney's portfolio of activities was its decision to build a new town, called Celebration, on 20 square kilometres of land located near the Disney Resort in Florida. Disney was the driving force behind the establishment of this new community, which currently has a population of around 11,000 people. Celebration involved Disney in town planning, housing developments, the design of business premises and the provision of facilities like shops, libraries and schools. The Disney CEO Michael Eisner was keen to develop a town 'worthy of the Disney brand and legacy that extended to Walt Disney's vision of an Experimental Prototype Community of Tomorrow (EPCOT)'.[60] Whilst

◀ at first sight this development appears far removed from Disney's core business, closer examination of the development of Disney's capabilities over time reveals that this has stronger links to Disney's other activities than it might first seem. The company's ownership and operation of Disneyland resorts has involved it in real estate development, project management, attraction design, engineering support and master planning services. Building a new town capitalised on many of these capabilities and also enabled Disney to set up Disney Imagineering, to sell these kinds of services to other firms.

Extending vertical scope

Disney has not only extended its product scope, it has also expanded along the media supply chain. Through its Studio Entertainment division Disney continues to produce animated movies but, in addition, makes and acquires the rights to other film, direct-to-video, musical and theatrical content. Through its Media Network segment, which comprises US television and radio stations, international cable networks and distribution and publishing operations, it distributes media content to households. Disney growth in this area was mainly achieved through acquisition. Of particular note was Disney's acquisition of Capital Cities/ABC in 1995 for the sum of US$19 billion. Capital Cities/ABC was a media company that owned and produced content for a range of TV and radio stations. This move was strategically important because gaining access to distribution is a key success factor in the media industry. The high fixed costs of making films or television programmes means that profitability depends on gaining as broad a distribution network as possible. If a company controls both content and distribution it can promote its own content and control access to other people's. Over time the media sector has come to be dominated by a few large media conglomerates like Time Warner and Bertelsmann. If Disney remained an independent content producer without direct access to networks and viewers it ran the risk of being squeezed out by its downstream rivals.

There are, of course, drawbacks as well as benefits to this kind of forward vertical integration. Audiences want the most entertaining content available and this is unlikely to always come from within a firm's own studios. Similarly studios with good content want to get in front of the largest possible audiences and restricting distribution to the group's own channels and networks limits the number of viewers. The other claimed drawback is a reduction in creativity. Speaking in 2002, Peter Chernin, the then president of News Corporation, argued that 'All the benefits of size, whether it's leverage, synergy or scope, are fundamentally the enemies of creativity'.[61]

Future challenges

Disney's continuing success depends on its ability to consistently create and distribute films, broadcast and cable programmes, online material, electronic games, theme park attractions, hotel and other resort facilities, travel experiences and consumer products that meet the changing preferences of a wide range of consumers, a growing number of whom are located outside the United States. The linkages between businesses mean that success or failure in one part of the business can affect other parts. For example if entertainment offerings, like *Who Wants to be a Millionaire* or *High School Musical* cease to be popular with audiences then revenue from advertising, which is based in part on programme ratings, falls and so does revenue from merchandising. In the worst-case scenario if the firm experienced successive content failures then viewers might cancel their subscriptions to cable channels or reduce their visits to entertainment parks where the themed rides are seen as passé. At the same time changes in technology and different delivery formats such as television, DVDs, computer and web-based formats are affecting not only the demand for the company's entertainment products but also the cost of producing and distributing them.

Disney has grown through a variety of means: organically through merger and acquisition and through collaborative arrangements with partner firms. Its brand has been stretched across myriad different activities many of which are very tenuously connected to its 'family entertainment' core. It remains to be seen whether Disney's senior management can continue to successfully manage this complex portfolio of businesses and retain the ability to produce the kind of creative content that is at the heart of the enterprise.

Case questions

- How does the concept of 'economies of scope' help to explain Disney's diversification strategy?

- What are the pros and cons for Disney of operating television and cable networks?

- In 2009 Disney announced that it had acquired Marvel Entertainment, a comic book and action hero company for US$4 billion. How would you evaluate the value-creating potential of this decision?

- What are the key challenges Disney's senior management faces in running such a diverse set of businesses?

1 *Tesco Annual General Report 2010.*

2 *Tesco Annual Report 2010.*

3 M. Potter, 'Tesco to outpace growth at rivals. Reuters [online]. http://uk.reuters.com/article/2011/02/17/uk-tesco-igd-idUKTRE71G01220110217. Accessed 14 April 2011.

4 http://en.wikipedia.org/wiki/Tesco. Accessed 4 August 2011.

5 *The Independent*, 'A trip to Alton Towers? That'll be £2000 please', (14 August 2005).

6 S. Mauch, 'From A(pples) to Z(oom lenses): extending the boundaries of multi-channel retailing at Tesco.com', INSEAD Case Study (2007).

7 Tesco was awarded a banking licence in 1997.

8 See, for example, D. Prosser, 'The long wait for better competition in British banking', *The Independent* (24 March 2011).

9 A. Felsted, 'Retailers: trust the stores to get into banking'. *The Financial Times* (28 April 2010).

10 *Tesco Annual Report 2009.*

11 Economies of scope can arise in consumption as well as in production: customers may prefer to buy different products from the same supplier. See T. Cottrell and B. R. Nault, 'Product variety and firm survival in microcomputer software', *Strategic Management Journal* 25 (2004): 1005–26.

12 There is some evidence to the contrary. See H. Park, T. A. Kruse, K. Suzuki and K. Park, 'Long-term performance following mergers of Japanese companies: the effect of diversification and affiliation', *Pacific Basin Finance Journal* 14 (2006); and P. R. Nayyar, 'Performance effects of information asymmetry and economies of scope in diversified service firms', *Academy of Management Journal* 36 (1993): 28–57.

13 The role of capabilities in diversification is discussed in C. C. Markides and P. J. Williamson, 'Related diversification, core competencies and corporate performance', *Strategic Management Journal* 15 (Special Issue, 1994): 149–65.

14 S. Mesure, 'Tesco plans to break into house-building sector', *The Independent* (22 January 2007).

15 A. Chandler Jr, *The Visible Hand: The Managerial Revolution in American Business* (Cambridge: MIT Press, 1977).

16 R. H. Coase, 'The nature of the firm', *Economica* 4 (1937): 386–405.

17 The term *interaction costs* has also been used to describe 'the time and money expended whenever people and companies exchange goods, services or ideas'. See J. Hagel and M. Singer, 'Unbundling the corporation', *Harvard Business Review* (March–April 1999): 133–44.

18 F. W. Taylor, *The Principles of Scientific Management* (Bulletin of the Taylor Society, 1916).

19 J. K. Galbraith, *The New Industrial State* (Harmondsworth: Penguin, 1969).

20 J. P. Liebeskind, 'Internal capital markets: benefits, costs and organizational arrangements', *Organization Science* 11 (2000): 58–76.

21 D. Scharfstein and J. Stein, 'The dark side of internal capital markets: divisional rent seeking and inefficient investment', *Journal of Finance* 55 (2000): 2537–64; V. Maksimovic and G. Phillips, 'Do conglomerate firms allocate resources inefficiently across industries?' *Journal of Finance* 57 (2002): 721–67; R. Rajan, H. Servaes and L. Zingales, 'The cost of diversity: the diversification discount and inefficient investment', *Journal of Finance* 55 (2000): 35–84.

22 M. E. Porter, 'From competitive advantage to corporate strategy', *Harvard Business Review* (May–June 1987): 46.

23 M. Hayward and D. C. Hambrick, 'Explaining the premiums paid for large acquisitions', *Administrative Science Quarterly* 42 (1997): 103–27.

24 A study of 68 diversifying ventures by established companies found that, on average, breakeven was not attained until the seventh and eighth years of operation: R. Biggadike, 'The risky business of diversification', *Harvard Business Review* (May–June, 1979): 103–11.

25 J. Hughes, 'Banking on it', *Financial Times* (16 May 2008).

26 S. Butler, 'Do Britain's biggest retailers have the know-how to cash in on our lack of trust of high street banks?' *Management Today* (1 July 2009).

27 In 2011 Tesco announced that it was spending an additional £200 million on upgrading its banking IT systems (A. Mari, 'Tesco increases spend on banking IT', *Computer Weekly* (19 April 2011).

28 R. M. Grant, A. P. Jammine and H. Thomas, 'Diversity, diversification and performance in the British manufacturing industry', *Academy of Management Journal* 31 (1988): 771–801.

29 L. E. Palich, L. B. Cardinal and C. C. Miller, 'Curvi-linearity in the diversification-performance linkage: an examination of over three decades of research', *Strategic Management Journal* 22 (2000): 155–74.

30 N. Harper and S. P. Viguerie, 'Are you too focused?' *McKinsey Quarterly* (2002 Special Edition): 29–37.

31 J. D. Martin and A. Sayrak, 'Corporate diversification and shareholder value: a survey of recent literature', *Journal of Corporate Finance* 9 (2003): 37–57.

32 C. C. Markides, 'Consequences of corporate refocusing: ex ante evidence', *Academy of Management Journal* 35 (1992): 398–412; C. C. Markides, 'Diversification, restructuring and economic performance', *Strategic Management Journal* 16 (1995): 101–18.

33 R. P. Rumelt, *Strategy, Structure and Economic Performance* (Cambridge, MA: Harvard University Press, 1974).

34 See, for example, A. Michel and I. Shaked, 'Does business diversification affect performance?' *Financial Management* 13 (1984): 18–24; G. A. Luffman and R. Reed, *The Strategy and Performance of British Industry, 1970–80* (London: Macmillan, 1984).

35 G. F. Davis, K. A. Diekman and C. F. Tinsley, 'The decline and fall of the conglomerate firm in the 1980s: a study in the de-institutionalization of an organizational form', *American Sociological Review* 49 (1994): 547–70.

36 T. Khanna and K. Palepu, 'Why focused strategies may be wrong for emerging markets', *Harvard Business Review* (July–August, 1997): 41–51; D. Kim, D. Kandemir and S. T. Cavusgil, 'The role of family conglomerates in emerging markets', *Thunderbird International Business Review* 46 (January, 2004): 7–20.

37 The situation is different in aluminium cans, where aluminium producers such as Alcoa and Pechiney and users such as Coca-Cola and Anheuser-Busch are major producers of beverage cans.

38 For a review of empirical evidence on transaction costs and vertical integration see: J. T. Macher and B. D. Richman 'Transaction cost economics: an assessment of empirical research in the social sciences', *Business and Politics* 10 (2008): Article 1; M.D. Whinston, 'On the transaction cost determinants of vertical integration', *Journal of Law Economics and Organization* 19 (2003): 1–23.

39 K. Monteverde and J. J. Teece, 'Supplier switching costs and vertical integration in the car industry', *Bell Journal of Economics* 13 (Spring 1982): 206–13.

40 S. Masten, 'The organisation of production: evidence from the aerospace industry', *Journal of Law and Economics* 27 (October 1984): 403–17.

41 J. T. Macher, 'Technological development and the boundaries of the firm: a knowledge-based examination in semiconductor manufacturing,' *Management Science* 52 (2006): 826–43; K. Monteverde, 'Technical dialogue as an incentive for

vertical integration in the semiconductor industry', *Management Science* 41 (1995): 1624–38.

42 J. H. Dyer, 'Effective interfirm collaboration: how firms minimise transaction costs and maximize transaction value', *Strategic Management Journal* 18 (1997): 535–56; J. H. Dyer, 'Specialised supplier networks as a source of competitive advantage: evidence from the car industry', *Strategic Management Journal* 17 (1996): 271–92.

43 N. Owen and A. C. Jones, 'A comparative study of the British and Italian textile and clothing industries', Department of Trade and Industry (2003).

44 G. Lorenzoni and A. Lipparini, 'The leveraging of interfirm relationships as distinctive organisational capabilities: a longitudinal study', *Strategic Management Journal* 20 (1999): 317–38.

45 G. Lorenzoni and A. Lipparini, 'Organising around strategic relationships: networks of suppliers in the Italian motorcycle industry', in K. O. Cool *et al.* (Eds), *Restructuring Strategy* (Oxford: Blackwell, 2005): 44–67.

46 J. H. Dyer and K. Nobeoka, 'Creating and managing a high-performance knowledge-sharing network: the Toyota case', *Strategic Management Journal* 21 (2000): 345–68.

47 D. Farrell, 'Smarter offshoring', *Harvard Business Review* (June 2006): 85–92.

48 www.covisint.com; www.elemica.com; www.rockanddirt.com.

49 'The virtual corporation', *Business Week* (8 February 1993): 98–104; W. H. Davidow and M. S. Malone, *The Virtual Corporation* (New York: HarperCollins, 1992).

50 H. W. Chesborough and D. J. Teece, 'When is virtual virtuous? Organising for innovation', *Harvard Business Review* (May–June 1996): 68–79.

51 C. K. Prahalad and Gary Hamel, 'The core competences of the corporation', *Harvard Business Review* (May–June 1990): 79–91.

52 S. Brusoni, A. Prencipe and K. Pavitt, 'Knowledge specialization, organizational coupling and the boundaries of the firm: why do firms know more than they make?' *Administrative Science Quarterly* 46 (2001): 597–621.

53 'Boeing's Dreamliner delays are a nightmare' *SeekingAlpha,* http://seekingalpha.com/article/110735-boeing-s-dreamliner-delays-are-a-nightmare.

54 For a fuller discussion of the GE/McKinsey matrix see: 'Enduring Ideas: The GE-McKinsey nine-box matrix', *McKinsey Quarterly* (September 2008).

55 For a fuller discussion of the BCG matrix see: B. Henderson, 'The experience curve reviewed: IV. The growth share matrix or product portfolio', Boston Consulting Group (1973).

56 Booz Allen Hamilton claim that 'dog' businesses can offer promising potential (H. Quarls, T. Pernsteiner and K. Rangan, 'Love your dogs', Booz Allen Hamilton (15 March 2005).

57 M. Goold, A. Campbell and M. Alexander, *Corporate-Level Strategy: Creating Value in the Multibusiness Company* (New York: John Wiley & Sons Inc., 1994).

58 The economies of internalisation is merely a shorthand way of referring to the cost savings that result from undertaking activities and associated transactions within the firm rather than externally with third parties.

59 The Walt Disney Company Annual General Report 2010.

60 http://en.wikipedia.org/wiki/Celebration_Florida. Accessed 4 August 2011.

61 *The Economist*, 'Tangled webs: a special report on media conglomerates' (2002).

Global strategies and the multinational corporation

Introduction and objectives

At the beginning of August 2011, prices plummeted on stock markets across the world. London's FTSE index fell by 10%, Germany's DAX lost almost 13% and the Dow Jones index in New York fell by 5.8%.[1] Similar falls in share prices occurred in Japan, South Korea, China and India. The immediate cause of the problem was a fear that two European countries, Italy and Spain, might not be able to repay their debts because the costs of financing their budget deficits were rising. If a country spends more than it raises in taxation in a year then it has an annual deficit. Such deficits are usually financed by issuing bonds (in essence IOUs) that are held by banks and other investors, including foreign governments. It might be expected that the possibility of default would have an adverse affect on the share prices of European banks and other institutions holding Italian or Spanish government bonds but the impact was much wider than this. Because of trade and financial links, problems in one part of the global economy are now quickly transmitted around the world in a chain reaction. The concern was that European countries might react to this debt crisis by cutting back on their expenditure in order to reduce the size of their deficits, but in so doing there was the possibility that this could trigger a more general economic downturn. Many Asian economies are dependent on the exports of goods to the West and, similarly, Latin American and Middle Eastern countries are dependent on the export of resources like copper and petroleum, so cutbacks in Europe could have a cascading effect.

The fact that spending by the Italian government can have a significant impact on steel producers in India and farmers in Africa is a testament to the power of internationalisation to transmit and amplify local economic factors. Internationalisation is the most important and pervasive force that has reshaped the competitive environment of business during the past half-century. While recent events have identified internationalisation with global contamination, for most of the past 60 years, *internationalisation* has been a source of expanding opportunity for both firms and individuals. The opening of national markets has resulted in widening consumer choice, huge increases in efficiency and growth options for both large and small firms.

Internationalisation occurs through two mechanisms: *trade* and *direct investment*. The growth of world trade has consistently outstripped the growth of world output, increasing export/sales and import penetration ratios for all countries and all industries. For the OECD countries, total trade (imports and exports) rose from 11% of GDP in 1960 to 52% in 2007. The total stock of direct investment by OECD firms amounted to $13 trillion at the beginning of 2009 – equivalent to 34% of OECD GDP.[2]

The forces driving both trade and direct investment are, first, the quest to exploit market opportunities in other countries, and, second, the desire to exploit resources and capabilities located in other countries. The resulting 'globalisation of business' has created vast flows of international transactions comprising payments for trade and services, flows of factor payments (interest, profits and licensing fees) and flows of capital.

What does the internationalisation of the world economy mean for strategy analysis? As we shall see, internationalisation is both a threat and an opportunity. Internationalisation opens domestic markets to competitors from different countries – often with tragic consequences not just for individual firms but sometimes for entire domestic industries. Internationalisation also offers vast opportunity allowing firms with small domestic markets to become global leaders: Nokia (from Finland) in mobile phones, Swatch (from Switzerland) in watches, A.P. Moller-Maersk (from Denmark) in shipping, Anheuser-Busch InBev (from Belgium) in beer, BHP (from Australia) in metals mining and Research in Motion (from Canada) in smartphones. Most of all, the international dimension adds considerable complexity to our strategy analysis – not just in broadening the scope of markets (and competition) but also in complicating the analysis of competitive advantage.

By the time you have completed this chapter you will be able to:

● Discern patterns of internationalisation;

● Analyse the implications of a firm's national environment for its competitive advantage;

● Formulate strategies for exploiting overseas business opportunities, including overseas market entry strategies and overseas production strategies;

● Formulate international strategies that achieve an optimal balance between global integration and national differentiation;

● Design organisational structures and management systems appropriate to the pursuit of international strategies.

Opening case IKEA's international strategy

© IKEA

IKEA is one of the largest furniture makers and retailers in the world and is well known for its low-cost, stylish furniture and bold, sometimes controversial, advertising campaigns. Established by Swedish entrepreneur, Ingvar Kamprad in 1943, by 2010 the company had an estimated turnover of €23.1 billion, net profits of €2.7 billion and around 300 stores in 26 countries.[3]

Whilst IKEA has undoubtedly succeeded in foreign markets, establishing stores in countries as far apart as Australia and Romania, 80% of its sales still come from Europe and its overseas expansion has not always progressed as smoothly as it would have liked. Most recently it has sacked two of its senior executives in Russia for allegedly turning a blind eye to bribes paid to a sub-contractor[4] and has been involved in acrimonious disputes with labour unions in France over its pay offers.[5]

A brief company history

Brought up in a small farming community in southern Sweden, Kamprad was an enterprising individual who even as a boy sold small items like matches and Christmas cards to his neighbours. He came up with the name, IKEA, by combining his initials (IK) with the first letters of the name of the farm and village in which he grew up (Elmtaryd, Agunnaryd). At first IKEA was a vehicle for Kamprad's trading and mail-order activities. He added furniture to his product lines in 1947 mainly by accident but quickly recognised that there was a growing demand in post-war Sweden for inexpensive household goods. Due to problems with Swedish manufacturers, the company started to procure furniture from Poland and found this to be a cost-effective strategy. By 1951 Kamprad decided to discontinue sales of other products and focus exclusively on furniture. The first IKEA showroom was opened in Sweden in 1953 to allow mail-order customers to establish the quality of the items they were ordering by seeing and touching them. In 1955 the company started designing its own products and a few years later opened retail stores.

The company offered well-designed, stylish items that drew on Swedish design traditions at inexpensive prices. Costs were kept down by designing furniture with a target price in mind. Furniture was flat-packed to minimise transportation costs, assembled by the customer to keep operating costs low and production was sourced from low-cost locations. IKEA became known for its cost-minimising approach and its associated capabilities in cost-efficient design, sourcing and logistics. The founder's passion for making his company's products affordable is still reflected in the company's mission which is to 'offer a wide range of well-designed, functional home furnishing products at prices so low that as many people as possible will be able to afford them'.[6]

Pattern of internationalisation

The company's forays into international markets began first by opening stores in nearby Scandinavian countries but, as Table 8.1 indicates, the company quickly moved farther afield. In the early years the formula for international expansion was a simple one. The company identified markets with the potential for high sales volumes and then purchased cheap land on the outskirts of a big city to establish a base. A tight-knit team of trusted and experienced Swedish managers (sometimes referred to as IKEA missionaries) relocated to the country in question and supervised the building of the new store, led the operational team and ran the business until it was deemed mature and could be handed over to local managers. Once a beachhead was established, IKEA tended to cluster further stores in the same geographical area.

In its first phase of internationalisation IKEA entered new markets by keeping its product catalogue and its management processes the same. There were sometimes minor adjustments to items to reflect national differences, for example standard bed sizes tended to differ between countries, but the overwhelming majority of the products sold by IKEA were common across countries. The Swedish roots of the company were celebrated as a source of distinctiveness not only in the design of the firm's products but also in its management style. Managers across the organisation were strongly encouraged to adopt a Swedish, open and non-hierarchical management style because Kamprad felt that this mode motivated employees and had universal appeal. A pragmatic problem-solving style and egalitarian approach to decision making became the cornerstone of IKEA's unique culture and was referred to by the founder and his team as the 'IKEA way'.[7]

◀ **Table 8.1** Year in which the first IKEA store was opened

Year	Country	Location
1958	Sweden	Älmhult
1963	Norway	Oslo (Nesbru)
1969	Denmark	Copenhagen (Ballerup)
1973	Switzerland	Zürich (Spreitenbach)
1974	Germany	Munich (Eching)
1975	Australia	Artamon
1975	Hong Kong	Hong Kong (Tsim Sha Tsui)
1976	Canada	Vancouver (Richmond)
1977	Austria	Vienna (Vösendorf)
1978	Netherlands	Rotterdam (Sliedrecht)
1978	Singapore	Singapore
1980	Spain	Gran Canaria (Las Palmas)
1981	Iceland	Reykjavik
1981	France	Paris (Bobigny)
1983	Saudi Arabia	Jeddah
1984	Belgium	Brussels (Zaventem and Ternat)
1984	Kuwait	Kuwait City
1985	United States	Philadelphia
1987	United Kingdom	Manchester (Warrington)
1989	Italy	Milan (Cinisello Balsamo)
1990	Hungary	Budapest
1991	Poland	Platan
1991	Czech Republic	Prague (Zlicin)
1991	United Arab Emirates	Dubai

1992	Slovakia	Bratislava
1994	Taiwan	Taipei
1996	Finland	Esbo
1996	Malaysia	Kuala Lumpur
1998	China	Shanghai
2000	Russia	Moscow (Chimki)
2001	Israel	Netanya
2001	Greece	Thessaloniki
2004	Portugal	Lisbon
2005	Turkey	Istanbul
2006	Japan	Tokyo (Funabashi)
2007	Romania	Bucharest
2007	Cyprus	Nicosia
2009	Ireland	Dublin
2010	Dominican Republic	Santo Domingo
2011	Bulgaria	Sofia
2011	Thailand	Bangkok

Source: IKEA's website: http://franchisor.ikea.com/worldmap/interactive.html. Accessed 9 June 2011.

The challenges of internationalisation

As the company moved further from its Scandinavian base and became more dependent on overseas operations so the pressure for the company to be more nationally responsive grew. One of IKEA's biggest challenges came when it entered the US market. The company expected its standard range to sell as well as it did in Europe but that was not the case. American tastes were different. Americans were used to purchasing furniture from high-end retailers who offered free delivery, interior design advice and other value-added services and many found the design and dimensions of the furniture a poor fit with their requirements. Whilst recognising the need to adapt some of its products to local demands,

◀ IKEA's low-cost business model depended on the high volume sales that came from standardisation. The IKEA headquarters team recognised the need for some country-specific adaptations and made it possible for area managers to put forward suggestions but to achieve economies of scale, the extent of adaptation was limited to 5–10% of the product range.

As well as adapting the company's product lines, there was also pressure to adapt the management style. The democratic approach to management characteristic of Swedish organisations was not perceived as favourably as the top team expected. Grol and Schoch,[8] for example, point out that in Germany Swedish management was considered peculiar. Older workers felt uncomfortable calling managers by their first names and employees, in general, disliked the lack of formality. Similarly in France rather than seeing IKEA's flat organisation structure as enabling, many employees saw it as stripping them of status and removing opportunities for promotion. The fact that the key decision-making and training centres were located in Sweden (and required managers to be fluent in Swedish) made it very difficult for non-Scandinavians to progress to the higher echelons of management.

More recently IKEA has faced a different set of challenges in its entry into China.[9] The company has always positioned itself as a low-cost provider but in China it is seen as an expensive brand by its target market of young professionals. Import duties and exchange rate fluctuations make it difficult for IKEA to compete with domestic furniture producers on cost and IKEA's designs are quickly copied and products undercut by local producers. Whilst China has a huge market potential for IKEA because of its population's growing affluence and a surge in home ownership, it is very difficult to maintain a low-cost market position in this environment. Faced with this dilemma IKEA has cut its prices significantly and sacrificed short-term profitability for long-term growth. In China some IKEA products sell at prices 70% lower than in other countries and some tables cost less than a Starbucks' latte. A number of commentators have doubted the wisdom of this move. Rein,[10] for example, suggests that, in China, IKEA has become an entertainment destination rather than a serious place to shop for furniture. The stores are crowded and consumers pick up free catalogues, get ideas for home decoration and enjoy the benefit of their children playing in an air-conditioned environment but make few purchases. Those that do shop buy only low-value items like drinking glasses or bathmats. The middle-class consumers that might spend money in the stores are deterred by the crowds so as Rein puts it, in China 'IKEA is too expensive for the majority of consumers but too cheap for the real spenders'.

Patterns of internationalisation

Internationalisation occurs through *trade* – the sale and shipment of goods and services from one country to another – and *direct investment* – building or acquiring productive assets in another country. On this basis we can identify different types of industry according to the extent and mode of their internationalisation (see Figure 8.1):

Internationalisation occurs through *trade* – the sale and shipment of goods and services from one country to another – and *direct investment* – building or acquiring productive assets in another country.

- **Sheltered industries** are served exclusively by indigenous firms. They are sheltered from both imports and inward direct investment by regulation, trade barriers or because of the localised nature of the goods and services they offer. The forces of internationalisation have made this category progressively smaller over time as the example box on Toni & Guy illustrates. Sheltered industries are primarily fragmented service industries (dry cleaning, car repair, funeral services), some small-scale manufacturing (handicrafts, residential construction) and industries producing products that are non-tradable because they are perishable (fresh milk, bread) or difficult to move (four-poster beds, garden sheds).

- **Trading industries** are those where internationalisation occurs primarily through imports and exports. If a product is transportable, not nationally differentiated

Figure 8.1 Patterns of industry internationalisation

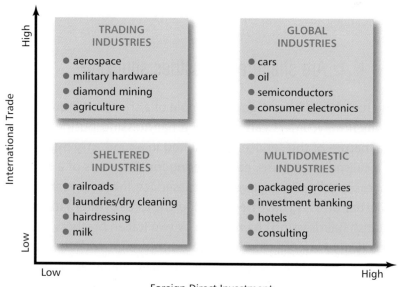

and subject to substantial scale economies, exporting from a single location is the most efficient means to exploit overseas markets. This would apply, for example, to commercial aircraft, shipbuilding and defence equipment. Trading industries also include products whose inputs are available only in a few locations: diamonds from South Africa, caviar from Iran and Azerbaijan.

- **Multidomestic industries** are those that internationalise through direct investment – either because trade is not feasible (as in the case of service industries such as retail banking, consulting or hotels) or because products are nationally differentiated (e.g., frozen meals, recorded music).

- **Global industries** are those in which both trade and direct investment are important. Most large-scale manufacturing industries tend to evolve towards global structures: in cars, consumer electronics, semiconductors, pharmaceuticals and beer, levels of trade and direct investment are high.

By which route does internationalisation typically occur? In the case of manufacturing companies, internationalisation typically begins with exports – mostly to countries with the least 'psychic distance' from the home country. Later a sales and distribution subsidiary is established in the overseas country. Eventually the company develops a more integrated overseas subsidiary that undertakes manufacturing and product development as well.[11] In service industries, internationalisation may involve replication (McKinsey & Company), acquisition (HSBC), or franchising (McDonald's).[12] With the advent of the internet, some companies have gone global from their inception. Companies that internationalise early are often found in high-tech industries[13] with inadequate domestic markets.

Example 8.1 Are sheltered industries shrinking?

Hairdressing has always been a good example of a sheltered industry. The relative ease with which newcomers can start up a hairdressing business together with the personal nature of the service has resulted in an industry made up of a large number of localised small firms, each catering for the needs of a slightly different clientele but essentially offering a very similar service. In recent years, however, even industries like hairdressing have begun to feel the force of internationalisation. Toni & Guy is a British hairdressing chain set up by two Italian brothers, Giuseppe (Toni) and Gaetano (Guy) Mascolo who immigrated to the UK with their parents in the early 1960s. From a humble start the brothers have managed to build a business with an annual turnover of £175 million and over 500 salons in 42 countries.[14]

The brothers have achieved this success by creating a standardised service and a brand that they have franchised across the globe. Whilst everyone's hair is different and there have always been recognisable national and local differences in hairstyles and treatments, the advent of mass media and the internet has resulted in the rapid transmission of fashion trends between countries. This has resulted in a degree of convergence in consumer preferences, particularly of young adults, around appearance. This convergence has created the opportunity for Toni & Guy to create an international brand.

To achieve consistency in hairdressing services all Toni & Guy hairdressers are trained at one of the company's 24 academies around the world. The salons are designed to a common template and use the range of hair-care products developed by the firm. The growth of the firm has provided the resources necessary to undertake advertising campaigns, to develop online booking systems and style galleries for clients and to extend its product range. The success of the firm has spawned a number of imitators and though it is unlikely that international chains will replace local independent businesses in the near future, the nature of competition in the industry is changing and an industry that was once sheltered is beginning to see the growth of international competition.

Analysing competitive advantage in an international context

The growth of international competition over the past 20 years has been associated with some stunning reversals in the competitive positions of different companies. In 1989, US Steel was the world's biggest steel company; in 2009 ArcelorMittal based in Luxemburg and India was the new global giant. In 1989, IBM, Compaq and Apple were world market leaders in PCs. By 2009, Hewlett-Packard and Acer were the new brand leaders; however, ASUSTeK was the biggest manufacturer of PCs.

To understand how internationalisation has shifted the basis of competition, we need to extend our framework for analysing competitive advantage to include the influence of

Figure 8.2 Competitive advantage in an international context

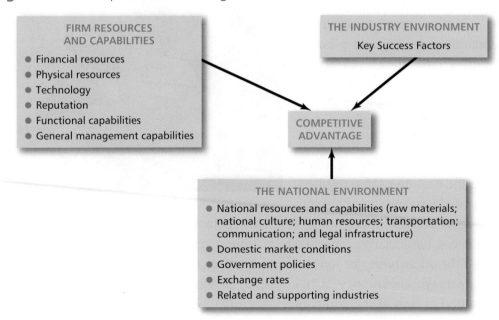

FIRM RESOURCES
AND CAPABILITIES
- Financial resources
- Physical resources
- Technology
- Reputation
- Functional capabilities
- General management capabilities

THE INDUSTRY ENVIRONMENT
Key Success Factors

COMPETITIVE
ADVANTAGE

THE NATIONAL ENVIRONMENT
- National resources and capabilities (raw materials; national culture; human resources; transportation; communication; and legal infrastructure)
- Domestic market conditions
- Government policies
- Exchange rates
- Related and supporting industries

firms' national environments. Competitive advantage, we have noted, is achieved when a firm matches its internal strengths in resources and capabilities to the key success factors of the industry. In international industries, competitive advantage depends not just upon a firm's internal resources and capabilities, but also its national environment – in particular, the availability of resources within the countries where it does business. Figure 8.2 summarises the implications of internationalisation for our basic strategy model in terms of the impact both on industry conditions and firms' access to resources and capabilities.

> In international industries, competitive advantage depends not just upon a firm's internal resources and capabilities, but also its national environment – in particular, the availability of resources within the countries where it does business.

National influences on competitiveness: comparative advantage

The role of national resource availability on international competitiveness is the subject of the theory of **comparative advantage**. The theory of comparative advantage states that a country has a comparative advantage in those products that make intensive use of those resources available in abundance within that country. Thus, Bangladesh has an abundant supply of unskilled labour. The United States has an abundant supply of technological resources: trained scientists and engineers, research facilities and universities. Bangladesh has a comparative advantage in products that make intensive use of unskilled labour, such as clothing, handicrafts, leather goods and assembly of consumer electronic products. The United States has a comparative advantage in technology-intensive products, such as microprocessors, computer software, pharmaceuticals, medical diagnostic equipment and management consulting services.

> A country has a comparative advantage in those products that make intensive use of those resources available in abundance within that country.

The term comparative advantage refers to the *relative* efficiencies of producing different products. So long as exchange rates are well behaved then comparative advantage translates into competitive advantage. Trade theory initially emphasised the role of natural resource endowments, labour supply and capital stock in determining comparative advantage. More recently emphasis has shifted to the central role of knowledge (including technology, human skills and management capability) and the resources needed to commercialise knowledge (capital markets, communications facilities and a legal system).[15] For industries where scale economies are important, a large home market is an additional source of comparative advantage (e.g. the US in aerospace).[16]

Research and development (R&D) activities have tended historically to be undertaken in a firm's home country so we would typically expect the research centre of a Dutch company like Philips to be located in the Netherlands and the research centre for Apple to be located in the United States. However, reductions in communication and travel costs together with the growing economic importance of new industrialised and emerging economies have caused companies to rethink their location strategies. In a recent study, Tellis *et al.* investigated where the world's top companies located their R&D centres.[17] They took the country where a firm's headquarters was located to be its home country. They found significant and widespread globalisation of innovation in developed economies with firms headquartered in developed economies having 50% or more of their R&D centres located offshore.

Porter's national diamond

Michael Porter has extended our understanding of comparative advantage by examining the dynamics through which particular industries within a country develop the resources and capabilities that confer international competitive advantage.[18] Porter's national diamond framework identifies four key factors which determine a country's competitive advantage within a particular sector (see Figure 8.3):[19]

Figure 8.3 Porter's national diamond framework

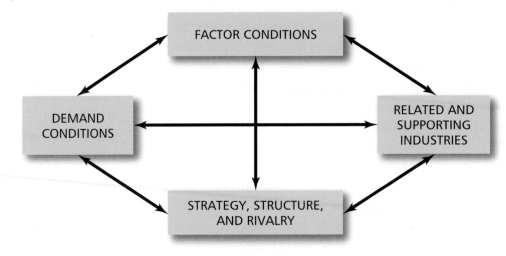

FACTOR CONDITIONS   Whereas the conventional analysis of comparative advantage focuses on endowments of broad categories of resource, Porter emphasises the role of highly specialised resources many of which are 'home-grown' rather than 'endowed'. For example, in analysing Hollywood's superiority in film production, Porter points to the local concentration of highly skilled labour, including the roles of UCLA and USC schools of film. He also suggests that resource constraints may encourage the development of substitute capabilities: in post-war Japan, raw material shortages spurred miniaturisation and low-defect manufacturing; in Italy, restrictive labour laws have stimulated automation.

RELATED AND SUPPORTING INDUSTRIES   One of Porter's most striking empirical findings is that national competitive strengths tend to be associated with **clusters** of industries. Silicon Valley's cluster comprises semiconductor, computer, software and venture capital firms. For each industry, closely related industries are sources of critical resources and capabilities. Denmark's global leadership in wind power is based upon a cluster comprising wind turbine manufacturers, offshore wind farm developers and operators and utilities.

DEMAND CONDITIONS   Demand conditions in the domestic market provide the primary driver of innovation and quality improvement. For example, Switzerland's pre-eminence in watches is supported by the obsessive punctuality of the Swiss. Japan's dominant share of the world market for cameras by companies owes much to Japanese enthusiasm for amateur photography and their eager adoption of innovation in cameras. German dominance of the high-performance segment of the world car industry through Daimler, BMW, Porsche and VW-Audi reflects German motorists' love of quality engineering and their irrepressible urge to drive on autobahns at terrifying speeds.

STRATEGY, STRUCTURE AND RIVALRY National competitive performance in particular sectors is inevitably related to the strategies and structures of firms in those industries. Porter puts particular emphasis on the role of intense domestic competition in driving innovation, efficiency and the upgrading of competitive advantage. The international success of the Japanese in cars, cameras, consumer electronics and office equipment is based upon domestic industries which feature at least six major producers all strongly competitive with one another.

Consistency between strategy and national conditions

Establishing competitive advantage in global industries requires congruence between business strategy and the pattern of the country's comparative advantage. In audio equipment, it is sensible for Chinese producers, such as Skyworth and Desay, to concentrate on the low end of the market and to supply Western mass retailers under their own brands. For Bose, international competitiveness requires exploiting US strengths in basic research. For Danish consumer electronics maker Bang & Olufsen, international competitiveness requires exploiting European strengths in design and high-end marketing. Japanese producers such as Sony and Matsushita compete most effectively in the broad mid-market exploiting national strengths in consumer electronic technology.

> Establishing competitive advantage in global industries requires congruence between business strategy and the pattern of the country's comparative advantage.

Limitation of the diamond model

Since it was published in 1990, Porter's diamond framework has had a significant influence on business practitioners and government policy-makers but it has also been the source of much critical debate. Criticism of the model has mainly come from two different perspectives. The first perspective (associated with the work of academics such as Rugman[20] and Dunning[21]) sees the diamond model as omitting key factors. In particular it is argued that the model fails to take into consideration the attributes of the home country's largest trading partners, isn't applicable to most of the world's smallest nations and ignores the role of multinational corporations in influencing the competitive success of nations. These critics suggest that the diamond framework needs to be expanded and amended, for example, Rugman and D'Cruz[22] propose a 'double diamond' framework, which incorporates both a national and a global diamond. The argument they put forward is that small countries like Korea and Singapore don't just target markets and resources in a domestic context but in a global context too.[23]

Singapore, for example, has been the recipient of inbound foreign direct investment by foreign multinationals attracted by the country's well-educated workforce and efficient infrastructure of roads, airports and telecommunications. Singaporean firms have also invested directly in other countries that have provided access to cheap labour and natural resources. In other words, the competitive advantage of many Singaporean firms depends not only on their domestic diamond (the factor and demand conditions, related and supporting industries etc. in Singapore) but also on the international diamond relevant to its firms (the factor and demand conditions, related and supporting industries etc. in countries in which its firms operate). The second perspective (associated with the work of academics such as Waverman[24] and Davies and Ellis[25]) suggests that the diamond model is so general that it lacks value. These critics argue that by trying to explain all aspects of trade and competition the model ends up explaining nothing because it is insufficiently precise to generate testable predictions.

Case Insight 8.1
Does IKEA gain a competitive advantage from being Swedish?

Porter's diamond model explains why some nations have an international competitive advantage with respect to particular industries. We can use this model to explore whether the national home base of IKEA has provided it with some advantages that it has been able to exploit on a global scale.

Factor conditions – Sweden has always had a plentiful supply of timber. It is Europe's second biggest afforested area after Russia and today the forestry business accounts for around 12% of the country's exports.[26] Until the 1900s Sweden was predominantly an agriculture society and its proximity to the Arctic Circle meant its farming communities faced long, harsh winters. Farmers had to be independent and self-sufficient and during the winter months, when little could be done on the land, they would make furniture and utensils, using the timber that was easily available.[27] As skills and craftsmanship improved, supplying furniture to nearby towns became a way of supplementing income and Sweden developed a strong base of skilled furniture makers. In addition, Sweden has a long tradition of design appreciation. Swedish designs are known for their simplicity, clean lines and light minimalist look. The country boasts many design schools and university courses in furniture design.

Related and supporting industries – the favourable conditions for furniture making have produced a number of furniture clusters in Sweden. For example the Tibro cluster in Västra Götaland comprises more than 70 furniture companies and includes producers of kitchen and office furniture, design and handicraft firms and centres for wood technology. The geographical proximity of companies facilitates the exchange of information and means that innovative ideas are quickly disseminated. Firms pool resources like marketing and logistics, and work in partnership with the regional government. In its early years IKEA benefited from the presence of these regional clusters and, even today, seeks to produce its own clusters in the markets it enters.

Demand conditions – firms are generally sensitive to their closest customers and the design preferences of Swedish consumers have been particularly important in shaping the type of furniture produced. Swedish customers are sensitive to environmental considerations and are concerned with sustainability. Waste wood and cellulose matter from furniture production is incinerated to produce energy and strict codes of conduct are in place to make sure that forests are managed in a responsible manner. The environmental concerns of IKEA's Swedish customers are reflected in the company's commitment to environmental stewardship. IKEA argues that its goes for low cost but not at a cost to the environment and this is a message that is increasingly appreciated by consumers around the world. It has also been suggested that the values of IKEA's founder, who was brought up in Småland, a poor rural community in Southern Sweden, have shaped the firm's ethos. Smålanders are known for working hard and making the best possible use of limited resources; they demand value for money. This 'frugality' is seen by many as the basis of the 'IKEA way'.

Local firm strategy, structure and rivalry – historically furniture manufacturing was highly localised because furniture is bulky and costly to transport over long distances and in Sweden there was significant competition between small local producers. IKEA's development of 'flat pack', non-assembled furniture together with reductions in transportation costs moved competition beyond regional and national boundaries. It is estimated that the Swedish furniture industry comprises around 800 firms, most of whom make intensive use of technology to produce their finished products. They face significant rivalry from other Scandinavian producers located in Denmark, Finland and Norway but increasingly Swedish manufacturers, including IKEA, face competition from low-cost manufacturers in China and other parts of Asia. This rivalry has been a stimulus to IKEA to redouble its efforts to reduce costs. For example even something as small as IKEA's 'Bang' mug has been redesigned several times to fit more into pallets and reduce transportation costs.

Applying the framework: international location of production

To examine how national resource conditions influence international strategies, we look at two types of strategic decision in international business: first, where to locate production activities; and second how to enter a foreign market. Let us begin with the first of these.

Firms move beyond their national borders not only to seek foreign markets, but also to access the resources and capabilities available in other countries. Traditionally, multinationals established plants to serve local markets. Increasingly, decisions concerning where to produce are being separated from decisions over where to sell. For example, ST Microelectronics, the world leader in application-specific integrated circuits (ASICs) is headquartered in Switzerland; production is mainly in France, Italy and Singapore; R&D is conducted mainly in France, Italy and the US; the biggest markets are Singapore, the Netherlands, the US and Japan.

> Increasingly, decisions concerning where to produce are being separated from decisions over where to sell.

Choosing where to locate production

The decision of where to locate production requires consideration of four sets of factors:

- *National resource availability.* Where key resources differ between countries in their availability or cost, then firms should manufacture in countries where resource

Table 8.2 Hourly compensation costs in US dollars for production workers in manufacturing 1997 and 2009

Hourly compensation rates				
	In US dollars		US =100	
Country	1997	2009	1997	2009
US	22.67	33.53	100	100
UK	18.24	30.78	80	92
Germany	29.24	46.52	129	139
France	24.99	40.08	110	120
Australia	19.12	34.62	84	103
Japan	22.28	30.36	98	91
Korea	9.42	14.2	42	42
Taiwan	7.04	7.76	31	23
Poland	3.13	7.5	14	22
Mexico	3.3	5.38	15	16

Source: US Department of Labor, Bureau of Labor Statistics

supplies are favourable. For the oil industry this means exploring in Kazakhstan, offshore Angola and the Gulf of Mexico. In most areas of manufacturing, offshoring by companies in the older industrial nations has been driven primarily by the quest to lower wage costs. Table 8.2 shows differences in employment costs between countries. However, for many industries, gaining access to specialised knowhow is a critical consideration.

- *Firm-specific competitive advantages.* For firms whose competitive advantage is based on internal resources and capabilities, optimal location depends on where those resources and capabilities are situated and how mobile they are. Wal-Mart has experienced difficulty recreating its capabilities outside of the US. Conversely, Toyota and Goldman Sachs have successfully transferred their operational capabilities to their overseas subsidiaries.

- *Tradability.* The more difficult it is to transport a product and the more it is subject to trade barriers (such as tariffs and quotas) or government restrictions (such as import licences), the more production will need to take place within the local market. Services – hairdressing, restaurant meals and banking – typically need to be produced in close proximity to where they are consumed.

- *Political considerations.* Government incentives, penalties and restrictions affect location decisions.

Location and the value chain

> A key feature of recent internationalisation has been the international division of value chains as firms seek to locate to countries whose resource availability and cost best match each stage of the value e-chain.

The production of most goods and services comprises a vertical chain of activities where the input requirements of each stage vary considerably. Hence, different countries offer advantages at different stages of the value chain. In the consumer electronics industry: component production is research and capital intensive and is concentrated in the US, Japan, Korea and Taiwan; assembly is labour intensive and is concentrated in China, Thailand and Latin America.

A key feature of recent internationalisation has been the international division of value chains as firms seek to locate to countries whose resource availability and cost best match each stage of the value e-chain.[28] The globally dispersed value chain of ECCO, a footwear manufacturer, is illustrated in the example box below.

Example 8.2 The globally dispersed value chain: ECCO A/S

ECCO is the world's second biggest supplier of 'leisure casual branded footwear' behind Clarks and ahead of Rockport and Geoxx. ECCO was founded in Denmark in 1963 by Karl Toosbuy and is now owned and managed by his daughter Hanni and her husband. Its shoe-making operations are characterised by their vertical integration ('from cow to consumer') and a proprietary process technology in which the shoe's sole and heel is moulded directly onto the upper. Production was initially based in its home country, but its activities now span the globe:

- *Design* is based primarily at the company's headquarters in Bredebro, Denmark.

- *R&D* is centred in Portugal.

- *Leather production* takes place at three tanneries in the Netherlands, Indonesia and Thailand.

- *Production of shoe uppers* is a relatively labour-intensive activity and is concentrated in specialised factories in Thailand, Indonesia and China.

- *Shoe production* used ECCO's direct injection technology and was fairly capital intensive. The main plants are in Thailand, China, Slovakia, Portugal and Indonesia. The Portuguese plant was the most technically advanced deploying robotic production and laser technology.

- *Primary distribution centres* are in the Netherlands and Hong Kong.

- *Regional sales organisations* are based in the Netherlands (Western Europe), Denmark (Central Europe), Poland (Eastern Europe and Middle East), the USA (the Americas) and Hong Kong (Asia Pacific).

- *Retail distribution* is undertaken both by exclusive franchised retailers and independent retailers serviced by wholesalers.

Sources: www.ecco.com; B. B. Nielsen, T. Pedersen and J. Pyndt, ECCO A/S – Global Value Chain Management, Ivey School of Business Case 908M14 (2008).

However, cost is just one factor in offshoring decisions: because cost advantages are vulnerable to exchange rate changes, it is important to consider underlying issues concerning the availability and quality of resources and capabilities. For most Western and Japanese companies it is the potential for overall operational efficiency rather than local wage rates that is the key criterion influencing choice of location. The modern laptop is the epitome of a globally dispersed value chain where every component and every process is located according the best combination of cost and technical knowhow. Figure 8.4 summarises the relevant criteria in location decisions.

Case Insight 8.2
The globalisation of IKEA's supply chain

IKEA's founder, Ingvar Kampard, recognised the benefit of an internationally distributed supply chain very early on when he changed from Swedish to Polish sources of supply in order to cut costs. As the company grew and entered new markets, its value chain became more distributed. Whilst product design remained in Sweden, the company moved its headquarters to the

▶

Netherlands in 2001 and located its European logistics centre in Germany. IKEA has its own manufacturing subsidiary, Swedwood, which manufactures and distributes wooden furniture and controls the entire value chain by managing and operating long-term forest contracts, saw mills, board factories as well as producing and distributing self-assembly furniture. Swedwood itself has internationalised and now owns and operates facilities in a number of countries including the US and Russia. In addition IKEA has a network of about 2000 other suppliers distributed around the globe. Suppliers are chosen primarily for their ability to provide specified products at low cost and IKEA closely monitors their adherence to its product and process specifications.

How should a firm enter foreign markets?

Firms enter foreign markets in pursuit of profitability. The profitability of entering a foreign market depends upon the attractiveness of that market and whether the firm can establish a competitive advantage within it. While market attractiveness can be a magnet for foreign multinationals – the size and growth of the Chinese economy has been irresistible to many Western companies – over the longer term, the key determinant

Figure 8.4 Determining the optimal location of value chain activities

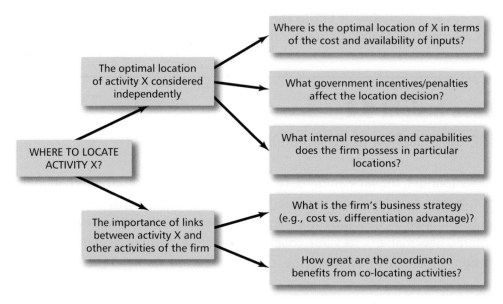

Figure 8.5 Alternative modes of overseas market entry

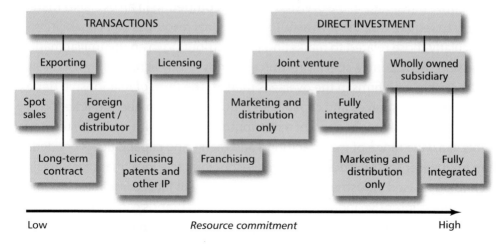

of profitability is likely to be the ability to establish competitive advantage vis-à-vis local firms and other multinationals.

A firm's potential for establishing competitive advantage has important implications for the means by which it enters a foreign market. The basic distinction is between market entry by means of *transactions* and market entry by means of *direct investment*. Figure 8.5 shows a spectrum of market entry options arranged according to the degree of resource commitment by the firm. Thus, at one extreme there is exporting through individual spot-market transactions; at the other, there is the establishment of a wholly owned, fully integrated subsidiary.

How does a firm weigh the merits of different market entry modes? Five key factors are relevant.

1   *Is the firm's competitive advantage based on firm-specific or country-specific resources?*
    If the firm's competitive advantage is country based, the firm must exploit an
    overseas market by exporting. Thus, to the extent that Tata Motors' competitive
    advantage in Western car markets is its low domestic cost base, it must produce
    in India and export to foreign markets. If Toyota's competitive advantage is its
    production and management capabilities, then as long as it can transfer and
    replicate these capabilities, Toyota can exploit foreign markets either by exports or
    by direct investment.[29]

2   *Is the product tradable and what are the barriers to trade?* If the product is not
    tradable because of transportation constraints or import restrictions, then accessing
    that market requires entry either by investing in overseas production facilities or by
    licensing the use of key resources to local companies within the overseas market.

3 *Does the firm possess the full range of resources and capabilities for establishing a competitive advantage in the overseas market?* Competing in an overseas market is likely to require that the firm acquires additional resources and capabilities, particularly those related to marketing and distributing in an unfamiliar market. Accessing such country-specific resources is most easily achieved by establishing a relationship with firms in the overseas market. The form of relationship depends, in part, on the resources and capabilities required. If a firm needs marketing and distribution, it might appoint a distributor or agent with exclusive territorial rights. If a wide range of manufacturing and marketing capabilities is needed, the firm might license its product and/or its technology to a local manufacturer. In technology-based industries, licensing technology to local companies is common. In marketing-intensive industries, firms with strong brands can license their trademarks to local companies. Alternatively, a joint venture might be sought with a local manufacturing company. US companies entered the Japanese market by joint ventures with local companies (e.g., Fuji-Xerox, Caterpillar-Mitsubishi). These combined the technology and brand names of the US partner with the market knowledge and manufacturing and distribution facilities of the Japanese firm.

4 *Can the firm directly appropriate the returns to its resources?* Whether a firm licenses the use of its resources or chooses to exploit them directly (either through exporting or direct investment) depends partly on appropriability considerations. In chemicals and pharmaceuticals, the patents protecting product innovations tend to offer strong legal protection, in which case patent licences to local producers can be an effective means of appropriating their returns. In computer software and computer equipment, the protection offered by patents and copyrights is looser, which encourages exporting rather than licensing as a means of exploiting overseas markets. With all licensing arrangements, key considerations are the capabilities and reliability of the local licensee. This is particularly important in licensing brand names, where the licenser must carefully protect the brand's reputation. Thus, Cadbury-Schweppes licensed to Hershey the trademarks and product recipes for its Cadbury's range of chocolate bars for sale in the United States. This arrangement reflects the fact that Hershey has production and distribution facilities in the US that Cadbury cannot match and that Cadbury views Hershey as a reliable business partner.

5 *What transaction costs are involved?* A key issue that arises in the licensing of a firm's trademarks or technology concerns the transaction costs of negotiating, monitoring and enforcing the terms of such agreements as compared with internationalisation through a fully owned subsidiary. In expanding overseas, Starbucks owns and operates most of its coffee shops while McDonald's franchises its burger restaurants. McDonald's competitive advantage depends primarily upon the franchisee faithfully replicating the McDonald's system. This can be enforced effectively by means of franchise contracts. Starbucks believes that its success is achieved through creating the 'Starbucks experience' which is as much about ambiance as it is about coffee. It is difficult to articulate the ingredients of this experience, let alone write it into a contract.

Issues of transaction costs are fundamental to the choices between alternative market entry modes. Barriers to exporting in the form of transport costs and tariffs are forms of transaction costs; other costs include exchange rate risk and information costs. Transaction cost analysis has been central to theories of the existence of multinational corporations. In the absence of transaction costs in the markets either for goods or for resources, companies exploit overseas markets either by exporting their goods and services or by selling the use of their resources to local firms in the overseas markets.[30] Thus, multinationals tend to predominate in industries where:

- firm-specific intangible resources such as brands and technology are important (transaction costs in licensing the use of these resources favour direct investment);

- exporting is subject to transaction costs (e.g., through tariffs or import restrictions);

- customer preferences are reasonably similar between countries.

International alliances and joint ventures

Strategic alliances – collaborative arrangements between firms – have become an increasingly popular means of accessing foreign markets. International strategic alliances take many forms: some are information collaborative arrangements; some involve one partner taking an equity stake in the other; others may involve equity cross-holdings. An international venture is where partners from different counties form a new company which they jointly own.

The traditional reason for cross-border alliances and joint ventures was the desire by multinational companies to access the market knowledge and distribution capabilities of a local company, together with the desire by local companies to access the technology, brands and product development of the multinationals. Western banks entering China's booming credit card market have usually formed marketing alliances with local banks, often reinforced with an equity stake.[31] Governments in emerging market countries often oblige foreign companies to take a local partner in order to encourage the flow of technology and management capabilities to the host country.

By sharing resources and capabilities between the partners, alliances not only economise on investment, they also allow access to more highly developed resources and capabilities

> By sharing resources and capabilities between the partners, alliances not only economise on investment, they also allow access to more highly developed resources and capabilities than a firm could create for itself.

than a firm could create for itself. Thus, the Freemove alliance formed by Telefónica Móviles (Spain), TIM (Italy), T-Mobile (Germany) and Orange (France) created a seamless third generation, wireless communication network across Europe at a fraction of the cost incurred by Vodafone; it also allowed each firm access to the mobile network of the leading operator in at least five major European markets.[32] Fiat's alliance with Chrysler gives Fiat access to the North American market while allowing Chrysler to expand its product range by building and marketing Fiat-designed small cars.[33]

Some companies have based their international strategies almost entirely on alliances with foreign partners. For Gazprom, the Russian gas giant, alliances relate to shared pipeline projects with Eni (Italy), CNPC (China), EON (Germany), PDVSA (Venezuela) and MOL (Hungary); liquefied natural gas projects with PetroCanada and Sonotrach (Algeria); and long-term supply arrangements with Gaz de France.

While the strategic rationale is strong, the success of cross-border alliances (including joint ventures) has been mixed. The Fuji–Xerox copier joint venture, the Sony–Ericsson mobile phone joint venture, the Renault–Nissan alliance and the collaboration between Hewlett Packard and Canon in printers have been very successful. Conversely, BT and AT&T's Concert alliance, the GM–Fiat alliance and Swissair's network of airline alliances were all disasters. Disagreements over the sharing of the contributions to and returns from an alliance are a frequent source of friction, particularly in alliances between firms that are also competitors. When each partner seeks to access the other's capabilities, 'competition for competence' results.[34] In several of the alliances between Japanese and Western firms, the Japanese partner was better at appropriating the benefits of the alliance.[35]

Case Insight 8.3
IKEA's foreign entry strategy

IKEA is a private company with a complex ownership and control structure. INGKA Holdings is the parent organisation that controls the IKEA Group of companies. IKEA Systems BV, one of the companies under the INGKA Holdings umbrella, owns the IKEA concept and trademark, and designs and controls its strategy for entering foreign markets. The decision to enter a new market is based on very detailed market research and IKEA operates a franchise system with each of the IKEA stores having a franchise agreement with IKEA Systems BV. In 2010 there were 316 IKEA stores in 39 countries – around 280 of these franchises were with stores inside the IKEA Group and the remainder with independent franchisees. The franchise model allows IKEA to raise capital, benefit from royalties and tap into local knowledge. The group carefully monitors the performance of each of its stores because poor performance in one retail outlet could have a damaging effect on the IKEA brand as a whole.

Multinational strategies: global integration vs. national differentiation

So far, we have viewed international expansion, whether by export or by direct investment, as a means by which a company can exploit its competitive advantages, not just in its home market but also in foreign markets. However, international scope may itself be a source of competitive advantage over geographically focused competitors. In this section, we explore whether, and under what conditions, firms that operate on an international basis are able to gain a competitive advantage over nationally focused firms. What is the potential for such 'global strategies' to create competitive advantage? In what types of industry are they likely to be most effective? And how should they be designed and deployed in order to maximise their potential?

> International scope may itself be a source of competitive advantage over geographically focused competitors.

The benefits of a global strategy

A global strategy is one that views the world as a single, if segmented, market. Global players win out over their national competitors for two reasons. First, supplying the world market allows access to scale economies in product development, manufacturing and marketing. Second, the key barrier to exploiting these scale economies, locally differentiated customer preferences, are fast disappearing in

the face of the uniformity imposed by technology, communication and travel. Levitt observed:[36]

> *Everywhere everything gets more and more like everything else as the world's preference structure is relentlessly homogenized.*

Subsequent contributions to the analysis of global strategy have elaborated Levitt's analysis of the potential for global strategies to create value.[37] Five major benefits have been proposed:

COST BENEFITS OF SCALE AND REPLICATION   One of the primary sources of scale economy is product development – Boeing and Airbus in commercial aircraft and Microsoft and SAP in computer software have to operate on a global scale to spread their huge investments in developing new products. In industries where internationalisation occurs through direct investment rather than exporting, the major cost efficiencies from international operation derive from economies in the replication of knowledge-based assets – including organisational capabilities.[38] When a company has created a knowledge-based asset or product – whether a recipe or a piece of software or an organisational system – subsequent replication costs a fraction of the original. With Disneyland theme parks in Tokyo, Paris, Hong Kong and soon Shanghai, as well as Anaheim and Orlando, Disney can achieve significant economies in developing new rides. Similarly with McDonald's: it developed its business system within the US and has subsequently replicated it across some 200 countries throughout the world.

SERVING GLOBAL CUSTOMERS   In several industries – investment banking, audit services, advertising – the primary driver of globalisation has been the need to service global customers.[39] Thus, the internationalisation of car parts manufacturers has tended to follow the internationalisation patterns of the car assemblers.

EXPLOITING NATIONAL RESOURCES – ARBITRAGE BENEFITS   As we have already seen, global strategy does not necessarily involve production in one location and then distributing globally. Global strategies also involve exploiting the efficiencies from locating different activities in different places. As we have seen, companies internationalise not just in search of market opportunities but also in search of resource opportunities. Traditionally this has meant a quest for raw materials and low-cost labour. Increasingly it means a quest for knowledge. For example, among semiconductor firms, a critical factor determining the location of overseas subsidiaries is the desire to access knowledge within the host country.[40]

LEARNING BENEFITS The learning benefits of multinational operation refer not only to MNCs' ability to access and transfer localised knowledge but also integration of knowledge from different locations and the creation of new knowledge through interacting with different national environments. IKEA's expansion has required it to adjust to the Japanese style and design preferences, Japanese modes of living and Japanese fanatical quality-consciousness. As a result, IKEA has developed its capabilities with regard to both quality and design that it believes will enhance its competitiveness worldwide. According to the CEO of IKEA Japan, 'One reason for us to enter the Japanese market, apart from hopefully doing very good business, is to expose ourselves to the toughest competition in the world. By doing so, we feel that we are expanding the quality issues for IKEA all over the world'.[41]

Recent contributions to the international business literature suggest that this ability of MNCs to develop knowledge in multiple locations, to synthesise that knowledge and transfer it across national borders may be their greatest advantage over nationally focused companies.[42] The critical requirement for exploiting these learning benefits is that the company possesses some form of global infrastructure for managing knowledge that permits new experiences, new ideas and new practices to be diffused and integrated.

COMPETING STRATEGICALLY A major advantage of the Romans over the Gauls, Goths and other barbarian tribes, was the Romans' ability to draw upon the military and economic resources of the Roman Empire to fight local wars. Similarly, multinational companies possess a key strategic advantage over their nationally focused competitors: multinationals can fight aggressive competitive battles in individual national markets using their resources (cash flows in particular) from other national markets. At its most simple, this **cross-subsidisation** of competitive initiatives in one market using profits from other markets involves *predatory pricing* – cutting prices to a level that drives competitors out of business. Such pricing practices are likely to contravene both the World Trade Organisation's antidumping rules and national antitrust laws. More usually, cross-subsidisation involves using cash flows from other markets to finance aggressive sales and marketing campaigns.[43] There is some evidence that Asian electronics firms use the profits from higher prices at home to subsidise expansion in Western markets.[44]

Strategic competition between MNCs presents more complex opportunities for attack, retaliation and containment.[45] The most effective response to competition in one's home market may be to retaliate in the foreign MNC's own home market. Fuji Film's incursion into Kodak's backyard was symbolised by Fuji's sponsorship of the 1984 Olympic Games in Los Angeles. Kodak responded by expanding its marketing efforts in Japan.[46] To effectively exploit such opportunities for national leveraging, some overall global coordination of competitive strategies in individual national markets is required.

Kenichi Ohmae has argued that to become effective global competitors, multinationals must become true insiders in all of the world's leading economic centres. This used to mean positioning within the 'triad': North America, Europe and Japan.[47] This doctrine has been weakened, first, by the rise of new industrial powers (notably China and India) and, second, the disappointing outcomes of several attempts to build 'triad power' – e.g. Daimler-Benz's acquisitions of Chrysler in the US and Mitsubishi in Japan.

National differences in customer preferences continue to exert a powerful influence in most markets: products designed to meet the needs of the 'global customer' tend to be unappealing to most consumers.

The need for national differentiation

For all the advantages of global strategy, the evidence of the past decade is that national differences in customer preferences continue to exert a powerful influence in most markets: products designed to meet the needs of the 'global customer' tend to be unappealing to most consumers. Moreover, costs of national differentiation can be surprisingly low if common basic designs and common major components are used. Most car firms have abandoned attempts to create global car models in favour of common platforms.[48] Flexible manufacturing systems have reduced the costs of customising products to meet the preferences of particular customer groups.

Domestic appliances provide an interesting refutation of the globalisation hypothesis. In washing machines, national preferences have shown remarkable resilience: French and US washing machines are primarily top loading, elsewhere in Europe they are mainly front loading; the Germans prefer higher spin speeds than the Italians; US

machines feature agitators rather than revolving drums; and Japanese machines are small. The pioneers of globalisation in domestic appliances, such as Electrolux and Whirlpool, still struggle to outperform national and regional specialists.[49] Similarly in retail banking, despite some examples of successful internationalisation (Banco Santander, HSBC), most of the evidence points to few economies from cross-border integration and the critical need to adapt to local market conditions.[50]

Every nation represents a unique combination of distinctive characteristics. How can we recognise and assess the extent of similarities and differences between countries? Pankaj Ghemawat proposes four key components: cultural distance; administrative and political distance; geographical distance; and economic distance – his 'CAGE' framework (see Table 8.3).[51]

Ghemawat's broad categories are only a starting point for exploring the national idiosyncrasies that make international expansion such a minefield. For consumer products firms, the structure of distribution channels is likely to be a critical barrier to global marketing and distribution. P&G must adapt its marketing, promotion and distribution of toiletries and household products to take account of the fact that, in the US, a few chains account for a major share of its US sales; in southern Europe, most sales are through small, independent retailers; while in Japan, P&G must sell through a multi-tiered hierarchy of distributors. The closer an industry to the final consumer, the more important cultural factors are likely to be. It is notable that so few retailers have become successful abroad. With the exception of IKEA, H&M and a handful of others, there are few international retailers that are truly global and few that have been as successful overseas as at home. For many, franchising has provided a lower risk internationalisation strategy.

> The closer an industry to the final consumer, the more important cultural factors are likely to be.

Reconciling global integration with national differentiation

Choices about internationalisation strategy have been viewed as a trade-off between the benefits of global integration and those of national adaptation (see Figure 8.6).[52] Industries where scale economies are huge and customer preferences homogeneous call for a global strategy (e.g. jet engines). Industries where national preferences are pronounced and where customisation is not prohibitively expensive favour a 'multi-domestic' strategy (e.g. retail banking). Indeed, if there are no significant benefits from global integration, then we may see these industries supplied almost entirely by locally specialised firms (as in funeral services and hairdressing). However, some industries may be low on most dimensions – cement and car repair services are fairly homogeneous worldwide, but also lack significant scale economies or other major benefits from global presence. Conversely, other industries offer substantial benefits from operating at global scale (telecommunications equipment, military hardware), but national preferences and standards may also necessitate considerable adaptation to the needs of specific national markets.

Reconciling conflicting forces for global efficiency and national differentiation represents one of the greatest strategic challenges facing MNCs. Achieving 'global localisation' involves standardising product features and company activities where scale economies are substantial and differentiating where national preferences are strongest

Table 8.3 Ghemawat's CAGE framework for assessing country differences

	Cultural distance	Administrative and political distance	Geographical distance	Economic differences
Distance between two countries increases with	• Different languages, ethnicities, religions, social norms • Lack of connective ethnic or social networks	• Absence of shared political or monetary association • Political hostility • Weak legal and financial institutions	• Lack of common border, water way access, adequate transportation or communication links • Physical remoteness • Different	• Different consumer incomes • Different costs and quality of natural, financial and human resources • Different information or knowledge
Industries most affected by source of distance	Industries with high linguistic content (TV, publishing) and cultural content (food, wine, music)	Industries viewed by government as strategically important (e.g. energy, defence, telecommunications)	Product with low value-to-weight (cement), that are fragile or perishable (glass, milk) or where communications are vital (financial services)	Products whose demand is sensitive to consumer varies by income (luxury goods). Labour- intensive products (clothing)

Source: Adapted from P. Ghemawat, 'Distance still matters: the hard reality of global expansion', *Harvard Business Review* (September 2001). Reproduced by permission of Harvard Business Review.

Figure 8.6 Benefits of global integration versus national differentiation

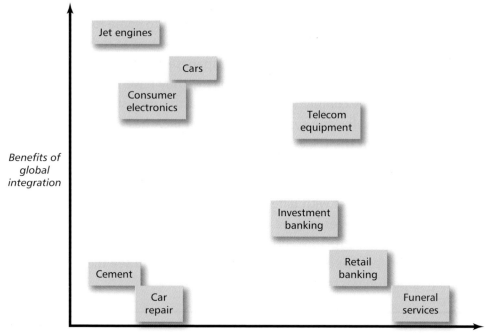

and where achieving them is not over-costly. Thus, a global car such as the Honda Civic (introduced in 1972 and sold in 110 countries of the world) now embodies considerable local adaptations – not just to meet national safety and environmental standards, but also to meet local preferences for leg room, seat specifications, accessories, colour and trim. McDonald's too meshes global standardisation with local adaptation, for example introducing more vegetarian and spicy options in India (e.g. McCurry Pan and McAloo Tikki) and a range of wraps in Australia (e.g. the seared chicken wrap).

Case Insight 8.4
IKEA goes glocal

IKEA has sought to introduce its Swedish-style home decor to the world by standardising not only its stores and its product range but also its management practices in all countries in which it operates. On the outside IKEA stores look the same regardless of where they are located. They are all painted blue and

▶

yellow reflecting the colours of the Swedish flag and all offer much the same retail experience. Nonetheless, IKEA has had to adapt to some local conditions. In Japan, for example, space is at a premium. IKEA has had to reduce the size of many of its furniture items so that they fit Japanese rooms which are typically smaller than those in other countries.[53] Similarly they have had to ensure that their kitchen cabinets comply with Japanese earthquake standards by fitting them with automatic locking systems. In contrast IKEA has had to increase the size of its furniture in the US. European beds are narrower than Americans are used to and cabinet drawers too shallow to take bulky sweaters.

IKEAs has also faced pressure to make adjustments to its management practices which have met with different responses in different countries. Whilst many European employees may be comfortable with the company's somewhat paternalistic style, flat structure and informality, employees in some parts of the world have been less happy with these arrangements and see the flat structure as limiting opportunities for progression.

Reconciling global efficiency with appealing to customer preferences in each country also means looking at the globalisation/national differentiation trade-off for individual products and individual function. In retail banking, different products and services have different potential for globalisation. Credit cards and basic savings products such as certificates of deposit tend to be globally standardised; current accounts[54] and mortgage lending are much more nationally differentiated. Similarly with business functions: R&D, purchasing, IT and manufacturing have strong globalisation potential; sales, marketing, customer service and human resource management need to be much more nationally differentiated. These differences have important implications for how the MNC is organised.

Strategy and organisation within the multinational corporation

The same issues – the benefits from global integration and need for national differentiation – that influence the design of international strategies also have critical implications for the design of organisational structures and management systems to implement these strategies. As we shall see, one of the greatest challenges facing the senior managers of MNCs is aligning organisational structures and management systems and their fit with the strategies being pursued.

The evolution of multinational strategies and structures

Over the past 100 years, the forces driving the internationalisation of companies have changed considerably; the trade-off between the benefits of global integration and those of national differentiation has shifted markedly. During different periods international firms have adopted different strategies and different structural configurations. Yet, even though some firms have adapted to change, many others have maintained their old structures. Structural configurations have tended to persist over time not only because organisations are subject to some inertia but also because of the complexity MNCs face in trying to execute structural change. To a large extent MNCs are captives of their history: their strategy–structure configurations today reflect choices they made at the time of their international expansion. Radical changes in strategy and structure are difficult: once an international distribution of functions, operations and decision-making authority has been determined, reorganisation is slow, difficult and costly – particularly when host governments become involved. Bartlett and Ghoshal argue that

> MNCs are captives of their history: their strategy–structure configurations today reflect choices they made at the time of their international expansion.

the 'administrative heritage' of an MNC – its configuration of assets and capabilities, its distribution of managerial responsibilities and its network of relationships – is a critical determinant of its current capabilities and a key constraint upon its ability to build new strategic capabilities.[55]

Bartlett and Ghoshal identify three eras in the development of the MNC (see Figure 8.7).

- *Early 20th century: era of the European multinational.* European companies such as Unilever, Shell, ICI and Philips were pioneers of multinational expansion. Because of the conditions at the time of internationalisation – poor transportation and communications, highly differentiated national markets – the companies created 'multinational federations': each national subsidiary was operationally autonomous and undertook the full range of functions, including product development, manufacturing and marketing.

- *Post-World War II: era of the American multinational.* US economic dominance was the basis for the pre-eminence of US multinationals such as GM, Ford, IBM, Coca-Cola, Caterpillar and P&G. While their overseas subsidiaries were allowed considerable autonomy, this was within the context of the dominant position of their US parent in terms of capital, new product and process technology, management capabilities and management systems. US-based resources and capabilities were their primary competitive advantages in world markets.

Figure 8.7 The development of the multinational corporation: alternative parent–subsidiaries relations

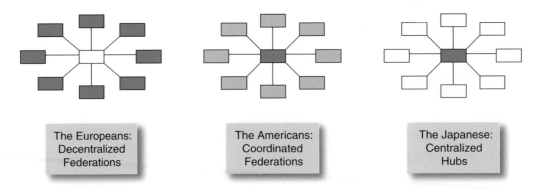

Note: The density of shading indicates the concentration of decision making.

Source: C. A. Bartlett and S. Ghoshal, *Managing Across Borders: The Transnational Solution* (Boston: Harvard Business School Press, 1998). Reproduced by permission of Harvard Business Review.

● *The 1970s and 1980s: the Japanese challenge.* Japanese MNCs – Honda, Toyota, Matsushita, NEC and YKK – pursued global strategies from centralised domestic bases. R&D and manufacturing were concentrated in Japan; overseas subsidiaries were responsible for sales and distribution. Globally standardised products manufactured in large-scale plants provided the basis for unrivalled cost and quality advantages. Over time, manufacturing and R&D were dispersed – initially because of trade protection by consumer countries and a rising value of the yen against other currencies.

The different administrative heritage of these different groups of MNCs continues to shape their organisational capabilities today. The strength of European multinationals is adaptation to the conditions and requirements of individual national markets. The strength of the US multinationals is their ability to transfer technology and proven new products from their domestic strongholds to their national subsidiaries. That of the Japanese MNCs is the efficiency of global production and new product development. Yet, these core capabilities are also core rigidities. The challenge for European MNCs has been to achieve greater integration of their sprawling international empires – for Shell and Philips this has involved reorganisations over a period of more than two decades. For US MNCs such as Ford and P&G it has involved nurturing the ability to tap their foreign subsidiaries for technology, design and new product ideas. For Japanese MNCs such as Nomura, Hitachi and NEC the challenge is to become true insiders in the overseas countries where they do business.

Reconfiguring the MNC: the transnational corporation

CHANGING ORGANISATION STRUCTURE For North American and European-based MNCs, the principal structural changes of recent decades have been a shift from organisation around national subsidiaries and regional groupings to the creation of worldwide product divisions. For most MNCs, country and regional organisations are retained, but primarily for the purposes of national compliance and customer relationships. Thus, Hewlett-Packard conducts its business through global product groups: Technology Solutions Group (comprising Enterprise Storage and Servers, Services and Software), Personal Systems Group (its personal computer and entertainment business) and Imaging and Printing Group (printers and cameras). At the same time, it maintains three regional headquarters: for the Americas (located in Houston); for Europe, Middle East and Africa (located in Geneva); and for Asia Pacific (located in Singapore).

NEW APPROACHES TO RECONCILING LOCALISATION AND GLOBAL INTEGRATION However, the formal changes in structure are less important than the changes in responsibilities, decision powers and modes of coordination within these structures. Escalating costs of research and new product development have made global strategies with global product platforms essential. At the same time, meeting consumer needs in each national market and responding swiftly to changing local circumstances requires greater decentralisation. Accelerating technological change further exacerbates these contradictory forces: despite the cost and 'critical mass' benefits of centralising research and new product development, innovation occurs at multiple locations within the MNC and requires nurturing of creativity and initiative throughout the organisation. 'It's the corporate equivalent of being able to walk, chew gum and whistle at the same time', notes Chris Bartlett.

According to Bartlett, the simultaneous pursuit of responsiveness to national markets and global coordination requires, 'a very different kind of internal management process than existed in the relatively simple multinational or global organisations. This is the *transnational organisation*'.[56] The distinguishing characteristic of the transnational is that it becomes an integrated network of distributed and interdependent resources and capabilities (see Figure 8.8). This necessitates that:

● Each national unit is a source of ideas, skills and capabilities that can be harnessed for the benefit of the total organisation.

● National units access global scale economies by designating them the company's world source for a particular product, component or activity.

● The centre must establish a new, highly complex managing role that coordinates relationships among units but does so in a highly flexible way. The key is to focus

Figure 8.8 The transnational corporation

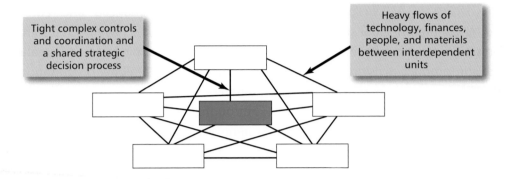

less on managing activities directly and more on creating an organisational context that is conducive to the coordination and resolution of differences. Creating the right organisational context involves 'establishing clear corporate objectives, developing managers with broadly based perspectives and relationships and fostering supportive organisational norms and values.'[57]

Balancing global integration and national differentiation requires that a company adapts to the differential requirements of different products, different functions and different countries. P&G adopts global standardisation for some of its products (Pringles potato chips and high-end perfumes, for example); for others (hair care products and laundry detergent, for example) it allows significant national differentiation. Across countries, P&G organises global product divisions to serve most of the industrialised world because of the similarities between their markets, while for emerging market countries (such as China and India) it operates through country subsidiaries in order to adapt to the distinctive features of these markets. Among functions, R&D is globally integrated while sales are organised by national units that are differentiated to meet local market characteristics.

The transnational firm is a concept and direction of development rather than a distinct organisational archetype. It involves convergence of the different strategy configurations of MNCs. Thus, companies such as Philips, Unilever and Siemens have reassigned roles and responsibilities to achieve greater integration within their traditional 'decentralised federations' of national subsidiaries. Japanese global corporations such as Toyota and Matsushita have drastically reduced the roles of their Japanese headquarters. American multinationals such as Citigroup and IBM are moving in two directions: reducing the role of their US bases while increasing integration among their different national subsidiaries.

MNCs are increasingly locating management control of their global product divisions outside their home countries. When Philips adopted a product division structure, it located responsibility for medical electronics in its US subsidiary and leadership in consumer electronics in Japan. Nexans, the world's biggest manufacturer of electric cables, has moved the head office of five of its 20 product divisions outside of France. For example, the head of ships' cables is based in South Korea – the world leader in shipbuilding.[58] Aligning structure, strategy and national resources may even require shifting the corporate headquarters – HSBC moved from Hong Kong to London, Tetra Pak from Lund, Sweden to Lausanne, Switzerland.[59]

ORGANISING R&D AND NEW PRODUCT DEVELOPMENT
Probably the greatest challenges facing the top managers of MNCs are organising, fostering and exploiting innovation and new product development. Innovation is stimulated by diversity and autonomy, while its exploitation and diffusion require critical mass and coordination. The traditional European decentralised model is conducive to local initiatives – but not to their global exploitation. Philips has an outstanding record of innovation in consumer electronics. In its TV business, its Canadian subsidiary developed its first colour TV; its Australian subsidiary developed its first stereo sound TV and its British subsidiary developed teletext TVs.

> Probably the greatest challenges facing the top managers of MNCs are organising, fostering and exploiting innovation and new product development.

However, lack of global integration constrained their success on a global scale. Building a globally integrated approach to new product development has been a major priority of the past two decades.

Assigning national subsidiaries global mandates allows them to take advantage of local resources and develop distinctive capabilities while exploiting globally the results of their initiatives.[60] For example, P&G, recognising Japanese obsessiveness over cleanliness, assigned increasing responsibility to its Japanese subsidiary for developing household cleaning products. Its 'Swiffer' dust-collecting products were developed in Japan (using technology developed by other firms) then introduced into other markets. Where a local unit possesses unique capabilities, it can be designated a *centre of excellence*.[61]

Summary

Moving from a national to an international business environment represents a quantum leap in complexity. In an international environment, a firm's potential for competitive advantage is determined not just by its own resources and capabilities but also by the conditions of the national environment in which it operates. The extent to which a firm is positioned in a single market or multiple national markets also influences its competitive position.

Our approach in this chapter is to simplify the complexities of international strategy by applying the same basic tools of strategy analysis that we developed in earlier chapters. For example, to determine whether a firm should enter an overseas market, our focus has been the profit implications of such an entry. However, establishing the potential for a firm to create value from internationalisation is only a beginning. Subsequent analysis needs to design an international strategy: do we enter an overseas market by exporting, licensing or direct investment? If the latter, should we set up a wholly owned subsidiary or a joint venture? Once the strategy has been established, then a suitable organisational structure needs to be designed.

The fact that so many companies that have been outstandingly successful in their home market have failed so miserably in their overseas expansion demonstrates the complexity of international management. In some cases, the companies have failed to recognise that the resources and capabilities that underpinned their competitive advantages in their home market could not be readily transferred or replicated in overseas markets. In others, the problems were in designing the structures and systems that could effectively implement the international strategy.

As the lessons of success and failure from international business become recognised and distilled into better theories and analytical frameworks, so we advance our understanding of how to design and implement strategies for competing globally. We are at the stage where we recognise the issues and the key determinants of competitive advantage in an international environment. However, there is much that we do not fully understand. Designing strategies and organisational structures that can reconcile critical trade-offs between global scale economies versus local differentiation, decentralised learning and innovation versus worldwide diffusion and replication and localised flexibilities versus international standardisation remain key challenges for senior managers.

Summary table

Learning Objectives	Summary
Discern patterns of internationalisation	Industry can be categorised on the basis of their internationalisation – sheltered, trading, multi-domestic and global – and also on the basis of the different routes by which firms internationalise

Analyse the implications of a firm's national environment for its competitive advantage	Porter's diamond model explores the processes through which particular industries within a country develop the resources and capabilities that confer an international competitive advantage. The four key factors highlighted by Porter are factor conditions, related and supporting industries, demand conditions and strategy, structure and rivalry. There needs to be consistency between firm strategy and national conditions for firms to exploit national strengths
Formulate strategies for exploiting overseas business opportunities including overseas production and market entry strategies	Firms move across national borders to seek foreign markets and to access the resources and capabilities available in other countries. Increasingly decisions of where to produce are made independently of decisions about where to sell. Decisions on location depend on national resource availability, firm-specific advantages and tradability. Firms moving into new geographical markets also need to decide on their mode of entry, e.g. licensing, joint ventures, direct investment. There are advantages and disadvantages of each approach
Formulate international strategies that achieve an optimal balance between global integration and national differentiation	A global strategy views the world as a single market and confers a number of benefits. But national differences in consumer preferences exert a powerful pressure for firms to adapt their products to local needs. Reconciling these conflicting forces represents a significant challenge for most international firms and achieving an optimal balance depends on standardising product features and company activities where scale economies are substantial and differentiating where national preferences are strongest
Design organisational structures and management systems appropriate to the pursuit of international strategies	The trade-offs that firms make with respect to global integration versus local responsiveness influence firm structure. During different periods of time international firms have adopted different organisational structures and even when circumstances change they can be slow to change. Bartlett and Ghoshal have suggested that the simultaneous pursuit of global integration and local responsiveness requires firms to adopt very different kinds of internal management processes and to become 'transnational'

Further reading

To gain a deeper understanding of the models and frameworks that help us to understand the challenges of formulating and implementing global strategies it is well worth reading the original work by authors such as Christopher Bartlett and Sumantra Ghoshal, Ted

Levitt, Michael Porter. If time pressures prevent you from reading their books, many of their key ideas are captured in journal articles for example:

Bartlett, C. and Ghoshal, S. (2003). What is a global manager? *Harvard Business Review*, 81(8), 101–8.

Levitt, T. (1983). The globalisation of markets. *Harvard Business Review*, May–June, 92–102.

Porter, M. (1990). The competitive advantage of nations. *Harvard Business Review*, 68(2), 73–93.

Grant provides a useful critique of Porter's diamond model in:

Grant, R. C. (1991). Porter's competitive advantage of nations: an assessment. *Strategic Management*, 12(7), 535–54.

Ghemawat explores the central tension between global integration and national responsiveness in:

Ghemawat, P. (2007). Managing difference: the central challenge of global strategy. *Harvard Business Review*, March, 59–68.

QUIZ

Visit your enhanced ebook at **www.foundationsofstrategy.com** for self test quiz questions

Self-study questions

1   With reference to Figure 8.1 identify a 'sheltered industry' (i.e. one that has been subject to little penetration either by imports or foreign direct investment). Explain why this industry has escaped internationalisation. Explore whether there are opportunities for profitable internationalisation within the industry and, if so, the strategy that would offer the best chance of success.

2   According to Michael Porter's *Competitive Advantage of Nations*, some of the industries where British companies have an international advantage are advertising, auctioneering of antiques and artwork, distilled alcoholic beverages, hand tools and chemical preparations for gardening and horticulture.

Some of the industries where US companies have an international competitive advantage are: photo film, aircraft and helicopters, computer hardware and software, oilfield services, management consulting, cinema films and TV programmes, healthcare products and services and financial services.

For either the UK or the US, use Porter's national diamond framework (Figure 8.3) to explain the observed pattern of international competitive advantage.

3   How does McDonald's balance global standardisation and national differentiation? Should it offer its franchisees in overseas countries greater initiative in introducing products that meet national preferences? Should it also allow greater flexibility for its overseas franchisees to adapt store layout, operating practices and marketing? What aspects of the McDonald's system should McDonald's top management insist on keeping globally standardised?

4   You are the founder of an internet service in the US that helps people to rent rooms. You are thinking of extending your service to clients in Germany and then other parts of Europe. What are the key challenges you are likely to face in internationalising your business?

5   Visit the website www.nestle.com and consider the way in which the company is organised (see the General Organisation of Nestlé SA diagram in the company's Corporate Governance Report). What additional information would you need to be able to judge whether Nestlé could be considered to be a transnational organisation?

GLOSSARY

Visit your enhanced ebook at **www.foundationsofstrategy.com** for key term flashcards

Closing case Sharp and the Production of Liquid Crystal Displays (LCDs)

The Sharp Corporation is one of the world's leading manufacturers of electronic products and components. Founded in 1915 by Tokuji Hayakawa who invented the 'Ever-Sharp Pencil', the company had net sales of just under ¥3 billion in 2010 and produced a wide range of products including television sets, electronic calculators, microwave ovens, solar panels and LED lights. The company first experimented with liquid crystal displays (LCDs) in the 1960s when it licensed the technology from RCA. LCD technology seemed unpromising at first because displays were expensive to produce and small but Sharp, along with a number of other firms in the industry, invested in research and development and over time barriers were overcome. By the 2000s LCD technology had become the dominant technology in flat-screen television displays and Sharp had developed a strong reputation for capability in the broad area of optoelectronics (the fusion of light and electronics).

In the early days of development the major players in the electronics industry had collaborated on LCD technology and breakthroughs were disseminated quickly but as the technology matured, competition intensified. Lehmberg points out that: 'By the time production technology reached its fifth generation, it had been improved to the point that firms with little LCD experience could buy a new plant and get it to function well with limited outside help'.[62] Firms based in countries with lower labour costs such as Taiwan and Korea started to compete. In response, Sharp, afraid that its core technology might be at risk, sought to wall off its proprietary knowledge. The company implemented a policy of secrecy and no outsiders, even suppliers, were allowed to visit Sharp's LCD plants.

Sharp's business model was based on manufacturing in Japan and selling overseas and for a long time this strategy served the company well. Prior to the 2000s the main market for Sharp's electronics products was Japan and a significant proportion of its LEDS went into its own products, the remainder being sold to other producers of electronic goods. The company was able to benefit from the geographical closeness of its plants and its proximity to a cluster of small and medium sized suppliers in an area known as 'Crystal Valley'. These firms supplied key inputs into the LCD production process, for example, 'steppers' – machines that etch circuitry into LCD panels – and specialised adhesives and films. Sharp's 'make in Japan' policy meant that it was able to consolidate production and exploit available economies of scale. Successive generations of LCD technologies required larger and larger investments and Sharp achieved efficiency gains by investing in new plants. In 2009 it opened its ¥430 billion (US$5 billion), state-of-the-art factory at Sakai in Japan which produced large tenth-generation LCDs that were primarily used in flat screen television sets.[63]

As Sharp internationalised, however, the drawbacks of its 'export' model became evident. Whilst in 2004 34% of sales had been in overseas markets by 2009 that figure was 54%, dropping back to 48% in 2010. LCDs were expensive to ship by air and transport by sea was slow. The LCD market was very competitive and prone to significant fluctuations in demand and supply causing prices to be volatile. Sharp faced higher taxes and labour costs than many of its non-Japanese rivals and the rapid appreciation of the yen in the latter part of the 2000s meant that Sharp received less revenue from overseas sales designated in foreign currencies. At the same time the Korean won depreciated giving an advantage to Korean competitors such as Samsung. To add to the company's problems, sales of electronic products like televisions that utilised LCDs were severely affected by the global recession and in 2009, for the first time, Sharp announced a loss in net income. Whilst markets recovered somewhat in 2010 the strongest market growth was in China and India. In addition Sharp received approaches from several Chinese electronics firms who were interested in purchasing and operating plant to manufacture older generations of LCDs.

In an interview in 2009[64] Sharp's president, Mikio Katayama, announced a change in business strategy. He declared that Sharp was moving away from its Japanese-centric policy to one based more on the concept of 'chisan chishou' – local production for local consumption. Following the example of Japanese car makers Sharp planned to change its global production strategy to one based more on the establishment of LCD and TV assembly plants abroad. He argued that Sharp's core technology wasn't making LCD panels or assembling LCD TVs, it was production technology. By inference the company was beginning to place less emphasis on investment in big production plants and giving greater emphasis to its intellectual property and specialised knowledge. The vulnerability of Sharp's

▶

strategy was also highlighted in 2011 when a devastating earthquake and tsunami hit Japan. Sharp was not as badly affected as many other firms because its plants were located some distance from the epicentre but it needed to shut down its new plant at Sakai for a time and supplies from the many smaller firms that produced components for LCDs were disrupted.

Case questions

- What factors should the Sharp Corporation take into consideration when deciding where to location its LCD production? What are the advantages and disadvantages of changing its 'make in Japan, sell overseas' strategy?

- If Sharp decides to relocate some of its production, what alternative approaches to entry into new countries are available to it? What are the potential costs and benefits of engaging in joint ventures with Chinese electronics manufacturers?

- Critically evaluate President Katayama's suggestion that Sharp should place greater emphasis on its knowledge assets rather than its physical resources.

Notes

1 www.bbc.co.uk/news/business-14418539. Accessed 8 August 2011.

2 *OECD in Figures 2008* (Organisation for Economic Cooperation and Development, 2008). Note that the OECD members comprise the world's advanced industrialised countries.

3 A. Ward, 'IKEA takes a cautious approach on China', *Financial Times* (13 January 2011).

4 *IKEA Annual Report 2010.* www.ikea.com/ms/en_CN/about_ikea/press/press_releases/annual_report.html. Accessed 30 June 2011.

5 www.swedishwire.com/business/2966-ikea-turned-a-blind-eye-to-russia-bribery. Accessed 5 August 2011.

6 www.ikea.com. Accessed 4 May 2011.

7 I. Kamprad and B. Torekull, *Leading by Design: The IKEA Story* (HarperBusiness, 1999).

8 P. Grol and C. Schoch, 'IKEA: culture as competitive advantage' (Paris: Group ICPA Case Study, 1998).

9 See, for example, P. Girija and S. Chaudhuri, 'IKEA in China: competing through low-cost strategies (IBSCDC Case Study, 2006).

10 www.cnbc.com/id/42409434/IKEA_A_Mini_Disneyland_for_Cash_Starved_Chinese. Accessed 20 June 2011.

11 This process was proposed by J. Johanson and J.-E. Vahlne, 'The internationalisation process of the firm', *Journal of International Business Studies* 8 (1977): 23–32. See also L. Melin, 'Internationalisation as a strategy process', *Strategic Management Journal* 13 (1992 Special Issue): 99–118.

12 S. L. Segal-Horn, 'Globalisation of service industries', in J. McGee (Ed.) *The Blackwell Encyclopedia of Management: Strategic Management* (Oxford: Blackwell Publishing, 2005): 147–154.

13 A. Kundna, G. Yip and H. Barkema, 'Born global', *Business Strategy Review* Winter (2008): 38–44.

14 'City Interview: Toni Mascolo still a cut above at hairdressing empire Toni & Guy', www.thisismoney.co.uk/money/markets/article-2034792/CITY-INTERVIEW-Toni-Mascolo-cut-hairdressing-empire-Toni--Guy.html. Accessed 16 May 2011.

15 A key finding was that *human capital* (knowledge and skills) was more important than *physical capital* in explaining US comparative advantage. See W. W. Leontief,

'Domestic production and foreign trade', in R. Caves and H. Johnson (Eds), *Readings in International Economics* (Homewood, IL: Irwin, 1968).

16 P. Krugman, 'Increasing returns, monopolistic competition and international trade', *Journal of International Economics* 9 (November 1979): 469–79.

17 G. Tellis, A. Eisingerich, R. Chandy and J. Prabhu, 'Competing for the future: patterns of global location of R&D centres by the world's largest firms', AIM Working Paper (2009).

18 M. E. Porter, *The Competitive Advantage of Nations* (New York: Free Press, 1990).

19 For a review of the Porter analysis, see R. M. Grant, 'Porter's *Competitive Advantage of Nations*: an assessment', *Strategic Management Journal* 12 (1991): 535–48.

20 A. M. Rugman, 'Porter takes the wrong turn', *Business Quarterly* 56 (1992): 59–64.

21 J. H. Dunning, 'The competitive advantage of nations and TNC activities: a review article', *Transnational Corporations* 191 (1992): 135–68.

22 A. M. Rugman and J. R. D'Cruz, 'The double diamond model of international competitiveness: Canada's experience', *Management International Review* 33 (1993): 17–39.

23 H. Moon, A. M. Rugman and A. Verbeke, 'A generalized double diamond approach to the global competitiveness of Korea and Singapore', *International Business Review* 7 (1998): 135–50.

24 L. Waverman, 'A critical analysis of Porter's framework on the competitive advantage of nations', in A. M. Rugman, J. Van den Broeck and A. Verbeke (Eds), *Research in Global Strategic Management Volume V: Beyond the Diamond* (Greenwich, CT: JAI Press, 1995).

25 H. Davies and P. Ellis, 'Porter's *Competitive Advantage of Nations*: time for the final judgement', *Journal of Management Studies* 37 (2000): 1189–213.

26 The Nordic Forestry Association. www.nordicforestry.org/facts/Sweden.asp#Sju. Accessed 16 May 2011.

27 www.interactmedia.co.za/component/content/article/74-current-design-a-technology/1153-a-swedish-success-story.html. Accessed 16 May 2011.

28 The linking of value-added chains to national comparative advantages is explained in B. Kogut, 'Designing global strategies and competitive value-added chains', *Sloan Management Review* (Summer 1985): 15–38.

29 The role of firm-specific assets in explaining the multinational expansion is analysed in R. Caves, 'International corporations: the industrial economics of foreign investment', *Economica* 38 (1971): 1–27.

30 D. J. Teece, 'Transactions cost economics and multinational enterprise', *Journal of Economic Behavior and Organisation* 7 (1986): 21–45. See also 'Creatures of imperfection,' in 'Multinationals: a survey', *The Economist* (27 March 1993): 8–10.

31 D. von Emloh and Y. Wang, 'Competing for China's credit card market', *McKinsey Quarterly* (November 2005), www.mckinseyquarterly.com.

32 'Freemove: creating value through strategic alliance in the mobile telecommunications industry', IESE Case 0-305-013 (2004).

33 'Fiat nears stake in Chrysler that could lead to takeover', *Wall Street Journal* (20 January 2009).

34 G. Hamel, 'Competition for competence and inter-partner learning within international strategic alliances', *Strategic Management Journal* 12 (1991): 83–103.

35 See R. Reich and E. Mankin, 'Joint ventures with Japan give away our future', *Harvard Business Review* (March–April 1986).

36 T. Levitt, "The globalization of markets", *Harvard Business Review* (May–June 1983): 92–102.

37 G. S. Yip, *Total Global Strategy II* (Upper Saddle River, NJ: Prentice Hall, 2003); C. Baden-Fuller and J. Stopford, 'Globalisation frustrated', *Strategic Management Journal* 12 (1991): 493–507; 'Rough and tumble industry', *Financial Times* (2 July 1997): 13.

38 S. G. Winter and G. Szulanski, 'Replication as strategy', *Organisation Science* 12 (2001): 730–43.

39 D. B. Montgomery, G. S. Yip and B. Villalonga, 'Explaining supplier behavior on global account management', Stanford Research Paper No. 1767 (November 2002). Available at SSRN: http://ssrn.com/abstract=355240.

40 P. Almeida, 'Knowledge sourcing by foreign multinationals: patent citation analysis in the US semiconductor industry', *Strategic Management Journal* 17, Winter Special Issue (1996): 155–65. See the McDonald's individual country websites, e.g., www.mcdonalds.com (US), www.mcdonalds.co.uk (UK), www.mcdonalds.fr (France).

41 Comments by Tommy Kullberg (IKEA Japan) in 'The Japan paradox', Conference organised by the European Commission, Director General for External Affairs (December 2003): 62–3. www.deljpn.ec.europa.eu/data/current/japan-paradox.pdf.

42 A. K. Gupta and P. Govindarajan, 'Knowledge flows within multinational corporations', *Strategic Management Journal* 21 (April 2000): 473–96; P. Almeida, J. Song and R. M. Grant, 'Are firms superior to alliances and markets? An empirical test of cross-border knowledge building', *Organisation Science* 13 (March–April 2002): 147–61.

43 G. Hamel and C. K. Prahalad, 'Do you really have a global strategy?' *Harvard Business Review* (July–August 1985): 139–48.

44 H. Simon and Y. Eriguchi, 'Pricing challenges for Japanese companies in the 21st century', *Journal of Professional Pricing* 14 (2005), www.pricingsociety.com; B. Y. Aw, G. Batra and M. J. Roberts, 'Firm heterogeneity and export – domestic price differentials: a study of Taiwanese electrical products', *Journal of International Economics* 54 (2001): 149–69.

45 I. C. Macmillan, A. van Ritten and R. G. McGrath, 'Global gamesmanship', *Harvard Business Review* (May 2003): 62–71.

46 R. C. Christopher, *Second to None: American Companies in Japan* (New York: Crown, 1986).

47 K. Ohmae, *Triad Power: The Coming Shape of Global Competition* (New York: Free Press, 1985).

48 The Ford Mondeo/Contour is a classic example of a global product that failed to appeal strongly to any national market. See M. J. Moi, 'Ford Mondeo: A Model T world car?' Idea Group (2001).

49 C. Baden-Fuller and J. Stopford, 'Globalisation frustrated', *Strategic Management Journal* 12 (1991): 493–507.

50 M. Venzin, *Building an International Financial Services Firm: How Successful Firms Design and Execute Cross-border Strategies* (Oxford: Oxford University Press, 2009).

51 P. Ghemawat, 'Distance still matters: the hard reality of global expansion', *Harvard Business Review* (September 2001).

52 Ghemawat (*Redefining Global Strategy* op. cit.) proposes a three-way rather than a two-way analysis. In his Adaptation–Aggregation–Arbitrage ('AAA') framework he divides integration into aggregation and arbitrage.

53 P. Indu and D. Purkayastha, 'IKEA: The Japanese misadventure and successful re-entry. Case Study: ICMR Center for Management Research (2008).

54 Referred to as 'checking' accounts in some parts of the world.

55 C. A. Bartlett and S. Ghoshal, *Managing Across Borders: The Transnational Solution*, 2nd edn (Boston: Harvard Business School Press, 1998).

56 C. Bartlett, 'Building and managing the transnational: the new organisational challenge,' in Michael E. Porter (Ed.), *Competition in Global Industries* (Boston: Harvard Business School Press, 1986): 377.

57 Ibid.: 388.

58 'The country prince comes of age,' *Financial Times* (9 August 2005).

59 J. Birkinshaw, P. Braunerhjelm, U. Holm and S. Terjesen, 'Why do some multinational corporations relocate their headquarters overseas?' *Strategic Management Journal* 27 (2006): 681–700.

60 J. Birkinshaw, N. Hood and S. Jonsson, 'Building firm-specific advantages in multinational corporations: the role of subsidiary initiative', *Strategic Management Journal* 19 (1998): 221–42.

61 T. S. Frost, J. M. Birkinshaw and P. C. Ensign, 'Centers of excellence in multinational corporations', *Strategic Management Journal* 23 (2002): 997–1018.

62 D. Lehmberg, 'Sharp Corporation: beyond Japan, Case Study, Richard Ivey School of Business (2011).

63 M. Williams, 'Inside the world's most advanced LCD factory', *PC World* (1 December 2009). www.pcworld.com/article/183422. Accessed 16 May 2011.

64 'Sharp adopts global production model', *Bloomberg Business Week* (8 April 2009). www.businessweek.com/globalbiz/content/apr2009/gb2009048_640568.htm.

Realising strategy

Introduction and objectives

'Great strategy; lousy implementation', is an epithet that has been applied to organisational failures from Philip II of Spain's attempted invasion of England with the Spanish Armada in 1588[1] to BP's disastrous handling of the Deep Water Horizon oil spill in the Gulf of Mexico. The idea that the formulation of strategy can be separated from its implementation has become institutionalised by the numerous strategic management texts that devote separate sections to strategy formulation and strategy implementation.

This supposed division between formulation and implementation is a fiction. At the most obvious level, formulating a strategy without taking into account the conditions under which it will be implemented will result in a poorly designed strategy. In addition, as we noted when discussing the work of Henry Mintzberg in the opening chapter of this book, realised strategy is usually a mix of the intended and unintended so we need to be open to the possibility that strategy itself evolves as it is executed.[2] Whilst intended strategies have implications for the way in which an organisation is structured, its norms and the way its staff are incentivised, we also need to be open to the possibility that things can happen in reverse order. The way the organisation is structured and its prevailing culture may influence the way in which organisational members see the world and how they view the strategic choices open to them. So rather than looking solely at the ways in which strategies conceived by top management teams are rolled out within the organisation, we focus instead on the factors that influence the ways in which strategy is realised.

Figure 9.1 illustrates our approach. The intended strategy of the organisation is implemented through the structure, systems and culture of the organization. However, the process of implementation involves a vast number of decisions which, in elaborating

Figure 9.1 The process by which strategy is realised

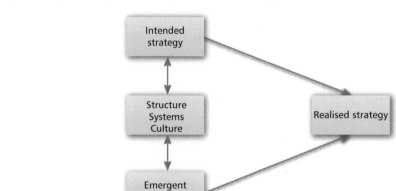

the strategy, also cause it to adapt—especially when circumstances are encountered that had not been envisaged by the intended strategy. In addition, the organisation's structure, systems and behaviour also shape the perceptions and priorities of top management that conditions their strategic intentions (hence, the feedback loop from structure, systems and culture to intended strategy).

In this chapter we focus on the ways in which strategy is realized in practice paying particular attention to the way in which three key factors—organisational structures, culture and systems are shaped by, and shape, strategy but first we need to explore the fundamental challenges of organising which these structures, culture and systems are designed to overcome.

By the time you have completed this chapter you will be able to:

- understand the ways in which strategy formulation and implementation are inextricably linked and be aware of the factors that mediate between planned and realised strategy;

- appreciate the key challenge of reconciling specialisation with coordination and cooperation and have an overview of the mechanisms managers employ to deal with these tensions;

- understand the basic principles of organisational design;

- be aware of different types of organisational structure and their fit with particular tasks and business environments;

- appreciate the forces that are causing companies to seek new organisational structures and management systems;

- comprehend the role of management systems in the coordination and control of corporations;

- understand the role that organisational culture plays;

- understand the role that organistional culture plays in the way strategy is realised in practice.

VIDEO

Opening case BP and the Deepwater Horizon Oil Spill

In April 2010 BP's Deepwater Horizon offshore oil rig in the Gulf of Mexico exploded and caught fire, causing 11 workers to lose their lives and triggering one of the worst environmental disasters in US history. By June 2010 BP's share price had almost halved in value and the company, confronted with an enormous bill for clean up and damages, faced the prospect of having to break up its business.[3]

The background

Deepwater Horizon was a floating drilling rig built by the South Korean firm, Hyundai Heavy Industries and owned by Transocean. BP leased the rig from Transocean and was drilling an exploratory well off the Louisiana coastline. The exploration required BP to drill far deeper than most underwater sites. At the time of the explosion BP and Transocean were in the process of closing the well in anticipation of bringing it into production at a later date. Halliburton Energy Services had been brought in to provide cement casings for the well and was completing the final stage of this project.

The explosion was thought to have been caused by a bubble of methane gas escaping from the well expanding quickly up the drill column and breaking through various barriers and cement casings. The subsequent fire caused the rig to sink and millions of barrels of crude oil were released into the ocean. Attempts to stem the flow of crude oil were unsuccessful because the blow-out preventer (a safety device fitted to the pipe that connects the well at the ocean floor to the rig on the surface) failed to operate. Oil continued to spill while BP sought to find an alternative way of capping the well until finally on 14 July 2010[4] a successful

solution was found. The escape of crude oil caused extensive damage to wildlife and the environment and adversely affected the livelihoods of the many communities dependent on the fishing, tourism and related industries in the area.

The US government held BP responsible for the incident and

accountable for the clean-up costs. Whilst BP accepted responsibility, in a report issued in September 2010 the company made it clear that in its view Transocean and Halliburton shared the blame for the disaster – a claim strongly denied by those companies.

The strategic and organisational background to the Deepwater Horizon disaster

For many commentators the Deepwater Horizon oil disaster represented a management rather than a technical failure and particular attention was focused on BP's structure, culture and style of leadership. The National Commission set up by the US president to examine the incident concluded that the accident was avoidable and that 'the immediate cause of the [. . .] blow-out can be traced to a series of identifiable mistakes by BP, Halliburton and Transocean that reveal such systematic failures in risk management that they place in doubt the safety culture of the entire industry'.[5]

Concerns about the safety culture at BP had preceded the Deepwater Horizon incident. In 2005 BP experienced a catastrophic explosion in its Texas City oil refinery which killed 15 people and injured 170.[6] In the following year BP reported a massive oil leak from its Prudhoe Bay pipeline in Alaska for which it was fined $20 million. Evaluations of both disasters had highlighted BP's strategy of cost cutting, its organisational structure and its culture as possible contributory factors.

In the late 1990s under the leadership of the then CEO, John Browne, BP became committed to creating value for its shareholders, revised its strategy and started to focus its exploration activities on 'new frontiers', such as Russia, Azerbaijan and Vietnam, as well as deep-sea locations such as the Gulf of Mexico. Accompanying the change in strategic focus was a move to create a flatter, more decentralised organisational structure at BP. In an interview for an academic paper[7] Browne explained that the whole purpose of his restructuring was to release creativity and empower the talented people who worked for the company, stating that BP wanted their staff to be 'entrepreneurs not bureaucrats doing exactly what they are told from above'. Whilst this restructuring undoubtedly unleashed a great deal of creative energy it also made the links between different parts of the business more tenuous and subtly altered the company culture, glorifying risk taking and the people, like the geologists, scientists and explorers, who worked in challenging, risky environments.

Under Browne's leadership, the driving force within BP was a new system of performance management with employees' pay increasingly linked to the achievement of financial targets through a system of bonuses. Ironically, whilst the structural changes were designed to decentralise decision making, the leadership style of Browne himself was described as autocratic. In 2007 when it was announced that Tony Hayward (the man in charge at the time of the Deepwater Horizon incident) was to take over from John Browne as BP's chief executive officer (CEO), Hayward was reported as saying, 'we have a leadership style that is too directive and doesn't listen sufficiently well. The top of the organisation doesn't listen to what the bottom is saying'.[8] This comment came to haunt Hayward when the same criticism was levelled against him and his top team with respect to the Gulf of Mexico oil spill.

On taking over as CEO Hayward continued to focus on cost cutting but also set out to simplify the organisation. One of his first acts as CEO was to commission a study from the consultancy group, Bain and Co. These consultants reported that BP was the most complicated organisation they had ever come across, having mapped more than 10,000 organisational interfaces[9] in a firm that employed around 100,000 people. On the basis of this report, Hayward introduced his 'forward agenda' with the mantra 'more is less'.[10] His change programme took operational efficiency as its main focus with the aim of turning BP into a more efficient and simpler organisation. To that end Hayward eliminated regional structures and greatly simplified the company's functional structures. He also reduced the number of senior executives from 650 to 500, at the same time introducing 'new blood'. In an interview in 2009[11] he reported that 50% of his senior team were new to their roles and 30% were from outside the company.

Despite the changes in organisation structure and personnel, safety was still cited as a priority within BP and Hayward and his team felt they had made progress in improving both the company's financial performance and its safety records. The company's profits immediately prior to the Deepwater Horizon accident had been better than analysts had expected and the senior management team had publicly celebrated the reduction in accidents on various site visits. Unfortunately subsequent analysis of the Deepwater Horizon spill by various agencies suggested that whilst the company paid attention to improvements in the avoidance of everyday injuries, for example slipping on wet stairways or being injured by machinery, the management of the risks associated with major catastrophic events was weak. Within the industry it appeared to be common practice for personnel to be trained on the job or to attend short one-week safety courses with the consequence that safety tended to be framed in terms of relatively minor incidents. Commentators pointed to a whole series of avoidable lapses in the lead up to the major disaster that might have been avoided if better risk management procedures had been in place. These lapses included the failure to identify a faulty seal at the base of the well, the decision to ignore a failed pressure test, the replacement of heavy drilling mud with seawater and the failure to respond to adverse indicators on monitors.[12]

The decision to ignore the negative results of a pressure test prior to the explosion serves to illustrate some of the problems the organisation faced. The rejection of the 'bad' reading was rationalised as an aberrant result without any reference to any higher authority or shared body of expertise. Testimony given to the National Academy of Engineering and National Reasearch Council that investigated the accident revealed that decision making on the rig was a negotiated team process with no clear identification of authority.[13] In a complex decentralised organisation like BP, or for that matter any other oil company, self-managed teams are often considered an efficient and effective way of organising, particularly given the physical separation between onshore management staff and offshore engineers and the multiplicity of specialist service contractors involved in exploration projects. Within BP team leaders were responsible for costs and schedules as well as safety issues and were regularly confronted with tough decisions on trade-offs. This led to the charge being levelled against the company that it had allowed short-term financial considerations to take precedence over health and safety issues.

As the disaster unfolded Tony Hayward remarked, 'What have we done to deserve this? A comment that ultimately lost him his job but which raised a question that will, no doubt, be puzzled over by analysts and policy-makers for many months to come.

The organisational challenge: reconciling specialisation with coordination and cooperation

Firms exist because they are efficient institutions for the organisation of economic activities, particularly the production of goods and services. However, as Henry Mintzberg has pointed out:

> Every organised human activity – from making pots to placing a man on the moon – gives rise to two fundamental and opposing requirements: the division of labor into various tasks and the coordination of these tasks to accomplish the activity.[14]

Unfortunately these two requirements are difficult to reconcile simultaneously and tackling the trade-off between them is one of the central problems for all organisations.

Specialisation and division of labour

The fundamental source of efficiency in production is **specialisation** through the division of labour into separate tasks. The classic statement on the gains due to specialisation is Adam Smith's description of pin manufacture:

One man draws out the wire, another straightens it, a third cuts it, a fourth points it, a fifth grinds it at the top for receiving the head; to make the head requires two or three distinct operations; to put it on is a peculiar business, to whiten the pins is another; it is even a trade by itself to put them into the papers.[15]

Smith's pin makers produced about 4800 pins per person each day. 'But if they had all wrought separately and independently and without any of them having been educated to this peculiar business, they certainly could not each have made 20, perhaps not one pin, in a day'. Similarly, Henry Ford achieved huge productivity gains by his assembly line system that assigned individuals to highly specific tasks. Between the end of 1912 and early 1914, the time taken to assemble a Model T fell from 106 hours to 6 hours.

But specialisation comes at a cost. The more a production process is divided between different specialists, the more complex is the challenge of integrating the efforts of individual specialists. Integrating the efforts of specialist individuals involves two organisational problems: there is the *cooperation problem* – that of aligning the interests of individuals who have divergent goals – and the *coordination problem* – even in the absence of goal conflict, how do individuals harmonise their different activities?

The cooperation problem

The economics literature analyses cooperation problems arising from differing goals in terms of the concept of *agency*.[16] An **agency relationship** exists when one party (the principal) contracts with another party (the agent) to act on behalf of the principal.

The problem for the principal is ensuring that the agent acts in his or her interest. Economics scholars usually focus on the agency problem between owners (shareholders) and managers and see the main issue for today's businesses as ensuring that professional managers run companies in ways that maximise shareholder wealth. During the 1990s, changes in the ways top management were rewarded – in particular placing greater emphasis on share options – were intended to align the interests of managers with those of shareholders.[17] However, at Enron, WorldCom and other companies, these incentives induced managers to manipulate reported earnings rather than to work for long-term profitability.

Agency problems do not just exist between managers and owners of firms. For individual employees, systems of incentives, monitoring and appraisal are designed to encourage the pursuit of organisational objectives and overcome employees' tendency to do their own thing or simply to take it easy. The way an organisation is structured can add to the challenge. Organisational departments frequently have their own subgoals and these can be at odds with those of other departments. The classic conflicts are between different functions: sales wishes to please customers; production wishes to maximise output; R&D wants to introduce mind-blowing new products; while finance worries about profit and loss.

> Organisational departments frequently have their own subgoals and these can be at odds with those of other departments.

Managers can use several mechanisms to try and align the goals of different individuals and groups within organisations:

- *Bureaucratic controls* go hand in hand with hierarchy. In this context **hierarchy** merely refers to an ordered grouping of people with an established pecking order. Those at the top of the pecking order supervise the behaviour and performance of those lower down through the establishment of rules and procedures. They require subordinates to seek approval for actions that lie outside their defined area of discretion – managers supervise workers, senior managers direct the activities of middle managers and so on. Weber,[18] the father of organisational theory, suggested that rules could be rationally designed by hierarchical superiors who occupy their posts on merit, i.e. by virtue of their expertise, knowledge or experience. Control is enforced through positive and negative incentives: the primary positive incentive is the opportunity for promotion up the hierarchy; negative incentives are dismissal and demotion.

  > Critics of bureaucracy argue that bureaucratic control reduces the extent to which those lower down the organisation can exercise their personal judgement.

  These days it is more common, however, to hear complaints about excessive bureaucracy rather than to hear voices celebrating bureaucracy as a reliable and efficient way of running organisations.[19] Critics of bureaucracy argue that bureaucratic control reduces the extent to which those lower down the organisation can exercise their personal judgement about how to do their work and, in certain circumstances, reduces the role of subordinates to that of cogs in a machine.[20] The standardised, impersonal procedures that characterise some bureaucracies can result in subordinates feeling alienated. There is also the danger that the observation of the rules becomes an end in its own right rather than a means to an end. Even when those in high-ranking positions within the organisation are appointed on the basis of their experience and expertise, it can be difficult for those in top positions within administrative hierarchies to establish appropriate rules or to give explicit instructions if the tasks that organisational members are required to undertake are complex and unpredictable. In these circumstances employees need to be flexible and use their personal judgement and intuition.

- *Performance incentives* link rewards to outputs: these kinds of incentives include piece-rates for production workers and profit bonuses for executives. Such performance-related incentives are seen as having two main benefits: first, they are *high powered* – that is to say they relate rewards directly to output – and second, they economise on the need for costly monitoring and supervision. Output controls are different from bureaucratic controls because they prescribe what organisational members should achieve by completing a task rather than specifying how they should do that task. However, to incentivise performance, organisations first have to be able to decide what constitutes desirable output or outcomes and that is not

always as straightforward as it might at first seem. For any given task there are usually a range of possible objectives that can be used for control purposes.

For example in a telephone call centre, good performance by operatives might be viewed as answering incoming calls quickly, providing accurate and appropriate advice, dealing with queries efficiently or closing sales effectively. Output controls tend to give prominence to particular aspects of performance, for example, in a call centre it may be difficult to assess individuals' performance with respect to all potential metrics, so certain indicators will be highlighted because they are easier to measure. But by selectively defining what is seen as 'good' or 'bad' performance output controls can, inadvertently, encourage inappropriate behaviour. For example if the performance of call centre operatives is measured on the speed with which they deal with calls, they may find ways of 'accidentally' disconnecting callers who look as if they have long, complex queries so that calls get rerouted to someone else. Pay-for-performance also becomes more difficult where employees work in teams or where output is difficult to measure, for example, in the provision of public services such as care for the elderly.

● *Shared values.* Some organisations are able to achieve high levels of cooperation and low levels of goal conflict without extensive explicit control mechanisms or performance-related incentives. Churches, charities, clubs and voluntary organisations typically display a commonality of purpose and values among members. Given that the presence of shared core values appears to be a key influence on sustained success,[21] it is not surprising that this approach to goal alignment has grown in popularity since the 1980s.[22] Efforts are increasingly being made by senior managers to generate and maintain shared cultures throughout their organisations by clearly articulating the firm's goals and by making explicit the kind of behaviours and attitudes the firm wishes to encourage. Performance evaluation becomes a matter of assessing organisational members' behaviour and attitudes in relation to the organisation's stated goals and norms.

The key strength of this approach from the perspective of its senior management team is that it encourages organisational members to develop an emotional attachment to the organisation and to internalise company values. Rather than having to engage in detailed monitoring and supervision of subordinates' work activities, organisational members act in the best interests of the company because they are driven by internal commitment and strong identification with company goals. Employees are able to use their initiative and be creative in their work because their personal goals are aligned with the organisation's goals.

> Organisational members act in the best interests of the company because they are driven by internal commitment and strong identification with company goals.

Organisational theorists[23] have, however, pointed out the promotion of 'shared values' and a 'corporate culture' is a form of control with a potential dark side. Kunda,[24] for example, suggests that there is a danger that people are manipulated and coerced into acting in particular ways without being aware of it, that cultural control is insidious and results in significant informal pressure for people to conform. Of course, this assumes that it is possible for managers to engineer changes in organisational cultures and that organisational members 'buy in' to the organisation's goals and values. Experience shows getting this 'buy in' is often very difficult. For example, when in 1999 Carly Fiorina took over as chief executive officer of Hewlett Packard, the computer company, she met a great deal of resistance when trying to change the existing company culture, commonly referred to as 'the HP way'. This was one of the contributory factors that led to her being replaced in 2005 by a new CEO – Mark Hurd. We return to the important issues of strategy and culture and the linked issue of managing change later in this chapter.

The coordination problem

> Unless individuals can find ways of coordinating their efforts, production doesn't happen.

The desire to cooperate is not enough to ensure that organisational members integrate their efforts – it is not lack of a common goal that causes Olympic sprint teams to drop the baton. Unless individuals can find ways of coordinating their efforts, production doesn't happen. Among the mechanism for coordination, the following can be found in all firms:

- *Rules and instructions.* A basic feature of the firm is the existence of general employment contracts under which individuals agree to perform a range of duties as required by their employer. This allows managers to exercise authority by means of *general rules* ('Secret agents on overseas missions will have essential expenses reimbursed only on production of original receipts') and *specific instructions* ('Miss Moneypenny, show Mr Bond his new cigarette case with 4G communication and a concealed death ray').

- *Routines.* Where activities are performed recurrently, coordination based on mutual adjustment and rules becomes institutionalised within organisational routines. As we noted in Chapter 3, these 'regular and predictable sequences of coordinated actions by individuals' are the foundation of organisational capability. If organisations are to perform complex activities at extreme levels of efficiency and reliability, coordination by rules, directives or mutual adjustment is not enough – coordination must become embedded in routines.

- *Mutual adjustment.* The simplest form of coordination involves the mutual adjustment of individuals engaged in related tasks. In soccer, each player coordinates with fellow team members without any authority relationship among them. Such mutual adjustment occurs in leaderless teams and is especially suited to novel tasks where routinisation is not feasible.

The relative roles of these different coordination devices depend on the types of activity being performed and the intensity of collaboration required. Rules tend to work well for activities where standardised outcomes are required – most quality control procedures involve the application of simple rules. Routines form the basis for coordination in most activities where close interdependence exists between individuals, whether a basic production task (supplying customers at Starbucks) or a more complex activity (performing a heart bypass operation or implementing a systems integration project for a multinational corporation).

Case Insight 9.1
The cooperation and coordination problem at BP

BP, like all companies, faces significant cooperation and control issues. Some of these issues are evident in the opening case. If we assume that BP engages in deep water drilling in order to enhance its profitability, then we might rationally argue that the company should weigh the benefits of adopting a stronger safety strategy against the costs. The benefit of a stronger safety strategy would include the reduction in the risk of a major spill and the avoidance of the costs associated with such a spillage. The costs would include increased expenditure in staff training, greater investment in safety equipment and 'blow-out prevention' and the loss of working time associated with safety simulations and practices. In reality few firms in the industry are likely to have (or admit to having) formulated their safety strategies in this manner. Given the potentially catastrophic consequences of safety breaches for human life and the environment, it is more likely that firms in this industry will try to prioritise safety above all other strategic objectives. But espousing safety as a key objective and making this aim a reality requires an organisation to find ways of achieving cooperation and coordination.

Cooperation problems arise because of the existence of principals and agents with conflicting interests. It is perfectly possible to envisage a situation in which a principal might wish to commit more (or fewer) resources to safety than an agent. For example it might be in shareholders' long-term interests to minimise the risks of a catastrophic incident that would adversely affect the share price and dividend payments but in managers' interests to trim back on safety in order to meet performance targets that affect bonus payments. Shareholders would probably find it very difficult to properly assess the risks of a major incident or to monitor managers' performance with respect to safety in a way that allowed for a proper alignment of incentives.

In addition it might be difficult for BP to align its interests with that of its subcontractors. On the one hand BP has a strong incentive to adopt tough safety standards because it has a reputation to defend and risks a strong backlash from governments (through the withdrawal of licences to explore for oil) and the consumers of its products (who might boycott its retail outlets) if major accidents occur. On the other hand contractors like Halliburton (the subcontractor commissioned to put cement casings and caps in place) might have a weaker incentive than BP to promote safety because the company would be unlikely to be liable for the full costs of damages and clean up.

Even if there was no conflict in the goals of those involved with the Deepwater Horizon project, harmonising the activities of various contributors to the project still represents a formidable challenge. The project involved leading edge oil-drilling technology and, whilst some of the activities on the rig were coordinated through rules and routines, much of the work required those with specialist expertise to coordinate their efforts through mutual adjustment. The investigation report following the accident suggested that there were limits to mutual adjustment and that a lack of coordination of critical procedures and the failure to refer decisions to higher authorities resulted in warning signs of imminent danger going undetected.[25]

The tensions that we have just discussed between specialisation on the one hand and cooperation and coordination on the other influence the way in which businesses design their organisational structure and management systems and attempt to shape their corporate cultures. In the next section we explore each of these aspects in more detail. It is worth reiterating the point we made earlier that realised strategy emerges through a dynamic process by which formal plans, structures and systems are interpreted and acted on by organisational members in ways that make sense to them, but which often produce unexpected consequences, new ideas and subtle changes to intended strategy. So when we look at structures, systems and culture it is important to remember that they are not only shaped by strategy but can also influence the way strategy is formed.

Organisational design

We have already noted that one of the means by which companies seek to achieve control, when individuals and groups specialise in different tasks, is through bureaucracy and hierarchy. The way in which an organisation arranges its lines of authority and communications and allocates decision-making power and responsibilities involves establishing a particular pecking power or hierarchy. Hierarchy is such a fundamental feature of business organisations that it merits a more detailed consideration. In this section we address two main issues: the advantages of using hierarchies to achieve

Figure 9.2 How hierarchy economises on coordination

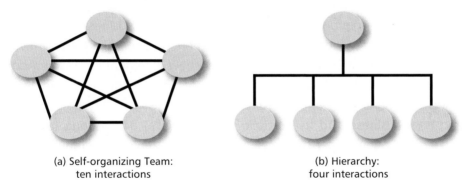

(a) Self-organizing Team:
ten interactions

(b) Hierarchy:
four interactions

coordination as well as control and the different ways in which organisations can be structured along hierarchical lines. We go on to consider different types of organisational structures and the trend towards less hierarchical organisational designs.

Hierarchy and coordination

We have already seen that hierarchy together with bureaucratic controls can be used to align the different goals of members of a business organisation, but introducing hierarchical structures can also reduce the costs of coordination. Figure 9.2 provides a simple illustration. Figure 9.2(a) represents a self-organising team – imagine yourself, for example, as part of a group of five students coming together to complete an assignment. In this team coordination is achieved by mutual adjustment – you negotiate with each other about who does what to complete the group assignment. No member of the team is given superior status or given the authority to direct the work of other team members. Figure 9.2(a) illustrates that this requires 10 interactions. In configuration B – a hierarchy is established. As a team you appoint a leader and agree that this person can direct who does what. Figure 9.2(b) illustrates that only four interactions need to be managed. At this simple level the reduction in the number of interactions lowers the cost of communication.

In the group assignment example we considered hierarchy as a way of coordinating the activities of individuals, but when we think about hierarchies within organisations we are usually thinking about the way in which specialised units are coordinated and controlled by a superior unit. Hierarchies are a flexible way of coordinating activities because they allow specialist units to act independently of each other.

> Hierarchies are a flexible way of coordinating activities because they allow specialist units to act independently of each other.

Proctor & Gamble (P&G) groups its activities into two key global business units – beauty and grooming products and household care. These business units are further divided into sub-categories, for example 'household care' contains the sub-divisions fabric and baby care. If P&G wishes to develop a new detergent for washing clothes it need only involve the relevant section of its organisation (the fabric care division), reducing communication and coordination costs. This flexibility also extends to adding new businesses to its portfolio (Gillette, Wella) or divesting itself of old ones (Folgers Coffee, paper products), which can be achieved without disrupting the whole.[26]

Although we have argued that hierarchies offer a number of advantages in terms of coordinating and controlling organisational activities, in essence this merely amounts to saying that there are benefits to organisations of creating specialist units that are coordinated and controlled by superior units. The more difficult questions are on what basis should specialist units be defined; how should decision-making authority be allocated and what kind of relationships should there be between different organisational units? We address these issues in the next sections of this chapter.

Defining organisational units

In creating a hierarchical structure, on what basis are individuals assigned to organisational units within the firm? This issue is fundamental and complex. Multinational, multiproduct companies are continually grappling with the issue of whether they should be structured around product divisions, country subsidiaries or functional departments and periodically they undergo the disruption of changing from one to another. Some of the principal bases for grouping employees are common tasks, products, geography and process:

● *Tasks.* Organisational units can be created around common tasks. This usually means grouping together employees who do the same job – thus, a firm might create a machine shop, a maintenance department, a secretarial pool and a sales office.

● *Products.* Where a company offers multiple products, these can provide a basis for structure. In a department store, departments are defined by products: kitchen goods, bedding, lingerie and so on. PepsiCo comprises three main product groups: PepsiCo Beverages, Frito-Lay (snack foods) and Quaker Foods (cereals and processed foods).

● *Geography.* Where a company serves multiple local markets, organisational units can be defined around these localities. Wal-Mart is organised by individual stores, groups of stores within an area and groups of areas within a region. The Roman Catholic Church is organised into parishes, dioceses and archdioceses.

● *Process.* A process is a sequence of interlinked activities. An organisation may be viewed as a set of processes: the product development process, the manufacturing process, the sales and distribution process and so on. A process may correspond closely with an individual product, or a process may be dominated by a single task. Functional organisations tend to combine task-based and process-based grouping.

How do we decide whether to use task, product, geography or process to define organisational units? The fundamental issue is achieving the coordination necessary to integrate the efforts of different individuals. This implies grouping individuals according to the intensity of their coordination needs. Those individuals whose tasks require the most intensive coordination should work within the same organisational unit.

> How do we decide whether to use task, product, geography or process to define organisational units? The fundamental issue is achieving the coordination necessary to integrate the efforts of different individuals.

● In a geographically dispersed organisation where communication across distance is difficult, it is advantageous to base the organisation on local units. For example, consultancy companies are often organised on this basis.

● Where an organisation is not particularly diversified in relation to products and does not need to be differentiated by location but possesses strong functional specialisations, then a grouping around functional tasks is appropriate. For example, British Airways is organised primarily around functions: flight operations, engineering, marketing, sales, customer service, human resources, information and finance.

● Where a company is diversified over many products and these products are substantially different in terms of technology and markets, it is vital that individuals who work on the same product should interact closely – a product-based organisation is the appropriate structure. Virtually all diversified companies – General Electric, 3M, Sony, Siemens and Unilever – are organised by product divisions.

Figure 9.3 GM Corporation: organisational structure 1997

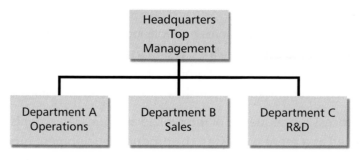

Alternative structural forms

On the basis of these alternative approaches to grouping tasks and activities, we can identify three basic organisational forms: the functional structure; the multidivisional structure; and the matrix structure.

THE FUNCTIONAL STRUCTURE   Single-business firms tend to be organised along functional lines (see Figure 9.3). Grouping together functionally similar tasks is conducive to exploiting scale economies, promoting learning and capability building and deploying standardised control systems. Since cross-functional integration occurs at the top of the organisation, functional structures are conducive to a high degree of centralised control by the CEO and top management team.

However, even for single-product firms, functional structures are subject to the problems of cooperation and coordination. Different functional departments develop their own goals, values, vocabularies and behavioural norms which make cross-functional integration difficult. As the size of the firm increases, the pressure on top management to achieve effective integration increases. Because the different functions of the firm tend to be *tightly coupled* rather than *loosely coupled*, there is limited scope for decentralisation. In particular, it is very difficult to operate individual functions as semi-autonomous profit centres.

The real problems arise when the firm grows its range of products and businesses. Once a functionally organised company expands its product range, coordination within each product area becomes difficult. The trend among very large companies has been for product-based, divisionalised companies to replace functionally organised ones but the trend is not entirely one way.

THE MULTIDIVISIONAL STRUCTURE   The product-based, multidivisional structure has emerged during the 20th century in response to the coordination problems caused by diversification. The key advantage of divisionalised structures (whether product

Figure 9.4 General Electric: organisational structure 2009

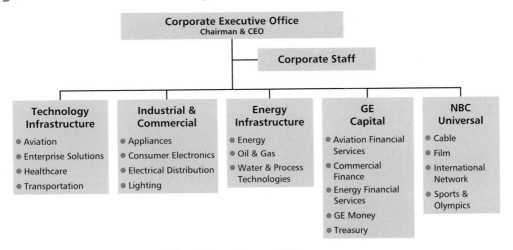

Source: based on information in General Electric Annual Report, 2008

based or geographically based) is the potential for decentralised decision making. The multidivisional structure is the classic example of a form of organisation that allows business-level strategies and operating decisions to be made at the divisional level, while the corporate headquarters concentrates on corporate planning, budgeting and providing common services.

Central to the efficiency advantages of the multidivisional corporation is the ability to apply a common set of corporate management tools to a range of different businesses. Divisional autonomy also fosters the development of top management leadership capability among divisional heads – an important factor in CEO succession.

The large, divisionalised corporation is typically organised into three levels: the corporate centre; the divisions; and individual business units, each representing a distinct business for which financial accounts can be drawn up and strategies formulated. Figure 9.4 shows General Electric's organisational structure at the corporate and divisional levels.

MATRIX STRUCTURES   Whatever the primary basis for grouping, all companies that embrace multiple products, multiple functions and multiple locations must coordinate across all three dimensions. Organisational structures that formalise coordination and control across multiple dimensions are called *matrix structures*.

Figure 9.5 shows the Shell management matrix (prior to reorganisation in 1996). Within this structure, the general manager of Shell's Berre refinery in France reported to his country manager, the managing director of Shell France, but also to his business sector head, the coordinator of Shell's refining sector, as well as having a functional relationship with Shell's head of manufacturing.

Figure 9.5 Royal Dutch Shell Group: pre-1996 matrix structure

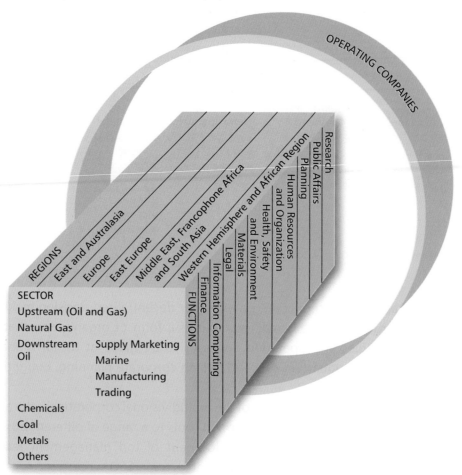

Many diversified, multinational companies, including Philips, Nestlé and Unilever, adopted matrix structures during the 1960s and 1970s, although in all cases one dimension of the matrix tended to be dominant in terms of authority. Thus, in the old Shell matrix the geographical dimension, as represented by country heads and regional coordinators, had primary responsibility for budgetary control, personnel appraisal and strategy formulation.

During the past two decades, most large corporations have dismantled or reorganised their matrix structures. Shell abandoned its matrix during 1995–6 in favour of a structure based on four business sectors: upstream; downstream; chemicals; and gas and power. During 2001–2, the Swiss-Swedish engineering giant ABB abandoned its much-lauded matrix structure in the face of plunging profitability and mounting debt. In fast-moving business environments companies have found that the benefits from formally coordinating across multiple dimensions have been outweighed by excessive complexity, larger head office staffs, slower decision making and diffused authority.

Bartlett and Ghoshal observed that matrix structures:

led to conflict and confusion; the proliferation of channels created informational logjams as a proliferation of committees and reports bogged down the organisation; and overlapping responsibilities produced turf battles and a loss of accountability.[27]

Yet, all complex organisations that comprise multiple products, multiple functions and multiple geographical markets need to coordinate within each of these dimensions. The problem of the matrix organisation is not that it attempts to coordinate across multiple dimensions – in complex organisations such coordination is essential – but that this multiple coordination is over-formalised, resulting in excessive corporate staffs and over-complex systems that slow decision making and dull entrepreneurial initiative. The trend has been for companies to focus formal systems of coordination and control on one dimension, then allowing the other dimensions of coordination to be mainly informal.[28] Thus, while Shell is organised primarily around four business sectors and these sectors exercise financial and strategic control over the individual operating companies, it still has country heads, responsible for coordinating all Shell activities in relation to legal, taxation and government relations within each country; and functional heads, responsible for technical matters and best-practice transfer within their particular function, whether it is manufacturing, marketing or HR.

Beyond hierarchical structures

For several decades consultants and management scholars have proclaimed the death of hierarchical structures in business firms.

In 1993, two of America's most prominent scholars of organisation announced:

the new organisational revolution is sweeping one industry after another . . . quantum changes in manufacturing and computer-mediated communication technologies have given managers radical new options for designing organisations.

The new organisations featured:

flatter hierarchies, decentralised decision making, greater tolerance for ambiguity, permeable internal and external boundaries, empowerment of employees, capacity for renewal, self-organising units, self-integrating coordination mechanisms.[29]

As noted in earlier sections, there have been substantial changes in the way in which corporate hierarchies have been organised. Layers have been removed; mechanistic

formality has been replaced by organic informality. Yet, hierarchy remains as the basic structural form of almost all companies. Are there alternative modes of organisation?

Several organisational forms have been identified which, although they comprise some hierarchical elements, are sufficiently distinctive to be regarded as alternative organisational forms:

- *Adhocracies.* In some organisations, the presence of shared values, motivation and willingness to participate, mutual respect and communication effectiveness may allow a high level of coordination with little need for hierarchy, authority or tools of control. These organisations, which Henry Mintzberg calls **adhocracies**,[30] feature flexible, spontaneous coordination and collaboration around problem solving and other non-routine activities. Adhocracies tend to exist among organisations where expertise is prized. In research organisations, new product development groups, jazz bands and consulting firms, each specialist is valued for his or her expertise and there is little exercise of authority.

- *Team-based and project-based organisations.* Flexibility and adaptability can also be achieved in project-based organisations – common in sectors such as construction, consulting, oil exploration and engineering services – where business takes the form of projects of limited duration. Because every project is different and every project goes through a changing sequence of activities, each project needs to be undertaken by a closely interacting team that relies on problem solving and mutual adjustment as well as rules and routines. Increasingly, companies are introducing elements of team- and project-based organisations into their conventional divisional and functional structures. For example, in most divisionalised corporations, new product development, change management, knowledge management and research is organised in projects and undertaken by teams.

> Increasingly, companies are introducing elements of team- and project-based organisations into their conventional divisional and functional structures.

- *Networks.* Localised networks of small, closely interdependent firms have been a feature of manufacturing for many hundreds of years. In Italy such networks are prominent in the clothing industry of Prato, near Florence and in packaging equipment.[31] Hollywood movie making[32] and microelectronics in Silicon Valley have similar structures – highly specialised firms that coordinate to design and produce complex products. Often these networks feature a central firm that acts as a 'systems integrator',[33] as in the case of Benetton and Toyota.[34] In fast-moving industries, the ability of highly specialised, knowhow intensive firms to reconfigure their relationships can be conducive to innovation, product differentiation and rapid new product development. In the developing world, such networks can be a viable alternative to industrial development where large enterprises are lacking.[35]

These different organisational forms share several common characteristics:

1   *A focus on coordination rather than control.* In contrast to the 'command-and-control' hierarchy, these structures focus almost wholly upon achieving coordination. Financial incentives, culture and social controls take the place of hierarchical control.

2   *Reliance on coordination by mutual adjustment.* Central to all non-hierarchical structures is their dependence on voluntaristic coordination through bilateral and multilateral adjustment. The capacity for coordination through mutual adjustment has been greatly enhanced by information technology.

3   *Individuals in multiple organisational roles.* Reconciling complex patterns of coordination with high levels of flexibility and responsiveness is difficult if job designs and organisational structures are rigidly defined. Adhocracies and team-based organisations feature individuals switching their organisational roles and occupying multiple roles simultaneously. For example, for most of the 1990s, AES had no finance function, no HR function, no safety or environmental affairs functions and no public relations department. These functions were performed by teams of operatives and line managers.

> Adhocracies and team-based organisations feature individuals switching their organisational roles and occupying multiple roles simultaneously.

Case Insight 9.2
BP's organisational structure

As one of the world's largest companies employing close to 80,000 people[36] and operating in more than 100 countries, it is not surprising that BP's organisational structure has evolved and changed over time. John Roberts of Stanford Graduate School of Business,[37] who made a detailed study of the company, described its organisational structure in the 1980s as follows: 'BP was a highly politicized, top-heavy bureaucracy managed through a cumbersome matrix structure. The company was spread across numerous distinct lines of business, the result of its not having yet completely undone the conglomerate diversification in which it had indulged in the 1970s. Financial proposals required 15 signatures before they could be accepted; head office staff filled a 32-storey building; and meetings of 86 committees absorbed top executives' days'. Needless to say the company's financial performance at this time was deteriorating.

During the late 1980s and 1990s BP transformed itself by focusing on three basic businesses – oil and gas exploration; refining and marketing; and petrochemicals – and by acquiring two large competitors, Amoco and Arco. Changes in organisational structure accompanied these changes in strategy with some of the biggest transformations taking place under the leadership of John Browne who took over as BP's chief executive officer in 1995. Browne focused on the exploration part of the business and set about making this the driving force of BP. To realise his vision for the company, he argued that BP needed to adopt a less bureaucratic and more entrepreneurial style. To achieve this he decentralised decision making and drastically reduced the size of the headquarters. The managers of oil fields were given the authority to run their operations the way they wanted as long as they met the performance targets negotiated annually with top management. Local managers could decide on their own suppliers, outsource activities and decide where and how to drill. Rather than information flowing vertically up and down a chain of command, a system of peer assistance was instigated whereby groups of managers involved in similar activities met to disseminate information horizontally, to collaborate to solve problems and to challenge each other.

As the opening case illustrated, when Tony Hayward succeeded John Browne he committed himself to continuing in much the same way. His emphasis remained on simplifying organisational structure and shifting authority and responsibility away from the centre. Whilst this form of organisation undoubtedly contributed to long-term improvements in BP's performance, as we see in the Deepwater Horizon case it also had some potential drawbacks. The leanness of that top meant that there were fewer headquarters staff to offer advice when technical or commercial problems arose and the increasing use of outsourcing and extensions to spans of control had the potential to increase complexity at a local level as the expert knowledge within the company became more diffused. The change from bureaucratic controls to performance or output-based controls also appeared to have had unintended consequences and may have been a contributory factor in the accident.

Management systems

It is not only organisational structures but also management systems that influence the ways in which intended strategies get realised in practice. Management systems provide the mechanisms of communication, decision making and control that allow companies to coordinate and integrate activities. Systems like organisational structure are shaped by strategy but also influence the ways in which strategy is interpreted by organisational members. Four management systems are of primary importance: the information systems; the strategic planning systems; the financial systems; and the human resource management systems. We consider each briefly.

Information systems

Information is fundamental to the operation of all management systems. Communication technology – the telephone and telegraph – was essential for the emergence of the modern corporation. The computer has had an equally dramatic impact during the past half century. Accounting systems are key components of firms' information systems. They collect, organise and communicate financial information to top management and other parts of the organisation.

Administrative hierarchies are founded on vertical information flows: the upward flow of information to the manager and the downward flow of instructions. The trend towards decentralisation and informality in organisations rests on two key aspects of increased information availability: information feedback to the individual on job performance, which has made self-monitoring possible and information networking, which has allowed individuals to coordinate their activities voluntarily without hierarchical supervision. For example, a central element of total quality management has been recognition that regular, real-time, performance feedback to employees permits them to take responsibility for quality control, reducing or eliminating the need for supervisors and quality controllers. During the past decade, corporate intranets, web-based information systems and groupware have transformed organisations' capacity for decentralised coordination.

Strategic planning systems

Small enterprises can operate successfully without an explicit strategy. The firm's strategy may exist only in the head of the founder and, unless the founder needs to write a business plan in order to attract outside financing, the strategy may never be articulated. Most large companies have a regular (normally annual) strategic planning process. For a multi-business company, the strategic planning process creates business plans for the

Whether formal or informal, systematic or ad hoc, documented or not, the strategy formulation process is an important vehicle for achieving coordination within a company.

individual divisions that are then integrated into a corporate plan.

Whether formal or informal, systematic or ad hoc, documented or not, the strategy formulation process is an important vehicle for achieving coordination within a company. As discussed in Chapter 1, the strategy process brings together knowledge from different parts of the company, to try and ensure consistency between the decisions being made at different levels and in different parts of the company.

A strategic plan typically comprises the following elements:

- *A statement of the goals* the company seeks to achieve over the planning period with regard to both financial targets (e.g. targets for revenue growth, cost reduction, operating profit, return on capital employed, return to shareholders) and strategic goals (e.g. market share, new products, overseas market penetration and new business development). For example, in BP's February 2006 strategy statement, the company established that its 'primary objective is to deliver sustainable growth in free cash flow', which it would achieve through 'growing production by about 4% a year to 2010' and 'delivering further improvements in return on average capital employed relative to our peer group'.[38]

- *A set of assumptions or forecasts* about key developments in the external environment to which the company must respond. For example, BP's 2006–10 strategic plan assumed an oil price of $40 a barrel.

- *A qualitative statement* of how the shape of the business will be changing in relation to geographical and segment emphasis and the basis on which the company will be establishing and extending its competitive advantage. For example, BP's 2011–16 strategy placed safety and operational risk management at the heart of the company and emphasised the need to rebuild trust following the Deepwater Horizon incident. To this end the company announced its resumption of dividend payments to shareholders and commitment to the active management of its business portfolio through a phased $30 billion divestment programme and a doubling of expenditure on exploration.[39]

- *Specific action steps* with regard to decisions and projects, supported by a set of mileposts stating what is to be achieved by specific dates. For example, BP's strategic commitments included 32 project start-ups by 2016 and 1 Mboe (million barrels of oil equivalent) of new production and new forms of partnership with resource holders.

- *A set of financial projections,* including a capital expenditure budget and outline operating budgets. For example, BP's 2010 strategy statement set a capital expenditure budget of $20 billion per year, a shareholder quarterly dividend level of 7 cents per share and a $2 billion pre-tax performance improvement by the end of 2012.

Although strategic planning tends to emphasise the specific commitments and decisions that are documented in written strategic plans, the most important aspect of strategic planning is the **strategy process**: the dialogue through which knowledge is shared and ideas communicated, the consensus that is established and the commitment to action and results that is built.

Increasing turbulence in the business environment has caused strategic planning processes to become less formalised and more flexible.

> The most important aspect of strategic planning is the strategy process: the dialogue through which knowledge is shared and ideas communicated, the consensus that is established and the commitment to action and results that is built.

Financial planning and control systems

Financial flows form the life blood of the enterprise. Revenues from customers provide the funds to pay suppliers and employees and any surplus remunerates owners. If inflows are insufficient to cover outflows, the firm becomes insolvent. Hence, financial systems are inevitably the primary mechanism through which top management seeks to control the enterprise. At the centre of financial planning is the budgetary process. This involves setting and monitoring financial estimates with regard to income and expenditure over a specified time period, both for the firm as a whole and for divisions and departments. Budgets are in part an estimate of incomes and expenditures for the future, in part a target of required financial performance in terms of revenues and profits, and in part a set of authorisations for expenditure up to specified budgetary limits. Two types of budget are set: the capital expenditure budget and the operating budget.

THE CAPITAL EXPENDITURE BUDGET   **Capital expenditure budgets** are established through both top-down and bottom-up processes. From the top down, strategic plans establish annual capital expenditure budgets for the planning period both for the company as a whole and for individual divisions. From the bottom up, capital expenditures are determined by the approval of individual capital expenditure projects. Companies have standardised processes for evaluating and approving projects. Requests for funding are prepared according to a standardised methodology, typically based on a forecast of cash flows discounted at the relevant cost of capital (adjusted for project risk). The extent to which the project's returns are sensitive to key environmental uncertainties is also estimated. Capital expenditure approvals take place at different levels of a company according to their size. Projects up to $5 million might be approved by a business unit head, projects up to $25 million might be approved by divisional top management, larger projects might need to be approved by the top management committee, while the biggest projects require approval by the board of directors.

THE OPERATING BUDGET The **operating budget** is a pro forma profit and loss statement for the company as a whole and for individual divisions and business units for the upcoming year. It is usually divided into quarters and months to permit continual monitoring and the early identification of variances. The operating budget is part forecast and part target. It is set within the context of the performance targets established by the strategic plan. Each business typically prepares an operating budget for the following year that is then discussed with the top management committee and, if acceptable, approved. At the end of the financial year, business-level divisional managers are called upon to account for the performance over the past year.

Human resource management systems

> Ultimately, strategic and financial plans come to nothing unless they influence the ways in which people within the organisation behave.

Strategies may arise from principles, formulae or divine inspiration, but their implementation depends on people. Ultimately, strategic and financial plans come to nothing unless they influence the ways in which people within the organisation behave. To support strategic and financial plans, companies need systems for setting goals, creating incentives and monitoring performance at the level of the individual employee. Human resource management has the task of establishing an incentive system that supports the implementation of strategic plans and performance targets through aligning employee and company goals and ensuring that each employee has the skills necessary to perform his or her job. The general problem, we have noted, is one of agency: how does a company encourage employees to act in line with its goals?

The problem is exacerbated by the imprecision of employment contracts. Unlike most contracts, employment contracts are vague about employee performance expectations. The employer has the right to assign the employee to a particular category of tasks for a certain number of hours per week, but the amount of work to be performed and the quality of that work are unspecified. Employment contracts give the right to the employer to terminate the contract for unsatisfactory performance by the employee, but often the employer has imperfect information as to employees' work performance – in team production, individual output is not separately observable.[40]

We have seen at the start of this chapter that firms attempt to gain the employee's compliance with organisational goals using direct supervision or performance incentives such as sales commission or profit sharing. We have also noted that there are difficulties associated with each of these different types of control. For example we noted earlier that designing compensation systems that do not distort overall performance is difficult and that direct supervision becomes problematic when tasks are not routine and predictable. In the face of these challenges there has been a trend amongst business organisations to try and influence the way in which employees think and behave by developing a strong corporate culture. It is to this topic we turn next.

Case Insight 9.3
Management systems at BP

The changes that have occurred over time in BP's strategy and structure were accompanied by changes to its management systems, particular those involving strategic and financial planning and human resource management. BP, like most other petroleum companies, has always had a dual planning process with strategic planning concentrating on the medium and long term and financial plans looking more at short-term performance. Over time, however, the emphasis placed on these complementary processes changed. While for many years the planning process was driven by specialists located in the strategic planning team at BP's headquarters, as the company moved towards a flatter, more decentralised structure so its emphasis moved towards financial rather than strategic control.

Financial control was achieved by linking performance targets to financial indicators and was reinforced by aligning the company's system of rewards and incentives with these targets. In interviews that took place between BP managers and federal investigators following the Deepwater Horizon accident, mention was made of the fact that the performance evaluations of drilling rig managers included a category called 'Every Dollar Counts and Simplification'. Under this heading managers were encouraged to outline the ways in which they had saved the company money. Similarly contractors on the rig explained how their bonuses depended in part on how fast repairs were completed. In their final report the Deepwater Horizon Study Group concluded that those involved in the project were 'trading something that was in their estimation unlikely for something that was sure. They were trading sure savings in terms of time and money – and perhaps quicker returns on investment – for what they took to be the unlikely possibility of a blow-out and its unimaginable consequences'.

Corporate culture

Edgar Schein defines **organisational culture** as: 'A pattern of shared basic assumptions that was learned by a group as it solved its problems of external adaptation and internal integration, that has worked well enough to be considered valid and, therefore, to be taught to new members as the correct way you perceive, think and feel in relation to those problems'.[41] Deal and Kennedy put it more simply as 'the way things get done around here'.[42] It is common to distinguish between corporate culture and organisational culture. The term **corporate culture** is typically used to refer to the values and ways of thinking that senior managers wish to encourage within their organisation, whereas organisational culture refers to the diverse cultural patterns that exist in the informal organisation. In addition commentators refer to strong and weak culture. A strong culture is one in which key values and attitudes are widely shared and intensely held. For example, companies such as Starbucks, Shell, Nintendo and Google endeavour to create a strong sense of identity among their employees. A weak culture, in contrast, is one where people tend to hold different views, have different values and may interpret and respond to signals in very different ways. Most organisations contain sub-cultures within the whole – in an advertising company, for example, the 'suits' are likely to have a different sub-culture from the 'creatives'; in a university administrative staff may have a different sub-culture from academics.

Describing and classifying cultures

Numerous ways of describing cultures have been developed, together with many different classifications of organisational types. Johnson,[43] for example, has identified a number of elements that can be used to describe organisational cultures which he labels a cultural web. These include the organisation's paradigm (its mission and values), its control systems, organisational structures, power structures, rituals and routines and stories and myths. By identifying these elements managers may be able to influence them.

Schein[44] suggests that culture can be understood at three different levels.

- The first level comprises the organisational attributes that an outsider visiting the company for the first time might see, hear or feel. Schein refers to these features as artefacts. Artefacts include corporate logos, the way people dress, the premises in which the firm's activities are located, the stories people tell about the organisation, even the look and feel of the washrooms! We can see something of these differences between companies if we compare the images of Google's and Microsoft's logos. Google deliberately attempts to portray itself as a playful and informal organisation whereas Microsoft comes across as more traditional.

- The second level refers to the values and attitudes that organisational members express. Managers often try to articulate the values they desire organisational members to share in mission statements or codes of conduct.

- The third and deepest level is that of 'unspoken rules' and tacit beliefs. Some attitudes and beliefs become so deeply ingrained in the organisation that they are taken for granted and moved beyond expression and challenge. It is this third facet of culture that is considered by Schein and others to be the most influential but also the most difficult to change.

Featured example 9.1   Is Nokia's culture to blame for its failure in the smartphone market?

Some commentators argue that Nokia's engineer-driven culture is to blame for its failure to make headway in the smartphone market. In an interview for the *New York Times*, Adam Greenfield, a former head of design direction at Nokia said, 'The engineers at Nokia brag about the number of megapixels a new phone has but they don't understand that if you can't find the button to use the camera on the phone, it doesn't matter how many megapixels it is.'[45] In other words the claim is that the engineering perspective is so embedded in Nokia's psyche that obvious factors in the design of phones are ignored.

A full discussion of many different typologies of culture and framework for assessing organisational cultures is beyond the scope of the chapter but the key questions for strategists are: Can organisational cultures be changed in ways that better align them with firm strategy and is it ethical to try to do so? Is there any evidence that a strong corporate culture has a significant impact on firm performance? In the following sections we will examine these questions.

Can organisational cultures be changed?

With regard to the first question, we have seen that the development of a strong culture can act as an efficient and effective coordinating device because if employees share the same values there is less need for direct supervision and employees can act on their own initiative. Strong corporate cultures play to employees 'hearts' rather than their 'heads' and encourage loyalty and commitment. They are built by recruiting the 'right' people, holding induction events, establishing corporate rites and ceremonies that reinforce the approved ways to behave (e.g. annual dinners or employee of the month awards), holding team briefings, organising social activities and paying attention to symbols (e.g. the architecture of buildings or the design of the corporate logo). Critics argue that emphasis given to building strong corporate cultures is misplaced – it represents an attempt to 'engineer' employees' 'souls' and is profoundly unethical.[46] Others point out that management attempts to 'engineer' a corporate culture is unlikely to succeed because the company can never completely shut out other cultural influences on employees. People are not machines, easily subject to managerial manipulation. Any attempts to change values that are not seen as authentic tend to be met with cynicism and resistance. For example corporate statements that declare 'people are our most valuable assets' or 'excellence in all we do' that do not ring true with organisational members' own experiences, tend to be treated as meaningless slogans. From the manager's point of view it is impossible to know whether an employee has truly internalised the desired norms and values or merely pays lip service to them.

> Strong corporate cultures play to employees 'hearts' rather than their 'heads' and encourage loyalty and commitment.

Corporate culture and organisational performance

With regard to our second question there is limited empirical evidence on the links between corporate culture and organisational performance, in part because of the difficulties of measuring these broad concepts. Those studies that have been attempted[47] suggest that organisations with strong corporate cultures do have better long-term financial performance than those that do not, but the methods that have been used to test this assertion have attracted significant criticism. Regardless of whether or not a link between corporate culture and firm performance has been established statistically, a large number of business practitioners believe that corporate culture and performance are linked. For example in a recent survey that Heskett undertook, asking questions about the relative importance of strategy, execution and culture in an organisation's success, culture came out on top by a wide margin.[48] We shouldn't forget, however, as Barney[49] has pointed out, that for an organisation's culture to confer a competitive advantage it needs to be valuable, rare and inimitable. If it were easy to engineer then it would cease to be rare and inimitable and all companies could create a 'strong' culture. On the other hand if culture is difficult to manipulate then, whilst having a 'superior' culture can confer an advantage on the firm, the basis of its advantage would be luck because culture would be outside managerial control.

Case Insight 9.4
Exploring BP's organisational culture

As a starting point for exploring BP's culture we could look at some of the symbols the company uses and value statements it selects to publicise on its website. The company's current logo was introduced in 2000 and designed as a representation of the Greek sun god Helios. The Helios design was chosen to replace the old shield because it was suggestive of light, heat and nature, reinforcing the company's portrayal of itself as progressive and environmentally concerned. However, even though these symbols (what Schein would call artefacts) tell us something about the company, unless the values expressed in the company's documentation are evident in the day-to-day behaviour of its senior team and are embedded in its structure, processes and practices they are more likely to be seen as part of BP's public relations efforts rather than indications of BP's corporate culture.

Large organisations are typically made up of many different cultures or sub-cultures. In BP, for example, interviews that took place with operatives following the Deepwater Horizon incident revealed that engineers and managers viewed risk and safety in very different ways. The Deepwater Horizon Study Group[50] suggested that the engineers tried to quantify risks by calculating probabilities and evaluating possible consequences, whereas managers saw risk in terms of 'risk and reward', that is to say the bigger the reward the bigger the risk that was worth taking. Some of those commenting on the disaster suggested that the managerial interpretation of risk had come to dominate the organisation and that over time BP's strategy had become one of 'elephant-hunting' – that is to say the company focused its efforts and resources on the biggest, most lucrative (and, by inference, the riskiest) prospects whilst ignoring more conventional projects.[51] This, it was argued, gradually resulted in the emergence of a culture in which it was legitimate to 'cut corners' in order to reduce costs. In the words of a recent report 'BP forgot to be afraid'.[52] This claim was strongly denied by BP who pointed out that there was no evidence whatsoever that any individual had put cost saving and profit above safety. From BP's point of view the accident was unprecedented and unforeseeable. Whilst few would argue that BP made a conscious decision to put cost cutting above safety, the debate centres on whether the 'unconscious mind' or deeply engrained culture of the company contributed in any way to the accident.

Summary

In this chapter we have explored two themes. First we have noted that there is often a discrepancy between planned strategy and realised strategy, in part, because strategy is interpreted by organisational members in the light of the organisation's structure, systems and culture. Second we have sought to explore key issues that underpin the design of an organisation's structures and systems and influence the ways in which an organisation attempts to develop strong corporate cultures. These two themes are closely interconnected. Organisational structures, cultures and systems are integral to strategy not only because they are shaped by it but also because they influence it. We saw in the BP case that BP's structure, systems and culture influenced the way in which employees interpreted safety strategy and viewed risk. In turn, the meaning employees and partners gave to the signals from senior managers influenced the way in which safety procedures were enacted in practice. Our focus within this chapter has, in the main, been on the way in which managers can approach designing appropriate organisational structures, aligning systems and processes and shaping corporate culture; but we have also pointed to some of the ethical dilemmas managers face in their search for ways of achieving effective coordination and control.

Summary table

Learning Objectives	Summary
Understand the ways in which strategy formulation and implementation are inextricably linked and be aware of the factors that mediate between planned and realised strategy	Whilst businesses need to set clear objectives and undertake analysis to identify the best ways of achieving those objectives, there is often a discrepancy between planned and realised strategy. Planned strategies are interpreted by organisational members through the filters of organisational structures, cultures and systems and are often changed in the process. It is usual to think of structures, cultures and systems following strategy but these factors can also subtly influence how strategies are framed
Appreciate the key challenge of reconciling specialisation with coordination and cooperation and have an overview of the mechanisms that managers employ to deal with these tensions	Allowing individuals to specialise greatly enhances the efficiency with which tasks are completed but at the same time creates the challenge of ensuring cooperation and coordination. Several mechanisms are available to managers to manage this challenge. Control mechanisms include the hierarchical supervision, shared values and performance incentives. Coordination mechanisms include rules and directives, routines and mutual adjustment
Understand the basic principles of organisational design and the types of organisational structure suited to particular tasks and particular business environments	The basic design for complex organisations is hierarchy but companies still need to grapple with the bases on which divisions or business units are established and what the relationships between these different divisions of entities should be. Three main organisational forms have been identified – functional, multi-divisional and matrix – each with different advantages and disadvantages and with a different degree of fit with different business contexts
Understand the role that organisational culture plays in achieving coordination and control	We have explored what is meant by organisational culture and the different levels at which it operates. We have seen how in recent years culture has been seen as an important way of controlling and coordinating work activity but we have also recognised that there are significant limits to managers' ability to influence culture
Comprehend the role of management systems in the coordination and control of corporations	We have explored four primary management systems – information systems, strategic planning systems, human resource management systems and financial planning and control systems – and outlined the ways in which these systems may be used to provide mechanisms of communication, decision making and control that allow companies to achieve cooperation and coordination

Further reading

The following article by Harold Leavitt is a good place to start to understand the role that hierarchies play in organising business activity:

> Leavitt, H. J. (2003). Why hierarchies thrive. *Harvard Business Review*, 81(3), 96–102.

Henry Mintzberg has also written extensively on organisational design:

> Mintzberg, H. (1980). Structure in fives: a synthesis of the research on organisation design. *Management Science*, 26(3), 322–41.

Mintzberg has also made a significant contribution to the debate on strategic planning systems:

> Mintzberg, H. (1994). The rise and fall of strategic planning. *Harvard Business Review*, January–February, 107–14.

In terms of more recent organisational forms Bartlett and Ghoshal's work on matrix organisations remains a classic:

> Bartlett, C. and Ghoshal, S. (1990). Matrix management: not a structure, a frame of mind. *Harvard Business Review*, July–August, 138–47.

DeFilippi and Arthur extend the discussion to project-based organisations:

> DeFilippi, R. and Arthur, M. (1998). Paradox in project-based enterprise: the case of film making. *California Management Review*, 40(2), 125–40.

For those wishing to understand the debates around cultural control the article by Grugulis *et al.* provides an illuminating insight into employment practices within a consultancy company:

> Grugulis, I., Dundon, T. And Wilkinson, A. (2000). Cultural control and the culture manager: employment practice in a consultancy. *Work, Employment and Society*, 14(1), 97–116.

QUIZ

Visit your enhanced ebook at **www.foundationsofstrategy.com** for self test quiz questions

Self-study questions

1   You are employed as a manager by a fashion retail chain and have been asked to put forward suggestions about ways in which the organisation can encourage

sales staff to offer better customer service. Suggest some of the alternative control mechanisms the firm might put in place and outline the advantages and disadvantages of each.

2 Can a firm's organisational structure contribute to the acceleration of innovation? If so, how?

3 Draw an organisation chart for an organisation with which you are familiar. How would you characterise this structure (e.g. functional, multi-divisional, matrix)? What suggestions would you make to reorganise the structure to make the organisation more efficient and effective?

4 Whereas in the past many universities were organised as self-organising collectives of scholars, today most have well-formulated strategic plans. What are the benefits to a university of having formalised planning and budgetary systems? What are the limitations?

5 Google regularly features towards the higher end of the Fortune 500 list of the top 100 companies to work for. Use the internet to research the key features of Google's corporate culture and explain why this culture is attractive to new recruits. What might be the downsides of working in this type of culture?

GLOSSARY

Visit your enhanced ebook at **www.foundationsofstrategy.com** for key term flashcards

VIDEO **Closing case** Designing and Redesigning Cisco

Cisco Systems Incorporated is a multinational company, headquartered in the US, that designs and sells consumer electronics, networking, video and voice communication technologies and services. For a short while in early 2000 Cisco was the most valuable company in the world by market capitalisation, but its time in the top spot was short lived as the bursting of the dot.com bubble saw its share price drop dramatically. Since that time Cisco has faced mixed fortunes. Like many other companies it has been adversely affected by the turbulence in the world economy following the banking crises of 2008 and by increased competition and as a result its financial performance has been somewhat lacklustre in recent years. Despite its change in fortune since the heady days of the early 2000s, in 2010 Cisco still employed more than 70,000 employees and had an annual sales revenue of around US $40 billion.[53]

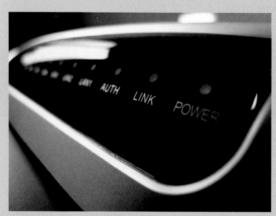

Cisco built its reputation and sustained its early growth by designing and selling equipment – the routers and switchers that guide data through the internet. As this market matured and margins were squeezed, Cisco branched out into new product areas such as wireless equipment, internet telephony and optical networks. Whilst the decision by a company located in maturing markets to diversify is unremarkable, Cisco is interesting because it explored many new markets, pursuing 30 or more opportunities, in what the company labelled 'market adjacencies', simultaneously.

In the early years, following its start-up in 1984, Cisco organised its business on the basis of its product lines but as the business grew it moved towards a more customer-focused structure. In 1997 it re-organised its business into three main divisions based on its three main customer segments – telecom operators; large businesses; and small businesses. The aim was to provide customers with complete end-to-end solutions including integrated software, hardware and network management. Over time, however, this structure proved problematic.

As markets matured and greater emphasis was placed on cost reduction this structure was increasingly seen as inefficient. The product requirements of different customer segments were becoming increasingly blurred and the structure was resulting in different lines of business developing similar routers independently of each other.

The dip in Cisco's financial performance following the dot.com crash resulted in the company finding itself under pressure to further reduce its costs and to achieve this aim it undertook more restructuring – this time moving to a more traditional functional structure. The functional groupings included marketing, engineering, R&D, operations and customer service; the rationale behind this structure being that it would: facilitate the design of equipment that used a standard architecture; allow economies of scale to be realised; and enhance knowledge sharing across Cisco's product groups. Whilst the functional structures did deliver some efficiency gains, like all organisational structures it also had some drawbacks. The emphasis on cost cutting and standardisation meant that the company was less in touch with the needs of its consumers and as functions developed their own sub-cultures, cooperation between functions became more problematic.

Instead of going back to one of its earlier structural forms, based on customers or products, in 2007 the chief executive officer, John Chambers, announced a new 'technology organisation' designed to make the most of the opportunities and to counter the challenges, created by the next phase of internet growth. The new structure comprised an elaborate system of committees made up of 'councils', 'boards' and 'working groups' with their membership drawn from managers operating in different business functions. There were initially around 12 councils that looked after new markets that might reach sales of US$10 billion in the future. There were more than 40 boards focused on prospective markets of around US$1 billion and both boards and councils were supported by temporary project teams called 'working groups'. Many managers had roles on both councils and boards and how well managers performed in these teams contributed to their annual bonuses.[54]

The opinions of the company's managers and industry observers were very mixed about whether this new structure would work. On the one hand the hierarchy of cross-functional teams made it easier for the organisation to react quickly to new opportunities and to innovate. On the other hand there was a real danger that the whole structure was too complex and would slow down decision making and lead to 'burn out' for senior managers. As a consequence

◀ of the restructuring a number of senior managers left the company, citing frustration with the 'councils' as part of their reasons for going.[55] In May 2011, following uninspiring financial results, Cisco announced it was to restructure yet again. Chambers announced that the councils and boards were to be reduced in number and the company would instead focus on five key areas it was targeting for growth.[56] This new announcement has left commentators wondering whether Cisco represents the firm of the future – flexible and not afraid to quickly reorganise in the face of new challenges – or whether John Chambers had just got it wrong and should step down.

Case questions

● Why has Cisco chosen to change its organisational structure on such a frequent basis?

● What are the advantages and disadvantages of the different organisational structures Cisco has adopted over time?

● In your opinion how might Cisco avoid the problems that matrix organisations typically face?

Notes

1 G. Parker, *The Grand Strategy of Philip II* (New Haven: Yale University Press, 1998).

2 It is worth noting that whilst academics tend to use the term strategic implementation, practitioners often talk about strategy execution.

3 'BP canvassing investors on possible break-up.' www.reuters.com/article/2010/07/18/us-bp-breakup-idUSTRE66H0WW20100718. Accessed on 25 May 2011.

4 'Gulf of Mexico oil spill timeline', *The Daily Telegraph* (26 May 2011).

5 The National Commission on the BP Deep Water Horizon Oil Spill and Offshore Drilling, 'The BP Deep Water Horizon oil disaster and the future of offshore drilling – report to the president' (January 2011).

6 'The Report of the BP U.S. Refineries Independent Safety Review Panel' (January 2007).

7 Joel Podolny and John Roberts, *British Petroleum (A2): Organizing for Performance at BPX*, case study S-IB-16A2 (Graduate School of Business Stanford University, revised 2 April 2002): 7.

8 'Hayward shares candid views on 2006', *The Daily Telegraph* (12 January 2007).

9 'Louisiana oil spill threatens turnaround efforts by BP CEO Tony Hayward', *Wall Street Journal* (3 May 2010).

10 N. O'Regan and A. Ghobadian, 'Revitalizing an oil giant: an interview with Dr Tony Hayward, chief executive of BP', *Journal of Strategy and Management* 3 (2009): 174–83.

11 O'Regan and Ghobadian (2009) op. cit.

12 S. Goldenberg, 'US oil spills chief slams BP's culture of complacency', *The Guardian* (9 November 2010).

13 'Interim report on causes of the Deepwater Horizon oil rig blowout and ways to prevent such events', National Academy of Engineering and National Research Council (16 November 2010).

14 H. Mintzberg, *Structure in Fives: Designing Effective Organisations* (Englewood Cliffs: Prentice Hall, 1993): 2.

15 A. Smith, *The Wealth of Nations* (London: Dent, 1910): 5.

16 S. Ross, 'The economic theory of agency', *American Economic Review*, 63 (1973): 134–9; K. Eisenhardt, 'Agency theory: an assessment and reviews', *Academy of Management Review*, 14 (1989): 57–74.

17 R. Grant, 'Organizational restructuring within the Royal Dutch/Shell Group', in *Contemporary Strategy Analysis*, 6th edn (Chichester: John Wiley & Sons, 2007).

18 M. Weber, *Economy and Society: An Outline of Interpretive Sociology* (Eds: G. Roth and C. Wittich), (Los Angeles: University of California Press, 1978).

19 An exception here is the work by Paul du Gay. See, for example, P. du Gay, *In Praise of Bureaucracy* (London: Sage, 2000).

20 Bureaucratic control of labour processes has long been associated with forms of work study that standardise work flows with detailed division of labour and job descriptions. Often this entails the application of technology, for example the technology of assembly lines, to programme the pace, sequencing and nature of tasks that employees are directed to undertake.

21 T. Peters and R. Waterman, *In Search of Excellence* (New York: Harper & Row, 1982).

22 Stephen Wood has referred to this trend as 'new wave management'. See, for example, S. Wood, 'New wave management?' *Work, Employment and Society* 3 (1989): 379–402.

23 See, for example, H. Willmott, 'Renewing strength: corporate culture revisited', *Management* 6 (2003): 73–87 or I. Grugulis, T. Undon and A. Wilkinson, 'Culture control and the "culture manager": employment practices in a consultancy', *Work, Employment and Society* 14 (2000): 97–116.

24 See, for example, G. Kunda, *Engineering Culture: Control and Commitment in a High-Tech Corporation* (Philadelphia: Temple University Press, 1992).

25 K. Salazar, 'Interim report on the causes of the Deepwater Horizon oil rig blowout', National Academy of Engineering and the National Research Council (2010).

26 Modularity in organisations is explored in: R. Sanchez and J. T. Mahoney, 'Modularity, flexibility and knowledge management in product and organisational design', *Strategic Management Journal* 17, Winter Special Issue (1996): 63–76; M. A. Schilling, 'Toward a general modular systems theory and its application to interfirm product modularity', *Academy of Management Review* 25 (2000): 312–34; and C. Baldwin and K. Clark, 'Managing in an age of modularity', *Harvard Business Review* (September–October 1997): 84–93.

27 C. A. Bartlett and S. Ghoshal, 'Matrix management: not a structure, a frame of mind'. *Harvard Business Review* (July–August 1990): 138–45.

28 'A survey of the company: the new organisation' *The Economist* (21 January 2006).

29 R. Daft and A. Lewin, 'Where are the theories for the new organisational forms?' *Organization Science* 3 (1993): 1–6.

30 H. Mintzberg, op. cit.: Chapter 12.

31 M. H. Lazerson and G. Lorenzoni, 'The firms that feed industrial districts: a return to the Italian source', *Industrial and Corporate Change* 8 (1999): 235–66; G. Lorenzoni and A. Lipparini, 'The leveraging of interfirm relationships as a distinctive organisational capability: a longitudinal study', *Strategic Management Journal* 20 (1999): 317–38; A. Grandori, *Interfirm Networks* (London: Routledge, 1999).

32 R. J. DeFilippi and M. B. Arthur, 'Paradox in project-based enterprises: the case of film making', *California Management Review* 42 (1998): 186–91.

33 G. Lorenzoni and C. Baden-Fuller, 'Creating a strategic center to manage a web of partners', *California Management Review* 37 (1995): 146–63.

34 J. H. Dyer and K. Nobeoka, 'Creating and managing a high-performance knowledge-sharing network: the Toyota case', *Strategic Management Journal* 21 (2000): 345–67; A.

Camuffo, P. Romano and A. Vinelli, 'Back to the future: Benetton transforms its global network', *Sloan Management Review* 43 (Fall 2001): 46–52.

35 D. Wheeler, K. McKague, J. Thomson, R. Davies, J. Medalye and M. Prada, 'Sustainable local enterprise networks', *Sloan Management Review* (Fall 2005): 33–40.

36 www.bp.com. Accessed 8 August 2011.

37 J. Roberts, 'Organizing for performance: how BP did it' (2005) www.gbs.stanford.edu/news/bmag/sbsm0502/feature_bp.shtml. Accessed 8 August 2011.

38 BP Strategy and Fourth Quarter 2005 Results Presentation, 7 February 2006 (www.bp.com).

39 BP 2010 Results and Investor Update (www.bp.com).

40 A. Alchian and H. Demsetz, 'Production, information costs and economic organization', *American Economic Review* 62 (1972): 777–97.

41 E. Schein, *Organizational Culture and Leadership* (San Francisco: Jossey Bass, 2004): 17.

42 T. Deal and A. Kennedy, *Corporate Cultures: The Rites and Rituals of Corporate Life* (Harmondsworth: Penguin Books, 1982).

43 G. Johnson, 'Strategy through a cultural lens', *Management Learning* 31(2000): 403–27.

44 Schein, op. cit.

45 N. Bilton, 'The engineer-driven culture at Nokia', *New York Times* (1 June 2011). Retrieved 1 June 2011 from http://bits.blogs.nytimes.com/2011/02/11/for-nokia-design-will-be -key-to-future.

46 See, for example, J. Lozano, 'Ethics and corporate culture: a critical relationship', *Ethical Perspectives* 5 (1998): 53–70.

47 See, for example, T. Peters and R. Waterman, *In Search of Excellence* (New York: Profile Books, 1982) or D. Denison, 'Bringing corporate culture to the bottom line', *Organizational Dynamics* 13 (1984): 5–22.

48 J. Heskett, *The Culture Cycle: How to Shape the Unseen Forces that Transform Performance* (London: FT Press, 2011).

49 J. Barney, 'Organizational culture: can IT be a source of sustained competitive advantage?' *Academy of Management Review* 11 (1986): 656–65.

50 W. E. Gale, 'Perspectives on Changing Safety Culture and Managing Risk', Deepwater Horizon Study Group Working Paper (January 2011). Retrieved 3 June 2011 from http://ccrm.berkeley.edu/pdfs_papers/DHSGWorkingPapersFeb16-2011/Perspective-on-ChangingSafetyCulture-and-Managing-Risk-WEG_DHSG-Jan2011.pdf.

51 D. Greising, 'Troubles run deep at oil gulf platform', *Chicago Tribune* (28 May 2007).

52 Final Report of the Investigation of the Macondo Well Blowout. Deepwater Horizon Study Group (1 March 2011): 76.

53 Cisco Systems Inc. 2010 Annual General Report. Retrieved 3 June 2011 from: https://materials.proxyvote.com/Approved/17275R/20100920/AR_67529/images/ Cisco-AR2010.pdf .

54 'Reshaping Cisco: the world according to Chambers', *The Economist* (27 August 2009).

55 P. Burrows and J. Galante, 'Cisco reins in management system that spurred exodus at the top', *Bloomberg Business Week* (5 May 2011). Retrieved 3 June 2011 from: www. businessweek.com/news/2011-05-05/cisco-reins-in-management-system-that- spurred-exodus-at-top.html.

56 J. Duffy, 'Cisco restructures and streamlines operations', *Network World* (5 May 2011). Retrieved 3 June 2011 from www.networkworld.com/news/2011/050511-cisco- reorginization.html.

10

Current trends in strategic management

Introduction and objectives

The early years of the 21st century have been characterised by the increasing levels of economic, political and social turbulence. In 2008 the failure of Lehman Brothers (an investment bank) and the collapse of a large insurance company, the American International Group (AIG), heralded the start of a full-blown crisis in the financial sector that went on to engulf many economies around the world. A number of the structures and institutions that had previously underpinned the global financial system came under severe pressure and central banks and governments across the world took unprecedented steps to offset the potential damage by introducing radical monetary and fiscal measures to stimulate economic activity. Just as the world economy seemed to be recovering from these events, political upheavals in a number of Arab states, an earthquake and tsunami in Japan and debt crises in the Eurozone produced further shocks.

In this final chapter we assess some of the key changes that have taken place in the business environment in recent times and discuss their implications for strategic management. Unlike other chapters of the book we will not be introducing tried and tested strategy tools and techniques, instead our approach is more speculative. We identify some of the forces that are reshaping the business environment and introduce a number of concepts and approaches that are influencing current thinking in strategy. We look to draw lessons from leading-edge companies about strategies, organisational forms and management styles that could prove effective during a period of rapid, unpredictable change and introduce you to some new ideas that are emerging in the field of strategic management.

By the end of this chapter you will:

● be familiar with some of the key changes that have occurred in the business environment in recent years;

● understand why the 2008 financial crisis has led to calls for change in a number of areas of management practice;

● be aware of some of the latest developments in strategic thinking;

● appreciate the forces that are driving changes in organisational design;

● be alert to the approaches and initiatives that are being developed across an array of different firms in response to turbulence in the business environment.

The new external environment of business

One of the defining features of the early 21st century will undoubtedly be increasing levels of economic turbulence associated with the global financial crisis, often referred to as the Credit Crunch or Great Recession, that hit the world economy in the latter part of the 2000s. At the time much news coverage was devoted to the collapse of financial institutions, such as Lehman Brothers and Fannie Mae/Freddie Mac in the US and Northern Rock and the Royal Bank of Scotland in the UK, but the crisis had a much wider impact, leading to falls in output, increases in unemployment and rises in house repossessions around the globe. There were even country casualties with Iceland, following failures in its three main banks, coming close to national bankruptcy. The economic crisis was not, however, the main cause of turbulence. Rather it highlighted and amplified a series of complex economic, political, social and technological changes that over time significantly altered the business environment. Nonetheless, the economic crisis ushered in a new era characterised by shifting patterns of global economic activity and increased societal pressure for change in business practices. To shed light on this new external environment of business we look first at the causes and consequences of the global financial crisis together with some of the other factors triggering change.

The global financial crisis

The immediate cause of the crisis was attributed to the collapse in the housing market in the US. As a result of low interest rates, demand for home ownership increased and house prices started to rise. This rise in house prices fuelled speculation that prices would increase even further and led to what has been described as a 'gold rush mentality'.[1] As more and more households attempted to jump on the housing bandwagon hoping to benefit from the rapid increase in house values, financial institutions, wishing to keep cash flowing into the market, turned mortgages into securities. These securities were particularly attractive to financial investors because they offered attractive returns and there was also a plentiful supply of funds available in money markets from governments and individuals in economies with large sovereign surpluses and high savings rates, like China.

The creation of these new mortgage-backed securities was made possible, in part, because the regulatory systems in the US and the UK were relatively 'light touch' and encouraged innovation. By pooling and packaging mortgage debts in sophisticated ways based on mathematical models, new securities called **collateralised debt obligations** (CDOs) were created. CDOs were merely promises to pay money to investors based on the cash flow generated by the assets on which the CDOs were based, namely the flow of mortgage repayments. CDOs were split into different risk classes – senior, mezzanine and junior – and in the event of the flow of cash into the CDO being insufficient to meet the claims of all investors, for example because some householders with mortgages had defaulted on their repayments, those holding the highest class of CDO (senior) were paid first. These products seemed a pretty safe bet because they were based on US real estate and they had been ranked favourably by credit rating agencies. To summarise, banks borrowed money from the short-term money markets and lent this money to those seeking a mortgage. These mortgages, which were assets from the banks' point of view, were then pooled to create CDOs. The CDOs were sold to investors and this enabled the banks to repay the money they had borrowed from the money markets. The repayments made by those who had taken out mortgage loans provided income to CDO investors.

The market in CDOs grew dramatically between 2000 and 2006 because, on the surface at least, these securities appeared safe and offered attractive returns. Unfortunately underneath they contained complex hidden risks. Tempted by the returns available from these new mortgage instruments, lenders relaxed their rules and allowed those seeking to buy properties to take out mortgages with little or no deposit and also permitted homeowners the ability to refinance their homes with little regard to their ability to repay. Loans made to people with a higher than average likelihood of default were known as 'sub-prime' loans. Needless to say sub-prime borrowers were charged higher interest rates or given less favourable terms to compensate lenders for the risk they were taking, but as the US housing market was booming there was a plentiful supply of households in the sub-prime category who were willing to take on mortgage debt. Eventually, as with all property booms, the market began to slow and the bubble burst as people began to default on their loans. Banks and other organisations with large exposure to CDOs found themselves facing huge losses and financial institutions became much more cautious in their approach to lending, particularly with regard to short-term money markets. Those that depended on obtaining money from this source found that their access to funds had dried up, in turn causing their depositors to fear that their own monies were at risk. This complex chain of events triggered the reappearance of runs on banks, the 'credit crunch' and a global recession with devastating consequences for many people around the globe.

Commenting on events a US Federal Inquiry Commission's report asked to look into the causes of the crisis stated that the global financial system 'had become vulnerable and interconnected in ways that were not understood by either the captains of finance or the system's public stewards'.

THE BACKGROUND TO THE CRISIS   Although the immediate source of the crisis lay in the US's sub-prime mortgage market, the seeds of the crisis were probably sown a decade earlier. At the end of the 1990s the stock markets in industrialised countries rose rapidly on the basis of significant growth in the internet sector and the formation of a large number of new companies with the prefix .com (dot.coms). On 10 March 2000 the NASDAQ stock market index hit its all time high but within a month the speculative boom was over and the ensuing meltdown of internet, technology, media and telecom stocks provided the first evidence that US credit expansion would not be enough to sustain the investment bubbles that had built up during the roaring 1990s. One of the consequences of the dot.com crash was that share prices fell across the board and remained sluggish for a considerable period, removing the opportunity for banks to make attractive returns from more traditional forms of investment and encouraging them to seek new, more innovative ways of making money (e.g. through the creation of financial instruments like CDOs).

The CDO debacle prompted a debate on the ethics of offering loans to those who were faced with a higher than average risk of default. Also the general public had had an earlier indication that corporate ethical standards were not always as they should be during the Enron scandal. Enron was one of the US's most successful and admired companies of the 1990s but in late 2001 it filed for bankruptcy. It was subsequently revealed that the company's financial position had been deliberately falsified through a system of false accounting. This was the first of a series of financial scandals that was to surround companies on both sides of the Atlantic and reveal the downside of the aggressive pursuit of shareholder value through financial engineering and high-powered management incentives.

THE IMMEDIATE AFTERMATH OF THE CRISIS   The immediate response around the world to the global financial crisis was to pump money into the global financial system to kick start economic activity. At the time this book was completed the effect of these massive monetary and fiscal initiatives was not fully known, but seemed to be patchy. Whilst the experience of different countries has varied, overall the growth rates of the rich industrialised nations have been very modest. In contrast emerging economies like China and India have proved more resilient and although their growth rates were slowed by the global financial crisis, national output and income have continued to rise. In many advanced economies the recession that followed in the immediate wake of the financial crisis was the deepest experienced since the 1930s, leaving lots of underutilised capacity and unemployed workers. Although, in most economies, output stopped shrinking, by 2010 growth had not revived sufficiently to take up the slack. As the immediate problems associated with the 'freezing up' of short-term money markets appeared to recede, so new concerns emerged. Government deficits and debt levels in European countries such as Greece, Ireland, Portugal and Italy have caused alarm in financial markets prompting fears of another financial crisis, this time focused on European sovereign debt. In addition the downgrading by Standard & Poor (a global credit rating agency) of the status of US government debt has resulted in turbulence in global stock markets and raised concerns that Western economies are heading towards a second recession.

Other sources of turbulence

> The start of the 21st century has not only been characterised by the economic and financial turbulence but also by social and political upheaval.

The start of the 21st century has not only been characterised by the economic and financial turbulence but also by social and political upheaval.

When terrorists hi-jacked four commercial airliners and crashed two of them into the Twin Towers of the World Trade Center in New York on 11 September 2001, they set in train a series of events with long-term repercussions. 9/11 was followed by the invasion of Afghanistan and Iraq and further bombings in Bali, Madrid, London and Mumbai, all of which had a major impact on world trade, financial flows, political tensions and risk perceptions. 2011 saw a new source of turbulence with a wave of demonstrations and civil uprising in Arab states against ruling elites, referred to in the media as the Arab Spring. To date there have been changes in political leadership in Tunisia and Egypt,

Credit: Getty Images.

a civil war in Libya, civil protests in Bahrain, Syria and Yemen as well as minor protests elsewhere. The UK also experienced unprecedented social disturbance when rioting and episodes of looting took place in London and a number of other English cities in August 2011. All these changes are set against the much larger backdrop of a changing world order with a shift in economic power taking place from West to East. Many commentators predict that China will overtake the US as the world's largest economy some time during the next decade.

The natural world has also emerged as a source of instability. A slew of scientific evidence suggests that climate change has reached 'tipping point', triggering rapidly accelerating global warming accompanied by greatly increased risks of natural disasters. The increasingly interconnected nature of the world economy also amplifies the effect of local disasters. When a volcano erupted in Iceland, air passengers were stranded around the world as many international flights were suspended because of the ash cloud. More tragically, given the loss of life and destruction, when Japan was hit by an earthquake and tsunami in March 2011, equity markets around the world declined and manufacturers of products as diverse as semiconductors and steel, and as far apart as the US and South Korea, were affected.

In addition, rapid developments in digital and communications technologies prompted a transition from an industrial to a knowledge economy, where software rather than hardware is the primary source of value. The digitally driven knowledge revolution has also created what Brian Arthur calls the 'casino of technology', where markets are transformed and established market leaders deposed.[2] The ability of two maverick entrepreneurs operating out of Estonia, Niklas Zennstrom and Janus Friis, to initiate revolutions in two industries – recorded music through their Kazaa file sharing system and telephony through their Skype VoIP internet telephony system – exemplifies the disruptive potential of new internet-based business models.[3]

Digital technologies are also causing competition to intensify through the dissolution of industry barriers and causing industry boundaries to blur. In hand-held devices Apple's iPod, Windows smartphones, Nintendo's Game Boy and RIM's BlackBerry are increasingly sharing functions and competing in a shared marketplace. These technologies are also creating new challenges for firms. In 2011 the Sony Corporation revealed that an attack on its online PC games network had resulted in the security surrounding some aspects of customers' personal and credit card details being breached. This resulted in the company shutting its online network for a period of time and had obvious legal, reputational and profit implications.

Societal pressures

All of the sources of instability that we have outlined – economic, social, political and technological – have led to societal pressures for change. For organisations to survive and prosper requires that they adapt to the values and expectations of society and retain what organisational sociologists refer to as **social legitimacy**.[4] One of the most profound impacts of the recent financial crisis on business may be implications for the legitimacy of particular types of business – which influences acceptability among consumers, motivation of employees, willingness of investors and financiers to provide funding and government support. Loss of social legitimacy may be as great a threat to the survival of commercial and investment banks as their weak balance sheets.[5]

> Loss of social legitimacy may be as great a threat to the survival of commercial and investment banks as their weak balance sheets.

The notion that the business enterprise is a social institution which must identify with the goals and aspirations of society has been endorsed by several leading management thinkers – including Peter Drucker, Charles Handy and Sumantra Ghoshal.[6] The implication is that when the values and attitudes of society are changing, so must the strategies and behaviours of companies.

While anti-business sentiment has for the most part been restricted to the fringes of the political spectrum: neo-Marxists, environmentalist and anti-globalisation activists, the corporate scandals of the early part of the decade and the financial crisis of 2008–9 have moved disdain for business corporation and their leaders into the mainstream of public opinion. Three issues have been paramount: equity, ethics and sustainability.

Equity – there has been increasing public concern about the widening gap in pay between those at the top of organisation, chief executives and their top management teams and those at the bottom. In 2009 a report from Income Data Services suggested that the average pay of CEOs in the UK's largest companies was 81 times that received by the average worker and in the US a report in the same year by the Economic Policy Institute suggested CEOs made 271 times the salary of average workers.[7] The argument that high salaries and bonuses were necessary to align top management incentives with shareholder value creation was no longer viewed as credible, particularly given that the excesses of the bonus culture in the financial services sector were viewed as a strong contributory factor in the 2008 financial crisis. Disquiet turned to public outrage when senior executives and top traders in firms like the Royal Bank of Scotland and JP Morgan Chase, that had been bailed out by taxpayers during the financial crisis, were awarded large bonuses. This has led to calls for even tighter scrutiny of executive compensation packages by shareholders and government.

Ethics – the confidence of the general public in business corporations was dented not only by the financial crisis but also by a series of scandals that preceded and succeeded it. A great deal of publicity surrounded three scandals in particular – Enron, Worldcom and the Madoff affair. The Enron Corporation was a US energy company and in 2001 it was discovered that the company had misled investors by falsifying its accounts. The incident not only revealed shortcomings within the company but also in the auditing process. The reputation of the company's auditors, Arthur Andersen, one of the largest auditing companies in the world, was severely damaged by this failure and Arthur Andersen subsequently ceased business. The following year a large telecommunications operator, Worldcom, came into the spotlight when an internal audit uncovered serious irregularities that had resulted in the financial performance of the firm being significantly overstated. A number of the directors of the company were found guilty of fraud and conspiracy to commit fraud. This failure raised the question of why no one in the company had complained or disclosed management misconduct earlier. The answer was claimed to lie, at least in part, in the company culture that was viewed as excessively materialistic and subtly coercive, preventing employees from challenging corporate practices. The 'Madoff affair' centred on the activities of Bernard Madoff, a well-respected investment advisor, who in 2009 admitted to running one of the largest fraudulent investment schemes in history. Madoff was found to have run a Ponzi scheme, that is to say a fraudulent investment operation that pays returns to investors not on the basis of income generated by the profits of the company but on the basis of the investors' own money and money paid in by subsequent investors. Ponzi schemes require ever increasing flows of money from investors and are eventually destined to fail.

Naturally these and other scandals have prompted questions about the ethical standards of company boards and management and have resulted in numerous calls for increased scrutiny of company activities and for board members and managers to receive greater training in, and to declare a stronger commitment to, corporate social responsibility.

Environmental sustainability – the clamour for firms to exhibit greater social responsibility also extends to 'green' issues. Public concern over the degradation of the natural environment continues to grow together with demands for companies to adopt more environmentally sustainable policies. A number of companies have been forced into action following public responses to issues that they may not immediately have recognised as their concern. For example, Nestlé became a major target in the global debate about access to fresh water because of its bottled water sales and fast-food companies like MacDonald's have found themselves at the heart of a public debate on obesity.

Adapting to society's growing demands for fairness, ethics and sustainability presents challenges for business leaders that extend beyond the problems of reconciling societal demands with shareholder interests. Should a company determine unilaterally the values that will govern its behaviour, or does it seek to reflect those of the society in which it operates? Companies that embrace the values espoused by their founders are secure in their own sense of mission and can ensure a long-term consistency in their strategy and corporate identity (e.g. Walt Disney Company and Wal-Mart with respect to founders Walt Disney and Sam Walton). However, there is a risk that these values become out of step with those of the society as a whole or with the requirements for business effectiveness. Thus, Marks & Spencer's paternalism towards employees and suppliers became a source of rigidity rather than competitive advantage. Conversely, seeking to embrace the concerns and values of society presents the challenge of identifying what these values are in a society characterised by diversity and rapid change.

Managing in the aftermath of the global financial crisis

Although the worst effects of the financial crisis and the ensuing recession seem to have passed, the changes that have occurred in the business environment and in the demands that society is now placing on businesses mean that many important challenges remain. We have already noted the acceleration in the shift in the balance of power between the developed West and the emerging East, the emergence of populist uprisings in a number of countries around the world, the deterioration in trust in business and concerns continue to grow about the sustainability of our natural environment,. The legacy of the 'great recession' remains, creating anxieties about spiralling government debt, high levels of unemployment and inflationary trends. Given all these factors it seems highly likely that the levels of volatility and unpredictability that we have experienced in recent years will continue into the future. A key feature of the global economy is the high level of interconnectedness that results from high levels of trade, internationalisation of financial markets, flexibility of exchange and interest rates and speed of communication. As predicted by systems theory, high levels of interconnectedness increase the tendency for the system to amplify small initial movements in unpredictable ways. The concern captured recently by a McKinsey & Company global managing director, is that the most consequential outcome of the recent turbulence 'is a challenge to capitalism itself'.[8] Whilst the debate is a very broad one and a full debate is beyond the scope of this chapter, we focus attention on three particular issues – the prioritisation of long-term over short-term goals; the fitness for purpose of current corporate governance arrangements; and the adoption of different styles of leadership.

> Interconnectedness increases the tendency for the system to amplify small initial movements in unpredictable ways.

Short-term versus long-term goals – one of the common explanations of what went wrong with the global economy is that late 20th-century firms, particularly financial institutions, were seduced by short-term gains. The emergence of short-termism is seen to have its roots in the broad acceptance in Western industrialised nations that shareholder value maximisation should be the main goal of firms. The pursuit of shareholder value has resulted in major gains in cost efficiency and a wave of corporate restructuring involving divestment, outsourcing and delayering, but the unremitting quest for shareholder value has also had unforeseen and undesired consequences. Rather than maximise the flow of profits on which stock market valuation depends, many companies focused excessively on short-term earnings. Short-term decision making is blamed for many companies' and countries' failure to invest in projects crucial to long-term competitiveness and for creating an environment in which it was very tempting to misrepresent company financial data for personal gain.

However, these assertions do not necessarily imply that the goal of maximising the value of the firm is misguided. Maximising shareholder value is essentially about maximising the present value of economic profit over the lifetime of the firm. The key issue is how it is translated into strategy. The problem for many public companies is that shareholder value creation has been interpreted by management to mean the management of a firm's stock market value. Management cannot create stock market value – only the stock market can do that. What management can do is to generate the stream of profits that the stock market translates into market value. The danger is that CEOs' obsession with their companies' share price can divert them from the task of long-term profit maximisation. Long-term thinking is

> Long-term thinking is necessary for long-term success and the critical focus of top management should be less on profits and more upon the factors that drive profits.

necessary for long-term success and the critical focus of top management should be less on profits and more upon the factors that drive profits: operational efficiency, customer satisfaction, new product development and the like.

The implication is not that firms abandon shareholder value maximisation in favour of a broad, difficult-to-define notion of stakeholder satisfaction, but they focus more determinedly on identifying the basic drivers of value creation and seek to manage them. There is no inherent tension between creating *long-term* value and serving the interests of employees, customers, suppliers, communities and the environment. Some have referred to this as the triple bottom line of economic, social and environmental performance, proposing that it is in a firm's self-interest to avoid short-term behaviour that is socially detrimentally and environmentally wasteful. This line of reasoning suggests that the answer to the present crisis of confidence in business leaders lies not in some new model of capitalism, but on putting in place incentives that encourage companies to take a long-term view and to refocus on the fundamentals of strategic management.

Corporate governance – **corporate governance** refers to the set of processes, institutions, regulations and policies that affect the way companies are directed, administer and controlled. The 2008 financial meltdown called into question the extent to which existing governance arrangements were fit for purpose. Attention was directed particularly towards remuneration, risk management, the operation of boards of directors and the effectiveness of regulatory institutions.

Much newspaper coverage at the time of the crash was devoted to the role that pay and incentive systems played in triggering the financial meltdown. The 'bonus culture' was blamed for encouraging excessive risk taking and, indeed, making risk taking the norm.

Since the crisis, governments in the UK and the US have tried to regulate bonuses through taxation policies but financial institutions have argued strongly that they operate in highly competitive markets and if they change their remuneration policies they will lose or be unable to recruit talented individuals. The claim is also made that national competitiveness will be damaged as firms seek to relocate their activities to other parts of the world.  Whilst many would dispute the arguments, it has none the less proved difficult to change this culture and despite a public outcry, bonuses have been paid to senior staff even in companies that have racked up large losses and been partially nationalised.

The global financial crisis highlighted not only the fact that excessive risks were being taken but perhaps, more importantly, that few within banking circles comprehended the true nature and extent of the risks. The complexity of the new financial instruments that had been created and the high-powered mathematics that underpinned them meant that few truly understood how these instruments worked or how long the string of effects had become. Whilst boards of directors had, in principle, the duty to oversee risks and to provide an early warning of potential problems, the make-up of many boards made this difficult. Independent board members often lacked expert knowledge about the specifics of the industry and were typically appointed on a part-time basis, limiting the time they could devote to scrutinising detailed and complex issues. Since the financial crisis there have been calls for greater attention to be paid to the basis of directors' competencies, for risk to be more clearly incorporated into performance metrics and for boards to be given the authority to request independent specialist advice on business risk, paid for by the company.

The financial crisis was also blamed on lax regulation by financial authorities. In the UK governments of all political persuasions were pleased to see the financial services sector booming because the sector constituted an important part of the economy and, as the sector was flourishing, there was no reason to interfere with the City's tradition of self-regulation. In the US the Clinton administration repealed laws which had originally been introduced in 1933 to curb speculation. Previously it had been a legal requirement for investment banking to be separated from retail banking but the repeal of this law eased the restrictions on what retail banks could do with their depositors' money. Needless to say following the financial debacle there were many calls to reinstate the previous legislation and this triggered a wider debate on the role of government in free market economies, including a discussion on whether some firms had become too big to fail. Whilst the full consequences of the crisis for organisational strategies are not yet known, at the very least it looks likely that there will be pressure for companies to make their activities more transparent and for these activities to be subject to greater government and public scrutiny.

New forms of leadership – the era prior to the financial crisis is often characterised as one of restructuring and shareholder focus associated with high profile 'change-masters'[9] – highly visible CEOs, with hard-driving management styles such as Lee Iacocca at Chrysler, John Browne at BP, Michael Eisner at Disney and Rupert Murdoch at News International. These leaders have been, first and foremost, strategic decision-makers, charting the direction and redirection of their companies and making key decisions over acquisitions, divestments, new products and cost cutting. The changing circumstances of management we have outlined imply that the 'buck-stops-here' peak decision-making role may no longer be feasible, let alone desirable. One simple observation is that most companies are too complex for the CEO to be able to access the information necessary to act as peak decision-maker. Recent contributions to the literature on leadership suggest that modern business leaders need to create organisational environments that encourage adaptability and flexibility.

Gary Hamel argues the need to redefine the work of leadership:

The notion of the leader as a heroic decision maker is untenable. Leaders must be recast as social-systems architects who enable innovation . . . In Management 2.0, leaders will no longer be seen as grand visionaries, all-wise decision makers and ironfisted disciplinarians. Instead, they will need to become social architects, constitution writers and entrepreneurs of meaning. In this new model, the leader's job is to create an environment where every employee has the chance to collaborate, innovate and excel.[10]

If strategy is founded in organisational identity and common purpose and if organisational culture is the bedrock of capability, then a key role of top management is to clarify, nurture and communicate the company's purpose, heritage, personality, values and norms. To unify and inspire the efforts of organisational members, leadership requires providing meaning to people's own aspirations. Ultimately this requires attention to the emotional climate of the organisation.[11]

> To unify and inspire the efforts of organisational members, leadership requires providing meaning to people's own aspirations.

If business leadership is less about decision making and more about guiding culture, identity and vision, then managers will require different knowledge and skills. Research into the psychological and demographic characteristics of successful leaders has identified few consistent or robust relationships – successful leaders come in all shapes, sizes and personality types. However, research based upon McClelland's *competency modelling* methodology pointed to the role of a set of personality attributes that have been referred to by Daniel Goleman as **emotional intelligence**.[12] These comprise: *self-awareness* – the ability understand oneself and one's emotions; *self-management* – control, integrity, conscientiousness and initiative; *social awareness* – particularly the capacity to sense others' emotions (empathy); and *social skills* – communication, collaboration and relationship building.

Jim Collins' concept of 'Level 5 Leadership' also emphasises individual qualities – notably a combination of personal and intense resolve.[13] This combination allows business leaders to avoid the hubris and megalomania associated with outsized egos and to devote themselves to team building and organisational development. Philip Morris's Joseph Cullman, Kimberly-Clark's Darwin Smith, Nucor's Ken Iverson, P&G's L. G. Laffey and IBM's Sam Palmisano are all transformational leaders who did not succumb to the cult of personality.

Probably the greatest error in Western thinking about leadership in organisations is the heavy emphasis on the role of individuals. Tappin and Cave argue that *team leadership* is best suited to today's troubled times where the top management team members are bound together by close bonds of fellowship. Their model is the Nokia leadership team that comprised Jorma Ollila, Matti Alahuhta, Pekka Ala-Pietilä, Sari Baldauf and his replacement as president and chief operating officer, Olli-Pekka Kallasvuo. An effective top management team comprises, ideally, just three or four people who share extensively and openly, have specialised roles, but are also able to cover for one another.[14]

However, it is important to acknowledge that, despite the urge to uncover 'the secrets of leadership', there is no dominant model of leadership or profile of the successful leader. The main lesson from empirical research is that successful leadership is associated with many different leadership approaches and many different characteristics of the individual leader. At the same time, different situations will respond to different leadership approaches.

New directions in strategic thinking

New challenges encourage new ways of thinking and as we have entered more turbulent times, new approaches have come to the fore. In this section we look briefly at three recent developments in strategic thinking – the real options approach, complexity theory and strategy-as-practice, each of which adds additional dimensions to our study of strategy.

Managing options

Deploying shareholder value maximisation also means recognising that shareholder value derives not only from the net present value of profits, but also from *real options*. Timothy Luehrman, in an influential article written in 1998, explains real options using the metaphor of a tomato grower.[15] He suggests that a gardener looking at his tomatoes during the summer months will find some that are ripe and ready to pick and others that are rotten and need to be discarded. In between, however, there will be a range of tomatoes with differing prospects. Some tomatoes could be picked now and would be edible but they would benefit from further ripening on the vine. By leaving them to mature, however, the gardener runs the risk that they might be attacked by pests or ruined by bad weather. Others aren't ripe enough to pick yet but given enough water, sun and plant food could do well. The active gardener inspects his tomatoes regularly and cultivates them to get the best possible crop. The message is, of course, that managing strategic opportunities (real options) in firms is analogous to being a tomato grower. During turbulent times, keeping 'one's options open' is important because options are likely to become increasingly important as sources of value.

Analysis of strategy in terms of option creation has focused on particular types of strategic decisions – for example, R&D decisions,[16] acquisitions,[17] and alliance formation.[18] However, application of real options thinking to strategic analysis at a broader level has been limited to broad generalisations, such as the value of flexibility. If we are to take on board options thinking more widely, then we need to reconsider most of our core strategy models and strategy techniques. For example:

- Industry analysis has taken the view that decisions about industry attractiveness depend on profit potential. However, if industry structure becomes so unstable that forecasting industry profitability is no longer viable, it is likely that industry attractiveness will depend much more on option value. From an options perspective, an attractive industry is one that is rich in options – for example, an industry that produces a number of different products, is composed of multiple segments, has many strategic groups, utilises a diversity of alternative technologies and raw materials and where internal mobility barriers tend to be low. Thus, consumer electronics, semiconductors, packaging and investment banking would seem to be more attractive in terms of options than electricity or steel or car rental.

- An options approach also has major implications for the analysis of resources and capabilities. In terms of option value, an attractive resource is one that can be deployed in different businesses and support alternative strategies. Owning a patent on a breakthrough in nanotechnology is likely to offer greater option value than owning blast furnace. Similarly with capabilities: highly specialised capabilities such as expertise in the design of petrochemical plants offers less option potential than expertise in the marketing of fast-moving consumer goods. Dynamic capabilities are important because they can create new options:

Dynamic capabilities are the organisational and strategic routines by which firms achieve new resource combinations as markets emerge, collide, split, evolve and die.[19]

Dealing with complexity theory

Organisations – like the weather, ant colonies, flocks of birds, human crowds and seismic activity – are complex systems whose behaviour results from the interactions of a large number of independent agents. This behaviour has a number of interesting features:

- *Unpredictability.* The behaviour of complex adaptive systems cannot be predicted in any precise sense. There is no tendency to stable equilibria; cascades of change are constantly interacting and reshaping competitive landscapes. Patterns of change tend to follow power-law distributions:

small changes typically result in small consequences but may also trigger major movements – dropping grains of sand onto a sand pile results in small movements interspersed by occasional major landslides.[20]

● *Self-organisation.* Complex systems – especially biological and social systems – have a capacity for self-organising. A bee colony or shoal of fish shows coordinated responses to external threats and opportunities without anyone giving orders. Humans too can often do as well as bees and ants in organising themselves, adapting to change and creating new structures and systems without any formal authority. Quite sophisticated synchronised behaviour can be achieved through adopting just a few simple rules. For human organisations there are three main requirements for self-organisation: *identity* that permits a common sense-making process within the organisation; *information* that provides the possibility of synchronised behaviour; and *relationships* that are the pathways through which information is transformed into intelligent, coordinated action. The more access individuals have to one another, the greater the possibilities for organised activity.[21]

● *Inertia and chaos.* Evolutionary processes can produce orderly outcomes where change is so limited that the system falls into stasis, or disorder leading to chaotic outcomes. In between is an intermediate region where disturbances produce both small and large shifts (with a power-law distribution) that achieves the most rapid evolutionary adaptation. These results point to the advantages of systems that are positioned at the *edge of chaos* – they are capable of small, localised adaptations, but also have the potential to make larger leaps toward higher *fitness peaks*.[22]

The implications of these ideas for strategic management are radical and far-reaching. Complexity implies that business is inherently unpredictable – not only is it impossible to forecast the business environment, but managers cannot predict with any certainty what the outcomes of their actions will be. The concept of the CEO as the peak decision maker and strategy architect is not only unrealistic, it is undesirable. Managers must rely on the self-organising properties of their companies. The critical issues are how they can select the structures, systems and management styles that will allow these self-organising properties to generate the best outcomes. Some of the recommendations arising from applications of complexity theory to strategic management include:[23]

> Complexity implies that business is inherently unpredictable.

● *Setting up conditions for both incremental and radical change.* Kaufman's *NK model* and the *fitness landscapes* that it generates is a widely used tool for exploring the implications of choices of strategy, organisational form and management behaviour.[24] Achieving the highest level of adaptive performance typically requires a combination of incremental changes with occasional radical leaps. Management systems can be designed to encourage these outcomes. For example the reorientation of companies' strategic planning systems from resource allocation decisions to agreeing performance targets is likely to encourage incentives for incremental measures – cost reduction and continuous improvement – while establishing conditions where serious performance shortfalls trigger corporate intervention involving major strategic changes. NK models also show that the optimal balance between incremental and radical management measures depend upon the degree of interdependency of the organisational environment: the stronger the linkages, the more rugged the landscape and the greater the need for major strategic leaps to move to new performance peaks.

- *Establishing simple rules.* If the coordinated behaviours of complex systems (e.g. the flying formations of flocks of birds) can be simulated with a few simple rules, it seems feasible companies can be managed by a few simple rules and very little managerial direction. For instance, rather than plan strategy in any formal sense, rules of thumb in screening opportunities (*boundary rules*) can locate the company where the opportunities are richest. Thus, Cisco's acquisitions strategy is guided by the rule that it will acquire companies with fewer than 75 employees of which 75% are engineers. Second, rules can designate a common approach to how the company will exploit opportunities (*how-to rules*). Thus, Yahoo! has a few rules regarding the look and functionality of new web pages, but then gives freedom to developers to design new additions. Third, companies have rules to determine priorities in resource allocation (*priority rules*).[25] Jack Welch's corporate initiatives at GE – 'Be number 1 or number 2 in your industry', 'Six-sigma', 'Destroy-your-business-dot-com' – fulfilled a similar role. They were not directives, but guidelines to stimulate and focus decentralised adaptation.[26]

- *Accelerating evolution through flexibility.* Organisational structures tend to become fixed over time as power centres build and interactions become institutionalised. Periodic large-scale corporate reorganisations are not enough: to exploit innovation and entrepreneurial initiative, flexibility in organisational structure is essential. Eisenhardt and Brown use the term 'patching' to describe a process in which new organisational units are continually being created, merged and redefined to foster initiative.[27] Achieving flexibility may require leaving structures only partially defined. This may be especially effective in assisting collaboration between different business units within a company. Rather than attempt to manage business unit

> Periodic large-scale corporate reorganisations are not enough: to exploit innovation and entrepreneurial initiative, flexibility in organisational structure is essential.

linkages from the corporate level, it may be better for corporate managers to create a context within which businesses can co-evolve. This requires allowing considerable autonomy to business units while keeping their boundaries porous to permit a multiplicity of voluntary collaborations between individuals across the businesses. Walt Disney Company exemplifies co-evolution between different internal divisions. Disney's *Lion King* movie spawned videos, theme park attractions, a stage musical and over 150 kinds of merchandise. These spinoffs were not planned by corporate strategists; they occurred through voluntary cooperation across Disney's different divisions.[28]

● *Using adaptive tension to position at the edge of chaos.* If too little tension produces inertia and too much creates chaos, the challenge for top management is to create a level of adaptive tension that optimises the pace of organisational change and innovation. Bill McKelvey interprets Jack Welch's management style from a complexity viewpoint – by imposing initiatives ('Be number 1 or number 2 in your industry') and powerful performance incentives, he turned up the level of pressure in the organisation to the point where changes began occurring spontaneously.[29]

Complexity theory provides an intellectual basis for ideas of 'emergence' in strategy making. Changes in large companies' strategic planning practices in recent years – reduced formality, emphasis on performance goals, focus on direction rather than content – are consistent with the tenets of complexity theory.[30]

Paying attention to processes and practice

The theme of emergence also surfaces in the approach to strategy adopted by a group of scholars who have come together under the loose label of 'strategy-as-practice'. As we saw in Chapter 9 strategic plans rarely come to fruition in the way senior managers anticipate, rather they emerge through iterative processes of planning, trial-and-error learning and top-down/bottom-up dialogue. Whilst we know quite a lot about the analytics that underpin strategy, the actual processes and practices by which strategies are formulated have tended to be overlooked. As Clegg *et al.* explain:

> *What is left out of the picture is the work of strategy – the people whose task it is to produce strategy, the tools they use, the workshops in which strategic ideas are born and the language they deploy to make strategic sense of the world and to legitimate their views as strategic.[31]*

The notion of strategy developed by the strategy-as-practice group is that strategy is something that people 'do' and, as such, it is best referred to by a verb rather than a noun – hence they prefer to talk about strategising rather than strategy. The focus of much of the work is on the day-to-day details of strategising, that is to say the nature of the meetings people attend, the way reports and presentations are constructed, capital expenditure and budgeting is conducted and language is used to position these activities as strategic. While the work of this group is designed to aid understanding through description rather than prescription, for some it offers a route to finding 'more helpful models of managing',[32] for example by uncovering some of the interpersonal skills that assist an individual to become a successful strategist.

Redesigning the organisation

As business environments become more complex, more competitive and less predictable, survival requires that companies perform at a higher level with a broader repertoire of capabilities. Building multiple capabilities and achieving excellence across multiple performance dimensions requires managing dilemmas that cannot be resolved as simple trade-offs. A company must produce at low cost, while also innovating; it must deploy the massed resources of a large corporation, while showing the entrepreneurial flair of a small start-up; it must achieve high levels of reliability and consistency, while also being flexible. All of these dilemmas are aspects of the underlying conflict between achieving operational efficiency today and adapting for tomorrow. Reconciling these conflicts within a single organisation presents huge management challenges. We know how to devise structures and incentive systems that drive cost efficiency; we also know the organisational conditions conducive to innovation. But how on earth do we do both simultaneously?

> A company must produce at low cost, while also innovating; it must deploy the massed resources of a large corporation, while showing the entrepreneurial flair of a small start-up; it must achieve high levels of reliability and consistency, while also being flexible.

Changes in organisational design are being driven by two major forces: first, the need for organisations to deploy more capabilities developed to a higher level; second, the need to respond quicker to external change.

Capability-based structures

If we accept that most enterprises need to deploy multiple capabilities and the coordination needs of different capabilities vary, it follows that our organisational structure must encompass different patterns of interaction. Hence, most business enterprises are unlikely to be successful with a unitary structure and will need to encompass multiple structures.

BEYOND UNITARY STRUCTURES Developing multiple capabilities requires that organisational members coordinate in different ways for different purposes which requires structures that simultaneously support multiple patterns of coordination.[33] Matrix structures – organising to develop capabilities around businesses, geographical markets and functions – have been around for a long time. But these dimensions of the traditional matrix relate primarily to operational activities. The literature on organisational learning and knowledge management distinguishes productive activities according to whether they are building the firm's stock of knowledge or deploying that knowledge: the former is referred to as *exploration*, the latter as *exploitation*.[34] When exploration activities were carried out by specialised functions – R&D, market research, strategic planning – organisations could simply differentiate these departments to meet the organisational requirements of exploration. Increasingly, however, these functions are not the preserve of specialised departments but are diffused across the organisation.

Adding exploration activities – product development teams, innovation initiatives, communities of practice – on top of the standard dimensions of the organisational matrix requires additional structures to support coordination. Structures directed towards acquiring new knowledge and promoting change within the formal organisation have been described as parallel learning structures.[35] They are designed to foster communication and interaction, but typically involve little specialisation or rules.

> 3M has a parallel structure for new product development whereby individuals are encouraged to 'bootleg' time, materials and use of facilities to work on new product ideas. Promising new products that emerge from this informal structure are ultimately taken up by the formal structure.
>
> The 'Work-Out' programme implemented by Jack Welch at GE was a parallel structure designed to effect change within the formal structure. During Work-Out sessions the norms that governed the formal organisation were suspended and free interchange of ideas was encouraged.
>
> IBM's massive, online '*Innovation Jam*' creates a temporary organisation that administers a biannual, 72-hour online session involving tens of thousands of contributors from inside and outside the company , then harvesting the results.[36]

TEAM-BASED, PROJECT-BASED AND PROCESS-BASED STRUCTURES The structures needed to support coordination are different from those required to ensure compliance and control. Increased reliance on teams reflects the recognition that routines require patterns of interaction that are spontaneous and poorly understood – hence, they cannot be 'managed' in any directive sense. Flexible, team-based structures can achieve

the kinds of adaptable integration that are the basis of dynamic capabilities, yet, beyond some very basic requirements of team structure, we know little about the dynamics of team interaction.[37]

More companies are organising their activities less around functions and continuous operations and more around time-designated projects where a team is assigned to a specific project with a clearly defined outcome and a specified completion date. While construction companies and consulting firms have always been structured around projects, a wide range of companies are finding that project-based structures featuring temporary cross-functional teams charged with clear objectives are more able to achieve innovation, adaptability and rapid learning than more traditional structures.

About half of Google's employees – including almost all of its software engineers – are organised into teams comprising three or four people. Team leadership revolves, individuals work on multiple teams and individuals can move between teams without HR approval. According to Shona Brown, Google's head of operations: 'If at all possible, we want people to commit to things, rather than be assigned to things . . . If you see an opportunity, go for it'.[38]

W. L. Gore, the supplier of Gore-Tex and a wide range of hi-tech fabric products, also has a team-based structure with minimal top-down direction – there are no formal job titles and leaders are selected by peers. Employees ('associates') may apply to join particular teams and it is up to the team members to choose new members. The teams are self-managed and team goals are not assigned from above but are agreed through team commitments. Associates are encouraged to work on multiple teams.[39]

Non-hierarchical, team-based organisations can achieve high levels of innovation, flexibility and employee motivation. But absence of hierarchical control can also produce chaos. Oticon, the Danish manufacturer of hearing aids, initiated radical decentralsation, abolished most formal controls and reorganised around over 100 self-directed project teams.[40] Within six years, lack of coordination, confused incentives and excessive internal politicking caused Oticon to dismantle much of its 'spaghetti organisation' and reinstitute hierarchical control.[41]

To improve coordination across, between and within organisational capabilities has encouraged companies to align their structures more closely with their internal processes. While business process reengineering directs attention to the microstructure of processes, a focus on organisational capabilities fosters an integrated view of processes that explores how individual processes fit together in sequences and networks of complementary activities. For example, a company's order fulfilment process may span a whole chain of activities from supplying information to potential customers, to customer selection and ordering, to manufacturing, through to distribution. Similarly, the customer relations process embraces the entirety of a company's interactions with its customers through marketing and after-sales services. These macro processes often extend beyond the company: supply-chain management links internal logistics with those of suppliers and suppliers' suppliers. Volvo reorganised ordering, production planning, supply chains, distributor and dealer relations into an integrated order fulfilment process with the goal of a 14-day cycle between customer order and customer receipt of a customised car.[42]

Organising for adaptability

The need for organisations to coordinate in multiple ways for multiple purposes inevitably means that company structures become more complex. Despite the propensity for CEOs to echo Thoreau in their call to 'Simplify, simplify', typically the emphasis has been, first, replacing formal systems by informal systems; second, relying less on continuous supervision and more on setting performance goals against which individuals are periodically appraised.

> Loosening the structure may be a critical step toward building the ambidextrous organisation – one that can combine multiple capabilities and accommodate both gradual change and occasional revolutionary leaps.

HANDS-OFF MANAGEMENT COMPLEXITY THEORY This theory supports the idea that organisations may be able to do complex things without necessarily resorting to complex structures. Notions of *self-organisation* and the power of *simple rules* support the idea that human beings are capable of being interested in complex patterns without the need for managers telling them what to do. Loosening the structure may be a critical step toward building the **ambidextrous organisation** – one that can combine multiple capabilities and accommodate both gradual change and occasional revolutionary leaps.[43]

The paradox of simplicity is that reducing complexity at the formal level can foster greater variety and sophisticated coordination at the informal level. At GE, Jack Welch's emphasis on 'Speed, Simplicity, Self-confidence' resulted in reformulating control systems around just a few performance indicators and using periodic corporate initiatives ('growth', 'boundarylessness' and 'six-sigma') to drive change. Yet, this paring down of formal systems fostered more complex patterns of coordination and collaboration within GE.[44] In general, the greater the potential for reordering existing resources and capabilities in complex new combinations, the greater the potential for 'consensus-based hierarchies' that emphasise horizontal communication over 'authority-based hierarchies' that emphasise vertical communication.[45]

IDENTITY Substituting informal structures and systems for formal structures and systems requires focus on organisational context over organisational structure. To manage the organisational context includes influencing social and behavioural norms, but these depend on some shared cognition of what the organisation is and an emotional attachment towards what the organisation represents. These ideas are components of what has been termed **organisational identity** – a collective understanding of what is presumed core, distinctive and enduring about the character of an organisation.[46] A strong consensus around organisational identity provides a powerful basis for coordinated action that permits flexibility and responsiveness to be reconciled with continuity and stability. At some point, organisational identity becomes an impediment to, rather than a facilitator of, change. (IBM's identity as a vertically integrated supplier of mainframe computers to large organisations hampered adaptation to microcomputing, networking and web-based computing). Organisational identity creates an important linkage between a firm's internal self-image and its market positioning. With increasing symbolic influences on consumer choices the linkage between product design, brand image and organisational identity becomes increasingly important. For companies such as Nokia, Apple, Alessi and Bang & Olufsen, product design is an important vehicle for establishing and interpreting organisational identity.[47]

> Organisational identity creates an important linkage between a firm's internal self-image and its market positioning.

BREAKING DOWN CORPORATE BOUNDARIES Even with informal coordination mechanisms, modular structures and sophisticated knowledge management systems, there are limits to the range of capabilities that any company can encompass. Indeed, converging technologies and the need for rapid new product development mean that outsourcing capabilities is often preferable to developing them internally. The implication is less distinction between what happens within the firm and more what happens outside it. Inter-firm networks permit stable yet flexible patterns for integrating the capabilities of different firms while also sharing risks. 'Contingent workforces' – comprising people who work for companies but are not covered by long-term employment contracts – similarly permit access to a wide range of skills while avoiding fixed costs.

While localised networks of firms – such as those which characterise Italy's clothing, furniture and industrial machinery industries – offer potential for building trust and inter-firm routines, web-based technologies permit much wider networks of collaboration. Powerful information and communications technologies enable firms to draw upon ideas and expertise across the globe. Increasingly innovation requires the combination of very different technologies: the Nike 1 iPod Sport Kit involving sensors in Nike running shoes providing real-time information that can be read on an Apple iPod – is just one example of a phenomenon that is breaking down barriers between industries as well as between companies.[48] Cisco Systems has pioneered the development of web-based business integration with its suppliers, customers and collaborations. The collaborative potential of the internet is most strongly revealed in open-source communities that build highly complex products such as Linux and Wikipedia through global networks of individual collaborators.[49]

Inter-firm networks facilitate the design and production of complex products that require a wide range of technical and commercial capabilities in sectors subject to rapid change. In cars, fashion clothing, aerospace, machine tools and telecom equipment, networks allow each firm to specialise in a few capabilities while providing the close linkages needed to integrate these different capabilities. The flexibility of these linkages offers the potential for the capabilities resident within an inter-firm network to be reconfigured in order to adapt quickly to external change.[50]

Summary

In responding to the environments in which their companies find themselves, business leaders experience two major difficulties. First the outlook for the future is highly uncertain. The last decade has been characterised by high levels of turbulence and while many people do have clear expectations about what they think will happen in the wake of recent events their expectations are highly divergent. For example people's views are often based more on emotional factors, such as the extent to which individuals are optimistic or pessimistic in their outlook, rather than upon objective analysis. We simply do not know what the aftermath of recent economic crises will be: the long-term economic, political and social repercussions are likely to differ significantly between countries and might lead to fundamental changes in the capitalist system.

Second, the capacity for managerial action has been confounded by a conflict between short-term and long-term forces. Over the longer term, several forces for change are influencing our thinking about strategy and management in general. These include increasing competition (arising in particular from internationalisation), turbulence, technology and changing social attitudes. In the short term the emphasis is on cost cutting and survival.

The central problem is that the two sets of challenges require responses that are often conflicting. While meeting the challenges of increased competition and technological change is likely to require developing new capabilities, short-term survival is likely to focus on cash conservation and inhibit investment. Similar observations can be made about styles of leadership. Complex organisations operating at high levels of evolutionary fitness require leaders that foster decentralised adaptation and initiative. Yet, in the financial crisis of 2008–9, in many companies, effective leadership involved a dramatic recentralisation of power in order to 'circle the wagons'.

In many ways this dilemma of reconciling short-term survival with longer term fitness is merely an extreme example of the paradoxes that almost define the challenge of management in the 21st century. It was over 15 years ago that Charles Handy identified paradox as the fundamental feature of business – and, indeed, society – yet it is recently that the challenges of reconciling cost cutting with innovation, global integration with local differentiation, scale with responsiveness and systematisation with improvisation have been acknowledged.

Yet, emerging concepts and theories – real options, complexity thinking, self-organisation, organisational identity, open-source innovation and distributed leadership as well as research into strategy processes and practices – offer the potential for us to augment our existing standard tools of strategic management. Even more encouraging is the fact that experimentation and innovation at the coal-face of management practice is offering new approaches to dealing both with old problems and with emerging ones. Radical corporate initiatives such as IBM's 'Innovation Jam', Google's emergent approach to business development and W. L. Gore's self-managed teams tend to be found among companies whose survival is not under serious threat. But even among firms that are primarily focused upon survival, management actions are going beyond conventional approaches to restructuring and cost cutting. These include novel forms of financing which are independent of traditional financial institutions, new approaches to employee relations, scenario-based financial planning and building strategy around options rather than projects.

One of the challenges for strategic management scholars is to be alert to the initiatives and innovations that are being developed across a vast array of different firms, to identify the critical features of these initiatives and innovations and to deploy the tools of management and social science theory to draw out their significance and potential for diffusion. A key consequence of this type of activity is that, while strategic management continues to draw heavily on concepts and theories drawn from economics, sociology, psychology, biology, systems theory and other disciplines, in the analysis of competition, competitive advantage, organisational design, evolution and change, strategic management is increasingly taking a leading role in developing new conceptual thinking.

Of course, many of the ideas that have developed over recent years – including the characteristics of the 'new economy', the potential for employee stock options to resolve agency problems and the potential for 'decoupling' from the world market – have been shown to be empty. While this reinforces our belief that the basic tools of strategy analysis – industry analysis and the analysis of resources and capabilities – remain valid and robust, it is clear that we need to continually develop our concepts and frameworks to meet the circumstances and challenges of tomorrow.

Summary table

Learning Objectives	Summary
Be familiar with some of the key changes that have occurred in the business environment in recent years	We have examined a range of economic, social, political and technological changes that together have changed the nature of the business environment making it volatile and uncertain. In particular we have looked at the major impact of the global financial crisis and subsequent recession
Understand why the 2008 financial crisis has led to calls for change in a number of areas of management practice	We have explored the causes and effects of the global financial crisis and how it has created societal pressure for greater fairness, ethical behaviour and environmental sustainability. We have focused particularly on how these pressures have led to the questioning of firms' goals, their corporate governance mechanism and the styles adopted by their leaders
Be aware of some of the latest developments in strategic thinking	We have looked briefly at some new approaches to strategic thinking including real options, complexity theory and research into strategy-as-practice
Appreciate the forces that are driving changes in organisational design	We have argued that changes in organisational design are being driven by two major forces – the need for organisations to deploy more capabilities developed to a higher level and the need to respond more quickly to external change
Be alert to the approaches and initiatives that are being developed across an array of different firms in response to turbulence in the business environment	We have seen how firms like Google, IBM, W. L. Gore, Oticom and many others have used innovative approaches to deal with the challenges they face

Further reading

The text by Clegg *et al.* (2011) takes a critical approach and explores alternative perspectives, issues of power and politics and strategy process in some detail:

Clegg, S., Carter, C., Kornberger, M. and Schweitzer, J. (2011). *Strategy: Theory and Practice*. London: Sage.

Rita McGrath has written extensively on strategy and real options, see for example:

McGrath, R. and Boisot, M. (2005). Option complexes: going beyond real options reasoning. *Emergence: Complexity and Organization*, 7(2), 2–13.

Paula Jarzakowski and Paul Spee provide a review of the strategy-as-practice literature in:

Jarzakowski, P. and Spee, P. (2009). Strategy-as-practice: a review and future directions for the field. *International Journal of Management Reviews*, 11(1), 69–95.

Heifetz *et al.* explore the challenges of business leadership in the aftermath of the financial crisis in:

Heifetz, R., Grashow, A. and Linsky, M. (2009). Leadership in a (permanent) crisis. *Harvard Business Review*, 87(7/8), 62–9.

Raisch *et al.* look at the issues of organisational flexibility and adaptation in:

Raisch, S. and Birkinshaw, J. (2008) Organisational ambidexterity: antecedents, outcomes and moderators. *Journal of Management*, 34(3), 375–409.

QUIZ

Visit your enhanced ebook at **www.foundationsofstrategy.com** for self test quiz questions

Self-study questions

1   Identify some of the key changes that have taken place in your national economy over the last five years and evaluate the impact these changes have had on the strategy adopted by one of the leading firms in your home economy.

2   In July 2011 News International, a subsidiary of the media company News Corporation announced the sudden closure of its best-selling UK tabloid newspaper, *The News of*

the World, which had been in print for 168 years. The closure was precipitated by a 'phone hacking' scandal that had resulted in the newspaper's major advertisers withdrawing their accounts. The employees of the newspaper were accused of illegally tapping mobile phones in the pursuit of the publication of sensational stories. The scandal raised wider questions about the ethics of the company under the ownership of Rupert Murdoch and the management standards at News International and its parent company, News Corporation. Could these problems have been avoided through better corporate governance arrangements? If so, what kind of arrangements needed, in your opinion, to be in place?

3   Critics of IKEA, the Swedish furniture retailer, have argued that the company minimises its tax payments, is very economical with the information it makes public and maximises the rewards that go to the Kamprads (the founder's family). In response Mr Kamprad, the founder, has argued that maximising tax efficiency is a natural corollary of IKEA's low-cost strategy. What ethical issues are raised by IKEA's strategy and Mr Kamprad's stance?

4   'Successful companies will work to establish and protect distinctive strategic positions even as they use more temporary competitive advantages as stepping stones to new advantages. They will be, so to speak, flexibly inflexible.' (N. G. Carr, *Does it Matter? Information Technology and the Corrosion of Competitive Advantage*. Harvard Business Review Press.) Discuss, giving examples of firms you feel have displayed both flexibility and focus.

5   Research suggests that chief executives consistently overestimate their influence on a company. Does the leadership style of a company's CEO matter? If so, why? If not, why not?

GLOSSARY

Visit your enhanced ebook at **www.foundationsofstrategy.com** for key term flashcards

Notes

1   The Financial Crisis Inquiry Commission. *The Final Report of the National Commission on the Causes of the Financial and Economic Crisis in the United States*. January 2011.

2   W. B. Arthur, 'Increasing returns and the new world of business', *Harvard Business Review* (July–August 1996): 101–8.

3   'The Skype guys', *Time* (30 April 2006).

4 A. Y. Lewin, C. B. Weigelt and J. D. Emery, 'Adaptation and selection in strategy and change', in M. S. Poole and A. H. Van de Ven (Eds), *Handbook of Organisational Change and Innovation* (New York: Oxford University Press, 2004): 108–60.

5 S. Jonsson, H. R. Greve and T. Fujiwara-Greve, 'Lost without deserving: the spread of legitimacy loss in response to reported corporate deviance', Working Paper (2008).

6 P. F. Drucker, *Managing in the Next Society* (New York: St Martin's Press, 2003); S. Ghoshal, C. A. Bartlett and P. Moran, 'A new manifesto for management', *Sloan Management Review* (Spring 1999): 9–20; C. Handy, *The Age of Paradox* (Boston: Harvard University Press, 1995).

7 M. Lee and M. Mather, 'U.S. labor force trends', *Population Bulletin* (June 2009).

8 D. Barton, 'Capitalism for the long term', *Harvard Business Review* 89 (2011): 85.

9 R. M. Kanter, *The Change Masters* (New York: Simon & Schuster, 1983).

10 G. Hamel, 'Moon shots for management?' *Harvard Business Review* (February 2009).

11 J. C. Collins and J. I. Porras, *Built to Last* (New York: Harper Business, 1996).

12 D. Goleman, 'What makes a leader?' *Harvard Business Review* (November–December 1998): 93–102. See also: J. C. Hayton and G. M. McEvoy, 'Developing and assessing professional and managerial competence', *Human Resource Management*, 45 (2006): 291–4.

13 J. Collins, 'Level 5 leadership: the triumph of humility and fierce resolve', *Harvard Business Review* (January 2001): 67–76.

14 S. Tappin and A. Cave, *The Secrets of CEOs: 150 Global Chief Executives Lift the Lid on Business, Life and Leadership* (London: Nicholas Brealey, 2008).

15 T. Luehrman, 'Strategy as a portfolio of real options', *Harvard Business Review* 76 (1998): 89–99.

16 R. G. McGrath, 'A real option logic for initiating technology positioning investment', *Academy of Management Review* 22 (1997): 974–96.

17 H. T. J. Smit, 'Acquisition strategies as option games' *Journal of Applied Corporate Finance* (2001): 79–89.

18 M. J. Leiblein and D. D. Miller, 'An empirical examination of the effect of uncertainty and firm strategy on the vertical boundaries of the firm' *Strategic Management Journal* 24 (2003): 839–60.

19 K. M. Eisenhardt and J. A. Martin, 'Dynamic capabilities: what are they?', *Strategic Management Journal* 21 (2000): 1105–21.

20 P. Bak, *How Nature Works: The Science of Self-Organised Criticality* (New York: Copernicus, 1996).

21 M. J. Wheatley and M. Kellner Rogers, *A Simpler Way* (Berrett-Koehler, 1996).

22 P. Anderson, 'Complexity theory and organisational science', *Organization Science* 10 (1999): 216–32.

23 Among the sources I draw upon are: S. L. Brown and K. M. Eisenhardt, *Competing on the Edge: Strategy as Structured Chaos* (Boston: Harvard Business School Press, 1998); W. McKelvey, 'Energizing order-creating networks of distributed intelligence: improving the corporate brain', *International Journal of Innovation Management* 5 (June 2001): 132–54; D. A. Levinthal, 'Adaptation on a rugged landscape', *Management Science* 43 (1997): 934–50.

24 S. A. Kaufman, *The Origins of Order: Self Organization and Selection In Evolution* (New York: Oxford University Press, 1993).

25 For discussion of the role of rules in strategy making, see K. M. Eisenhardt and D. Sull, 'Strategy as simple rules', *Harvard Business Review* (January–February 2001): 107–16.

26 W. McKelvey, 'A simple rule approach to CEO leadership in the 21st century' (Paper presented at the ISUFI Conference, Ostuni, Italy, September 11–13, 2003).

27 K. M. Eisenhardt and S. L. Brown, 'Patching: restitching business portfolios in dynamic markets', *Harvard Business Review* (May–June 1999): 72–84.

28 K. M. Eisenhardt and D. C. Galunic, 'Coevolving: at last, a way to make synergies work', *Harvard Business Review* (January-February 2000): 91–101.

29 W. McKelvey, 'A simple rule approach to CEO leadership' op. cit.

30 R. M. Grant, 'Strategic planning in a turbulent environment: evidence from the oil majors', *Strategic Management Journal* 24 (2003): 491–518.

31 S. Clegg, C. Carter, M. Kornberger and J. Schweitzer, *Strategy Theory and Practice* (London: Sage, 2011): 129.

32 See, for example, G. Johnson, L. Melin and R. Whittington, 'Guest editors' introduction: micro strategy and strategizing – towards an activity-based view', *Journal of Management Studies* 40 (2003): 3–22.

33 J. Strikwerda, 'The emergence of the multidimensional organisation' (April 2008). Available at SSRN: http://ssrn.com/abstract=1077363.

34 J. G. March, 'Exploration and exploitation in organisational learning', *Organization Science* 2 (1991): 71–8.

35 G. Bushe and A. B. Shani, *Parallel Learning Structures* (Reading, MA: Addison-Wesley, 1991).

36 O. M. Bjelland and R. C. Wood, 'An inside view of IBM's "Innovation Jam"', *MIT Sloan Management Review* (Fall 2008): 32–40.

37 J. R. Katzenbach and D. K. Smith, 'The discipline of teams', *Harvard Business Review* (March–April 1993): 111–20.

38 G. Hamel and W. Breen, *The Future of Management* (Boston: Harvard Business School Press, 2007): chapter 6.

39 Ibid.: chapter 5.

40 D. Ravasi and G. Verona, 'Organising the process of knowledge integration: the benefits of structural ambiguity', *Scandinavian Journal of Management*, 17 (2001): 41–66.

41 N. J. Foss, 'Internal disaggregation in Oticon: an organisational economics interpretation of the rise and decline of the spaghetti organisation' (Department of Industrial Economics and Strategy, Copenhagen Business School, October 2000).

42 S. Hertz, J. K. Johansson and F. de Jager, 'Customer-focused cost cutting: process management at Volvo' *Journal of Supply Chain Management* 6 (2001): 128–41.

43 C. A. O'Reilly III and M. L. Tushman, 'The ambidextrous organisation', *Harvard Business Review* (April 2004): 74–81; M. L. Tushman and C. A. O'Reilly III, 'The ambidextrous organisation: managing evolutionary and revolutionary change' *California Management Review* 38 (Summer 1996): 8–30.

44 'Jack Welch and the General Electric management system', in R. M. Grant, *Cases to Accompany* Contemporary Strategy Analysis, 6th edn (Oxford: Blackwell, 2008).

45 J. A. Nickerson and T. R. Zenger, 'The knowledge-based theory of the firm – a problem-solving perspective', *Organization Science* 15 (2004): 617–32.

46 D. A. Gioia, M. Schultz and K. G. Corley, 'Organisational identity, image and adaptive instability', *Academy of Management Review* 25 (2000): 63–81.

47 D. Ravasi and G. Lojacono, 'Managing design and designers for strategic renewal', *Long Range Planning*, 38 (February 2005): 51–77.

48 'Apple and Nike, running mates', *Business Week* (24 May 2006).

49 A. Wright, 'The next paradigm shift: open source everything', *Brighthand.com* (9 July 2008), www.brighthand.com/default.asp?newsID=14348.

50 R. Gulati, N. Nohria and A. Zaheer, 'Strategic networks', *Strategic Management Journal* 21 (2000): 203–15.

Glossary

Absolute cost advantages – a firm has an absolute cost advantage over a rival producing a similar product or providing a similar service when its average costs of production are lower than its rivals at all levels of output

Adhocracies – a type of organisation characterised by the absence of bureaucracy and hierarchy. Decision-making authority is diffused and located within organisational members' areas of specialisation. Co-ordination is achieved informally through mutual adjustment

Administrative mechanism – the process by which decisions concerning production and resource allocation are made by managers rather than the market

Agency relationship – the arrangement that exists when one person (known as the agent) acts on behalf of another (known as the principal). For example, the arrangements by which the managers of a firm (the agents) act on behalf of its owners (the principals)

Ambidextrous organization – an organisation that can handle both gradual and revolutionary change

Architectural capabilities – the ability of a firm to innovate at a product or systems level i.e. to change the way in which component parts fit together

Barriers to entry – the obstacles a firm faces in trying to enter a particular market

Barrier to exit – the obstacles a firm faces in trying to leave a particular market

Benchmarking – the process by which one organisation gathers information on other organisations in order to evaluate and improve its own performance

Bilateral monopolies – a single seller (a monopoly) and a single buyer (a monopsony) in the same market

Born global companies – a company that operates internationally on start-up

Brand extension – the use of an established brand name in a new product category

Business environment – all the external influences that affect a firm's decisions and performance

Business strategy – how a firm competes within a particular industry or market

Capabilities – what organisations are able to 'do'

Capital expenditure budget – that part of a company's overall financial plan that deals with expenditure on assets such as equipment and facilities

Causal ambiguity – the situation where it is difficult or impossible to map the connections between actions and results. When causal ambiguity exists the source of a successful firm's competitive advantage is unknown

Clusters – groups of firms that form part of a close networks, usually because of their geographic proximity to each other

Codifiable knowledge – knowledge that can be written down

Collateralized debt obligations (CDOs) – promises to pay money to investors based on the cash flow generated by the assets on which the CDOs are based, for example in the case mortgage backed CDOs the flow of mortgage repayments

Competencies modelling – involves identifying the set of skills, content knowledge, attitudes and values associated with superior performers within a particular job category, then assessing each employee against that profile

Common ownership – the shared possession of assets

Comparative advantage – a situation in which a country or a region can produce a particular good or service at a lower opportunity cost than rivals

Competitive advantage – the ability of one firm to earn (or have the potential to earn) a persistently higher rate of profit than rivals who operate in the same market

Complementary resources – mutually dependent assets that enhance the value of an industry's products, for example petrol stations are a complementary resource to cars

Component competencies – the ability of the firm to innovate at the level of component parts or sub-systems

Concentration ratio – the combined market share of the leading firms

Consumer surplus – the difference between the maximum price a consumer is willing to pay for a product or service and the amount he or she actually pays

Core competences – Corporate culture -refers to the values and ways of thinking that senior managers wish to encourage within their organisation

Corporate culture – the values and ways of thinking that are promoted by the senior management team within an organisation

Corporate governance – refers to the set of processes, institutions, regulations and policies that affect the way companies are directed, administer and controlled

Corporate incubators – are business developments established to fund and nurture new businesses, based upon technologies that have been developed internally, but have limited applications within a company's established businesses

Corporate planning – adopting a systematic approach to setting corporate objectives, making strategic decisions and checking progress towards achieving objectives

Corporate social responsibility – a business organisation's accountability for the social and environmental as well as the economic consequences of its activities and its commitment to having a positive impact on society

Corporate strategy – strategic decisions concerning the scope of the organization's activities in terms of the markets and industries in which it competes

Cost advantage – when a firm is able to supply an identical product or service to its rivals at a lower cost

Cost drivers – the determinants of a firm's unit costs (cost per unit of output) relative to its competitors

Creative abrasion – frictions or differences that generate new ideas

Cross-subsidization – using profits or surpluses generated by one part of a business to support other parts of the business that perform less well

De alio entrants – entrants that are established firms from another industry

De novo entrants – entrants that are new start-ups

Differentiation advantage – a competitive advantage that is built on providing something unique that is valuable to buyers beyond simply offering a low price

Distinctive competence – those things that an organisation does particularly well relative to its competitors

Diversification – the expansion of an existing firm into another product line or field of operation

Dynamic capabilities – a firm's ability to integrate, build or reconfigure its internal and external capabilities in response to rapidly changing environments

Economies of scale – reductions in unit costs that result from increases in the output of a particular product in a given period of time

Economies of scope – reductions in unit costs that result from increases in the output of multiple products i.e. using a resource across multiple activities

Emergent strategy – decisions that are derived from the complex process in which individual managers interpret the intended strategy and adapt to changing external circumstances

Emotional intelligence – the ability to perceive and understand one's own and others' emotions and to manage emotions in a way that facilitate communication, collaboration and relationship

Entrepreneurship – the process through which individuals identify opportunities, allocate resources, create value and assume risk for new ventures

Evolutionary strategy – a strategy that involves incremental rather than radical change. In the context of high-tech industries an evolution strategy is often used to describe the decision by a firm to retain backward compatibility with earlier products

Firm as property – a viewpoint that sees management's responsibility as acting in the interests of shareholders

Firm as social entity – a viewpoint that sees management's responsibility as acting in the interests of a broad set of stakeholders and making a positive contribution to society at large

First-mover advantage – refers to the advantages that an initial occupant of a strategic position or niche gains by pre-empting the best resources or by using early entry to build superior resources and capabilities

Fixed costs – costs that do not change when a firm's output changes

Franchise – a contractual agreement between the owner of a business system and trademark (the franchiser) and a licensee (franchisee) that permits the franchisee to produce and market the franchiser's product or service in a specified area

Functional analysis – identifying organisational capabilities in relation to each of the principal functional areas of the firm e.g. operations, sales and distribution etc.

Global industries – industries which internationalise through both trade and direct investment is important

Hierarchy – an ordered grouping of people with an established pecking order

Horizontal diversification – the extension of the firm's activities into areas that are at the same stage of the production process as its existing activities

Human resources – the people who staff and run an organisation

Hypercompetition – a situation characterised by intense and rapid competitive moves, where firms constantly strive to build [new] advantages and erode the advantages of their rivals

Incumbency advantage – the advantages experienced by existing competitors in an industry or market relative to new comers

Industry life cycle – the notion that industries, like products, go though distinct phases which comprise introduction, growth, maturity and decline

Innovation – is the initial commercialisation of invention by producing and marketing a new good or service or by using a new method of production

Intellectual property – creative products of the mind that have commercial value, for example literary or artistic works or ideas for new products or processes

Intended strategy – the strategy as conceived of by the top management team

Internal capital market – the mechanism by which the headquarters allocates funds to various divisions of the business

Internal environment – all the factors within an organisation that affect its strategic decision-making and performance for example, its organisational structure, management systems and human resources

Intangible resources – assets that you cannot touch or see but that add value

Invention – the creation of new products and processes through the development of new knowledge or from new combinations of existing knowledge

Isolating mechanisms – the barriers that protect a firm's profits from being driven down by the competitive process

Key success factors – those factors within the firm's market environment that determine the firm's ability to survive and prosper

Lead time – is the time it will take followers to catch up

Long-term contract – a contract involving a commitment to undertake agreed activity over several time periods

Market failure – the situation where resources cannot be allocated efficiently or effectively because of a break down in the price mechanism

Market mechanism – the process by which individuals and firms, guided by market prices, make independent decisions to buy and sell goods and services

Multidomestic industries – industries that internationalise through direct investment in overseas markets

Network effects – the effect that one user of a good or service has on the value of that good or service to other people

Network externalities – the change in the benefit that an individual derives from a good or service when the number of other individuals consuming the same good or service

Not-for-profit organisation – organisations that do not distribute the surplus funds that may result from their operations to those in control

Open innovation – market-based systems where companies buy in technology and also licensing out their own technologies rather than doing everything 'in-house'

Operating budget – A detailed projection of all estimated income and expenses based on forecasted sales revenue during a given period

Organisational capability – the firm's capacity to deploy resources for a desired end result

Organisational culture – the values, traditions and social norms that exist informally within organisations

Organisational complexity – when a business has many diverse but interdependent parts that are linked through dense sets of interrelationships

Organisational identity – refers to what is central, distinctive and enduring in an organization that determines organisational members collective sense of who they are

Organisational process – the sequence of actions through which a specific task is performed

PEST analysis – an environmental scanning framework that classifies external influences by source, i.e. political, economic, social and technological

Planned emergence – a strategy making process that combines design with emergence i.e. there is a planned strategy but this strategy is continually enacted through decisions that are made by every member of the organisation

Positive feedback – a response that results in self reinforcing cycle of amplification or growth

Producer surplus – the difference between the amount that a producer receives from the sale of a good and the lowest amount that producer is willing to accept for that good

Product life cycle – the notion that products go through distinct stages from their introduction to eventual withdrawal from the market

Property rights – the legal rules that govern how individuals can control, transfer and benefit from the assets they possess

Public goods a product that one individual can consume without reducing its availability to another individual and from which no consumer can be excluded

Public sector organisations that are owned and controlled by government

Realized strategy – the strategy that is pursued in practice

Regime of applicability – describes the conditions that influence the distribution of returns from an innovation

Relational capability – the ability to build and maintain social relationships, in particular by building trust, developing inter-firm knowledge-sharing routines and establishing mechanisms for coordination

Relational contracts – agreements based on informal social relationships between transacting partners rather than on formal legal documents

Resources – assets that the organisation 'has' and that it can use to pursue its objectives

Resource-based view – a theoretical perspectives that highlights the role of resources and capabilities as the principal basis for firm strategy

Resource leverage – utilising resources to the maximum advantage

Revolutionary strategy – a strategy that involves radical rather than incremental change. In the context of high-tech industries an re-evolutionary strategy is often used to describe the decision by a firm to produce products that are not compatible with its earlier offerings

Routinization – the process by which the regular activities performed by an organisation become a set of customary, standardised procedures

Scale economies – see economies of scale

Scenario analysis – a systematic way of thinking about how the future might unfold that builds on what is known about current trends and signals

Segmentation – the processes of partitioning a market on the basis of characteristics that are likely to influence consumers' purchasing behaviour

Sheltered industries – industries that are protected from international competition

Shared service organisations – organisations with central departments that supply common administrative and technical services to the operating businesses

Social enterprise – businesses that do not give primacy to shareholders' interests but instead have philanthropic goals

Social legitimacy – popular acceptance of business organisations' rights to behave in particular ways

Specialization – the division of labour into separate tasks

Spot contracts – a contract for the immediate sale and delivery of a commodity

Stakeholder analysis – the process of identifying, understanding and prioritising the needs of key stakeholders so that the questions of how stakeholders can participate in strategy formulation and how relationships with stakeholders are best managed can be addressed

Stakeholder approach – viewing the business organisations as a coalition of interest groups where top management's role to balance these different – often conflicting – interests

Strategy – the means by which individuals or organisations achieve their objectives

Strategy process – the way in which strategy is conceived and put in to practice

Strategic alliances – refers to collaborative arrangements between firms

Strategic innovation – creating value for customers from novel products, experiences or modes of product delivery

Strategic management – the label given to an approach that places less emphasis on corporate planning and focuses more on competition as the central characteristic of the business environment and competitive advantage as the primary goal of strategy

Substitutability – the extent to which goods or services can be interchanged or act as replacements for one another

Sunk costs – costs that have already been incurred that cannot be recovered regardless of future events

Tangible resources – assets that can be touched or seen

Standard – agreed, consistent rules about the way to doing something

Time-based competition – rivalry based on speed to market

Tipping – movement towards a market situation where the winner takes all i.e. a single firm dominates

Trading industries – industries in which internationalisation occurs primarily through imports and exports

Transaction costs – the costs associated with participating in a market e.g. the costs of searching for a particular product or negotiating a price

Uncertain imitability – the situation where there is ambiguity associated with the causes of a competitor's success

Value chain analysis – separates the activities of the firm into a sequential chain and explores the linkages between activities and to gain insight into the firm's competitive position and capabilities

Variable costs – costs that change when a firm's output changes

Vertical diversification – see vertical integration

Vertical integration – where a firm extends its activities into the preceding or succeeding stages of the production process

Virtual corporation – a firm whose primary function is to coordinate the activities of a network of suppliers and downstream partners. Co-ordination typically takes place through the use of information and communication technologies

Index

Note: Page references in *italics* refer to Figures; those in **bold** refer to Tables

www.foundationconstructiongycom